SPECIAL FORCES: A UNIQUE NATIONAL ASSET

"THROUGH, WITH AND BY"

DE OPPRESSO LIBER

MARK D. BOYATT

outskirtspress
DENVER, COLORADO

In Memory of
Lieutenant Colonel Robert J. Phillips
United States Army Special Forces
Comrade in Arms...
and my friend

Comments from Reviewers

"In *Through, With and By*, Colonel Boyatt has produced the definitive history/text/white paper/investigative analysis/field manual/adventure story of the U.S. Special Forces and unconventional warfare. Simply put: it is invaluable. You want to know what, why, who and how? Read this book!" -- *Frank Emerson, soldier, author, singer, patriot*

"Mark D. Boyatt's **Special Forces – A Unique National Asset** is a journalistic achievement of the highest order. His impeccably researched and crafted delivery will serve Special Operations Forces and the general public admirably in yet untold ways. Colonel Boyatt has masterfully taken us '*back to the future*' at a critical juncture in U.S. history with the passion, energy and authenticity of a tested professional. **Special Forces – A Unique National Asset** is destined to become required reading for serious students who seek to embrace every artifice of special warfare." *Anthony T. Reed, Sr., USAR Ambassador Emeritus (Major General Equivalent); Colonel, U.S. Army Special Forces (Ret); Senior Fellow, International Strategic Studies Association*

"This should be a textbook." *Vera Elizabeth Ross Boyatt, genealogy researcher, author and publisher*

"Mark Boyatt, former professional colleague while on active duty and now permanent friend, has produced, in **"Special Forces -- a Unique National Asset"** an excellent and comprehensive history of one of our nation's premier military tools. This is a vibrant description of how it works and how it can and should be used by our national leadership. He gets it right -- warts and all -- and it will be an invaluable teaching and reference tool for both military and civilian leaders interested in our national security." *David Passage, U.S. Ambassador/Retired, former NSC official and first Foreign Affairs Adviser to the Commander/USSOCOM.*

Colonel Boyatt was a Special Forces A Team Commander, a Special Forces Battalion Commander and a Special Forces Group Commander. He is a War College Graduate. He is a master of Counter-Insurgency, Foreign Internal Defense, indeed all the Special Forces missions. *Major Michael "Uncle West" Linnane, Special Forces Retired*

"through, with and by"

Mark D. Boyatt, U.S. Army Special Forces Colonel Retired. Colonel Boyatt is well known throughout the Special Operations community. In May 1976, he graduated first in his Special Forces Officers Qualification class as the Distinguished Honor Graduate and earned the Green Beret. Over a four year period from 1976-1979, he served as the commander of three different Special Forces Operational Detachments "A" in the 5th Special Forces Group (Airborne) --- a GREENLIGHT Special Atomic Demolition Team; a military freefall team; and was one of three BLUELIGHT counter-terrorist assault team leaders. He commanded the first Special Forces Mobile Training Team to then North Yemen in 1979. From December 1984-May 1987 he served as the Operations Officer (S-3), 5th SFGA, then in the U.S. Army Special Operations Agency in the Pentagon until 1989. In November, 1989 he assumed command of the 1st Battalion, 1st Special Forces Group forward deployed on Okinawa, Japan. From 1993-1994, he was the Chief of Staff of the United States Army John F. Kennedy Special Warfare Center and School (USAJFKSWCS). Subsequently, from 1994-1996, he was the Commander, 3rd Special Forces Group and commanded the Army Special Operations Task Force during Operation Uphold

Democracy in Haiti 1994-1995. He served as the Deputy Chief of Staff for Operations, G-3, for the United States Army Special Operations Command from 1996 -1998 and then as the Deputy Commander and Assistant Commandant USAJFKSWCS from April 1998 until his retirement in January 2000. *During his attendance at the Army War College in Carlisle, Pennsylvania 1992-1993, Colonel Boyatt published a thesis-level paper which originated and defined the term "through, with and by," which is currently codified in joint doctrine and is a base reference in the Special Operations community.*

Acknowledgements and thanks.

Major Michael "Uncle West" Linnane, Special Forces

Frank Emerson, soldier, author, singer, patriot

Major General James A. Guest, Special Forces

Major General Sidney Shachnow, Special Forces

Ambassador David Passage, Foreign Affairs Adviser

Command Sergeant Major David Clark, Special Forces

Master Sergeant Joseph Beasley, Special Forces

Assistant Secretary of Defense Bing West, author and a U.S. Marine

Captain Douglas A. Livermore, Special Forces

Colonel Tim Heinemann, Special Forces

Ph.D. Raleigh Bailey, Director Emeritus, Center for New North Carolinians

U.S. Army Reserve Ambassador Emeritus (MG Eqiv), Colonel Anthony T. Reed, Special Forces

Lieutenant Colonel Joseph J. Vonnegut, Judge Advocate General

Colonel Hy S. Rothstein, Special Forces

U.S. Navy Captain Dick Couch, Navy SEAL

Colonel Thomas M. Carlin, Special Forces

Vera Elizabeth Ross Boyatt, my mother, and genealogy researcher, author and publisher

and especially to my very supportive and patient wife, Nancy.

...and too many others to list them all.

Contents

Bottom Line Up Front

Through, with and by. Uniquely inherent to U.S. Army Special Forces, the "Green Berets." 1993. U.S. Army War College, Carlisle, Pennsylvania. The term or phrase was born.[1]

What does *"through, with and by"* mean? This phrase describes the manner in which Special Forces, working *"through, with and by"* other people, such as indigenous populations, rebels and revolutionaries, the oppressed and persecuted, displaced persons and refugees, accomplish the military and political objectives of the United States. However, most often Special Forces does the *"through, with and by"* with the militaries and civilian authorities of our friends and allies. Special Forces accomplishes this unique work by living with, training, fighting alongside and even, at times, leading these groups. Usually this is accomplished openly, but, at times, behind the scenes.

"With" is simple. It means working, eating, sleeping and living, side by side 24 hours per day, seven days a week, with those we are helping for as long as it takes -- years or generations -- to accomplish the objectives of both the people we are supporting and the USA; however, their objectives and conduct must, or certainly should, align morally and ethically with the United States. This *"with"* usually takes place overseas in the location of the people, but it can occur in surrounding areas or even in training locations within the United States. Regardless, it does mean that Special Forces go to war side-by-side with these people.

---

1   U.S. Army War College Military Studies Program Paper, *"Unconventional Operations Forces of Special Operations"* by the author, then LTC Mark D. Boyatt, 15 April 1993.

But what is the difference between *through* and *by*? "*Through*" is as simple as the Special Forces not working directly "*with*" the people, but working "*through*" surrogates (trusted third parties acting as intermediaries). This may happen when we wish to conceal U.S. support or when Special Forces are not permitted direct contact with the people we wish to help.

The "*by*" is when the indigenous people conduct the actual operations by themselves, but are supported and assisted by Special Forces who may work with them in remote, safe locations to train and prepare them, secure their equipment and supplies, but not accompany them when they return to their home location to conduct operations.

"*Through, with and by*" can be conducted in peace or conflict and, to be clear, some other organizations do "through, with and by" to some degree. But only Army Special Forces are specifically selected, assessed, trained and organized for "*through, with and by*" for long duration (years, generations) in foreign lands with foreign cultures in war and other conflicts, specifically in unconventional warfare.

Why is this unique to the Green Berets? You will discover this in detail in Chapter 1.

What is the purpose of this book?

The purpose of this book is to explain the uniqueness of Special Forces as a national asset, and second, to clarify the uniqueness of unconventional warfare as the sole realm of Special Forces.

BOTTOM-LINE: Unconventional warfare (UW) is a U.S. supported and conceivably inspired, insurgency or revolution. It is *total warfare* for the indigenous population who use every means at their disposal to effect *regime change* of their current masters. These masters may be a tyrannical government or an occupying power. To the indigenous population involved in UW, the survival of every man, woman and child is at stake. To this group, this is revolt or insurrection. This is revolutionary warfare. Contrary to some of our "conventional wisdom" and the official definition of UW, UW is *not* something that is used to coerce or influence a regime. For the U.S. to approach our support of a UW situation with the camouflaged intent of influencing or coercing rather that supporting the indigenous people in regime change is disingenuous, deceptive, immoral and unethical. To do this dooms the people to annihilation.

This book is written first and foremost for United States taxpayers. For every one of you who pays into the national treasury with your hard-earned money...

...but more importantly it is written for those who give their sons and daughters, the real national treasure, to the Nation's politicians to spend... to spend their blood.

This book is also written for Special Forces in particular, Special Operations Forces in general, and especially for those politicians, staffers, military leaders who have the power and responsibility for the expenditure of our national treasure – the blood and money of our citizens – and the lives and treasure of those to whom we make commitments, the "indig."

The main theme is the uniqueness of Special Forces and unconventional warfare. Second is the requirement for the <u>commitment of persistent national will</u> to the deployment and use of the military and specifically Special Forces and the understanding of the role of the interagency process as the conscience of the Nation. It is the responsibility of the interagency process, Congress and the military leadership to stress the moral and ethical considerations and responsibilities when engaging in unconventional warfare.

> "...that unconventional warfare is a major form of politio-military conflict equal in importance to conventional warfare." -- David Tucker, issue 14 of *The Letort Papers*.

The interagency process is always critical, but never more so than when planning for and consolidating the political success immediately upon military success. It is within this criticality that victory or defeat may be decided. Interagency composition varies according to each administration, but always consists of the six principal presidential advisors responsible for dealing with national security: the Secretaries of State,

Defense, and Treasury, the National Security Advisor, Director of National Intelligence, and Chairman of the Joint Chiefs of Staff. Most other departments are normally represented. The actual working groups consist of staff members with ultimate decision authority residing with the President.

The U.S. had no (viable) political plan ready to implement after we defeated the Taliban in Afghanistan in 2002 and the Iraqi army in 2003. These were key failures, and our inability to consolidate our military victories into political victories is the root cause of the quagmire in which we now find ourselves.

Our strategy must not only be to win the fight, but also to politically consolidate that victory. This end game must be inculcated into the education of our combat leaders in our current military schools and in the core psychic of all politicians.

Today, we continue to develop battlefield strategies, but, as yet, have no apparent political strategy for our small wars, and no political "country teams" ready to implement a well-defined political consolidation strategy immediately following battlefield wins. We win the fight, but lose the war.

- The core purpose of Special Forces is to accomplish Special Operations activities *through, with or by* indigenous populations. No unilateral[2] activities.
- Unconventional Warfare (UW) is the primary SF activity and it is only conducted *through, with or by* the indigenous population for the purpose of regime change.
- Unconventional warfare's only purpose is political victory.
- The military must understand and accept that UW is not a military operation, it is political.
- Unconventional warfare is political warfare conducted *through, with and by* indigenous populations to achieve a legitimate political solution and prevents the exposure of U.S. military except for those Special Forces soldiers that must be on the ground supporting, advising, and directing the indigenous population effort.
- Unconventional warfare is total war to the indigenous population involved. Anything short of regime change will result in the genocide or enslavement of those involved in the UW effort against the regime.
- If we do not have the political leadership with the political will to pursue the continuation of the UW campaign for as long as it may take, it is morally bankrupt to even begin a UW campaign.
- There is a moral and ethical imperative to unconventional warfare.
- The required premise for unconventional warfare is ubiquitous, persistent, continuous engagement.
- Internal defense and development/foreign internal defense/counterinsurgency operations all must be interagency-led operations that must be planned for and be put into effect simultaneous with any unconventional warfare operation.
- Regional orientation and regional focus is imperative for Special Forces.

---

2   unilateral - in this context it means U.S. personnel only; no foreign participation is allowed. For example, a raid or attack in which only U.S. personnel are involved. The point is that unilateral operations do not have the legitimacy that "through, with and by" operations have with those we are trying to help.

- Persistent, and continuous, forward presence/stationing is imperative for Special Forces.
- Unconventional warfare is generational war and there is little room for cultural errors.
- Every move must be culturally integrated.
- Special Forces units must remain focused on their area of responsibility.
- Without this regional focus there is no viable *"through, with and by"* with indigenous populations that will support national objectives in a timely manner.
- Interagency coordination and collaboration remains problematic.
- The definition of Special Forces is very definitive.

Are we kidding ourselves? Are we hoisting ourselves up by our own petard[3]?

To my Special Forces brethren from all eras, I salute you. *De Oppressor Liber.* Go tell the Spartans...

---

3   petard - an explosive device - hoisted by one's own petard is to be hurt, ruined, or destroyed by the very device or plot intended for another.

Definitions

Before proceeding, this is a good place to list the definitions of the key military acronyms that are used and you will see used throughout the book. The below listed definitions are all taken from the most current available joint publications published by the Department of Defense. The publications from which the definitions were drawn are listed with the definitions. The initials "JP" mean it is an official Joint Publication.

CD - Counterdrug Operational Support —Support to host nations and drug law enforcement agencies involving military personnel and their associated equipment, provided by the geographic combatant commanders from forces assigned to them or made available to them by the Services for this purpose. See also counterdrug nonoperational support; counterdrug operations. (JP 3-07.4) (JP 1-02, 8 November 2010, as amended through 15 January 2015)

Clandestine: Any activity or operation sponsored or conducted by governmental departments or agencies with the intent to assure secrecy and concealment. (JP 1-02, 8 November 2010 as amended through 15 January 2015)

COIN - Counterinsurgency — Comprehensive civilian and military efforts designed to simultaneously defeat and contain insurgency and address its root causes. Also called **COIN.** (JP 3-24) (JP 1-02, 8 November 2010, as amended through 15 January 2015)

Covert: an operation that is so planned and executed as to conceal the identity of or permit plausible denial by the sponsor. (JP 1-02, 8 November 2010 as amended through 15 January 2015)

DMO - Demining Operations - sometimes called Humanitarian Demining Assistance. The activities related to the furnishing of education, training, and technical assistance with respect to the detection and clearance of land mines and other explosive remnants of war. (JP 3-29) (JP 1-02, 8 November 2010, as amended through 15 January 2015)

FID - Foreign Internal Defense — Participation by civilian and military agencies of a government in any of the action programs taken by another government or other designated organization to free and protect its society from subversion, lawlessness, insurgency, terrorism, and other threats to its security. Also called FID. (JP 3-22) (JP 1-02, 8 November 2010, as amended through 15 January 2015)

Foreign Disaster Relief — Assistance that can be used to alleviate the suffering of foreign disaster victims that normally includes services and commodities as well as rescue and evacuation of victims; the provision and transportation of food, water, clothing, medicines, beds, and bedding, and temporary shelter; the furnishing of medical equipment, medical and technical personnel; and making repairs to essential services. See also foreign disaster. (JP 3-29) (JP 1-02, 8 November 2010, as amended through 15 January 2015)

HA - Foreign Humanitarian Assistance — Department of Defense activities conducted outside the United States and its territories to directly relieve or reduce human suffering, disease, hunger, or privation. Also called FHA. See also foreign assistance. (JP 1-02, 8 November 2010, as amended through 15 January 2015)

HADR - Humanitarian Assistance/Disaster Relief - This is an acronym which was once in common use that combined the above two like-type definitions

Humanitarian Demining Assistance, sometimes called **DMO** (demining operations) — The activities related to the furnishing of education, training, and technical assistance with respect to the detection and clearance of land mines and other explosive remnants of war. (JP 3-29) (JP 1-02, 8 November 2010, as amended through 15 January 2015)

IDAD - Internal Defense and Development — The full range of measures taken by a nation to promote its growth and to protect itself from subversion, lawlessness, insurgency, terrorism, and other threats to its security. Also called IDAD. See also foreign internal defense. (JP 3-22) (JP 1-02, 8 November 2010, as amended through 15 January 2015)

IW - Irregular Warfare - A violent struggle among state and non-state actors for legitimacy and influence over the relevant population(s). (Joint Publication 1–02; Department of Defense Dictionary of Military and Associated Terms; dated 8 November 2010 (as amended through 15 January 2015)

Overt: Activities that are openly acknowledged by or are readily attributable to the United States Government, including those designated to acquire information through legal and open means without concealment. Overt information may be collected by observation, elicitation, or from knowledgeable human sources.

PK - Peacekeeping, sometimes called **PKO** (peacekeeping operations)— Military operations undertaken with the consent of all major parties to a dispute, designed to monitor and facilitate implementation of an agreement (cease fire, truce, or other such agreement) and support diplomatic efforts to reach a long-term political settlement. See also peace building; peace enforcement; peacemaking; peace operations. (JP 3-07.3) (JP 1-02, 8 November 2010, as amended through 15 January 2015)

SA - Security Assistance — Group of programs authorized by the Foreign Assistance Act of 1961, as amended, and the Arms Export Control Act of 1976, as amended, or other related statutes by which the United States provides defense articles, military training, and other defense-related services by grant, loan, credit, or cash sales in furtherance of national policies and objectives. Security assistance is an element of security cooperation funded and authorized by Department of State to be administered by Department of Defense/Defense Security Cooperation

Agency. Also called SA. See also security cooperation. (JP 3-22) (JP 1-02, 8 November 2010, as amended through 15 January 2015)

SC - Security Cooperation - SA - Security Assistance — See definition above. These terms have the same definition in the referenced doctrinal authority.

Stability Operations —An overarching term encompassing various military missions, tasks, and activities conducted outside the United States in coordination with other instruments of national power to maintain or reestablish a safe and secure environment, provide essential governmental services, emergency infrastructure reconstruction, and humanitarian relief. (JP 3-0) (JP 1-02, 8 November 2010, as amended through 15 January 2015)

SFA - Security Force Assistance—The Department of Defense activities that contribute to unified action by the U.S. Government to support the development of the capacity and capability of foreign security forces and their supporting institutions. Also called **SFA.** (JP 3-22) (JP 1-02, 8 November 2010, as amended through 15 January 2015)

UW - Unconventional Warfare — Activities conducted to enable a resistance movement or insurgency to coerce, disrupt, or overthrow a government or occupying power by operating through or with an underground, auxiliary, and guerrilla force in a denied area. Also called **UW.** (JP 3-05, 8 November 2010, as amended through 15 January 2015)

Acronyms

FOR QUICK REFERENCE AS YOU READ.	
18A	Special Forces Detachment Commander
18B	Special Forces Weapons Sergeant
18C	Special Forces Engineer Sergeant
18D	Special Forces Medical Sergeant
18E	Special Forces Communications Sergeant
18F	Special Forces Intelligence Sergeant
18Z	Special Forces Senior Sergeant either a Sergeant Major or Master Sergeant
180A	Special Forces Warrant Officer – Detachment Executive Officer
A	
A2/AD	Anti-Air/Air Defense
ADP	Army Doctrine Publication
AFSOC	Air Force Special Operations Command
AIT	advanced individual training
AOR	Area of Responsibility often used to mean Area of Operations
APFT	Army Physical Fitness Test
ARI	Army Research Institute

ARSOF	Army Special Operations Command
ARSOAC	Army Special Operations Air Component
ASVAB	Armed Services Vocational Aptitude Battery (ASVAB)
ATP	Army Technical Publication
B	
BG	Brigadier General (Army)
C	
CAC	Combined Arms Center (Fort Leavenworth, KS)
CD	Counter-Drug Operational Support
CIF	CINC In-Extremis Force
CINC	Commander in Chief (old terminology for Geographic Combatant Commander - GCC)
CMF	Career Management Field - these are numerical designations -- 11 is infantry; 12 is engineer; 13 is field artillery; 14 is air defense artillery; 15 is aviation; 18 is Special Forces
CN	Counternarcotics
COE	contemporary operating environment
COI	Office of the Coordinator of Information (World War II)
COIN	Counterinsurgency
COL(R)	Colonel Retired
CONUS	The Continental United States (as opposed to OCONUS - Outside the Continental United States)

CT	Counterterrorism
CULEX	Culmination Exercise

	D	

DA	Direct Action or Department of the Army
DEROS	Date eligible for return from overseas
DLAB	Defense Language Aptitude Battery
DOD	Department of Defense
DOTD	Directorate of Training and Doctrine
DR	Foreign Disaster Relief

	E	

E&E	Evasion and Escape

	F	

FHA	Foreign Humanitarian Assistance
FID	Foreign Internal Defense
FM	Field Manual
FOB	Forward Operational Base - usually organized around a Special Forces Battalion headquarters
FSF	Foreign Security Forces
FSO	Full Spectrum Operations

	G	

GCC	Geographic Combatant Command
GW	Guerrilla Warfare

	H	

HA	Humanitarian Assistance

HUMINT	Human Intelligence
I	
IDAD	Internal Defense and Development
ISIL	Islamic State of Iraq and the Levant
ISIS	Islamic State of Iraq and Syria
IW	Irregular Warfare
J	
JIIM	Joint, Interagency, Intergovernmental, and Multinational
JP	Joint Publication
JRCC	Joint Recovery Coordination Center
JSOA	Joint Special Operational Area
JSOU	Joint Special Operations University, USSOCOM, MacDill AFB, FL
L	
LOCs	Lines of Communication
LTG	Lieutenant General
M	
MAAG	Military Assistance Advisory Group
MARSOC	U.S. Marine Special Operations Command
MG	Major General
MMPI	Minnesota Multifaceted Personality Inventory (MMPI) Test
MNF	Multinational Force
MOS	Military Occupational Specialty

N	
NATO	North Atlantic Treaty Organization
NAVSPECWARCOM	Naval Special Warfare Command
NCO	Non-commissioned officer (a sergeant)
NOFORN	No Foreign (a classification terminology distinction)
NPS	Naval Post Graduate School
NSA	National Security Agency
O	
OCONUS	Outside the Continental United States
ODA	Operational Detachment "A" - commanded by a Captain (12 soldiers)
ODB	Operational Detachment "B" - commanded by a Major (11-13 soldiers)
ODC	Operational Detachment "C" - commanded by a Lieutenant Colonel (usually has a full headquarters with support detachments plus 3xODBs and 18xODAs)
OGs	Operational Groups (part of OSS)
OSS	Office of Strategic Services
P	
PCS	Permanent Change of Station (vice temporary duty -TDY)
PERSCOM	U.S. Army Personnel Support Command
PK or PKO	Peace-Keeping Operations
R	
RAF	regionally aligned conventional forces

RTL	resistance training lab (part of SERE training)
	S
SA	Security Assistance (SA) programs
SAF original	Special Action Force
SAF current	Security Assistance Force or Stabilization Assistance Force
SC	Security Cooperation
SEAL	Sea, Air, Land (Navy)
SERE	Survival, Evasion, Resistance and Escape
SF	Special Forces (Army)
SFA	Security Force Assistance
SFAS	Special Forces Selection and Assessment
SFDOQC	Special Forces Detachment Officer Qualification Course (SFDOQC)
SFOB	Special Forces Operational Base - usually organized around a Special Forces Group headquarters
SFQC	Special Forces Qualification Course
SME	subject matter expert
SOF	Special Operations Forces
SOPC	Special Operations Preparation and Conditioning Course
SSE	Sensitive Site Exploitation
SR	Strategic Reconnaissance
SWCS	Special Warfare Center and School (Fort Bragg, NC) full title: United States Army John F. Kennedy Special Warfare Center and School (USAJFKSWCS)
SWTG	Special Warfare Training Group

	T
TDY	Temporary Duty (vice PCS-permanent change of station)
TRADOC	U.S. Army Training and Doctrine Command (USATRADOC)
TTL	Tag, Track, and Locate
TTPs	Tactics, Techniques, Procedures
	U
UAV	Unmanned Aerial Vehicle
UNMIH	United Nations Mission in Haiti
USASFC	United States Army Special Forces Command (Fort Bragg, NC)
USACDCSWA	United States Army Combat Developments Command Special Warfare Agency
USAJFKSWCS	United States Army John F. Kennedy Special Warfare Center and School (Fort Bragg, NC)
USASOC	United States Army Special Operations Command (Fort Bragg, NC)
USG	United States Government
USMC	United States Marine Corps
USSOCOM	United States Special Operations Command (Tampa, FL)
UW	Unconventional Warfare
UWOA	Unconventional Warfare Operational Area
	W
WMD	Weapon(s) of Mass Destruction

1

Special Forces

Defining "through, with and by"

A paper originally written in 1993 at the Army War College[4] introduced the term *"through, with and by."* Over the years it has become apparent that the meaning of these words is not clear and has been distorted, modified, and possibly lost in some interpretations. Below, the original meaning of the words and the term *"through, with and by,"* are clarified.

"Through, with and by:" This phrase describes the manner in which Special Forces, working *"through, with and by"* other people, such as indigenous populations, rebels and revolutionaries, the oppressed and persecuted, displaced people and refugees, and most often with the militaries and civilian authorities of our friends and allies, accomplish the military and political objectives of the United States. Special Forces does this unique work by living with, training, fighting alongside and even, at times, leading these groups. Usually this is done openly, but, at times, this work is accomplished behind the scenes.

"With" is simple. It means working, eating, sleeping and living, side by side 24 hours per day, seven days a week, with those we are helping for as long as it takes -- years or generations -- to accomplish the objectives of the people we are supporting; however, their objectives and conduct

---

4   U.S. Army War College Military Studies Program Paper, *"Unconventional Operations Forces of Special Operations"* by the author, then LTC Mark D. Boyatt, 15 April 1993.

must, or certainly should, align morally and ethically with the United States. This *"with"* usually takes place overseas in the location of the people, but it can occur in surrounding areas or even in training locations within the United States. Regardless, it means Special Forces go to war side-by-side with these people.

"Through" is as simple as the Special Forces not working directly *"with"* the people, but working *"through"* surrogates (trusted third parties acting as intermediaries). This may happen when we wish to conceal U.S. support or when Special Forces are not permitted direct contact with the people we wish to help. *"Through"* has two parts:

1) Special Forces effect operations by providing/coordinating equipment, training, logistics, fire support, aviation support, etc. to another party, a surrogate – not directly with the indigenous population seeking assistance. The surrogate then subsequently carries out the action in support of the indigenous population.

2) Special Forces effects operations by having a second party act as the cutout for a third-party that conducts the actual operations. (A cutout is a mutually trusted intermediary, usually only known to the source - the Special Forces - and through which the indigenous personnel, the information, supplies, equipment or other action is transmitted. The third-party, the indigenous population, would know the cutout intermediary; however, they would not know the Special Forces that were controlling the cutout intermediary.)

"With" is simply when Special Forces provides and/or coordinates the equipment, training, logistics, fire support, aviation support, etc. and conducts and accompanies operations directly with the affected party – the indigenous population seeking assistance. Plus, the Special Forces stand side-by-side with these people throughout the entire event; however many years. Of course, the event may be a peacetime training event or it could be conflict.

An example of *"with"* is T.E. Lawrence, Lawrence of Arabia in the First World War (see Annex A). Lawrence lived and fought with the Arabs and these successfully changed the regime (the Turks) when they won. Unfortunately, the winning Arabs did not survive their success and lost control to another group. Again, a failure of the Allies to consolidate the win.

"*By*" is simply that the Special Forces provides and/or coordinates the equipment, training, logistics, fire support, aviation support, etc. directly with the affected party (indigenous population) who then carries out the actions without active participation by Special Forces. The indigenous people conduct the actual operations totally by themselves, but are supported and assisted by Special Forces who may work with them in remote, safe locations to train and prepare them, get them equipment and supplies, but cannot accompany them when they return to their home location to conduct operations.

An example of *"through"* and also *"by"* is the Soviet-Afghan War 1979-1989. The United States supported the Mujahideen[5] by both using the Pakistanis as an intermediary and the U.S. also provided some training to the Mujahideen in Pakistan. No U.S. personnel accompanied the Mujahideen into Afghanistan, so no "with." If you don't wish to research history, just watch the movie "Charlie Wilson's War." Again, the Mujahideen did not enjoy their success as the U.S. did not continue support and the radical Taliban seized control. And so, we had 9/11 and the current quagmire of Afghanistan--another failed victory.

The *"through, with and by"* applies to all the Special Forces missions. It equally applies to unconventional warfare, foreign internal defense/internal defense and development, counterinsurgency operations, direct action, strategic reconnaissance, counterterrorism, and all of the other missions.

The only other definitive attempt at defining *"through, with and by,"* of which I am aware is a paper written in 2007 by then Marine Corps Major

---

5   Mujahideen - the plural form of mujahid, the term for one engaged in Jihad. In English usage, it mostly referred to the guerrilla type military outfits led by the Muslim Afghan warriors in the Soviet war in Afghanistan, but now it often refers to other jihadist outfits in various countries. The name was most closely associated with members of a number of guerrilla groups operating in Afghanistan that opposed invading Soviet forces and eventually toppled the Afghan communist government during the Afghan War (1979–92).

Travis L. Homiak[6] as a part of his degree program. Below is an excerpt from his paper that explains his point of view. It is a bit of a difficult read, but impressive that he took it on.

> What is really meant by the phrase "Through, With, and By?" The phrase "through, with, and by" can be explained by examining different relationships between two notional actors (i.e., Actor A and Actor B) and relative capacities and will for undertaking action. In broad terms, working "through, with, and by" refers to the idea that Actor A directly or indirectly builds Actor B' s *capacity* and *will* to take action to address a given problem, the resolution of which benefits both parties. Within this construct, capacity refers to an actor's ability to undertake action in a given situation, while *will* refers to an actor's freedom of choice. *Will* has three components: recognition of the problem, desire to take action, and determination to see that action through to completion. For clarity, the terms "through, with, and by" will be addressed from most to least visible with regard to the overt nature of underlying interactions, rather than defining them in the order in which they appear in the Joint UW definition.
>
> "With" is the most overt association in the methodology, necessitating a physical presence and associated interaction between Actors A and B. "Accompanied by or accompanying," best defines the concept of working "with" another agent. In a relationship defined as working "with," Actor A works alongside Actor B to address a given problem while providing Actor B with the capacity, will, or both capacity and will required to act. In this relationship, Actor A works shoulder-to-shoulder with Actor B, while facilitating the resolution of a mutual problem. Working "with" another actor is an on-the-scene activity where Actor A is physically present

---

6   USMC School of Advanced War-fighting, Marine Corps University; *Future War Paper: Working "Through, With, and By" Non-US Actors to Achieve Operational-Level Security Objectives(Draft)*; Major Travis L. Homiak; 26 April 2007.

with Actor B, sharing ideas, providing advice, and combining resources.

A Special Operations assistance mission whereby Actor A trains and equips (builds capacity) in Actor B and then fights alongside him (provides will) demonstrates working "with" in terms of a military task. An excellent historical example is provided by Special Operations Executive/Office of Strategic Services (SOE/OSS) operatives who equipped and fought alongside Tito's partisans in Yugoslavia during World War II. SOE/OSS operatives built the partisans' capacity for action through aerial-delivered equipment, bolstered their will through their presence as representatives of the Western Allies (at least initially), and fought side by side to defeat the Germans in the Balkans.

The second of the three relationships in order of observability is working "through" and refers to achieving an objective "by means of." Working "through" implies a relationship in which Actor A works behind-the-scenes to provide Actor B with the capacity, will, or both to take action against a given problem, the resolution of which benefits both actors. The key component to working "through" is Actor A's reduced level of direct involvement in efforts to address the shared problem. In a "through" relationship, Actor A employs Actor B as a surrogate, enabling actions intended to resolve a shared problem by precursor counsel, training, equipping, or combination thereof.

According to this definition of "through," capacity building is not restricted to increasing physical capability, but can also apply to empowering the actions of other actors. If Actor B possesses the physical capability to take action but lacks the freedom to do so, and Actor A can sanction Actor B's right to act, then Actor A is working "through" Actor B by granting Actor B permission to act. Furthermore, in contrast to working "with," working "through" necessitates sharing ideas and providing advice *without* overtly taking action against the common problem. While "through" demands cooperation between the actors, it has no requirement for combined action.

"By" is the indirect context's third and final relationship, promoting achievement of a desired outcome "through the agency or instrumentality of' another. "By" assumes that an actor, who possesses the capacity and will sufficient to address a given problem, is going to engage that problem. The essence of "by" is that Actor B takes action to achieve an objective desired by Actor A, without Actor A necessarily prompting Actor B to do so. One can reasonably expect Actor B to address the problem, because Actor B recognizes the problem and has both the capacity and will to undertake action toward resolving it.

When the relationship of "by" is operative in a system composed of at least three actors, the system can be considered to be 'self-regulating' because no input is required from Actor A to elicit action on the part of Actor B. What is required for "by" to function is that both actors recognize the problem and perceive that solving the problem will yield a beneficial outcome."By" is the least obtrusive of the three relationships because it may not require any initiating action on the part of Actor A. Actor B simply acts because it is in his interest to do so. In Actor B's mind, it may be merely coincidental that Actor A also benefits from B's actions. On the other hand, a relationship characterized as "by" can be the result of having previously worked "through" and "with" an actor, building the capacity and will required for the future action. Thus, working "through" and "with" may be viewed as stepping stones to creating a 'self regulating' system in which actors take care of problems that affect the entire system without the prompting or direct involvement of others to do so. (pages 3-7) (end of excerpt)

Clearly there is some divergence in the intricacies between the definitions above. Likewise, when you review the section on *Unconventional Warfare*

Definition Evolution in Chapter 3 and Annex D, you will see that there is further divergence and even places where the definitions only use the words "through and with." Obviously, this reduces the scope and meaning of the phrase *"through, with and by"* and subsequently, understanding Special Forces.

So what are indigenous populations?

indigenous -- adjective
- originating in and characteristic of a particular region or country; native (often followed by *to*)
- produced, living, or existing naturally in a particular region or environment

population -- noun
- All the inhabitants of a particular place
- A particular group or type of people living in a place:

Population, in human biology, is the whole number of inhabitants occupying an area (such as a country or the world) and continually being modified by increases (births and immigrations) and losses (deaths and emigrations). As with any biological population, the size of a human population is limited by the supply of food, the effect of diseases, and other environmental factors. Human populations are further affected by social customs governing reproduction and by the technological developments, especially in medicine and public health, that have reduced mortality and extended the life span.

The United Nations *Permanent Forum on Indigenous Issues* website provides the following information reference indigenous populations (not that I believe the UN is authoritative on *any* issue).

Who are indigenous peoples?
It is estimated that there are more than 370 million indigenous people spread across 70 countries worldwide. Practicing unique traditions, they retain social, cultural, economic and political characteristics that are distinct from those of the dominant soci-

eties in which they live. Spread across the world from the Arctic to the South Pacific, they are the descendants –according to a common definition--of those who inhabited a country or a geographical region at the time when people of different cultures or ethnic origins arrived. The new arrivals later became dominant through conquest, occupation, settlement or other means.

Among the indigenous peoples are those of the Americas (for example, the Lakota in the USA, the Mayas in Guatemala or the Aymaras in Bolivia), the Inuit and Aleutians of the circumpolar region, the Saami of northern Europe, the Aborigines and Torres Strait Islanders of Australia and the Maori of New Zealand. These and most other indigenous peoples have retained distinct characteristics which are clearly different from those of other segments of the national populations.

Understanding the term "indigenous"

Considering the diversity of indigenous peoples, an official definition of "indigenous" has not been adopted by any UN-system body. Instead the system has developed a modern understanding of this term based on the following:

- Self- identification as indigenous peoples at the individual level and accepted by the community as their member.
- Historical continuity with pre-colonial and/or pre-settler societies
- Strong link to territories and surrounding natural resources
- Distinct social, economic or political systems
- Distinct language, culture and beliefs
- Form non-dominant groups of society
- Resolve to maintain and reproduce their ancestral environments and systems as distinctive peoples and communities.

A question of identity

- According to the UN the most fruitful approach is to identify, rather than define indigenous peoples. This is based on the fundamental criterion of self-identification as underlined in a number of human rights documents.

- The term "indigenous" has prevailed as a generic term for many years. In some countries, there may be preference for other terms including tribes, first peoples/nations, aboriginals, ethnic groups, *adivasi, janajati*. Occupational and geographical terms like hunter-gatherers, nomads, peasants, hill people, etc., also exist and for all practical purposes can be used interchangeably with "indigenous peoples."
- In many cases, the notion of being termed "indigenous" has negative connotations and some people may choose not to reveal or define their origin. Others must respect such choices, while at the same time working against the discrimination of indigenous peoples.

Culture and Knowledge

Indigenous peoples are the holders of unique languages, knowledge systems and beliefs and possess invaluable knowledge of practices for the sustainable management of natural resources. They have a special relation to and use of their traditional land. Their ancestral land has a fundamental importance for their collective physical and cultural survival as peoples. Indigenous peoples hold their own diverse concepts of development, based on their traditional values, visions, needs and priorities.

Political participation

Indigenous peoples often have much in common with other neglected segments of societies, i.e. lack of political representation and participation, economic marginalization and poverty, lack of access to social services and discrimination. Despite their cultural differences, the diverse indigenous peoples share common problems also related to the protection of their rights. They strive for recognition of their identities, their ways of life and their right to traditional lands, territories and natural resources. (end of excerpt)

So, indigenous populations often, but not necessarily always, share the same ethnicity, culture, morals and values, goals and objectives, political orientation, language, etc. Therefore, it would not be feasible to effectively conduct operations *through with and by* without an almost visceral understanding of these characteristics. Achieving this understanding requires intense and focused education, focused, continuous regional engagement and preferably immersion in the population.

So why is it necessary to go into the detail of explaining these terms? The answer is both simple and complex. Since the end of the Vietnam War, working with foreign indigenous populations has been looked at by many in both the Department of Defense and the Department of State, as a bad way to conduct the business of the United States. As such, the conventional military has seen much of what Special Forces did in Vietnam and is organized to do in the future as a "pitiful sideshow.[7]" Because of this perception, some in Special Forces also viewed working *through, with and by* indigenous populations as less than desirable.

Beginning in the mid to late '70s, there was a deliberate movement away from *through, with and by* and into/toward unilateral operations such as direct action missions and special reconnaissance missions. While this was a survival tactic to keep Special Forces alive during the post-Vietnam drawdown, it created a unilateral[8] culture that continued through the recent (and still ongoing?) engagements in Iraq and Afghanistan. Unilateral operations are high visibility, immediate gratification missions, well within the cultural comfort zone, and easily identified with by most people, most importantly the conventional Army. Special Forces repeatedly conducted and still conducts these unilateral operations; however, they do so by sacrificing expertise and competence in *through, with or by* operations such as unconventional warfare, foreign internal defense/internal defense and development, counterinsurgency operations, etc.

Arguably, immediately following 9/11 in the early stages of operations in Afghanistan, Special Forces, with CIA and Air Force special tactics combat

---

7   This may or may not have changed due to the Iraq and Afghanistan experiences 2001-2015.
8   unilateral - in this context it means U.S. personnel only; no foreign participation is allowed, no "through, with or by." It meant changing focus to direct support of the conventional Army in conventional warfare.

controllers, conducted unconventional warfare operations (entering the UW conflict at stage 3—see Annex K) with the Northern Alliance early on during September through December 2001. Subsequently, with the collapse of the Taliban in Afghanistan, unconventional warfare gave way to foreign internal defense and counterinsurgency operations. Obviously, internal defense operations (the military conceived a term called *combat* foreign internal defense which sounds like an attempt to "*warriorize*" foreign internal defense to make it more "manly") by definition are conducted *through, with and by the indigenous personne*l; however, the same is not always true with counterinsurgency operations. Many, if not most, of the Special Forces counterinsurgency operations were conducted unilaterally[9]. This consisted mostly of unilateral direct action missions after high value individual target or groups of Taliban or Al Qaeda. This unilateral execution of counterinsurgency was for many reasons, such as expediency, source of intelligence, lack of trust and confidence in the indigenous assets, among others.

The other SOF units[10], particularly the national SOF[11], receive specific resourcing to train, equip and organize for unilaterally executed missions. To consider Special Forces for **unilateral** tasks should be a last choice. Rather than being considered *first* for *any* unilateral mission, Special Forces should be considered *only* if other SOF or conventional forces are unavailable. Special Forces' unique capabilities lie in conducting missions and tasks **through, with or by indigenous personnel and populations**.

This uniqueness of Special Forces lies in its cultural aspects and the selection, assessment, experience, maturity and training of the personnel (see Chapter 7: Selection and Assessment). These aspects apply equally to the requirements of teaching or the conduct of military operations in a culturally sensitive environment. To conduct effective operations **through, with or by indigenous populations** requires detailed ethnographic[12] knowledge and understanding of the indigenous population through

---

9   unilateral - in this context it means U.S. personnel only; no foreign participation is allowed.

10   Such as SEALs, Rangers, Marine Special Operations Command, Army and Air Force Special Operations Aviation.

11   These are selected units specifically focused on counterterrorism.

12   ethnography - a branch of anthropology dealing with the scientific description of individual cultures including the details of day-to-day life that provide real insight into the meaning of social and cultural change.

dedicated regional focus and, most importantly, a unique attitude --- the core ideology (see Chapter 2: Core Ideology).

Next, key elements of effective **through, with or by operations** are language training, cultural studies, continuous forward presence and regional engagement (see Chapter 6: Regional Focus) and an understanding of the ethnography of the population. When Special Forces units focus on a unilateral mission, these complex ethnographic capabilities and understandings are the first areas to suffer. To achieve adequate proficiency in these cultural aspects requires intensive focus, training, regional expertise and persistent forward presence. Key to understanding the conduct of *"through, with and by"* activities[13] is that these activities require a degree of proficiency in the unilateral missions such as direct action (DA) and strategic reconnaissance (SR). These areas are not ignored. They are only approached with a different training focus and attitude. The uniqueness of Special Forces is in executing all these missions **through, with or by indigenous personnel.** (Note – *Everything* SF does is strategic in effect)

Why care about focusing the SF mission on the "through, with and by" missions of UW and IDAD (FID/ /COIN)? Why not focus on unilateral operations? Surely, the reasoning is becoming clearly evident. Clarity of purpose, scarce resources and security through continual regional engagement world-wide can only be achieved with this single-minded focus, and it must be single-minded. "Through, with and by" operations are too complex and time consuming to take vacations into unilateral missions. Too often enthusiasm is confused as competence – – a saying attributed to General Peter Schoomaker[14]. There is also a mistaken belief that the potential to conduct a given mission equals the capability to execute it competently -- also attributed to General Schoomaker.

Rarely are there excess resources for preparation...any type of preparation. The prime resource is time. Even given the years of recent experience in Iraq and Afghanistan, many SF units (battalions and teams) still focus

---

13   UW/FID/IDAD/COIN.
14   General Peter J. Schoomaker. Started out in the Army as an Armored Cavalry officer, volunteered for and successfully accomplished selection into Delta Force, became the Commander of the United States Army Special Operations Command, Cmdr. U.S. Special Operations Command in Tampa, and the 35th Chief of Staff of the Army.

on unilateral DA, SR, or CT. Accordingly, much of their training time is spent perfecting their *unilateral* capabilities in these areas at the expense of time that should be focused on the "through, with and by" activities of UW an IDAD (FID/COIN). By so narrowly focusing on the unilateral DA, SR, or CT missions, these elements continue to degrade their ability to be truly effective in the more complex activities of UW and IDAD (FID/COIN). Yes, more complex than unilateral actions. Why?

Unilateral actions, in the grand scheme of things, are relatively simple. When U.S. elements unilaterally conduct a mission, they do so in a common language, a relatively common cultural background, shared understanding of doctrinal principles, tactics, techniques, purpose and goals. Unilateral missions have crystal-clear and well-defined parameters of operation and execution. Unilateral missions have a relatively clear timeline. Furthermore, unilateral missions have the advantage of being terminated or canceled at any point in time, usually even after commencement of the operation. None of these things are simple or easy to do when operating *through with or by* indigenous personnel or populations.

So, units that have a unilateral training focus cannot make the transition from a unilateral focus without significant effort and time or the risk is greatly increased. And by risk I don't mean just to the unit's conduct in the operation. Placing U.S. forces with an indigenous population is a decision that it is made at the highest levels of command and as part of national policy with interagency guidance. The risk of employing marginally trained, focused, culturally attuned units in a strategic environment with indigenous populations is fraught with disaster for the United States and the indigenous people. Working *through, with and by* indigenous populations cannot be an enterprise conducted by tourists.

Likewise, units effectively trained in UW and FID/COIN will not be able to transition rapidly to effective *unilateral* DA, SR or CT. These, too, are complicated missions requiring intensive training and best reside with the SOF units that are exclusively unilaterally focused; Rangers, Delta, SEALs, Marine Special Operations Command and selected Army and Air Force Special Operations Aviation elements.

The execution of activities unilaterally should never be a task or mission for Special Forces. Special Forces should neither be assumed to nor required to act unilaterally. The regional combatant commanders (the four star generals or admirals) must require SF to maintain a persistent forward presence during peacetime/pre-conflict in their assigned regions, with the specific task of cultivating relationships to identify the capability, availability and potential of indigenous assets. These assets might conduct missions alone or they may be organized, trained, equipped and led by SF. However, to effectively accomplish this requires years of persistent presence and engagement to establish the cultural knowledge, credibility, legitimacy and trust of the indigenous population. Unilateral action by SF is the method of last, and most ineffective and inefficient, choice.

Human intelligence (HUMINT) is a category of intelligence derived from information collected and provided by human sources (this means people on the ground, in the area), vice intelligence collected by technical means (think here National Security Agency (NSA), Star Wars, satellites, drones, etc). This is battlefield intelligence, not the James Bond foreign intelligence collection which is information relating to capabilities, intentions, and activities of foreign powers, organizations, or persons (this is the realm of the CIA, NSA and others). Undoubtedly, this is insulting the "techies," but nothing trumps human intelligence collected *through, with or by* the indigenous population.

Why is HUMINT gathered through indigenous assets trained by SF the most dependable way of conducting information collection for the on-the-ground, in-your-face daily operations? Because, if properly used, SF should have been on the ground for years, have developed trust, understanding and empathy through daily physical contact (vs texting). People primarily do things for other people...not governments, not money, not for fame...but for people.

As for the people-oriented missions of UW and IDAD (FID/COIN), these are complex activities with interrelated capabilities that require dedicated attention and training to achieve and maintain proficiency. To dilute and divert the efforts and resources of the Special Forces to *unilateral* CT, DA and SR as primary missions severely degrades the ability of SF and degrades this unique capability for the nation.

Surprisingly, it is the conventional forces and Congress that seem to have grasped the unconventional approach while the Special Operations Command (USSOCOM) and, to a degree, Army Special Operations Command (USASOC) remain rooted in and fixated on the unilateral missions. The SOF community continues the fifty plus years of neglect of the unique capability of *through, with and by.*

(Testimony on Special Operations Forces, 11 July 2012, Linda Robinson, Adjunct Senior Fellow for U.S. National Security and Foreign Policy Council on Foreign Relations, House Committee on Armed Services Subcommittee on Emerging Threats and Capabilities Hearing on the Future of Special Operations Force and Author of "Masters of Chaos: The Secret History of the Special Forces") The indirect approach should be the primary area of focus for improvements at this time. It is my assessment that while incremental steps have been taken in recent years, the indirect approach is still sub-optimized and the forces primarily charged with carrying it out are not properly resourced, organized or supported to fully maximize their potential.

Vague and confusing terminology, lack of emphasis on doctrine and operating concepts, and weak outreach to relevant partners in the government have all hampered the development and employment of SOF for maximum strategic or decisive impact. The indirect approach is an unfortunately vague term; in place of direct and indirect, the draft Army doctrinal publication 3-05 uses surgical strike and special warfare. To me, the distinguishing feature of the indirect approach (or special warfare) is partnered operations. The partner(s) can range widely from various government forces, to informal groups like tribes or community defense groups, or populations, with which civil affairs and other units routinely interact. The range of activities that SOF can engage in as part of the indirect approach is similarly broad (training, combat advising, intelligence and psychological operations, civil affairs projects) depending on the problem, the goals and the rules of engagement. But the key point is that the activities will always be ***with or through*** (emphasis added) other entities, so that they are empowered and eventually enabled to enact the solutions on their own. To achieve lasting, decisive impact the activities cannot be episodic and unconnected but must be deliberately planned, linked and sustained via a campaign design that is nested in the larger theater and mission plans and overall U.S. policy goals.

(Testimony on Special Operations Forces, 11 July 2012, Christopher J. Lamb, Distinguished Research Fellow Center for Strategic Research, Institute for National Strategic Studies, National Defense University, House Committee on Armed Services Subcommittee on Emerging Threats and Capabilities Hearing on the Future of Special Operations Force) There has been a tendency for conventional force commanders to assume their forces can relieve SOF of its indirect activities, particularly training and working with foreign forces. Worse, some SOF commanders have agreed and shunned such missions in favor of direct action. When this happens, both types of forces are saying they do not believe working ***"by, with and through"*** (emphasis added) host nation forces requires special skills, which is incorrect.

A prime reason for this is that *"through, with and by"* training is difficult to conduct, time intensive and expensive. Also, it is difficult to measure, validate and certify. It is easy and cheap in resources (time) to measure, validate and certify unilateral training. But the most likely reason *"through, with and by"* has been neglected is that it is difficult, long duration, can't be explained in a "sound bite." That it is more educationally-based than training-based, and requires years of seemingly snail-paced progress that does not read well in officer efficiency reports or budgets.

"The first is in terms of the training and SOF education programs, I think we need to start elevating the importance of the indirect approach so that people don't believe it's a second class set of missions relative to the direct action missions." *(Testimony on Special Operations Forces, 11 July 2012 House Armed Services Subcommittee on Emerging Threats and Capabilities Hearing on the Future of Special Operations Forces, Dr. Jacquelyn K. Davis, Executive Vice President, Institute for Foreign Policy Analysis)*

It is the "routine and not so glamorous" "*through, with and by*" which in fact contribute most to U.S. national security strategy in terms of their effect on long term national security objectives.

Special Forces elements have been training with their counterparts in many nations around the globe for many years. Through their presence in these countries, relationships and contacts have been established that have had far reaching effects. In many of these countries, the military counterparts with whom Special Forces have worked have eventually risen to various positions of power--in some cases even Head-of-State. These relationships have led to regional stability in some cases and access to critical facilities in others. In almost all cases, SF is viewed in these countries as informal ambassadors of the U.S. and positive examples of democracy.

The leverage gained in negotiations with foreign governments over our national security goals and objectives often staggers the imagination of the casual observer. For example, if one accepts the fact that one of our goals in Liberia was to gain and maintain the trust and confidence of its leader, President Doe, then the efforts of a single Special Forces sergeant (John Campbell) met and exceeded expectations. There are other operations, usually classified, where Special Forces *through, with and by* accomplishments far exceeded anything thought possible in terms of the long term positive impact on U.S./allied relations.

A compelling example of this contribution was the unconventional operations role SF played in Haiti. By any measure, the U.S. Army Special Forces mission in Haiti was an unqualified success. This success, however, was due to the extraordinary people in Special Forces, and not due to "*through, with and by*" preparation and training. Consequently, there were many mistakes corrected on-the-go through on-the-job experience.

Unfortunately, none of the lessons learned in Haiti were applied or, apparently even considered, in the planning or execution of the operations in Iraq or Afghanistan. Both SOF and the conventional forces repeated the errors of Haiti.

Never totaling more than 1,200 personnel (including support personnel), which comprised only 5% of the total U.S. force package, the Special Forces controlled 95% of the land mass and 80% of the population in Haiti.

The Special Forces detachments were dispersed all across the country. In fact, the only places Special Forces did not have the dominant role was within the cities of Port-au-Prince and Cap Haitian. The mission of the Special Forces was to support the Multi-National Force-Haiti (MNF-Haiti) in establishing and maintaining a stable and secure environment to facilitate the transition of the new Government of Haiti (GOH) to functional governance and to participate as required in the United Nations Mission in Haiti (UNMIH), and then hand over military operations to designated UNMIH forces and redeploy.

By 5 October 1994, the Special Forces detachments were spread throughout Haiti and physically occupying the FAd'H (Haiti's military) garrisons. The Special Forces divided Haiti into three Areas of Responsibility (AORs) - the Northern Claw, the Central Region and the Southern Claw. One SF battalion was assigned to each of the AORs. Each battalion AOR was sub-divided into at least two SF company AORs and these sub-divided into SF detachment AORs. The detachment (ODA) was the smallest element deployed and typically was comprised of 8-9 Special Forces soldiers plus attachments (units were not at full strength of twelve personnel for numerous reasons; this shortage greatly stressed the soldiers and required combining teams in some instances). The normal attachments were one U.S. military linguist if needed, a Civil Affairs detachment of 2-4 personnel usually led by a captain, and a Psychological Operations attachment of 1-2 personnel with a loudspeaker.

This typical SF detachment, with attachments, was required to control large areas. Some of the assigned AORs were 2,000-plus square kilometers in size, containing 8-11 major towns of 10,000 to 50,000 people each, with a total population of around 300,000 people in the AOR.

In each AOR, the SF were the only authority. There were no police, and the Haitian military was effectively disassembled. The town mayors, many of them Cedras appointees, had fled; the legal system was not operational; lawyers and judges were corrupt and many had fled; the prison system was atrocious; there was no border control; no port control; the electrical system was inoperative; the water system was destroyed. In short, the SF had to organize a complete political, legal, civil, and administrative infrastructure in 95% of Haiti. Again, the success of this operation depended not on prior UW focused training, but on the quality of the Special Forces soldiers[15].

"Through, with and by" operations, prudently and judiciously executed, can provide for regional stability through low-level U.S. presence. This presence can act as a brake on regional ambitions, demonstrate U.S. interest, support and bolster local legitimacy, possibly mitigate the spread of Weapons of Mass Destruction (WMD) and augment the counter-proliferation strategy.

As a nation and as a military, we cannot only focus on the *"conflict de jour."* We must put just as much emphasis and effort to promote and sustain *"through, with and by"* capabilities in all regions, simultaneously. Nations and indigenous populations that see or benefit from these *"through, with and by"* operations may become more convinced and assured of U.S. interest in and concern for a given region. This presence can foster diplomacy, whereas absence may foster conflict. Nations or regions that perceive themselves adrift from or outside the sphere of concern of the world's only super-power, feel compelled to pursue their own

---

15 Extract from After Action paper prepared by Colonel Mark D. Boyatt, Cdr 3rd Special Forces Group (Airborne) and the ARSOTF Commander Haiti for Operation Promote Democracy/Operation Uphold Democracy 1994-95.

independent means of national security. This can exacerbate regional arms races, proliferation of weapons of mass destruction and regional instability. Examples of this, unfortunately, abound around the globe.

U.S. foreign policy will always be in transition. This fact is an unfortunate result of our political process. It seems, more often than not, that our national focus is on the election rhetoric rather than stability and security. At best, it is difficult to anticipate world and regional events. Samuel Huntington[16] describes it thus:

> All in all, the emerging world is likely to lack the clarity and stability of the Cold War and to be a more jungle-like world of multiple dangers, hidden traps, unpleasant surprises and moral ambiguities.

"*Through, with and by*" operations can provide a window through which this "jungle-like world" can be viewed with greater clarity. This is the arena, the regionally focused arena, within which Special Forces thrive and can, if properly employed long term, provide a unique option in furthering the national security strategy of the United States.

Serious Business – Extremely Serious Business

It may be impossible for the United States to conduct unconventional warfare. UW just might fall within the purview of the "politically incorrect" and therefore can never become a viable tool for the United States.

UW requires the U.S. advisors (Special Forces) to become deeply embedded in the culture of those whom they are attempting to assist and influence, including and involving the whole population –men, women, children. In past lexicons this has been termed "going native." Numerous case examples show that this has never been accepted by the political or conventional military establishment. Cases in point: Lawrence of Arabia; Maj. Jim Gant in Afghanistan; US Special Forces in Vietnam with the

---

16   Samuel Huntington is an Eaton Professor of the Science of Government and Director of the John M. Olin Institute of Strategic Studies at the Center for International Affairs at Harvard University.

Montagnards; and CPT Doug Livermore's article *Broken Valor*. See *Annex A: Case Examples*.

SPECIAL FORCES: Who They Are

According to Army Special Operations doctrine[17], Special Forces are U.S. Army forces organized, trained, and equipped to conduct special operations with an emphasis on unconventional warfare capabilities. According to joint doctrine[18], Special Forces are U.S. Army forces organized, trained, and equipped to conduct special operations with an emphasis on unconventional warfare capabilities. Also, in accordance with Department of Defense dictionary[19], Special Forces are defined as — U.S. Army forces organized, trained, and equipped to conduct special operations with an emphasis on unconventional warfare capabilities; also called SF.

As one can see and determine from the definitions above, there is a consistency of definitions for Special Forces in all three of the listed doctrinal references. Also, as you may have noticed, the term and definition of Special Forces is not just an Army term. The definition of Special Forces is very definitive.

Unfortunately, the term "special forces" is constantly being misused by well-meaning, but ill-informed people including the news media, other pundits, and even people in the military. The Army's *Green Berets* are the only Special Forces in the United States military. There are plenty of Special Operations Forces and plenty of elements that claim themselves either Special or Special Operations Forces; but there is only one organization that is Special Forces—the *Green Berets*.

So how did Army Special Forces come to be known as the Green Berets?

The Green Beret was originally designed in 1953 by SF Major Herbert Brucker, a veteran of the OSS. Later that year, First

---

17 SOF Doctrine ADP (Army Doctrine Publication) 3-05, August 2012 and Joint Doctrine (JP 1-02. Source: JP 3-05)
18 Source: JP 3-05 April 2012. Also called **SF.** (JP 1-02. Source: JP 3-05)
19 (DOD Dictionary of Military and Associated Terms; 8 November 2010 (As Amended Through 15 April 2012)

Lieutenant Roger Pezelle adopted it as the unofficial headgear for his A-team, Operational Detachment FA32 (SF History | Special Forces Association). In the U.S. armed forces, the green beret may be worn only by soldiers awarded the Special Forces Tab, signifying they have been qualified as Special Forces (SF) soldiers. The Special Forces beret is officially designated "beret, man's, wool, rifle green, army shade 297" as described by the Defense Logistics Agency.

U.S. Special Forces wear the green beret because of a shared tradition which goes back to the British Commandos of World War II. The first Ranger unit, commonly known as Darby's Rangers, was formed in Northern Ireland during the summer of 1942. On completion of training at the Commando Training Depot at Achnacarry Castle in Scotland, those Rangers had the right to wear the British Commando green beret, but it was not part of the regulation uniform at the time and was disallowed by the U.S. Army.

The 10th Special Forces Group (Airborne) had many veterans of World War II in their ranks when it was formed in 1952. They began to unofficially wear a variety of berets while training, some favoring the crimson or maroon airborne beret, the black Ranger beret, or the green commando beret. The 10th Special Forces Group (Airborne) deployed to Bad Tolz, Germany in September 1953. The remaining cadre at Fort Bragg formed the 77th Special Forces Group. Members of the 77th SFG began searching through their collections of berets and settled on the Rifle Green color of the British Rifle Regiments (as opposed to the Lovat Green of the Commandos) from Captain Mike de la Pena's collection. Captain Frank Dallas had the new beret designed and produced in small numbers for the members of the Special Forces (History: Special Forces Green Beret, *Special Forces Search Engine* hosted by the Special Forces Association as retrieved 8 March 2007).

When the new green beret was first worn in June 1955 at a parade at Fort Bragg for Lieutenant General Joseph P. Cleland, the retiring commander of the XVIII Airborne Corps, many visitors thought the soldiers were a contingent from NATO.

In 1956 General Paul D. Adams, the post commander at Fort Bragg, banned its wear, even though it was worn surreptitiously when deployed overseas. This was reversed on 25 September 1961 by *Department of the Army Message 578636,* which designated the green beret as the exclusive headdress of the Army Special Forces.

When visiting the Special Forces at Fort Bragg on 12 October 1961, President John F. Kennedy asked Brigadier General William P. Yarborough to make sure that the men under his command wore green berets for the visit. Later that day, Kennedy sent a memorandum which included the line: *"I am sure that the green beret will be a mark of distinction in the trying times ahead."* By the time of America's entry into the Vietnam War, the green beret had become a symbol of excellence throughout the U.S. Army. On April 11, 1962 in a White House memorandum to the United States Army, President Kennedy reiterated his view: *"The green beret is a symbol of excellence, a badge of courage, a mark of distinction in the fight for freedom."* To no avail, both Yarborough and Edson Raff had previously petitioned the Pentagon to allow wearing of the green beret. The President, however, did not fail them (John F. Kennedy Presidential Library and Museum).

Special Forces are those United States Special Operations Forces (SOF) that are unique in their capability to conduct a wide range of activities, as opposed to those SOF elements whose special operations (SO) missions are more narrow and specialized.

These Special Forces roles consist primarily of teaching, training and organizing military, paramilitary or other indigenous elements in the conduct of unconventional warfare (UW), foreign internal defense operations (FID), internal defense and development (IDAD), counterinsurgency operations (COIN), humanitarian assistance (HA), peacekeeping (PK), demining, security assistance, counter-drug assistance (CN), etc. These efforts focus on nations, regions and populations that are important to U.S. national security strategy.

A Profile of a UW Practitioner

Now this is practicing without a license.

Following is an example of what I consider a type of profile of individuals who may be successful in unconventional warfare environments. I call it "unconventionalism"--- out-of-the-box thinking as a norm.

The term *unconventionalism,* we can agree is not an accepted word; however, it best describes the characteristics embodied in out-of-the-box thinking as a norm -- confidence without arrogance; flexibility; initiative and prudent risk-taking without foolhardiness; both mental and physical courage; decisiveness without impetuousness; integrity, but certainly not sainthood; independence in thought and action; and just plain common sense. Additionally, people skills and negotiation skills must be included.

It was December 1975 and I was assigned as a new candy striper to the 5th Special Forces Group, Fort Bragg, North Carolina. A "candy striper" was an individual who was assigned to a SF Group but waiting to go through the schoolhouse (the John F. Kennedy Special Warfare Center and School) and become Special Forces qualified. On their beret, instead of wearing the full flash of the Special Forces Group of assignment, they wore a thin stripe with the unit colors, but obviously it was not a full flash; therefore, they were unqualified "candy stripers."

My Special Forces Officers Course (SFOC - now changed and combined into the Special Forces Qualification Course - SFQC; see Chapter 8) class started in February 1976 at Camp Mackall, North Carolina. In 1976, the qualification course was divided in that the officers went to their own 13-week course, while the non-commissioned officers attended a separate Special Forces qualification course. The beginning phases and the ending phases of both courses were the same. It was just that the middle seven weeks or so of the officers' course was dedicated to what was determined at that time to be officer-related material. Conversely, the non-commissioned officers in between the beginning and ending phases, went to their respective military occupational specialty (MOS) specific training and varied in time according to their specialty (see Chapter 8: Training and Preparation) .

In my particular course, we had several foreign officers attending the training. The ad hoc detachment, in other words a student detachment, which I was a part of had two Pakistani officers as members. One of the tasks for our student detachment--all the student detachments–was to do a target analysis and target folder[20] on a selected target in or around Fort Bragg. Our detachment target was the National Guard Armory on Fort Bragg. We were to put all of our training to date to use in the development of this target folder.

Among other things, we used what is known as the CARVER formula for analysis:

- Criticality – or in other words target value to friendly, enemy and civilians
- Accessibility – can you get to the target and get away
- Recoverability – how long to replace, repair, or bypass the damage
- Vulnerability – do we have the capability to attack the target
- Effect – type in magnitude of the effect on military, political, economic, psychological, sociological, and on the population
- Recognizability – can you find the target in all kinds of weather conditions, etc.

So, an obvious factor is you have to know and understand the target and the target's impact not only on the enemy, but also on the indigenous population. And, of course, there are several ways of doing this. One of the criteria was to be able to observe the target for a sufficient period of time as to understand the ebb and flow of security, times of operation, through all periods of visibility both day and night and in good and bad weather. For some of the members of our team this meant getting binoculars and night vision devices and crawling to within sight of the target and observing it for a continuous 72 hour period from multiple vantage points.

Me, I was a bit lazy and looked for ways to have somebody else do the hard work. So we came up with some other ideas that we implemented in addition to the physical surveillance of the target.

---

20   A target folder is a detail analysis of a specific target and includes photos, historical information, drawing, reconnaissance reports, etc and follows a detailed outline and format.

First, with very little difficulty, we went to the post engineer's office and obtained the blueprints for the building using some innocuous excuse that was accepted without question. The blueprints assisted us with the rest of our approach to the target analysis.

Next, at the time I was dating a young lady that was a staff writer for the Fort Bragg *Paraglide* newspaper and I approached her to assist us. I proposed she write an article on the National Guard armory. She agreed for several reasons besides the fact that it would give her a good article to write for the *Paraglide*. The background research for her article on the National Guard Armory would include a visit to the facility and interviews with the commander and other key personnel in the facility. Accompanying her was one of our team members who acted as her photographer. Short story, he was able to get pictures of all the key personnel and all of the maintenance boards in the facility. This certainly greatly assisted us with understanding the supply chain and the critical components that impacted the maintenance of the 8-inch self-propelled howitzer weapons systems which were the main weapon system in the National Guard armory. Footnote, the article was published in the *Paraglide* along with photographs of the commander sitting in front of his maintenance boards.

Third, again using a very valid and innocuous approach, we went to the International Student Affairs Office and our two Pakistani officers arranged to be given a tour of the National Guard facility under the guise of understanding how our military reserve system works so they could take the knowledge back to improve their National Guard system. During their visit with the commander and his staff, they received full briefings on the entire operation, including the interior layout of the National Guard armory and its functions. They were able to see the inside of the facility and took their own set of photographs, which was allowed.

Next, through a contact with the post fire marshal and through his willing assistance, he agreed to conduct a no-notice fire inspection on the National Guard armory and allow one of our members to accompany him in the full camouflage of an assistant fire inspector. Under the fire marshal's cover, our individual was able to gain entry to all of the classified areas of the facility and into the arms room where he was able to identify the entire array of weapons and critical parts that were in the arms room.

We then were able to produce a very detailed, complete target folder to include that provided to us by our chigger-and-mosquito-bitten field observers. To be fair, the surveillance intelligence was in fact very important in determining the external security and vulnerable access points.

Thus, *unconventionalism* in action. Unfortunately, in today's "politically correct" environment, unconventional and independent thought is often penalized, even in the SOF community.

2

Special Forces Core Ideology[21]

If we in Special Forces are to have a firm grasp of who we are as an entity, we must clearly understand and succinctly articulate our core ideology.

In February 1997, General Peter Schoomaker, then commanding general of the U.S. Army Special Operations Command, or USASOC, challenged USASOC officers to read a professional-development book entitled *Built to Last: Successful Habits of Visionary Companies*, by James C. Collins and Jerry I. Porras. After having read the book, we formed a series of working groups that eventually codified the USASOC vision, goals and objectives.

An organization's core ideology is its enduring character — its stake fixed in the ground that says this is who we are; this is what we stand for; and this is what we are all about. Core ideology has two distinct sub-components: *core values* and *core purpose* and unless these are passionately held on a gut level, they are not core. Identifying core values and core purpose is not an exercise in wordsmithing. It is a defining process.

One does not create a core ideology. A core ideology is derived not by looking outside the organization, but rather by looking inside. You do

---

21   This is a Special Warfare magazine article Summer, 1998, written by the author, Colonel Mark D. Boyatt, titled *Special Forces: Who Are We and What Are We?*

not ask, "What core values *should* we hold?" You ask, "What core values *do* we hold?"

Core ideology must be pervasive; it must transcend any leader. Core ideology is for the people inside the organization, and it need only be meaningful and inspirational to them. Core ideology plays an essential role in determining who is inside the organization and who is outside it. A clear and well-articulated ideology will attract people whose values are compatible with the values of those who are inside the organization and will repel those whose values are contradictory. There are many examples of this both in the U.S. and around the world.

Core ideology is not to be confused with core competence. Core competence is a strategic concept that captures an organization's capabilities. Core ideology captures what one stands for and why one exists. You can, and as appropriate perhaps should, change anything that is not a core ideology.

The act of stating a core ideology influences behavior toward consistency with that ideology. The difference between success and failure of an organization can often be traced to how well that organization establishes a common purpose and shared values to bring out the energies and the talents of its people.

What is Special Forces' core ideology? This is not a frivolous question. What would be lost if Special Forces ceased to exist? Why is it important for Special Forces to exist now and in the future? What deeper sense of motivation keeps a person in Special Forces? When someone asks themselves why Special Forces is important, question each answer by asking "Why?" five times. What is the result? This is not a trick. Each person must do this for themselves.

Core values are essential and enduring tenets. If circumstances around us changed and we were penalized for holding a core value, would we still keep it? If our answer is no, then we did not have a core value. You do not change core values; you change strategies.

A core value is simple, clear, straightforward and powerful. It provides substantial guidance with piercing simplicity. People can discover their core values, but new core values cannot be instilled. Core values are not something a person buys into. A person must have a predisposition to hold them. Core values need no justification, nor do they come into or out of fashion.

What are the core values of Special Forces? They must be values equally valid 100 years from now.

Core purpose is the second component of core ideology. Core purpose is the organization's fundamental reason for being, and it is the more important of the two components. It must capture the soul, the essence. Do not confuse the core purpose with goals or strategies, which change over time.

You cannot fulfill a purpose. A purpose is like a guiding star on the horizon: forever pursued but never reached. A core purpose does not change; it inspires change. An organization can and usually does evolve into new areas, but it remains guided by its core purpose. What is the core purpose of Special Forces? What purpose defines Special Forces today and what they will be 100 years from now? What is the Special Forces reason for being?

What Special Forces does, where we do it, and at whose direction are all important issues. However, "*how*" we do the "*what*" sets us apart from other military organizations of the past, the present and certainly the future.

The core purpose of Special Forces is to accomplish Special Operations activities *through, with or by* indigenous populations. This is the SF enduring purpose — the guiding light on the horizon. The core purpose of Special Forces is never-changing, regardless of changing strategies or the problems that the belief in Special Forces may bring in the future. No other organization has a core ideology of working *through, with or by* indigenous populations.

The core values of Special Forces are unconventionalism[22] (out-of-the-box thinking as the norm), strength of character, doing what is right, and making a difference. These core values define Special Forces and what Special Forces will be 100 years from now, regardless of a changing world or the penalties encountered for holding these values. (See Annex B---SF Core Values; Army Values; SOF Truths; SOF Imperatives)

---

22 Unconventionalism. We agree that this is not an accepted word, but it best describes the characteristics embodied in out-of-the-box thinking as a norm; confidence without arrogance; flexibility; initiative and prudent risk-taking without foolhardiness; both mental and physical courage; decisiveness without impetuositys; integrity, but certainly not sainthood; independence in thought and action; and just plain common sense.

3

Unconventional Warfare

So you think you know unconventional warfare (UW)?

<u>BOTTOM-LINE</u> <u>UPFRONT</u>: Unconventional warfare is a U.S. supported and maybe, inspired, insurgency and is *total warfare* for the indigenous population using every means at their disposal to affect *regime change* of their current masters. These masters may be a tyrannical government or an occupying power. To the indigenous population involved in UW the survival of every man woman and child is at stake. To the indigenous population this is revolt or insurrection. This is revolutionary warfare. Contrary to some of our "conventional wisdom" of the definitions of UW, UW is *not*, I say again, *not* something that is used to coerce or influence a regime. For the U.S. to approach our support to a UW situation with the camouflaged intent of influencing or coercing rather that supporting the indigenous people in regime change is disingenuous, deceptive, immoral and unethical.

Unconventional warfare conducted as a default or as a spur of the moment "what's on the menu today," a *soup d'jour,* is not only unethical, it's dumb. Preparation for UW requires long-term effort. And this means *long-term.* The decision to execute unconventional warfare may be the result of a very short notice decision (for example, Afghanistan in 2001); however, it requires (or it should require) those who conduct unconventional warfare to have extensive preparation. Frivolously entering into

UW as a "tourist," without the regional and cultural preparation and most importantly, the training and focus of the Special Forces units, will always result in greater casualties to both the indigenous population and our soldiers.

> "People who do not understand the dynamics of UW are likely to give the wrong advice at critical times, and jump when they should have stood still. Unconventional warfare is primarily about politics but most often has a violent component. In theory, it is possible to adapt the conventional U.S. military structure to UW, but the reality is different."[23]

Executing UW without properly prepared personnel is a chaotic, dysfunctional operation both on-the-ground and in the interagency functionality. Again, look at Afghanistan 2001 .... we had little idea of who was who.... which "good guys" were "good guys" .... we certainly had little idea of the various ethnic groups, sub-groups, cultures, sub-cultures...hell, look at today. We still have not grasped that Afghanistan is not now and may never be a unified nation.

This does not mean we would always know in advance exactly where the occasion would arise for UW, but we should have a pretty good idea if we prepare. This requires a persistent, ubiquitous, continuous engagement around the globe through partnership events and training with those nations that also promote freedom, liberty and non-oppression of their people. Of course, not all of these will be democracies. Also, it will be impossible to have access to certain areas of anticipated disturbances. In these circumstances, we must maintain a presence in any surrounding friendly nation as described above and begin building contacts and networks with identified resistance potential in the pariah nations or occupied territories.

The required premise for UW is not only intense education of both the warriors and the interagency, but ethnographic expertise acquired through ubiquitous, persistent, continuous engagement and education.

---

23   *Afganistan & The Troubled Future of Unconventional Warfare* by Hy S. Rothstein, pgs 26-27. Hy Rothstein is a Ph.D, a USMA graduate, a 30 year career Special Forces officer, and a current professor at the Department of Defense at the Naval Postgraduate School, Monterey, CA.

This means a permanent commitment to IDAD, FID, COIN, security assistance or whatever…if not directly in the target nation-state, then with any "friends" or surrogates in the region preferable that border the target state. It also means a training and institutional base that focuses on ethnographic education.

Every time SF goes anywhere it is for the purpose of preparing for UW. IDAD (FID/COIN), while legitimate *through, with and by* missions in their own right, are preparation for UW.

The Special Forces position as a unique national asset is twofold. First, Army Special Forces is the only U.S. military organization specifically *selected and trained* to primarily operate *through, with and by* indigenous populations. Second, Special Forces is the only U.S. military ground combat organization specifically selected, trained, organized, and equipped, to conduct unconventional warfare.[24]

Operational SOF Mission Criteria (from the General Wayne Downing[25] days as Commander, U.S. Special Operations Command)

- Is this an appropriate SOF mission?
- Does it support CINC's[26] campaign plan?
- Is it operationally feasible?
- Are required resources available to execute?
- Does expected outcome justify risk?

As factually as history can demonstrate, political and diplomatic platitudes never successfully influence rogue or tyrannical regimes. The only

---

24   The U.S. Air Force Special Operations Command (AFSOC) 6th Special Operations Squadron (SOS) is a designated UW element.

25   General Wayne A. Downing. I first ran into General Downing when he was a Lt. Col. in commander of the 2nd Ranger Battalion. We were on an exercise in 1978 as part of the BLUELIGHT Force prior to the formation of Delta. His battalion was in support. He subsequently became the Commander of the Joint Special Operations Command; Commander of the U.S. Army Special Operations Command, and Commander of the U.S. Special Operations Command Tampa. Downing died on July 18, 2007, of meningitis and was buried in the *West Point Cemetery*, West Point, New York on September 27, 2007.

26   CINC - Commander-in-Chief; a 4-star general or admiral. On 24 October 2002, Secretary of Defense Donald H. Rumsfeld announced that in accordance with Title 10 of the US Code (USC), the title of "Commander-in-Chief" would thereafter be reserved for the President and the military CINCs would be known as "combatant commanders", as heads of the Unified Combatant Commands. Unified combatant command s are comprised of two or more services (Army, Air Force, Marine Corps, Navy) and there are currently nine of these.

other obvious method of helping an oppressed population achieve freedom, short of all-out war, is unconventional warfare–in other words an insurgency. It is imperative that the indigenous population be the engine of change or the result is not legitimate and will not endure. The most recent case in point is the result of the ten plus years we spent in Iraq and Afghanistan...dismal.

As different from unconventional warfare, IDAD (FID/COIN) and CT are conducted by a population that is threatened by an insurgency or invasion...they are not yet oppressed... yes, they are threatened, but they are still not subjugated. This is different than a population engaged in an insurgency and therefore receptive to unconventional warfare.

Unlike the American Revolution, most populations no longer enjoy the time/spatial advantage of distance and time as provided by oceans and great expanses of terrain, not to mention the speed and ubiquitous reality of communications. In our current digital, instantaneous world, support to UW must be long term and is almost impossible to keep covert[27]. While the United States may be able to sustain a façade of deniability, this is all it can practically accomplish given the current world of transparency enabled by the ubiquitous social media.

Even given a successful regime change by an indigenous population supported in their revolt by U.S. sponsored unconventional warfare, in today's world the indigenous people do not have the luxury of isolation in which to develop their fledging freedoms gained by UW. They require long term umbrella support and coverage for generations, yes, generations, under which to go through the developmental and evolutionary phases of growing into a free institution. And, yes, the term freedom is subjective. However, without long-term, multi-generational support and protection by the United States, the possibility of these indigenous populations successfully capitalizing on the overthrow of their oppressive regime is nearly impossible. Case in point is Iraq. After we abandoned them, any hope of any type of democracy fell apart with internecine

---

27   Covert -an operation that is so planned and executed as to conceal the identity of or permit plausible denial by the sponsor.

squabbling and fighting; not to mention the invasion by ISIS or ISIL[28], whichever term you prefer.

Providing this umbrella security for generations makes us responsible, not imperialistic. In his book, *Things That Matter*, Charles Krauthammer (as always) articulates this best:

> "Even Rome is no model for what America is today. First, because we do not have the imperial culture of Rome.....
>
> ...unlike Rome, unlike Britain and France and Spain and the other classic empires of modern times, in that *we do not hunger for territory.* The use of the word *empire* in the American context is ridiculous...
>
> That's because we are not an imperial power. We are a commercial republic. We don't take food; we trade for it. Which makes us something unique in history, an anomaly, a hybrid: a commercial republic with overwhelming global power...." (From Dr. Krauthammer's Irving Kristol Lecture to the American Enterprise Institute, Washington, D.C., February 10, 2004)

We are not imperialistic, but if supported only for the relatively brief period of time to affect the regime change (like Iraq), these new efforts at freedom most assuredly will have little chance to fend off internal and external threats. Likewise, if the United States does not remain the unassailable world power and commit to provide this security umbrella, then newly freed national institutions have little hope for long term survival.

So, what is the definition of success in UW? Regime change, of course, but to what? What type of new regime? Or is it easier or clearer to define what it should not be? It certainly must be legitimate to a majority of the population. How does it obtain legitimacy?

---

28   ISIS or ISIL: The Islamic State of Iraq and al-Sham (ISIS) or the Islamic State of Iraq and the Levant (ISIL). ISIS stands for Islamic State in Iraq and al-Sham, antonym of the region bordering the eastern Mediterranean Sea, usually known as the Levant or the region of Syria, Lebanon, Palestine/Israel, Jordan, Cyprus, Hatay Province. ISIL stands for Islamic State in Iraq and the Levant. The Levant is the historic name given to the entire region east of the Mediterranean from Egypt, east to Iran and to Turkey.

What type of new regime? First, in order to warrant the commitment of U.S. lives and resources, the new regime structure must guarantee freedom and liberty to all of its inhabitants and provide for independence of the individual and accountability and responsibility of both the individual and the government. What a novel idea. Maybe we should practice this?

Or is it easier or clearer to define what it should not be? Ralph Peters identifies seven deep flaws that condemn nations to failure in the modern world:

- restrictions on the free flow of information;
- the subjugation of women;
- inability to accept responsibility for individual or collective failure;
- the extended family or clan as the basic unit of social organization;
- domination by a restrictive religion;
- a low valuation of education;
- low prestige assigned to work.

UW support to any culture that reflects these flaws is probably not a good idea. Either the new nation will implode due to these faults or, we are just using these insurgents as throw-away pawns for a "grander" strategy which means, ultimately, betraying these very people. This means we accept the likely genocide of the indigenous people involved. It is nothing new for us to abandon and sacrifice our friends (see Annex A, Captain Douglas Livermore's article *Broken Valor* and Colonel Tim Heinemann's article *Our Forgotten Allies Stand in the Gap*). We must be better than this. We are better than this.

How does regime change and the new institution achieve legitimacy to a majority of the population? I suggest the below. You might recognize the passage:

> *When, in the course of human events, it becomes necessary for one people to dissolve the political bands which have connected them with another, and to assume among the powers of the earth, the separate*

and equal station to which the laws of nature and of nature's God entitle them, a decent respect to the opinions of mankind requires that they should declare the causes which impel them to the separation.

We hold these truths to be self-evident, that all men are created equal, that they are endowed by their Creator with certain inalienable rights, that among these are life, liberty and the pursuit of happiness. That to secure these rights, governments are instituted among men, deriving their just powers from the consent of the governed. That whenever any form of government becomes destructive to these ends, it is the right of the people to alter or to abolish it, and to institute new government, laying its foundation on such principles and organizing its powers in such form, as to them shall seem most likely to effect their safety and happiness.(The unanimous Declaration of the thirteen united States of America, July 4, 1776)

So what would it take to achieve this condition after a successful insurgency that resulted in the regime change of an oppressive, tyrannical state? As a starter, let's look at the United States after its War of Independence or Revolutionary War. First, that war lasted from 1775 at Lexington until Yorktown in 1781; however, the final peace treaty was not signed until 1783 at the Treaty of Paris. It was not until 1788 that the U.S. Constitution became adopted, 1789 for the first president, George Washington, to be elected and it took until 1791 for the Bill of Rights to be approved, adopted and effective (see Annex L: U.S. Constitution Time Line).

Shays rebellion of 1786 and 1787 was one of the postwar threats to the new American republic. This was an internal uprising brought about by financial difficulties from the Revolutionary War. This was totally an isolated internal affair that had no support from outside entities and was resolved before it disrupted the constitutional process. Still it was a threat to the new fledgling nation. However, it was nowhere near as threatening as that which will face and has faced newly emerging national entities in today's world.

So what is the purpose of this discussion about the timeline of the American Revolution and the constitutional timeline? Simply, that we had the benefit of time and distance in which to solidify regime change and develop and adopt a workable constitution. All done under the relative stability of an umbrella of security provided by time and distance and the distractions of European conflict.

Accordingly, what do we expect new fledgling successful insurgencies that are supported by the U.S. (such as Iraq and Afghanistan) to accomplish when immediately and constantly threatened by both internal and external threats from the moment of their existence? In a case in point, we immediately abandoned Iraq in December 2011 and by the spring of 2014, the nation of Iraq no longer effectively existed. Absent any security buffer, external and internal threats overwhelmed the fledgling Iraqi regime. Granted, in and of itself, the regime the U.S. left in place was corrupt and probably had little chance of success regardless. It had little legitimacy to the majority of the population.

So what is the parallel I am drawing here? The fledgling United States had 31 years from 1781 until 1812 (remember the War of 1812 with Britain?) in which to develop the fundamentals of our Republic in an essentially secure and safe environment without either serious internal (well, maybe Shay's Rebellion in 1786 – 87) or external threats to the Republic until the British in 1812. This is a 31-year buffer… a generation and a half. This type of buffer no longer exists in the world. At least not unless imposed by an outside agent with the ability and military might to enforce such a buffer in which to allow the new regime to grow and mature. In effect this means that the U.S. must stay in place providing security over any nation that they assist in achieving a regime change anywhere from two to three generations… maybe 50 years or more. To do otherwise is dishonorable, disingenuous, unethical and immoral.

Why so long? Because you have to give time for all of the internal institutions to develop, and for one to two generations of children who are born into this changed environment to mature, get an education, enter the workforce, and form and organize a large middle class–a tax-paying middle class. In my opinion, and probably validated by an economic study of history, it is impossible for the institution of freedom and liberty to exist without a large, healthy, taxpaying middle class. If you have a country like Haiti during the Duvalier years where less than 3% of the population lived in luxury while 97% lived in abject poverty, it's impossible for freedom and liberty to exist.

What are examples of regime change brought about by an insurgency... what were the resulting new regimes...did they result in freedom and liberty?

There are numerous examples of successful insurgencies, just not many that survived their own success. Many of these successful insurgencies were based on protestations of freedom and liberty. But many of these successful insurgencies did not survive the internal conflict arising from their success. The original intent of the insurgency was hijacked internally by a tyrannical or dictatorial element that usually eliminated those who led the original insurgency. Or the leaders of the insurgency misled or camouflaged their true intentions which only surfaced after the successful regime change and they consolidated their internal power (Castro and Cuba). Or they were pounced upon by a neighboring regime while weak and disorganized.

One of these cases was the Russian Revolution of 1917 which replaced the Tsarist autocracy with a provisional government which was then subsequently overthrown and replaced with a Bolshevik government led by Lenin which was then challenged by the "White" factions (anti-Bolsheviks, liberal and monarchist forces) which resulted in a continuing civil war for several years until the "Red" Leninist Bolsheviks finally won.

Another was the Mao Tse-tung (Zedong) led revolution in China culminating in 1949 when his communist forces defeated the Nationals who withdrew to Taiwan. When he died in 1976 as the head of the People's Republic of China, Mao Tse-tung is attributed with having caused the deaths of between 40 and 70 million people.

This is the old story of "be careful what you ask for, because you just may get it." It seems to be that those who lead the initial insurgency and affect regime change usually fail to survive the consolidation of their victory.

Examples mentioned earlier were the Arabs with Lawrence of Arabia and the Mujahideen in Afghanistan after their victory over the Russians in 1989.

So who in the indigenous population seem to be the instigators and leaders of the insurgencies that result in regime change? It would appear that while the masses which get involved in an insurgency often are the downtrodden and disenfranchised, the leadership appears to be extremely intelligent, well-educated, and in many cases part of the economic elite. The leadership seems to be at the top of the hierarchy of needs.

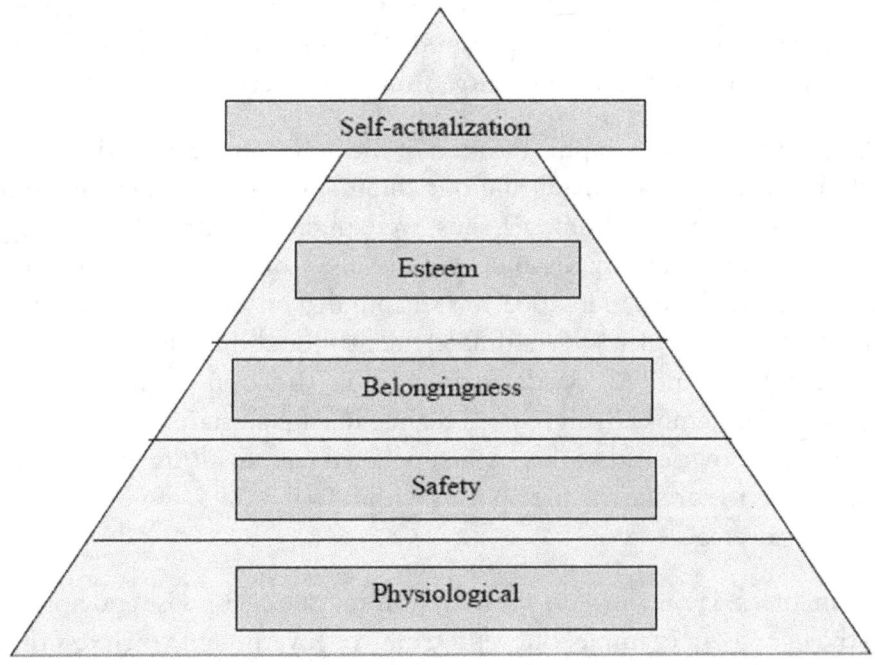

Hierarchy of needs... How does this play?

- **Self-actualization** – includes morality, creativity, problem-solving, etc.
- **Esteem** – includes confidence, self-esteem, achievement, respect, etc.
- **Belongingness** – includes love, friendship, intimacy, family, etc.

- **Safety** – includes security of environment, employment, resources, health, property, etc.
- **Physiological** – includes air, food, water, sex, sleep, clothing, shelter, other factors towards homeostasis, etc.

Arguably, it is very important to understand where the disaffected indigenous population ranks in the hierarchy of needs. Those caught in the very lowest level of needs, i.e. food, shelter, clothing... in other words the basic survival level, may not be able to nor desire to engage in an insurgency. On the other hand, with nothing to lose, they may be frothing to participate in revolt---regardless of who leads it. As an example, the American Revolution was led by those who had reached the top levels of the hierarchy of needs pyramid. On the other hand, the French Revolution of 1789 seemed to surge from the street.

Does the size and geographic location of the indigenous population make a difference? If so, what? During our colonial years, the American colonies, while not totally homogeneous, were under English rule on a large land mass, protected by distance and oceans. Conversely, the Northern Alliance in Afghanistan in 2001 was surrounded on all sides by unsympathetic nations, all of whom ultimately contributed directly or indirectly to the Taliban and Al Qaeda regimes. This situation continues today against the current U.S.-supported regime in Afghanistan. Just as in Iraq, it is abundantly clear that this U.S.-supported regime in Afghanistan will not be able to survive the precipitous withdrawal of U.S. forces and U.S. security coverage.

On an internal note, how do we, in the United States, espouse and hold up to the light as an example, our representative government when less than fifty percent of eligible voters vote in U.S. elections? Is our Constitution and Declaration of Independence sufficient? Can we explain our own government to an indigenous population? When was the last time we had serious formal education in our schools about civics, our Constitution, and our form of government? How well prepared are our Special Forces soldiers to address these issues to an indigenous population?

This points out a severe educational shortfall in our preparation for operations *through, with and by* indigenous populations. The U.S. was, and may still be, a melting pot. Also, although the Constitution is under significant internal attacks, the U.S. remains a haven for religious freedom and independence. Most of all, our Founding Fathers and the original colonists valued independence, freedom and liberty of the individual.

Okay, now that we've laid some groundwork, what is unconventional warfare (UW)? In the first chapter, we first saw the latest (as of January 2015) official definition of unconventional warfare:

> **Unconventional Warfare** — (JP 3-05) 8 November 2010 (As Amended Through 15 January 2015) Activities conducted to enable a resistance movement or insurgency to coerce, disrupt, or overthrow a government or occupying power by operating through or with an underground, auxiliary, and guerrilla force in a denied area. Also called **UW.**

Later in this chapter we will follow the evolution of the definitions of unconventional warfare. In the meantime we will try to come to grips with both the literal and the esoteric meaning of unconventional warfare.

Is unconventional warfare anything that is not conventional? So then what is conventional?

The Webster's dictionary defines conventional as: *con·ven·tion·al; adjective*

- used and accepted by most people: usual or traditional
- of a kind that has been around for a long time and is considered to be usual or typical
- common and ordinary: not unusual

That must mean anything that does not fall into this definition is to be considered unconventional: un·con·ven·tion·al: *adjective*

- very different from the things that are used or accepted by most people : not traditional or usual: not conventional

Full definition of *unconventional*

- not conventional: not bound by or in accordance with convention: being out of the ordinary <an *unconventional* outfit> <an *unconventional* thinker>

Okay then, unconventional warfare means any type of warfare that is not conventional. So conventional warfare is what? Conventional warfare is "regular" warfare? So this would lead one to assume that if you are not conducting regular warfare, you are conducting irregular warfare. Does this mean that irregular warfare is unconventional warfare?

In April and May 2007 I attended a symposium as a panel member for one effort to try to define and categorize irregular warfare. The symposium took place at the Joint Special Operations University (JSOU) in Hulbert Field. The symposium was titled *JSOU Second Annual Symposium Irregular Warfare (IW): Strategic Utility of SOF*, 30 April through 3 May 2007, Hurlburt Field, Florida. The symposium resulted in an abundance of good discussion, but there was no consensus reached on anything (see Annex G: Generational Warfare).

The definition of regular is: reg·u·lar: *adjective*

- happening over and over again at the same time or in the same way : occurring every day, week, month, etc.
- happening at times that are equally separated
- happening or done very often

Full definition of *regular*

- 1: belonging to a religious order
- 2:
  - *a* : formed, built, arranged, or ordered according to some established rule, law, principle, or type
  - *b (1)* : both equilateral and equiangular <a *regular* polygon> *(2)* : having faces that are congruent regular polygons and all the polyhedral angles congruent <a *regular* polyhedron>

- o *c of a flower* : having the arrangement of FLORAL parts exhibiting radial symmetry with members of the same whorl similar in form
- 3:
  - o *a* : ORDERLY, METHODICAL <*regular* habits>
  - o *b* : recurring, attending, or functioning at fixed, uniform, or normal intervals <a *regular* income> <a *regular* churchgoer> <*regular* bowel movements>
- 4:
  - o *a* : constituted, conducted, scheduled, or done in conformity with established or prescribed usages, rules, or discipline
  - o *b* : NORMAL, STANDARD: as *(1)* : ABSOLUTE, COMPLETE <a *regular* fool> <the office seemed like a *regular* madhouse> *(2)* : thinking or behaving in an acceptable, normal, or agreeable manner <was a *regular* guy>
- **5: of, relating to, or constituting the permanent standing military force of a state <the *regular* army> <*regular* soldiers>**

So anything not regular is irregular: ir·reg·u·lar: *adjective*

- not normal or usual : not following the usual rules about what should be done
- not even or smooth : not regular in form or shape
- happening or done at different times that change often

Full definition of *irregular*

- 1:
  - o *a* : not being or acting in accord with laws, rules, or established custom <*irregular* conduct>
  - o *b* : not conforming to the usual pattern of inflection <*irregular* verbs>
  - o *c* : not following a usual or prescribed procedure; *especially British* : celebrated without either proclamation of the bans or publication of intention to marry <*irregular* marriage>

- 2: **not belonging to or a part of a regular organized group; *specifically*: not belonging to a regular army but raised for a special purpose <*irregular* troops>**
- 3:
  - *a* : lacking perfect symmetry or evenness <an *irregular* coastline>
  - *b* : having one or more floral parts of the same whorl different in size, shape, or arrangement;
- 4: lacking continuity or regularity especially of occurrence or activity <*irregular* employment>

According to that 2007 Joint Special Operations University Executive Report, the Department of Defense's approved definition for irregular warfare was:

> Irregular warfare is a form of warfare that has as its objective the credibility and/or legitimacy of the relevant political authority with the goal of undermining or supporting that authority. Irregular warfare favors indirect approaches, though it may employ the full range of military and other capabilities to seek asymmetric approaches, in order to erode an adversary's power, influence, and will.

Since 2007 the definition of irregular warfare has been changed. In accordance with Joint Publication 1–02; Department of Defense Dictionary of Military and Associated Terms; dated 8 November 2010 (as amended through 15 January 2015) the current definition of irregular warfare is:

> A violent struggle among state and non-state actors for legitimacy and influence over the relevant population(s).

Now, in order to complete setting the stage, *DOD Instruction 3000.7 Irregular Warfare (IW) dated 28 August 2014* seems to solve the dilemma of the tangle revolving around the irregular/regular/conventional argument with a convenient definition for "traditional warfare."

> *Traditional warfare-- a form of warfare between the regulating militaries of states, or alliances of states, in which the objective is to defeat*

an adversary's armed forces, destroy an adversary's war-making capacity, or seize or retain territory in order to force a change in an adversary's government or policies.

Joint Publication 1-02, *Department of Defense Dictionary of Military and Associated Terms*, remains silent on "traditional warfare."

So, what does all this mean?

Unfortunately, or fortunately, depending on your point of view, definitions can be manipulated by the user. Extrapolating from the definitions above for regular and irregular, one could make a case that the U.S. Marine Corps, raised for a specific purpose, is not a regular force or, conversely, they are regular since they constitute a permanent standing military force of a state.

Likewise, there are questions about how to categorize special operations forces. If you choose to categorize special operations forces as irregular forces, therefore not regular, then they should not fall under the command and control of our regular military establishment. This type of terminology interpretation can lead one in the direction that SOF should all be established separate from the regular military and placed under an entirely separate organization such as the Office of Strategic Services (OSS) in the Second World War.

Now we get into talking about SOF. What are special operations forces (SOF)? In accordance with Joint Publication 1– 02: Department of Defense Dictionary Of Military And Associated Terms, 8 November 2010 (as amended through 15 January 2015):

> **Special Operations Forces** — Those Active and Reserve Component forces of the Services designated by the Secretary of Defense and specifically organized, trained, and equipped to conduct and support special operations. Also called SOF. See also Air Force special operations forces; Army special operations forces; naval special warfare forces. (JP 3-05)

As always, it seems that every definition requires more defining. So what is the definition for special operations? Again, according to the current (as of 2015) official documentations as stated above, the definition for special operations is:

> Operations requiring unique modes of employment, tactical techniques, equipment and training often conducted in hostile, denied, or politically sensitive environments and characterized by one or more of the following: time sensitive, clandestine, low visibility, conducted *with and/or through* indigenous forces, requiring regional expertise, and/or a high degree of risk. (JP 3-05)

As per these definitions there is a litany of units that are designated, or at least claim to be designated, SOF. There is significant confusion that results from the term SOF and in the term Special Forces (SF). Many people confuse the term "special operations forces" with "Special Forces." As clarified in Chapter 1, there is only one Special Forces entity in the entire U.S. military establishment. In accordance with Joint Publication 1– 02: Department of Defense Dictionary of Military and Associated Terms, 8 November 2010 (as amended through 15 January 2015):

> **Special Forces** — U.S. Army forces organized, trained, and equipped to conduct special operations with an emphasis on unconventional warfare capabilities. Also called **SF.** (JP 3-05)

> **Special Forces Group** — The largest Army combat element for special operations consisting of command and control, Special Forces battalions, and a support battalion capable of long duration missions. Also called **SFG.** (JP 3-05)

These are the Green Berets.

As a note, under the current Special Forces Group, of the four assigned Special Forces battalions, the battalion capable of long-term duration missions is the unconventional warfare battalion. The "unconventional warfare battalion" is a new restructuring internal to Special Forces. This will be a point of discussion later in this book; but briefly, it is the *strong* opinion of the author that the primary mission and purpose for *all* Special

Forces is unconventional warfare. Everything else is a subset. The designation of an independent unconventional warfare battalion, apart from the other Special Forces battalions, represents the rift in Special Forces between the unconventional warriors and the unilateral warriors. As we discussed in the first two chapters, the unique mission and capability of Special Forces is the ability to work *through, with and by* the indigenous populations. No other U.S. combat formation has this as its primary capability. This is what makes Special Forces a unique national asset.

All of the other missions assigned under various charters, beginning with the Goldwater – Nichols Department of Defense (DOD) Reorganization Act of 1986 and the Nunn-Cohen Amendment to the National Defense Authorization Act of 1987, to various additional definitions by various SOF commands, can be conducted by numerous SOF and conventional military forces. All of these missions can and usually are conducted *unilaterally* by the units involved. Unconventional warfare is a very specific and unique mission and *is never conducted unilaterally*, but always *through, with or by* indigenous populations for the purpose of regime change.

And, therefore, this is the origin of the confusion around UW. There are many units, SOF and conventional, that have claimed that they can and do conduct UW. That is because they don't understand or have corrupted the definition of UW. They have corrupted not only the meaning of UW, but how it is conducted. Many believe UW means anything behind enemy lines. This is totally incorrect.

Dick Couch in his book "*Chosen Soldier,*" provides a SEAL perspective of the differences between SEALs and SF. On page 53 he states, "SEAL training is difficult, perhaps more difficult on the pure pain-o-meter scale than Special Forces training. But the skill set of a Navy SEAL– in addition to his behind-the-gun proficiency, which is comparable to an SF soldier's – requires maritime training. Over one-third of basic SEAL training is in-water training; ongoing maritime/underwater certification and proficiency training also take a great deal of time. And the counter-insurgency skills, while being given more attention, are still not the focus of SEAL training nor a primary mission in their deployment locations."

On page 55 Couch continues, "Some Army and Marine Corps senior officers believe that with a little training, experience, and funding, they can cover the Special Forces mission. I couldn't disagree more strongly. I personally had no idea of just how difficult the SF mission was, nor the intensive skill set required to do the job. It took me ten months at Fort Bragg and Camp Mackall to appreciate what it takes to be *really* proficient at foreign internal defense and unconventional warfare."

Most importantly, the *through, with and by* strategy puts the legitimacy of the effort with the indigenous population and makes the solution, their solution. Unilateral direct action does nothing for legitimacy and, in fact, may do just the opposite by highlighting the inadequacies of the indigenous effort, especially if we don't treat this as a generational effort.

Later in this chapter the evolution of the definition of unconventional warfare is detailed as it has changed over time. You will see that in all the UW definitions there are very key elements missing. These definitions are typical of a synthesis of inputs from all of the services, the Joint Chiefs of Staff and the Department of Defense entities. In this joint environment, everything gets reduced to the lowest common denominator, and in this case, political correctness. ***There is no mention of regime change as the principal reason for unconventional warfare.*** Furthermore, there is no mention of the moral obligation owed the indigenous population once we have entered into a UW campaign. As I have said many times, the true definition of "political correctness" is moral cowardice... from which our military establishment is not immune.

> UW is the primary SF activity and it is only conducted *through, with or by* the indigenous population for the purpose of ***regime change***.

Given the two- or maximum four-year horizon of the U.S. political environment, it may be impossible to conduct UW. The conduct of UW requires the United States to be both moral and ethical, which of course we believe we are...regardless of the evidence. This is because UW is total war to the indigenous population involved. Anything short of regime change will result in the genocide, enslavement or, if they are lucky, oppression of those involved in the UW effort against the regime. If we don't have the moral and ethical backbone, commitment, and understanding of this, then our commitment to UW is disingenuous, patronizing, self-serving, dishonest, immoral, unethical, cruel….and maybe criminal.

UW obviously requires a long-term commitment which is likely impossible in the world of 20 second news sound bites and two-year political cycles --- which actually means after the election 50% of all effort goes to a reelection campaign and a bloated political reelection money chest. Everything is based on telling voters what they want to hear in order to win elections. Campaigning begins immediately after being elected. The political cycle makes any long-term commitment nearly impossible, thereby making an unconventional warfare campaign questionable.

None of the indigenous population to which a politician would have to commit in a UW effort helps them get reelected. Politicians are usually as willful as leaves on the wind. They blow in whatever direction their perceptions of the voters take them. And history shows that the general population in the United States wearies of overseas conflicts and engagements fairly rapidly or they dismiss the events to background noise that affects only a few … the less than 1% of the population in harm's way. Political correctness (i.e. moral cowardice) trumps moral and ethical behavior, or so our past history would lead one to believe (see Annex A: CPT Doug Livermore's article: *Broken Valor,* and Colonel Tim Heinemann's article *Our Forgotten Allies Stand in the Gap*).

Dick Couch further stated:

> "We invaded Iraq. That war, which we initiated, has become a nasty, protracted insurgency. Americans tend not to like lengthy military engagements; the insurgents know this, and even count on it.
>
> 'You watch news of the war on TV,' a detachment sergeant told me, 'and it's unlike anything we see here on a day-to-day basis. You also see the approval polls for the war, and it makes you wonder. I don't care how we got here--we're here. And we have to stay here and help these people until they can do it on their own.

For the nation, it's pulling out. For us, it's leaving behind friends you've promised to stand alongside until the job's done." Dick Couch in his book "*Chosen Soldier*, page 386-7.

I submit that for the nation, it is not "pulling out," it is betrayal. The conduct of UW (and we did change the regime in Iraq) requires the United States to be both moral and ethical. UW is total war to the indigenous population involved. To repeat, if we don't have the moral and ethical backbone, commitment, and understanding of this, then our commitment to UW is disingenuous, patronizing, self-serving, dishonest, immoral, unethical, and cruel....and maybe criminal.

We see today the betrayal in Iraq. A corrupt, divided, immature, incompetent, illegitimate government (for which we are responsible) falling to the fanaticism of the theocracy of ISIL. And if not ISIL, it would be something else because we abandoned Iraq. We declared victory and withdrew, leaving the Iraqi people to fend for themselves as sheep to a pack of wolves. Being responsible for regime change, we are then responsible to provide for the new regime to develop and mature, which takes 2-3 generations...not 2-3 years.

This is probably not the way to start out trying to sell unconventional warfare. But maybe that is the whole point.

The main theme here is the requirement for the **commitment of persistent _national will_** to the deployment and use of the military and specifically Special Forces and the understanding of the role of the interagency process as the conscience of the nation. It is the responsibility of the interagency process, Congress, and the military leadership to stress the moral and ethical considerations and responsibilities in engaging in unconventional warfare. And once the fervor and passion of the moment has waned (how long after 9-11 did it take for the car flags to disappear?), it remains the responsibility of the interagency process, Congress, and the military leadership to continue to remind the American public regardless of political cost...and you sign or laugh or both. Okay, so then it is the responsibility of the interagency process, Congress, and the military leadership to never commit the nation, the lives of our sons and daughters, the national treasure to UW... stick with the Powell Doctrine ... only overwhelming force, then get out and let the Devil take the hindmost.

****

But we will go on, at least as an esoteric discussion .....

Special Forces is the only U.S. entity that is selected, assessed, organized, trained, and equipped to conduct unconventional warfare. The core uniqueness of SF is *"through, with and by."* This is the core purpose of Special Forces. Other entities dabble at times with working with indigenous populations, but Special Forces is unique in that they accomplish the nation's security objectives *"through, with and by"* indigenous populations as their core approach.

Anything SF does "unilaterally," the conventional forces can do. The same is true of SOF in general. It is just a matter of degree and resourcing; for example, given resources, time, priority and focus, any combat unit can do unilateral direct action (DA). The SOF who have the direct action mission as a priority, are certainly more adept with finesse and surgical precision at this mission than Special Forces. On the other hand, it would take SOF a while to get ready to conduct a mechanized/armor mission. Every unit of the U.S. military is trained, equipped and organized to conduct a mission set. Special Forces are assessed, selected, trained, organized and equipped to conduct activities *"through, with and by"* indigenous populations.

To conduct activities *"through, with and by"* indigenous populations requires in-depth cultural awareness and understanding, regional expertise, and an applicable core ideology. Therefore, regional orientation and focus are an absolute must for Special Forces. Special Forces soldiers and SF units should not be utilized out of their area of focus except in cases of extreme emergency; only *in-extremis*. The Oxford Dictionary of the U.S. Military defines *in-extremis* as used to describe a situation *"of such exceptional urgency that immediate action must be taken to minimize imminent loss of life or catastrophic degradation of the political or military situation."*

The conduct of UW is not limited to war or a conflict in which the U.S. is openly engaged. Conducted with proper authorities, UW is most effective in preventing open warfare or open conflict. The U.S. support to UW can be completely open and visible or it may be clandestine or covert. Also, remember that the purpose of UW is regime change.

> "...UW is ultimately aimed at replacing an existing regime with a politically and militarily viable opposition ..."[29]

The U.S. has conducted UW in support of insurgent movements attempting to overthrow an adversarial regime as well as in support of resistance movements to defeat occupying powers (e.g., the Nicaraguan Contras and the Afghan Mujahedeen). UW was also successfully used against the Taliban in the initial stages of Operation ENDURING FREEDOM in Afghanistan (extract from Joint Pub 3-05, Chap II.e, pgII-9,10). This success in Afghanistan was not the result of large conventional forces, but small Special Forces teams with the CIA providing support coupled with the firepower delivered by the U.S. Air Force. The heavy fighting was done by the Afghan Mujahedeen and therefore provided the legitimacy of the effort and the results.

It is arguable that the Haiti operation in 1994 could have been a UW operation and totally precluded the U.S. and multi-national force invasion. Certainly, the outcome would have been no worse. Also, there are current opportunities for UW that debatably could result in a safer world with potentially much less loss of life and national treasure that may yet occur. Examples are Venezuela, Iran, Libya, Syria, and Egypt (several in danger of falling to the Muslim Brotherhood/ISIS/ISIL), Somalia (piracy), Sudan (a total human disaster), Burma (genocide), to name a few.

When unconventional warfare (*through, with and by* the indigenous population) is the solution to a threat, the result is legitimacy of the effort with and by the people. There are numerous examples of U.S. policy failures by "backing the wrong horse." Twice the U.S. has failed in Viet Nam in this very venue. First, by not supporting the people's choice (Ho

---

29   *Afganistan & The Troubled Future of Unconventional Warfare* by Hy S. Rothstein, pg 156. Hy Rothstein is a Ph.D, a USMA graduate, a30-year career Special Forces officer, and a current professor at the Department of Defense at the Naval Postgraduate School, Monterey, CA.

Chi Minh) after World War II and again in 1955 with the fraudulent election of Diem.

With the capitulation of Germany in May, 1945, Aaron Bank was reassigned to the Pacific theater, where he was inserted into Indochina and linked up with Ho Chi Minh, then leading the resistance to the Japanese. Bank spent considerable time traveling through Vietnam with Ho and was impressed with Ho's manifest popularity among the Vietnamese population. Bank advised the OSS of Ho's great popularity, recommended that Ho be allowed to form a coalition government, and predicted that Ho would win a popular election overwhelmingly if one was conducted. It is not known whether Bank's recommendations reached President Harry S. Truman, but American policy was contrary: Ho was a long-time Communist, having joined the party in the 1920s in Paris, and therefore was considered unacceptable as leader of a coalition government. Some French "Vichy" military forces remained in Indochina, and the United States now consented to the use of these residual forces to block Ho and reinstate Indochina as a French colony. President Truman and later President Dwight D. Eisenhower provided financial support to the French, thus leading to the Indochina War and ultimately the Vietnam War.

The State of Vietnam referendum of 1955 determined the future form of government of the State of Vietnam, the nation that was to become the Republic of Vietnam (widely known as South Vietnam). It was contested by Prime Minister Ngô Đình Diệm, who proposed a republic, and former emperor Bảo Đại. Bảo Đại had abdicated as emperor in 1945 and at the time of the referendum held the title of head of state. Diệm won the election, which was widely marred by electoral fraud, with 98.2% of the vote. In the capital Saigon, Diệm was credited with more than 600,000 votes, although only 450,000 people were on the electoral roll. He accumulated tallies in excess of 90% of the registered voters, even in rural regions where opposition groups prevented voting. Prime Minister of North Vietnam, Pham Van Dong, wrote to Saigon asking to begin negotiations over the specific details of the elections. While the Americans were happy to avoid elections because of fears of a communist victory, they hoped that

Diệm would enter the dialogue over planning matters and wait for North Vietnam to object to a proposal, and thus use it to blame Ho for violating the Geneva Accords. The Americans had earlier advised Diệm, who had been acting in defiance of Bảo Đại, that continued aid was contingent on Diệm establishing a legal basis for usurping the head of state's power. Having claimed the election was entirely without irregularities, the United States government hailed Diệm as a new hero of the "free world"[30].

Other "black eyes" include Fidel Castro in Cuba, Karzai in Afghanistan, and Iraqi Prime Minister al-Maliki. Of course whether or not Iraq and Afghanistan are legitimate nation-states is also arguable.[31] The problem continues to be that we look at these locations and peoples through our eyes and with our background and prejudices. The solution should be an indigenous population solution and therefore the most likely to be enduring. If properly used, it is Special Forces, *through, with and by* operations, ubiquitous and persistent presence, regional focus, area orientation, cultural awareness and understanding that can provide this insight.

"It had taken fewer than fifty days of concentrated military operations and only a few hundred soldiers to seize the country from the Taliban and its terrorist allies."[32] It was a unique time in the immediate aftermath of the 9/11 attacks and the unified fervor within the United States led to an unusual level of cooperation among agencies. It was this honeymoon of close collaboration among SOF, the interagency, and conventional force that helped bring about initial success in the first UW campaign conducted by U.S. SF and SOF in the 21st century. Unfortunately, this level of cooperation soon retrograded back into the usual entrenchment of

---

30   Karnow, Stanley (1997). *Vietnam: A history*. New York City, New York: Penguin Books. ISBN 0-670-84218-4; Tucker, Spencer C. (2000). *Encyclopedia of the Vietnam War*. ABC-CLIO. ISBN 1-57607-040-9. Buttinger, Joseph (1967). *Vietnam: A Dragon Embattled*. Praeger Publishers. Miller, Edward (2004). *Grand Designs, Vision, Power and Nation Building in America's Alliance with Ngo Dinh Diem, 1954–1960*.

31   Pakistani Army Major Mehar Omar Khan states in his 2009 article "Don't Try to Arrest the Sea: An Alternative Approach for Afghanistan" in Small Wars Foundation journal that the strategic intent is unclear and should be driven bottom-up from each valley rather than top-down for the country as a whole.

32   Dr. Richard W. Stewart, *Operation Enduring Freedom: The United States Army in Afghanistan, October 2001-March 2002* (Washington, DC: U.S. Army Center of Military History, 2004), CMH Pub 70-83-1, pp. 27, available at http://www.history.army.mil/brochures/Afghanistan/Operation%20 Enduring%20Freedom.htm.

agency prerogatives and competitive positions that adversely affected later events. Political correctness and bureaucratic infighting soon replaced cooperation, initially due to the distraction, maybe willingly so, of President Bush and, subsequently, the intentional retreat by the Obama administration.

Yes, UW TTPs (tactics, techniques, procedures) must keep up with the changing world and technology. Drones, and the use of drones, has been around for a long time in the U.S. military. However, since 9/11 and the conflicts in Afghanistan and Iraq, the use of drones and the subsequent drone technology have exploded and continues to advance at an exponential pace. This technology is not limited to the U.S. Countries all around the globe have increased their drone technology and usage. The sophistication of drones has dramatically improved the tactical, operational, and strategic reach and capabilities of our forces, and this is being mirrored everywhere. Not only will Special Forces be able to enhance their unconventional warfare operations and capabilities with the use of drones, a key for SF in a UW role is to find and develop counter or anti-UAV technology. With the proliferation of UAVs worldwide, this will be a significant element that will be used against any UW effort. This must be recognized and countered.

> *High-Low Mix of UAVs. SOF will need a mix of high- and low-end unmanned aviation capabilities to meet future challenges. This high-low mix should include both non-stealthy, short-range systems for uncontested air environments with adequate basing and stealthy, long-range systems to operate in denied airspace where regional basing is unavailable.*[33]

Another exploding technology and capability is the innovation of cutting edge technologies to tag, track, and locate (TTL) high value targets, conduct sensitive site exploitation (SSE), and collect biometric information.[34] In addition to UAVs, these are the same measures that can be used against a U.S. sponsored or U.S. supported UW effort. It must be

---

33 *"Beyond the Ramparts: The Future of U.S. Special Operations Forces"*; by Jim Thomas and Chris Dougherty; 2013 Center for Strategic and Budgetary Assessments.

34 *"Advance Policy Questions for Vice Admiral William H. McRaven,"* p. 40; Lamb and Munsing, "Secret Weapon," p. 13; and USSOCOM, USSOCOM Fact Book 2013, p. 45.

assumed that all of these capabilities are available to the regime which the UW effort is trying to change. We have to "RED TEAM" our capabilities in UW by looking at our own incredible capabilities to conduct counterterrorism (CT) and counterinsurgency (COIN). Remember, to the opposing regime, we are the terrorists and the insurgents. Accordingly, the regime will use every means at their disposal to maintain control. This includes severe and harsh population control measures.

Population control measures are evolving and take numerous forms, including restriction of movement, control of currency, identification papers and cards, rationing and ration cards, and proliferation of security cameras. With proliferation of biometrics and DNA testing, population control becomes more complex and covert operations become more problematic and are seriously at risk.

> In particular, the use of biometrics--the collection and analysis of unique biological signatures and characteristics such as fingerprints, iris scans, and even the gait of a person walking--has helped to deny enemies the anonymity they might otherwise have had while operating within civilian populations.[35]

> Identity Masking. The war on terror has prompted rapid development and proliferation of biometric technologies such as digital fingerprint and iris scanners. Together with advanced digital networks and interconnected databases, biometric technologies have enabled U.S. forces, and SOF in particular, to better track and identify persons of interest. Unfortunately, the proliferation of this technology designed to prevent terrorists and insurgents from hiding in plain sight has also hampered SOF's ability to operate clandestinely. "Cover" identities and disguises are unable to deceive advanced biometric capabilities. SOF operating clandestinely will therefore require counter-biometrics capabilities to disguise their signatures or deceive biometric sensors.[36]

---

35 "Beyond the Ramparts: The Future of U.S. Special Operations Forces"; by Jim Thomas and Chris Dougherty; 2013 Center for Strategic and Budgetary Assessments.

36 "Beyond the Ramparts: The Future of U.S. Special Operations Forces"; by Jim Thomas and Chris Dougherty; 2013 Center for Strategic and Budgetary Assessments.

Biometrics and DNA testing technologies and capabilities will only become more refined and more widespread in the future. If for no other reason, the ability of Special Forces to conduct unconventional warfare in a covert manner in the future is highly unlikely. The future of covert UW may very well hinge on the use of surrogates and members of the indigenous population operating under guidance and direction of the Special Forces from a third country location. Of course this has its own problems such as having to deal with the third nation government and their willingness to host such operations.

There is precedent for this type of use of a third nation to host UW. In the '60s, Special Forces detachments were training Iranian special forces and Kurdish tribesmen in the mountains of Iran while at the same time training Turkish special forces. There are antidotal stories of U.S. Special Forces teams in each country having the indigenous teams that they were training, infiltrating the opposing country and conducting operations, in effect against each other.

> *Beyond SR and direct-action missions in contested A2/AD environments, SOF could conduct UW either within, or more likely along, the periphery of a target state. These operations could involve fomenting insurrection in disaffected minority groups, conducting cross-border raids, and harassing or interdicting lines of communication (LOCs), electricity grids, and energy pipelines. In concert with maritime blockade operations, this could constrict a target nation's economy and cause it to dedicate significant forces to defend its territorial integrity and critical infrastructure, thereby diverting those resources from other objectives. Airpower is likely to remain a critical force-multiplier for UW operations; AFSOC and ARSOAC may therefore need to develop specialized platforms (likely clandestine or unmanned), communications capabilities, and operators to support far-forward UW operations in denied environments.[37]*

Regardless, UW is changing with technology and time, primarily from a rural-based operation to more of an urban/suburban-based operation.

---

37 "Beyond the Ramparts: The Future of U.S. Special Operations Forces"; by Jim Thomas and Chris Dougherty; 2013 Center for Strategic and Budgetary Assessments.

The phenomenon of the Internet, Facebook, Twitter and other social media is not only changing the world, it is also changing how we must look at UW. With the ubiquitous capability to collect, search, screen, read and analyze all forms of electronic media, Special Forces will require new and innovative means of communicating with their UW networks that take advantage of all means of social media. Not only can information messaging be hidden in social media, as in Egypt and the Ukraine, social media can be used to create flash mob type resistance or protests and demonstrations in a time sensitive manner before security forces can react. In the future, being "off the grid" will produce just as much a signature as improperly using the social media. The use of social networks in UW is an under-developed area.

> *Maintaining access to communications and social networks will likely be critical to conducting information operations, developing and maintaining popular support for U.S.-led coalition actions, conducting UW operations, and enabling irregular forces operating within hostile states.*[38]

As Lieutenant Colonel Brian Petit (U.S. Army) has observed, "Success in future UW campaigns will likely blend the understanding of social networking with the application of SF advisors and U.S. joint firepower in support of a resistance movement or insurgency."[39]

---

38   "Beyond the Ramparts: The Future of U.S. Special Operations Forces"; by Jim Thomas and Chris Dougherty; 2013 Center for Strategic and Budgetary Assessments.

39   See Lieutenant Colonel Brian Petit (U.S. Army), ³Social Media and UW," *Special Warfare,* 25, Issue 2, April-June 2012, p. 2_, available at http://www.dvidshub.net/publication/issues/10170.

Unconventional Warfare (UW) Definition Evolution

****

Since the 1950s, there have been eleven to fourteen different doctrinally approved definitions of UW, depending on who is counting, and numerous non-doctrinal definitions....a total of 43 (/-) variants detailed below.

UW is a specific type of operation enabling and supporting resistance movements and insurgencies against a governing authority for the purpose of regime change. UW operations can only successfully be conducted in an interagency environment. Regime change mandates interagency involvement and assistance in developing and preparing the complete indigenous array of diplomatic, infrastructural, military, economic, financial, informational, and law enforcement structures to replace the ousted regime.

Within this construct of UW, Special Forces will be involved in numerous activities. These activities predominantly include guerrilla warfare, subversion, sabotage, intelligence collection and escape and evasion. Additionally, SF working *through with and by* the indigenous elements will also conduct direct action, counterterrorism activities, strategic reconnaissance, and other activities as required in order to effect regime change.

The uniqueness of Special Forces is that the tactics, techniques, and procedures (TTPs) associated with working *through, with and by* indigenous populations greatly enables SF to perform a wide array of other special operations such as DA, CT, SR, FID and COIN. SF should never be used to conduct *unilateral* operations.

It is very important to understand that UW's sole purpose is regime change. If the objective is not regime change, for instance in FID or COIN, the use of irregular forces during the conduct of operations does not make these operations unconventional warfare.

There is now only one U.S. doctrinally approved definition and it is *morally bankrupt*. The only purpose of UW is regime change. The indigenous population is in a total war situation with the current regime. *To say that UW is to "coerce" or "disrupt" is disingenuous, deceptive, deceitful, unethical and morally bankrupt.* If we make the political decision to support the indigenous population and conduct UW, we inherit the moral obligation to sustain support to the indigenous effort until such time as regime change has been accomplished, to include the generations of continuing support, no matter what the cost. To do otherwise relegates the indigenous participants, men, women and children, to genocide and the fledgling new entity to failure.

The three definitions immediately below are the most current in the indicated doctrinal publication:

(JP 3-05; Special Operations; 16 July 2014) **Unconventional Warfare.** *Activities conducted to enable a resistance movement or insurgency to coerce, disrupt, or overthrow a government or occupying power by operating through or with an underground, auxiliary, and guerrilla force in a denied area. Also called* **UW.** *(Approved for incorporation into JP 1-02.)*

JP 1-02 (DOD Dictionary of Military and Associated Terms; 8 November 2010 (As Amended Through 15 January 2015) Unconventional Warfare — *Activities conducted to enable a resistance movement or insurgency to coerce, disrupt, or overthrow a government or occupying power by operating through or with an underground, auxiliary, and guerrilla force in a denied area. Also called* **UW.** *(JP 3-05)*

(SOF Doctrine ADP (Army Doctrine Publication) **3-05, 31 August 2012) Unconventional Warfare.** *Activities conducted to enable a resistance movement or insurgency to coerce, disrupt, or overthrow a government or occupying power by operating through or with an underground, auxiliary, and guerrilla force in a denied area. (JP 1-02. SOURCE: JP 3-05)*

****

Snapshot Evolution of the Definition of Unconventional Warfare

(Annex D tracks the historical evolution of the definition and context of Unconventional Warfare in more detail)

****

(1951) Army Field Manual 31-20 Organization and Conduct of Guerrilla Warfare October dated 1 February 1951

At the time of this publication, no "Special Forces" organization existed within the U.S. military.

On the 27th of March 1952, the Chief of Staff of the Army, General. Collins, gave his approval for the establishment of a Psychological Warfare and Special Forces Center at Fort Bragg North Carolina. On 29 May 1952 the Chief of Army Field Forces at Fort Monroe, Virginia, formally announced the activation of the Psychological Warfare Center at Fort Bragg. The 10th Special Forces Group was a subordinate unit of the Psychological Warfare School at Fort Bragg. The first Special Forces Group, the 10th SFG, was activated at Fort Bragg, NC on 19 June 1952 with Colonel Aaron Banks as its commander.

Likewise, unconventional warfare was not yet a term in use.

(1955 May) Army Field Manual Army Field Manual 31-21 Guerrilla Warfare dated May (23 March) 1955 (Supersedes 1951 Army Field Manual 31-21, 5 October 1951)

1ST USE

unconventional warfare-- unconventional warfare operations are conducted in time of war behind enemy lines by

predominantly indigenous personnel responsible in varying degrees to friendly control or direction in furtherance
of military and political objectives. It consists of the interrelated fields of guerrilla warfare, evasion and escape,
and subversion against hostile state (resistance).

**(1955 August) Army Field Manual 31-20 U.S. Army Special
Forces Group (Airborne) dated 10 August 1955
(Supersedes Army Field Manual 31-20, 1 February 1951)**

2ND USE

unconventional warfare: consists of the interrelated fields
of guerrilla warfare, escape and evasion, and subversion
against hostile states.

**(1958 May) Army Field Manual 31-21 Guerrilla Warfare and
Special Forces Operations dated 8 May 1958 (Supersedes
Army Field Manual 31-20, 10 August 1955, and Army
Field Manual 31-21, 23 March 1955)**

Chapter 1. Section 2. Explanation of Terms.

Guerilla warfare comprises that part of unconventional warfare which is conducted by relatively small
groups employing offensive tactics to reduce enemy
combat effectiveness, industrial capacity, and morale. Guerilla operations are normally conducted in
enemy-controlled territory by units organized on a
military basis. It must be emphasized that unconventional warfare is an activity which, in addition to
guerilla warfare, includes evasion and escape and subversion against hostile states.

**(1961) Army Field Manual 31-21 Guerrilla Warfare and Special
Forces Operations dated 29 September 1961 (Supersedes
Army Field Manual 31-21, 8 May 1958)**

3RD USE

unconventional warfare. The three interrelated fields of guerrilla warfare, evasion and escape, and subversion. (JCS Pub 1).

unconventional warfare forces. Forces who engage in unconventional warfare. For the purposes of this manual, UW forces include both U.S. forces (special forces detachments) and the sponsored resistance force (guerrillas, auxiliaries and the underground). Often used interchangeably with the area command.

Chapter 1. Section 2. Definition of Unconventional Warfare

Unconventional warfare consists of the interrelated fields of guerrilla warfare, evasion and escape, and subversion against hostile states (resistance).

Unconventional warfare operations are conducted in enemy or enemy-controlled territory by predominantly indigenous personnel usually supported and directed in varying degrees by an external source.

(1965 June) Army Field Manual 31-21 Special Forces Operations dated 5 June 1965 (Supersedes Army Field Manual 31-21, 29 September 1961, including C 1, 4 September 1963)

4TH USE

Unconventional warfare includes the three interrelated fields of guerrilla warfare, escape and evasion, and subversion. Unconventional warfare operations are conducted within enemy or enemy-controlled territory by predominantly indigenous personnel, usually supported and directed in varying degrees by an external source.

Unconventional warfare forces- U.S. forces having an existing unconventional warfare capability consisting of Army special forces and such Navy, Air Force, and Marine units as are assigned for these operations.

(1965 December) Army Field Manual 31-20 Special Forces Operational Techniques dated 30 December 1965 (This manual together with Army Field Manual 31 – 20A, 30 December 1965, supersedes Army Field Manual 31 – 20, 16 October 1964, including C 1, 13 February 1962 and C 2, 19 July 1962)

This manual does not have a definition for unconventional warfare. It presents the operational techniques for special forces operations primarily in the guerrilla warfare operating area (GWOA). This manual describes intelligence, psychological operations, infiltration, air operations, amphibious operations, communications, logistics, demolitions, Special Forces field maneuvers, medical aspects and other techniques.

(1969 February) Army Field Manual 31-21 Special Forces Operations - U.S. Army Doctrine dated 14 February 1969 (Supersedes Army Field Manual 31-21, 3 June 1965— Note: the referenced manual is actually dated 5 June 1965)

5TH USE

Unconventional warfare consists of military, political, psychological, or economic actions of a covert, clandestine, or overt nature within areas under the actual or potential control or influence of a force or state whose interests and objectives are inimical to those of the United States. These actions are conducted unilaterally by United States resources, or in conjunction with indigenous assets, and avoid formal military confrontation.

Concept: UW is conducted to exploit military, political, economic, or psychological vulnerabilities of the enemy. It is implemented by providing support and direct action to indigenous resistance forces where appropriate, or by unilateral operations of U.S. UW forces. Its conduct involves the application of guerrilla warfare and selected aspects of subversion, political warfare, economic warfare, and psychological operations in support of national objectives

Unconventional warfare operations may be covert, clandestine, or overt in nature. Covert operations are conducted in such a manner as to conceal the identity of the sponsor, while clandestine operations place emphasis on concealment of the operation rather than the identity of the sponsor. Overt operations do not try to conceal either the operation or the identity of the sponsor.

Unconventional warfare forces—U.S. forces have an effective UW capability consisting of Army, Navy, Air Force, and Marine Corps forces as they are assigned for these operations. Resources of the military services include-

a. U.S. Army Special Forces, a force developed and trained to fulfill requirements for the Army to participate in unconventional warfare.

b. Elements of the U.S. Navy, included Underwater Demolition teams (UDT), and Sea Air Land teams (SEAL Teams), plus selected reconnaissance elements of the U.S. Marine Corps, which have among their capabilities the conduct of UW on hostile shores, restricted waterways, or river areas in conjunction with naval operations or in coordination with other UW forces.

c. Elements of the U.S. Air Force, including Special Air Warfare units, which participate in unconventional warfare, principally by providing airlift and other air support to UW forces.

(1971) Army Field Manual 31-20 Special Forces Operational Techniques dated 12 February 1971(Supersedes Army Field Manual 31-20, 30 December 1965)

This manual does not have a definition for unconventional warfare. It presents the operational techniques for special forces operations primarily in the unconventional warfare operating area UWOA).

(1982) Book, Special Warfare, The Origins of Psychological and Unconventional Warfare, COL(R) Paddock

Between 1955-1961 the term UW began to appear in the doctrine over GW. Guerilla warfare was explained as that part of UW for which the Army retains responsibility. In a 1957 article entitled *Unconventional Warfare, the Psychological Role of Special Forces*, LTG Yarborough used the term *unconventional warfare* to describe the wider resistance efforts, of which the guerrilla element is merely a part. He stated,

> *"The nature of the unconventional warfare structure must be understood in order to appreciate the importance of the psychological component. Guerrillas are the action element of the total unconventional warfare system but they do not comprise it entirely. Moreover, guerrilla will not appear as the first manifestation of a well conceived and organized resistance movement."*

(1990) Army Field Manual 31-20 Doctrine for Special Forces Operations dated 20 April 1990 (Supersedes Army Field Manual 31-20, 30 September 1977)

6TH USE

Unconventional warfare - A broad spectrum of military and paramilitary operations conducted in enemy-held, enemy-controlled, or politically sensitive territory.

Unconventional warfare includes, but is not limited to, the interrelated fields of guerrilla warfare, evasion and escape, subversion, sabotage, and other operations of a low visibility, covert or clandestine nature. These interrelated aspects of unconventional warfare may be prosecuted singly or collectively by predominantly indigenous personnel, usually supported and directed in varying degrees by (an) external sources(s) during all conditions of war or peace. (JCS Pub 1-02)

This manual has a different version of unconventional warfare on page 3 – 1:

UW is a broad spectrum of military and paramilitary operations, normally of long duration, predominantly conducted by indigenous or surrogate forces who are organized, trained, equipped, supported, and directed in varying degrees by an external source. UW includes guerilla warfare (GW) and other direct offensive low-visibility, covert, or clandestine operations, as well as the indirect activities of subversion, sabotage, intelligence collection, and evasion and escape (E&E).

(1992) Joint Publication 3-05 Doctrine for Joint Special Operations dated 28 October 1992 (Supersedes Joint Test Pub 3-05, October 1990)

Unconventional warfare-- a broad spectrum of military and paramilitary operations conducted in enemy-held, enemy-controlled, or politically sensitive territory. Unconventional warfare includes, but is not limited to, the interrelated fields of guerrilla warfare, evasion and escape, subversion, sabotage, and other operations of a low visibility, covert or clandestine nature. These interrelated aspects of unconventional warfare may be prosecuted singly or collectively by predominantly indigenous personnel, usually supported and directed in varying degrees by (an) external source(s) during all conditions of war or peace.

Unconventional warfare

a. UW includes guerrilla warfare and other low visibility, covert, or clandestine operations, as well as subversion, sabotage, intelligence collection, and E&E.

(1) GW consists of military and paramilitary operations conducted by irregular, predominantly indigenous forces in enemy-held or hostile territory. It is the overt military aspect of an insurgency or other armed resistance movement. Guerrilla forces primarily employ raid and ambush tactics against enemy vulnerabilities. In the latter stages of a successful insurgency, guerrilla forces may directly oppose selected, vulnerable enemy forces while avoiding enemy concentrations of strength.

(2) subversion is an activity designed to undermine the military, economic, psychological, or political strength or morale of a regime or nation. All elements of the resistance organization contribute to the subversive effort, but the clandestine nature of subversion dictates that the underground elements perform the bulk of the activity.

(3) sabotage is conducted from within the enemy's infrastructure in areas presumed to be safe from attack. It is designed to degrade or obstruct the war-making capability of a country by damaging, destroying, or diverting war material, facilities, utilities, and resources. Sabotage may be the most effective or only means of attacking spacific targets that lie beyond the capabilities of conventional weapon systems. Sabotage selectively disrupts, destroys, or neutralizes hostile capabilities with a minimum expenditure of manpower and matériel. Once accomplished, these incursions can further result in the enemy spending excessive resources to guard against future attack.

(4) in UW, the intelligence function must collect, develop, and report information concerning the capabilities, intentions, and activities of the established government or occupying power and its external sponsors. In this context, intelligence activities have both offensive and defensive purposes and range well beyond military issues, including social, economic, and political information that may be used to identify threats, operational objectives, and necessary supporting operations.

(5) E&E is an activity that assists military personnel and other selected personnel to:

(a) move from an enemy held, hostile, or sensitive area to areas under friendly control,

(b) avoid capture if unable to return to an area of friendly control,

(c) once captured, escape. SO (special operations) personnel often will work in concert with the JRCC (joint recovery coordination center) of the JFC (joint force commander) while operating in an E&E network.

(1994) Joint Publication 1-02 Department of Defense Dictionary of Military and Associated Terms dated 23 March 1994 (Supersedes JP 1-02, 1 December 1989)

7TH USE

unconventional warfare-- a broad spectrum of military and paramilitary operations, normally of long duration, predominantly conducted by indigenous or surrogate forces who are organized, trained, equipped, supported, and directed in varying degrees by an external source. It includes guerrilla warfare and other direct offensive, low visibility, covert, or clandestine operations, as well as the indirect activities of subversion, sabotage, intelligence activities, and evasion and escape.

unconventional warfare forces-- United States forces having been existing with unconventional warfare capability consisting of Army Special Forces and such Navy, Air Force, and Marine units as are assigned for these operations.

(1995) Joint Publication 3-0 Doctrine for Joint Operations dated 1 February 1995

No definition of UW.

(1997) Joint Doctrine Encyclopedia dated 16 July 1997

Unconventional warfare-- a broad spectrum of military and paramilitary operations, normally of long duration, predominantly conducted by indigenous or surrogate forces who are organized, trained, equipped, supported, and directed in varying degrees by an external source. It includes guerrilla warfare and other direct offensive, low visibility, covert, or clandestine operations, as well as the indirect activities of subversion, sabotage, intelligence activities, and evasion and escape.

(1998) Joint Publication 3-05 Doctrine for Joint Special Operations dated 17 April 1998

Unconventional warfare-- a broad spectrum of military and paramilitary operations, normally of long duration, predominantly conducted by indigenous or surrogate forces who are organized, trained, equipped, supported, and directed in varying degrees by an external source. It includes guerrilla warfare and other direct offensive, low visibility, covert, or clandestine operations, as well as the indirect activities of subversion, sabotage, intelligence activities, and evasion and escape.

(1999 June) Joint Publication 1-02 Department of Defense Dictionary of Military and Associated Terms dated 23 March 1994 (As Amended through 29 June 1999)

Unconventional warfare-- a broad spectrum of military and paramilitary operations, normally of long duration, predominantly conducted by indigenous or surrogate forces who are organized, trained, equipped, supported, and directed in varying degrees by an external source. It includes guerrilla warfare and other direct offensive, low visibility, covert, or clandestine operations, as well as the indirect activities of subversion, sabotage, intelligence activities, and evasion and escape.

Unconventional warfare forces-- United States forces having been existing with unconventional warfare capability consisting of Army Special Forces and such Navy, Air Force, and Marine units as our assigned for these operations.

(1999 August) Army Field Manual 100-25 Doctrine for Army Special Operations Forces dated 1 August 1999

Unconventional warfare-- a broad spectrum of military and paramilitary operations, normally of long duration, predominantly conducted by indigenous or surrogate forces who are organized, trained, equipped, supported, and directed in varying degrees by an external source. UW includes guerrilla warfare and other direct offensive, low visibility, covert, or clandestine operations, as well as the indirect activities of subversion, sabotage, intelligence activities, and unconventional assisted recovery.

UW. SF organization, training, and equipment are ideally for this mission. SF are regionally oriented, language qualified, and specifically trained to develop and foreign nation insurgents they capabilities to sustain themselves after U.S. forces leave.

(2001 June) Army Field Manual 3-05.20 Special Forces Operations dated June 2001 (Supersedes Army Field Manual 31-20, 20 April 1990)

Unconventional warfare--a broad spectrum of military and paramilitary operations, normally of long duration, predominantly conducted by indigenous or surrogate forces who are organized, trained, equipped, supported, and directed in varying degrees by an external source. It includes guerrilla warfare and other direct offensive, low visibility, covert, or clandestine operations, as well as the indirect activities of subversion, sabotage, intelligence activities, and evasion and escape.

UWOA--Replaced by joint special operations area (JSOA)

(UWOA-- unconventional warfare operating area)

(2001) December) Joint Publication 3-05.1 21 Joint Tactics, Techniques, and Procedures for Joint Special Operations Task Force Operations dated 19 December 2001

Unconventional warfare--a broad spectrum of military and paramilitary operations, normally of long duration, predominantly conducted by indigenous or surrogate forces who are organized, trained, equipped, supported, and directed in varying degrees by an external source. It includes guerrilla warfare and other direct offensive, low visibility, covert, or clandestine operations, as well as the indirect activities of subversion, sabotage, intelligence activities, and evasion and escape.

(2003 April) Army Field Manual 3-05.201 Special Forces Unconventional Warfare Operations dated April 2003

Unconventional warfare--a broad spectrum of military and paramilitary operations, normally of long duration, predominantly conducted by indigenous or surrogate forces who are organized, trained, equipped, supported, and directed in varying degrees by an external source. It includes guerrilla warfare and other direct offensive, low visibility, covert, or clandestine operations, as well as the indirect activities of subversion, sabotage, intelligence activities, and evasion and escape.

(2003 June) Joint Publication 1-02 Department of Defense Dictionary of Military and Associated Terms dated 12 April 2001 (As Amended Through 5 June 2003)

Unconventional warfare-- a broad spectrum of military and paramilitary operations, normally of long duration, predominantly conducted by indigenous or surrogate forces who are organized, trained, equipped, supported, and directed in varying degrees by an external source. It includes guerrilla warfare and other direct offensive, low visibility, covert, or clandestine operations, as well as the indirect activities of subversion, sabotage, intelligence activities, and evasion and escape.

Unconventional warfare forces—U.S. forces having an existing unconventional warfare capability.

(2003 December) JP 3-05 Doctrine for Joint Special Operations dated 17 December 2003 *(This was the first definition change to through, with or by)*

8TH USE

Unconventional warfare-- a broad spectrum of military and paramilitary operations, normally of long duration, predominantly conducted ***through, with, or by*** indigenous or surrogate forces who are organized, trained, equipped, supported, and direct it in varying degrees by an external source. It includes but is not limited to, guerrilla warfare, subversion, sabotage, intelligence activities and unconventional assisted recovery.

(2006) Army Field Manual 3-05 Army Special Operations Forces dated 20 September 2006 (Supersedes FM 100-25, 1 August 1999)

The definition for UW as undergone numerous changes since the term was first used in the 1950s. Although struggles have occurred in defining the details surrounding UW operations, one concept has remained constant-- UW is a form of warfare that usually involves the cooperation of indigenous or surrogate personnel and their resources, coupled with United States Government (USG) assets, to defeat a State, an occupying force, or non-state actors.

9TH USE

JP 1-02 approaches the defining of UW is a "classic" sense. ARSOF broadens the definition by defining UW operations as "a broad range of military and/or paramilitary operations and activities, normally of long duration, conducted **through, with, or by** *indigenous* or other simulated forces that are organized, trained, equipped, supported, and otherwise directed in varying degrees by an external source. UW operations can be conducted across the range of conflict against regular and irregular forces. These forces may or may not be State-sponsored." This expanded definition includes the use of surrogates and the implementation of UW operations against non-State actors.

(2007 September) Army Field Manual 3-05.201 (S/NF) Special Forces Unconventional Warfare (U) dated 28 September 2007

10TH USE

Unconventional warfare--Operations conducted **by, with, or through** irregular forces in support of a resistance movement, an insurgency, or conventional military operations.

(2007 October) Joint Publication 1-02 Department of Defense Dictionary of Military and Associated Terms dated 12 April 2001 (As Amended Through 17 October 2007)

11TH USE

Unconventional warfare-- a broad spectrum of military and paramilitary operations, normally of long duration, predominantly conducted *through, with, or by* indigenous or surrogate forces who are organized, trained, equipped, supported, and directed in varying degrees by an external source. It includes, but is not limited to, guerrilla warfare, subversion, sabotage, intelligence activities, and unconventional assisted recovery.

Unconventional warfare forces—U.S. forces having an existing unconventional warfare capability.

(2008 February) Army Field Manual 3-0 Army Operations dated 27 February 2008

Unconventional warfare-- a broad spectrum of military and paramilitary operations, normally of long duration, predominantly conducted *through, with, or by* indigenous or surrogate forces who are organized, trained, equipped, supported, and directed in varying degrees by an external source. It includes, but is not limited to, guerrilla warfare, subversion, sabotage, intelligence activities, and unconventional assisted recovery.

Unconventional warfare forces--no definition or mention.

(2008 September) Army Field Manual 3-05.130 dated 30 September 2008 Army Special Operations Forces Unconventional Warfare

12TH USE

Unconventional warfare-- operations conducted **by, with, or through** irregular forces in support of a resistance movement, an insurgency, or conventional military operations.

Unconventional warfare operational-- a joint special operations area (JSOA) specifically designed for unconventional warfare operations. An unconventional warfare operational area is distinguished from other JSOAs by the intended involvement of non-DOD US interagency, multinational, and/or non-state partner elements, and the inherent political nature, typically protracted time frame, and usually discreet execution of UW.

page iv. Scope: ARSOF execute and are the functional component for UW under United States Special Operations Command Directive 10-1, *Terms of Reference for Component Commanders*, and other authorities. Currently, there exists **no authoritative interagency** or joint doctrine specifically for UW...

(2008 December) Department of Defense Directive 3000.07 Irregular Warfare dated 1 December 2008

Unconventional warfare-- a broad spectrum of military and paramilitary operations, normally of long duration, predominantly conducted **through, with, or by** indigenous or surrogate forces who are organized, trained, equipped, supported, and directed in varying degrees by an external source. It includes, but not limited to, guerrilla warfare, subversion, sabotage, intelligence activities, and unconventional assisted recovery.

(2009 April) Conference 7-9 April 2009 *(This was a big break in the definition after a large effort by a UW Working Group comprised of 25 representatives USSOCOM, USASOC, USASFC, SWCS,*

NPS, JSOU and CAC SOF Cell. This effort rescinded and re-placed the above definitions within SOF; but it took until 2012 to change JP 1-02)

(2009 October) Joint Publication 1-02 Department of Defense Dictionary of Military and Associated Terms dated 8 November 2001 (As Amended Through 31 October 2009)

Unconventional warfare-- a broad spectrum of military and paramilitary operations, normally of long duration, predominantly conducted *through, with, or by* indigenous or surrogate forces who are organized, trained, equipped, supported, and directed in varying degrees by an external source. It includes, but is not limited to, guerrilla warfare, subversion, sabotage, intelligence activities, and unconventional assisted recovery.

Unconventional warfare forces—U.S. forces having an existing unconventional warfare capability.

(2011 January) Training Circular (TC) 18-01 Special Forces Unconventional Warfare dated 28 January 2011

13TH CURRENT USE (AS OF 2014)

Unconventional warfare-- activities conducted to enable a resistance movement or insurgency to coerce, disrupt, or overthrow a government or occupying power by operating *through or with* an underground, auxiliary, and guerrilla force in a denied area.

(2011 January) Joint Publication 1-02 Department of Defense Dictionary of Military and Associated Terms dated 8 November 2010 (As Amended Through 31 January 2011)

Unconventional warfare-- a broad spectrum of military and paramilitary operations, normally of long duration, predominantly conducted **through, with, or by** indigenous or surrogate forces who are organized, trained, equipped, supported, and directed in varying degrees by an external source. It includes, but is not limited to, guerrilla warfare, subversion, sabotage, intelligence activities, and unconventional assisted recovery.

(2011 April) Joint Publication 3-05 Special Operations dated 18 April 2011

Unconventional warfare—activities conducted to enable a resistance movement or insurgency to coerce, disrupt, or overthrow a government or occupying power by operating ***through or with*** an underground, auxiliary, and guerrilla force in a denied area.

(2012 April) Joint Publication 1-02 Department of Defense Dictionary of Military and Associated Terms dated 8 November 2010 (As Amended Through 15 April 2012) *(This dropped the "by" from the definition)*

Unconventional warfare-- activities conducted to enable a resistance movement or insurgency to coerce, disrupt, or overthrow a government or occupying power by operating ***through or with*** an underground, auxiliary, and guerrilla force in a denied area.

(2012 August) Army Doctrine Publication 3-05 Special Operations dated 31 August 2012

Unconventional warfare-- activities conducted to enable a resistance movement or insurgency to coerce, disrupt, or overthrow a government or occupying power by operating ***through or with*** an underground, auxiliary, and guerrilla force in a denied area.

(2013 September) Army Techniques Publication (ATP) 3-05.1 Unconventional Warfare

Unconventional warfare-- activities conducted to enable a resistance movement or insurgency to coerce, disrupt, or overthrow a government or occupying power by operating *through or with* an underground, auxiliary, and guerrilla force in a denied area.

(2014 July) Joint Publication 1-02 Department of Defense Dictionary of Military and Associated Terms dated 8 November 2010 (As Amended Through 16 July 2014)

Unconventional warfare-- activities conducted to enable a resistance movement or insurgency to coerce, disrupt, or overthrow a government or occupying power by operating *through or with* an underground, auxiliary, and guerrilla force in a denied area.

(2014 July) Joint Publication 3-05 Special Operations dated 16 July 2014

Unconventional warfare-- activities conducted to enable a resistance movement or insurgency to coerce, disrupt, or overthrow a government or occupying power by operating *through or with* an underground, auxiliary, and guerrilla force in a denied area.

(2014 August) Joint Publication 1-02 Department of Defense Dictionary of Military and Associated Terms dated 8 November 2010 (As Amended Through 15 August 2014)

Unconventional warfare-- activities conducted to enable a resistance movement or insurgency to coerce, disrupt, or overthrow a government or occupying power by operating *through or with* an underground, auxiliary, and guerrilla force in a denied area.

(2014 August) Department of Defense Directive 3000.07 Irregular Warfare (IW) dated 28 August 2014

Unconventional warfare-- activities conducted to enable a resistance movement or insurgency to coerce, disrupt, or overthrow a government or occupying power by operating ***through or with*** an underground, auxiliary, and guerrilla force in a denied area.

(2015) Joint Publication 1-02 Department of Defense Dictionary of Military and Associated Terms dated 8 November 2010 (As Amended Through 15 January 2015)

Unconventional warfare-- activities conducted to enable a resistance movement or insurgency to coerce, disrupt, or overthrow a government or occupying power by operating ***through or with*** an underground, auxiliary, and guerrilla force in a denied area.

4

Special Forces and IDAD/FID/COIN

As an introduction, some excerpts from the chapter:

As it turns out, FID and COIN are subsets of IDAD.

FID programs, therefore, will only be implemented when a nation is experiencing internal security challenges or instability.

Joint doctrine recognizes that in supporting IDAD through FID, the military is normally focused on Counterinsurgency (COIN).....

FID is civil and military assistance that helps a country respond to a threat that it cannot handle on its own.

Just so you don't have to turn back to the front, here are the definitions again:

Internal Defense and Development (IDAD)— (JP 1-02, 8 November 2010, as amended through 15 April 2012) The full range of measures taken by a nation to promote its growth and to protect itself from subversion, lawlessness, insurgency, terrorism, and other threats to its security.

Foreign Internal Defense (FID) — (JP 1-02, 8 November 2010, as amended through 15 April 2012) Participation by civilian and military agencies of a government in any of the action programs taken by another government or other designated organization to free and protect its society from subversion, lawlessness, insurgency, terrorism, and other threats to its security.

Counterinsurgency (COIN) — (JP 1-02, 8 November 2010, as amended through 15 April 2012) Comprehensive civilian and military efforts taken to defeat an insurgency and to address any core grievances.

While UW is a unique Special Forces activity, there are other activities and missions assigned to Special Forces. Special Forces prepare for operations primarily by conducting training, operations and persistent engagement with nations that are important to U.S. national security strategy. In other words, SF helps to strengthen our friends and helps influence those with whom we wish to be friends. Likewise, this sends a notice to other nations and groups that may not have friendly intentions toward the United States. Concurrently, this engagement empowers cultural awareness and understanding, provides access adjacent to denied areas of interest, and establishes lasting personal relationships. Internal defense and development (IDAD), foreign internal defense (FID) operations, and counterinsurgency (COIN) are examples of these operations.

The above mentioned operations must continue around the globe even when there is a conflict in a specific location. This is an economy of force effort. Also these operations will occur within the conflict area of operation (AOR) both in and around the actual combat area. An example of the synergistic effect of this strategy is found in current operations. While some U.S. Army Special Forces are engaged in the Middle East, other Special Forces elements continue training and stability missions in Bosnia-Herzegovina, Macedonia, the "Stans" and Turkey, Africa, South/Central America and the Pacific and Asia, maintaining continuous engagement, cultural immersion and enhancing regional stability.

Internal defense and development/foreign internal defense/counterinsurgency operations are the operations, interagency-led operations, that must be planned for and be put into effect simultaneously with any unconventional warfare operation. This has been a repeated failure of U.S. policy from Haiti, Somalia, Afghanistan, Iraq twice, and the list goes on and on. This failure is tied to the U.S. head-in-the-sand belief that every conflict can be resolved with a short burst of overpowering U.S. military might (and ten years is a short burst), and then we walk away victorious, hold a parade, and everybody goes home and the world is well. And every time when we do this, chaos breaks out, and we are surprised.

IDAD/FID/COIN -- Are they all the same or, maybe, IDAD and COIN are subsets of FID? What is the difference between them? How is "combat FID" different from COIN?

"The modern COIN mindset is when one arrogantly goes to some foreign land and attempts to make those who live there a lesser version of one's self. The FID mindset is when one humbly goes to some foreign land and seeks first to understand, and then to help in some small way for those who live there to be the best version of their own self." *Colonel Robert C. Jones, U.S. Army Special Forces (Retired)*

In the purest sense, we have never conducted COIN in Afghanistan (or Iraq). We went in conducting UW, then shifted to a major in CT with a minor in FID. After a couple of years of that we elevated Karzai in a kangaroo election and promoted the production of a centralized form of government under the current constitution that left the Taliban government in exile no option but to wage revolutionary insurgency to regain some degree of influence in their homeland. At that point our FID effort grew in response to the growing revolutionary insurgency, which in turn promoted a growth of resistance insurgency to our growing presence and activities. A vicious circle. *Colonel Robert C. Jones, U.S. Army Special Forces (Retired)*

I'd suggest that what we're doing in Afghanistan is not COIN nor FID not CT, though it involves elements of all. It's still regime change. Regime change logically has three broad stages:
- Remove old government (generally pretty easy)
- Install a new government (generally pretty difficult)
- Shelter and support that new government until it is actually able to govern on its own... until it becomes an actual government, rather than a puppet extension of our presence.

That 3rd stage is very difficult indeed, and that's where we're still mired in Afghanistan, and to some extent in Iraq. -- *H.L. Mencken*

As it turns out, FID and COIN are subsets of IDAD. The below excerpt and figure are from an Army War College White Paper: *The Doctrinal Nesting of Joint and U.S. Army Terminology*; U.S. Army Peacekeeping and Stability Operations Institute; U. S. Army War College; 10 March 2011.

[begin excerpt]

Foreign Internal Defense (FID) and Counterinsurgency (COIN)[40]

The U.S. Government supports a host nation through that nation's internal defense and development (IDAD) programs. *The IDAD strategy is a whole of government approach_*"...to promote its growth and to protect itself from subversion, lawlessness, insurgency, terrorism and other threats to its security." (JP 3-22) The USG can support IDAD programs when the host nation experiences peace or conflict. During peace, the USG provides nation assistance support; however, when the nation falls into conflict, the USG focus applies a whole of government approach into FID programs. This is where differences begin with regards to interpreting FID. Will the USG apply FID programs when there is no instability or will it only apply security cooperation (SC) programs?

FID programs are conducted by civilian and military government agencies in support of another government, or designated organization, "to free and protect its society from subversion, lawlessness, insurgency, terrorism, and other threats to its security." (JP 3-22) This definition focuses USG support efforts during crises and instability and this instability would occur as a result of IW. The words "to free and protect" imply there is some level of crisis. **FID programs, therefore, will only be implemented when a nation is experiencing internal security challenges or**

---

40   Source: *White Paper: The Doctrinal Nesting of Joint and U.S. Army Terminology*; U.S. Army Peacekeeping and Stability Operations Institute; U. S. Army War College; 10 March 2011.

instability. The focus of FID assistance falls to the drivers of conflict and the ways to address the cause of instability.

Joint doctrine recognizes that **in supporting IDAD through FID, the military is normally focused on counterinsurgency (COIN),** but states that FID activities can also assist the host nation in areas such as civil disorder, drug trafficking, and terrorism. **FID is civil and military assistance that helps a country respond to a threat that it cannot handle on its own.** FID consists of three categories of programs: FID Indirect Support, FID Direct Support, and FID Combat Operations. FID indirect support provides equipment or training support in order to enhance the HN's ability to conduct its own operations. FID direct support involves U.S. forces actually conducting operations in support of the HN. In FID combat operations the U.S. military may be required to conduct operations directly in the place of HN forces, particularly if HN security force capacity is still being developed.

U.S. Army doctrine states that FID and COIN occur as part of Irregular Warfare. FM 3-0 also recognizes indirect and direct support within FID. Indirect support to FID works to build host nation self-sufficiency where direct support involves U.S. forces directly assisting the host nation's civilian populace or military forces. As part of FID, COIN involves activity taken by a government to defeat insurgency to reestablish the host nation government's legitimacy.

Since an insurgency can occur anytime there is a governing authority, therefore COIN can also occur anytime, as long as there is a governing authority to defend its legitimacy. U.S. military forces can conduct COIN operations in support of a host nation or when no host nation governance exists. COIN in support of a host nation can occur through any category of FID, whether separately or simultaneously. COIN can also occur outside FID programs when only supporting a military governing authority. Based on these explanations, COIN can occur as a part of IW, but is not an element of FID since it can occur with or without a host nation or civilian-coalition governance.

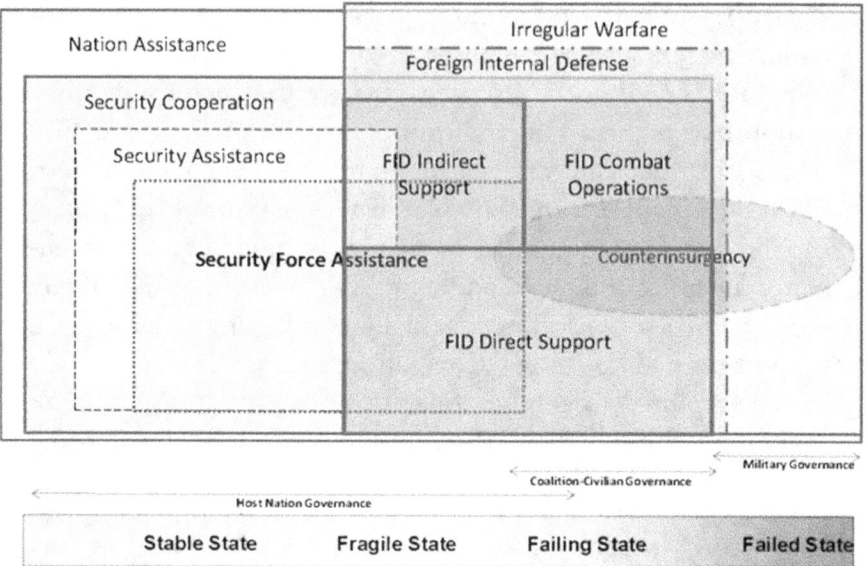

Nesting Relationships among NA, FID, SC, SA, SFA, IW and COIN**

(The figure above) does not show how offense, defense and stability cut through these concepts because as already stated above, in FSO[41] there are always continuous, simultaneous combinations of offensive, defensive, and stability tasks. [end excerpt] **Source: *White Paper: The Doctrinal Nesting of Joint and U.S. Army Terminology*; U.S. Army Peacekeeping and Stability Operations Institute; U. S. Army War College; 10 March 2011.

---

41 **Full Spectrum Operations (FSO)** – Combined use of offensive, defensive, and stability or civil support operations simultaneously as part of an interdependent joint force to seize, retain, and exploit the initiative, accepting prudent risk to create opportunities to achieve decisive results. They employ synchronized action—lethal and nonlethal—proportional to the mission and informed by a thorough understanding of all variables of the operational environment. Mission command that conveys intent and an appreciation of all aspects of the situation guides the adaptive use of U.S. Army forces. (FM 3-0)

Foreign Internal Defense (FID)

Combat FID, as found in *Beyond the Ramparts*[42], is an interesting term not currently supported in doctrine. The current doctrinal term as shown above is FID combat operations. In both Afghanistan and Iraq, after successful regime change, the U.S. was involved in building and training the winners' military capability while at the same time being involved in COIN, because the losers didn't quit.

Simultaneously, the interagency operation, with the State Department lead, should have been doing exactly the same thing in rebuilding the entire country's infrastructure both politically and economically. It did not. The U.S. was much unprepared for victory--again. It is a tragic educational void in both the U.S. military and the interagency operations, to not clearly understand when you conduct a regime change, unless it is conventional type surrender such as Germany and Japan in World War II, any remaining regime forces will probably revert to UW/insurgency ...voila! (or wa-la!), Iraq and Afghanistan.

Our Obama administration, the Bush administration, and our senior military leadership, totally missed this. Oh yes, there was the ill-fated effort under retired General Jay Garner during the first Iraqi war, to put together a group that was supposed to address this very issue. However, as was proven, they were totally inept, totally marginalized and were an utter failure in Iraq in doing this. And we still did not learn the lesson for the second Iraqi enterprise.

FID is a key mission for Special Forces, but Special Forces is not the lead agency in FID. Again, FID, like UW, should be an interagency-led process in that the impact is totally political. The legitimacy of the host nation is on the line. We do not conduct FID without a political decision, even if that political decision is made by the geographic combatant commander in accordance with the national security planning guidance from the Department of Defense which reflects the goals of the administration.

---

42   "Beyond the Ramparts: The Future of U.S. Special Operations Forces"; by Jim Thomas and Chris Dougherty; 2013 Center for Strategic and Budgetary Assessments.

The key to success is in ensuring the legitimacy of the host nation government. As stated above, "FID programs, therefore, will only be implemented when a nation is experiencing internal security challenges or instability." We can win all the fights we want to win in FID, but we will never win long-term if the perception is the host government was too weak to do anything without U.S. participation. All IDAD/FID/COIN activities must be closely coordinated and approved by the Ambassador and his country team.

> "Country teams" in embassies are made up of key figures from the State Department and other agencies who work under the direction of the ambassador and meet regularly to share information and coordinate their actions. This practice has been followed since May 29, 1961, when President John F. Kennedy wrote to all U.S. chiefs of mission saying, "You are in charge of the entire United States Diplomatic Mission and I shall expect you to supervise all of its operations. The mission includes not only the personnel of the Department of State and the Foreign Service, but also the representatives of all other United States agencies which have programs or activities in [your country]." Depending on embassy size and the nature of U.S. interests in a country, each country team may be configured differently—and some may include more than 40 agencies. (www.usdiplomacy.org)

Counterinsurgency (COIN)

Even after reading and digesting the white paper and the figure above I still have difficulty separating counterinsurgency operations from FID combat operations. To me they look the same. Using the old adage "if it looks like a duck, quacks like a duck, then it must be a duck." However, that's not what the doctrine says.

So, in Afghanistan and Iraq, COIN operations emphasized training and equipping those countries' national armies and police forces, which is the same thing FID does. To me all of this falls under the rubric of internal defense and development which is what the doctrine states per the above white paper. It is Special Forces selection, training, attitude, and mindset for UW that transcends the full IDAD arena.

And not only IDAD, but all of the missions which Special Forces would be, should be, involved with. Gaining the trust of the indigenous population, building their own internal security capability, improving and strengthening self-sufficiency, and establishing their legitimacy is exactly what Special Forces does for indigenous population in UW.

Counterterrorism (CT) and Direct Action (DA)

CT and DA are offensive measures conducted unilaterally by most forces. Special Forces conduct these, not unilaterally, but *through, with and by* indigenous (host nation) personnel, military or local security forces, as subsets, again, to IDAD in support of the efforts to stabilize and legitimize the host nation government. The primary mission of SF in this interagency activity is to apply UW skills to the IDAD environment.

CT missions are merely another form of direct action missions and therefore, if unilateral, they should never be conducted by Special Forces. There are numerous other SOF forces specifically organized, trained, and equipped to do CT and DA missions. If SF conduct or support a CT mission, then it is *through with or by* the indigenous population.

5

Other Special Forces Activities

The previous chapter discussed internal defense and development (IDAD), foreign internal defense (FID) operations, and counterinsurgency (COIN) operations. This chapter will discuss other activities in which SF participates. These activities and their definitions include:

Foreign Humanitarian Assistance (FHA) operations: (JP 1-02, 8 November 2010, as amended through 15 April 2012) Department of Defense activities, normally in support of the United States Agency for International Development or Department of State, conducted outside the United States, its territories, and possessions to relieve or reduce human suffering, disease, hunger, or privation.

Foreign Disaster Relief (DR): (JP 1-02, 8 November 2010, as amended through 15 April 2012) Prompt aid that can be used to alleviate the suffering of foreign disaster victims. Normally, it includes humanitarian services and transportation; the provision of food, clothing, medicine, beds, and bedding; temporary shelter and housing; the furnishing of medical materiel and medical and technical personnel; and making repairs to essential services.

Peacekeeping Operations (PKO): (JP 1-02, 8 November 2010, as amended through 15 April 2012) Military operations undertaken with the consent of all major parties to a dispute, designed to monitor and facilitate implementation of an agreement (cease-fire, truce, or other such agreement) and support diplomatic efforts to reach a long-term political settlement.

Humanitarian Demining Assistance: (JP 1-02, 8 November 2010, as amended through 15 April 2012) The activities related to the furnishing of education, training, and technical assistance with respect to the detection and clearance of land mines and other explosive remnants of war.

Stability Operations: (JP 1-02, 8 November 2010, as amended through 15 April 2012) An overarching term encompassing various military missions, tasks, and activities conducted outside the United States in coordination with other instruments of national power to maintain or reestablish a safe and secure environment, provide essential governmental services, emergency infrastructure reconstruction, and humanitarian relief.

Security Force Assistance (SFA): (JP 1-02, 8 November 2010, as amended through 15 April 2012) The Department of Defense activities that contribute to unified action by the U.S. Government to support the development of the capacity and capability of foreign security forces and their supporting institutions.

Counter-Drug (CD) Operational Support: (JP 1-02, 8 November 2010, as amended through 15 April 2012) Support to host nations and drug law enforcement agencies involving military personnel and their associated equipment, provided by the geographic combatant commanders from forces assigned to them or made available to them by the Services for this purpose.

Security Assistance (SA) programs (also called Security Cooperation): (JP 1-02, 8 November 2010, as amended through 15 April 2012) Group of programs authorized by the Foreign Assistance Act of 1961, as amended, and the Arms Export Control Act of 1976, as amended, or other related statutes by which the United States provides defense articles, military training, and other defense-related services by grant, loan, credit, or cash sales in furtherance of national policies and objectives. Security assistance is an element of security cooperation funded and authorized by Department of State to be administered by Department of Defense/Defense Security Cooperation Agency.

As you may have noted the above operations are fairly complex events. These are also the type of operations that greatly enhance support to those nations we wish to maintain as our friends. Accordingly, the above mentioned peacetime operations must continue during conflict as an economy of force effort, both within the operational and strategic area of responsibility (AOR) and around the globe. This is why the regional focus of the Special Forces units should never be compromised by sending them into operations in an area outside their regional focus.

For those units not involved in a specific regional conflict, there is an understandable desire to want to be involved, for many different reasons. Some of the reasons are noble and some are self-serving. For many of those in uniform, their sole desire is service to their country. And when their country is engaged in conflict, it is a natural desire of these individuals to wish to be involved and contribute.

Conversely, for some the reason is much more self-serving. It is a reality that those individuals who have been successful in a combat environment tend to be promoted ahead of those who were not in such an environment. It can be debated forever whether this is fair or not. The reality is it's a fact. Therefore, for those who are careerist and using the military as a pathway to fame and fortune, not missing out on the *conflict du jour* is an imperative[43].

Regardless, Special Forces units must remain focused on their area of responsibility. The activities outlined above are just as critical to our friends and allies around the world as is the conflict in which another ally may be involved. The point is, if we use Special Forces units in an area outside of their regional focus, our friends and allies in that region will feel abandoned and our enemies in that region will feel empowered. It is likely this will cause increased problems leading to instability and conflict in these abandoned regions.

---

43   A prime example is John Kerry in Vietnam as brilliantly exposed in the 2004 book "*Unfit for Command: Swift Boat Veterans Speak Out Against John Kerry*"

6

Regional Focus

Regional focus (area orientation, cultural awareness and understanding) is the reason for the existence of Special Forces. Without this regional focus there is no viable *"through, with and by"* with indigenous populations that will support national objectives in a timely manner.

> *The ability to conduct UW operations against a sophisticated opponent could require years, if not decades, of preparatory action. SOF must begin to lay the groundwork — for example, by building relationships with local partners, scouting locations for safehouses[44], and pre-positioning equipment — well in advance to provide an array of policy options available if and when they are needed. The United States must also assume that competitors and potential adversaries will engage in their own UW operations against states that choose to partner with the United States. Therefore, SOF may also need to conduct FID and security force assistance (SFA) in these countries preventively, with a particular focus on training partner SOF, to increase partner nations' abilities to withstand subversion or intimidation by hostile states.[45]*

---

44   safe house, n. an inconspicuous place for refuge or clandestine activities. An innocent-appearing house or premises established by an organization for the purpose of conducting clandestine or covert activity in relative security.

45   "Beyond the Ramparts: The Future of U.S. Special Operations Forces"; by Jim Thomas and Chris Dougherty; 2013 Center for Strategic and Budgetary Assessments.

As found in FM 3-05.20 dated June 2001:

REGIONAL ORIENTATION

1-16. Each SF group is oriented to a specific region of the world, which is within the area of responsibility (AOR) assigned by the Unified Command Plan to the geographically apportioned unified commands. These commands include United States Central Command (USCENTCOM), United States European Command (USEUCOM), United States Pacific Command (USPACOM), and United States Southern Command (USSOUTHCOM). Each SF group orients toward specific AORs. Within each group, individual battalions and operational detachments have an even more well-defined focus within their AORs. Orientation helps commanders focus their personnel and training toward the peculiarities of the region. Examples are language training, cultural familiarization, movement techniques, and military skills in various climates. Regional orientation is also the basis for the development of intercultural communication skills. Area orientation begins with formal qualification training in the different phases of the Special Forces Qualification Course (SFQC) and is reinforced through continued training and repeated deployments to an assigned AOR.

It is obvious that rotations or utilization out of the area of focus breaks the core *"through, with and by"* because it breaks the critical relationships with the indigenous population. This also creates a vacuum [i.e., the loss of Joint/Combined Exercises and Training (JCETs)] and broken relationships that required years to cultivate and build and, once broken, will require more years to rebuild and sustain.

This is generational engagement[46], to be measured by the influences on indigenous populations, generations of indigenous populations. Therefore, properly employed, through persistent engagement, Special Forces become the most embedded element at all societal levels within

---

46   See Annex K: Executive Report: JSOU Second Annual Symposium; Irregular Warfare: Strategic Utility of SOF; 1-3 May 2007.

an area. The cultural awareness and understanding attained is unequalled by any other agency or group. Every interagency move must be culturally integrated and no other element is better situated, prepared, integrated, or trusted as Special Forces.

The Country Team

Joint Publication (JP) 1-02, dated 8 November 2010, as amended through 15 April 2012, defines the country team as the senior, in-country, U.S. coordinating and supervising body, headed by the chief of the U.S. diplomatic mission (the U.S. Ambassador)[47], and composed of the senior member of each represented U.S. department or agency, as desired by the chief of the U.S. diplomatic mission. The http://www.usdiplomacy.org/ website describes country teams:

> "Country teams" in embassies are made up of key figures from the State Department and other agencies who work under the direction of the ambassador and meet regularly to share information and coordinate their actions. This practice has been followed since May 29, 1961, when President John F. Kennedy wrote to all U.S. chiefs of mission saying, "You are in charge of the entire United States diplomatic mission and I shall expect you to supervise all of its operations. The Mission includes not only the personnel of the Department of State and the Foreign Service, but also the representatives of all other United States agencies which have programs or activities in [your country]." Depending on embassy size and the nature of U.S. interests in a country, each country team may be configured differently—and some may include more than 40 agencies. In addition to State Department section chiefs and the head of the local USAID mission, the following are some agencies most frequently represented on a mission's country team.

---

47   The chief of the U.S. diplomatic mission is usually the U.S. Ambassador except in cases where there is no U.S. Embassy. Then maybe only a consul in charge of a Consulate. A country will have only one embassy, but could have several consuls.

DEPARTMENT OF AGRICULTURE

The mission of the Department of Agriculture (USDA) is to provide leadership on food, agriculture, natural resources and related issues based on sound public policy, the best available science and efficient management. At embassies, the Foreign Agricultural Service (FAS) is responsible for collecting, analyzing and disseminating information about global supply and demand, trade trends and market opportunities. FAS seeks improved market access for U.S. products, administers export financing and market development programs, provides export services, carries out food aid and market-related technical assistance programs, and provides links to world resources and international organizations. Its Animal and Plant Health Inspection Service (APHIS) also has offices in some overseas embassies.

DEPARTMENT OF COMMERCE

The mission of the Department of Commerce (DOC) is to foster, promote and develop the foreign and domestic commerce of the United States. It advances these objectives by participating with other government agencies in the creation of national policy, promoting and assisting international trade, strengthening the international economic position of the United States, promoting progressive business policies and growth, improving comprehension of the environment, ensuring effective use and growth of scientific and technical resources, and assisting states, communities and individuals with economic progress. Foreign Service Officers of the DOC Foreign Commercial Service (FCS) staff the commercial sections of embassies abroad.

DEPARTMENT OF DEFENSE

The mission of the United States Department of Defense (DOD) is to provide the military forces needed to deter war and to protect the security of the United States. This mission is achieved through war-fighting, humanitarian efforts, peacekeeping and evacuation operations. The Defense Department has employees located in more than 146 countries. Personnel of the Defense Intelligence Agency (DIA, a part of DOD), representing the service branches of the U.S. military, staff the Defense Attaché Offices (DAO) at embassies abroad.

DRUG ENFORCEMENT AGENCY

The mission of the Drug Enforcement Agency (DEA) is to enforce the controlled-substances laws and regulations of the United States and to bring to justice organizations involved in the growing, manufacture or distribution of such substances. It also supports non-enforcement programs aimed at reducing the availability of illicit controlled substances on domestic and international markets. Cooperation with foreign law enforcement agencies is essential to the DEA mission. To support international investigations, DEA operates abroad in more than 50 countries. Its special agents assist their foreign counterparts by developing sources of information, interviewing witnesses and working undercover to assist in surveillance efforts on cases that involve drug trafficking to the United States. DEA also seeks U.S. indictments against major foreign traffickers who have committed crimes against American citizens.

FEDERAL BUREAU OF INVESTIGATION

The mission of the Federal Bureau of Investigation (FBI) is to protect and defend the United States against terrorist and foreign intelligence threats, uphold and enforce the criminal laws of the United States and provide leadership and criminal justice service to federal, state, municipal and international agencies and partners. The globalization of crime – terrorism; international trafficking of drugs, contraband and people; and cyber crime – requires the FBI to integrate law enforcement efforts around the world to stop foreign crime as far from U.S. borders as possible and to help solve international crimes as quickly as possible. The FBI has more than 50 Legal Attaché offices (legats) in U.S. embassies and consulates abroad. Legats coordinate international investigations with their colleagues, cover international leads for domestic U.S. investigations, link U.S. and international resources in critical criminal and terrorist areas and coordinate FBI training classes for police in their geographic areas.

DEPARTMENT OF HOMELAND SECURITY

The Department of Homeland Security (DHS) was established to "provide the unifying core for the vast national network of organizations and institutions involved in efforts to secure our nation." It works to ensure safe and secure borders, welcome lawful immigrants and visitors, and promote the free flow of commerce. Its Citizenship and Immigration Services (USCIS), formerly the Immigration and Naturalization Service (INS), is responsible for immigration and naturalization adjudication as well as immigration services policies and priorities. USCIS has overseas field offices in about 25 countries.

DEPARTMENT OF TREASURY

The mission of the Department of the Treasury (DOT), "the steward of U.S. economic and financial systems," is "to promote the conditions for prosperity and stability in the United States and encourage prosperity and stability in the rest of the world." A major participant in the international economy, the DOT monitors economic trends and seeks "to influence global financial and economic issues whenever possible." Its Office of International Affairs supports economic prosperity at home by encouraging financial stability and sound economic policies abroad through engagement with financial market participants, foreign governments and international financial institutions. Officers in DOT's International Affairs sections perform surveillance and in-depth analysis of global economic and financial developments. Treasury Attaches are assigned at some large embassies abroad.

Now the following statement really gets into some rice bowls and gores some sacred oxen. First and foremost, every United States Ambassador should have a Special Forces team permanently assigned inside their country. At any given point in time, only part of the team will be in-country with the remainder in the United States (CONUS). Individual rotations with the U.S. based part of the team sustains connectivity, training and schools. The role of the SF team is as the key advisors to the American Ambassador and the country team for any and all activities, peace or war. The cultural expertise of the team touches all the elements of power; DIME, DIMEFIL, MIDLIFE, ASCOPE, and PMESII – see Annex F for definitions. All interagency entities should ensure coordination with the SF element (as part of the country team) before entering the operational space, in other words, before entering the country. As clarification, the SF are not in the approval loop. As members of the country team, they advise and assist the American Ambassador.

Some will say that this will cause deployment stress. This argument highlights a complete lack of understanding of regional focus for Special Forces. In peaceful situation, there is no rationale to not permit dependents to accompany the soldiers. In fact, dependents may help enhance the cultural understanding and integration.

The operations in Iraq and Afghanistan should have been totally conducted by the 5th Special Forces Group which is regionally oriented to that area. Of course, this would've required an increase in force structure for the 5th Special Forces Group. This is an illustrative case for the return to an expanded Special Action Force (SAF) (See Annex O). Also, just like with conventional forces, you increase to wherever you need in order to have your 2:1 dwell to deployment ratio[48].

The attempt by the SOF leadership to get "everybody in the game" has resulted in a potentially tragic loss of regional expertise and regional contact around the rest of the globe. Additionally, this constant rotation of different units into different areas and the changing interface with the indigenous population breaks the bonds of trust that then must be re-created with each new unit that deploys to an indigenous area. Again, this flies totally in the face of the use of Special Forces. It is this regional

---

48   2:1 dwell: This means for every soldier deployed, there are two with the same regional focus and military specialty in the United States, one of which is preparing to replace the deployed soldier and the other is in training, schools, on leave, etc.

focus in peacetime, and IDAD, FID and COIN, that enables conventional force projection, counterterrorism operations, and UW.

The 2:1 dwell ratio should be maintained at each unit level. Entire units should only be rotated in extreme situations. As an example, one SF ODA could have eighteen personnel instead of twelve. They would have three of each MOS, and over a period of time would rotate individuals into their deployed area. This ensures continuity of regional expertise and continuity of engagement with the indigenous population. This ensures the bonds of trust developed are maintained. This, in turn, ensures that the HUMINT nets are sustained. Human intelligence relationships are extremely personal and the handing off of intelligence assets to new persons, most often results in a disruption of the intelligence… at least until trust has been reestablished, which may never happen with constant turnover.

The piling-on of personnel and units into an area of conflict seems to be a natural phenomena. This is understandable due to the culture of the military. First, everyone wants to participate in the conflict because one of the primary reasons for joining the military is to defend the nation. Secondarily, our promotion system tends to favor those who have participated in a conflict environment over those who do not, regardless of the otherwise demonstrated capabilities of the individuals.

To date our senior leaders have lacked either the understanding and recognition of the current ruinous nature of the arbitrary rotation of non-regionally focused units into a region of conflict, or have lacked the willingness to cease this. And I say arbitrary, because they do not value, or at least in the past have not seemed to value, the importance of regional focus, cultural expertise, ethnographic understanding of the population, language immersion and the intense long-term dedicated preparation that goes into preparation of the environment and HUMINT.

Persistent human relationships are the foundation of partnerships and trust and the military is no different. This highlights the value of regional engagement and regional focus prior to a conflict. It's only through this long-term engagement prior to conflicts that the development of these human intelligence capabilities are possible. If you wait until the conflict begins, it takes a long time to develop these relationships and the cost is in lives. The only way to truly follow the ever-adapting terrorist network is through human intelligence (HUMINT). Nothing beats HUMINT, which is the indigenous populations on the ground working *through, with or by* Special Forces.

In the future resource-constrained military, the ubiquitous presence of SF forward deployed/ employed, working through the country team and other interagency partners, can form the relationships and information systems and networks that will provide the knowledge to enable a UW campaign to be implemented. However, this requires the discipline to leave these SF in place regardless of the situations that occur in other regions of the world. In other words, do not move SF from one region to another to participate in a conflict in another region. Only by having constant presence in all areas and regions with SF forward deployed can you mitigate surprise. This also means you do not have to jump-start every operation, but have a firm base of knowledge and information networks on the ground, already providing information and intelligence on a routine basis. And this is not covert/CIA type intelligence. This is intelligence gathered by ethnographic understanding, cultural sensitivity, personal relationships, and trust built over the years.

Regionally Aligned Forces

Like the Phoenix trying to rise from the ashes of Iraq and Afghanistan, the Army is exploring regional alignment. An article in the March 2012 edition of *Parameters, Regionally Aligned Forces: Business Not as Usual,* focuses on General Raymond T. Odierno's, *"Regionally Aligned Forces: A New Model for Building Partnerships,"* as described in *Army Live,* March 22, 2012, http://armylive.dodlive.mil/index.php/2012/03/ aligned-forces/; and General Odierno, *CSA's Strategic Intent,* February 5, 2013, http://www. army.mil/article/95729/. These documents lay out the (then) Chief of Staff of the Army's vision of regionally aligned conventional forces (RAF).

> RAF is integral to the Army vision of being "Globally Responsive and Regionally Engaged" and it is fundamental to our ability to "Prevent, Shape and Win" across the globe. It is essential to the U.S. defense strategy and represents the Army's commitment to provide culturally attuned, scalable, mission- prepared capabilities in a changing strategic environment characterized by combinations of nontraditional and traditional threats.

According to the Parameters article and the authors, BG Kimberly Field, British Army Colonel James Learmont, and U.S. Army Lieutenant Colonel Jason Charland, the conclusions are "Business Not as Usual."

> Regional alignment will take approximately five years to implement fully. The effects of the reduced budget and the pace of drawdown of U.S. forces from Afghanistan are the key constraints to quicker progress. However, as the concept matures through FY14, the Army's focus on regional alignment will increase across all combatant commands, to include increasing support to and integration with U.S. Special Operations Command. For soldiers, RAF means real-world missions in exciting places. For policymakers and strategists, RAF means a more agile, responsive, integrated Army. To combatant commanders, RAF means many of the Army's capabilities in the continental United States have, in effect, become a part of their areas of responsibility. And for America's role as a global leader, RAF offers a very real mechanism to shape the operational environment, on the land and among humans, more consistently and in conjunction with a range of strategic partners.

While an interesting idea, RAF for conventional Army units can never be more than a familiarization process. This certainly will help with the non-combat missions such as humanitarian assistance (HA), security assistance (SA), etc. But cultural expertise requires more micro-focus than Army brigades can reasonably manage. There is just too much of the world out there and there will always be too few brigades.

7

Selection and Assessment

This section describes the histories of the selection and assessment processes of the Office of Strategic Services in World War II and the United States Army Special Forces Selection and Assessment (SFAS) program. It further outlines the current SFAS program (as of 2015).

Special Forces differs from the rest of Special Operations Forces in that they are specifically selected, assessed, trained, equipped and organized to conduct special operations *through, with or by indigenous populations*.

> SOF's newfound status as a "crown jewel" within the Department of Defense's (DoD's) portfolio of capabilities is grounded in the attributes of the operators comprising the United States Special Operations Command (USSOCOM). More than any other capability in America's arsenal, it is the human dimension—both the people who serve and the domain for which they are optimized—that differentiates SOF from both conventional and nuclear forces. SOF's "First Truth is that "Humans are more important than hardware." The characteristics that make SOF operators "special" go far beyond the rigorous assessment, selection, and qualification processes of SOF units, which only a small fraction of candidates complete. Though SOF have exceptional physical and psychological stamina, those selected to serve in SOF are first and foremost problem-solvers distinguished

by their critical thinking skills and ingenuity. Most SOF operators are well-educated and hold college degrees, although highly
trained in the discriminate use of lethal force, *(for the remainder
of this diatribe, SOF/USSOCOM has hijacked the attributes only
found in Army Special Forces)* SOF(SF) are also known for their
political acumen and engagement skills, "winning hearts and
minds" by leveraging their cultural expertise and linguistic proficiency. Because they operate in the human domain, SOF (SF)
must also be adept at building relationships by understanding the
needs of others, showing empathy, and earning trust. SOF (SF)
are generally more experienced than their conventional counterparts, with SOF (SF) personnel typically spending eight years in
the conventional forces prior to their SOF (SF) qualification and
ranging in average age from twenty-nine (enlisted) to thirty-four
(officers).[49] (U.S. Special Operations Command (USSOCOM),
Fact Book 2013 (Tampa, Florida: USSOCOM, 2013), p. 55.

During World War II, the Office of Strategic Services (OSS) assessed approximately 5400 men and women at two locations in the United States
between December 1943 and August 1945. The United States Army
Special Forces Selection and Assessment (SFAS) program, instituted in
1988, assesses 1000-1500 men per year at Fort Bragg, North Carolina.

The OSS assessments were conducted primarily from two locations;
Station "S" in northern Virginia and Station "W" in Washington, D.C.
The majority of OSS recruits were assessed at Station "S" during a 3-day
assessment; the remainder in a one-day program at Station "W." The
Special Forces Selection and Assessment (SFAS) program is a 24-day pro-
gram primarily conducted in a field environment at the Special Forces
Rowe Training Facility, Camp MacKall, a subsidiary post at the western
reaches of Fort Bragg, North Carolina.

Using trained professional psychologists and psychiatrists as assessors in
an interactive social matrix environment, the OSS assessment process
focused on small classes of eighteen recruits with up to a 3:1 ratio of

---

49 "Beyond the Ramparts: The Future of U.S. Special Operations Forces"; by Jim Thomas and Chris
Dougherty; 2013 Center for Strategic and Budgetary Assessments.

assessors to assessed. The legacy SFAS process used experienced Special Forces soldiers who attend an Assessor Training Course. Stoicism characterized this process as non-interactive assessors worked with large classes (up to 300 recruits) at an average ratio of 1:15 assessor to assessed. A new program changes the "stoic" approach and provides for a long-term assessment through the use of tactical/advisor/counselors (TACs).

The OSS assessment process resulted in an average attrition rate of 25%, while the SFAS process averages 50+%. Comparably, while both programs use elementalistic[50] and organismic[51] methodology, the SFAS program incorporates physical stress and sleep deprivation to induce mental stress, where the OSS only used mentally stressful situational tests. The OSS assessors were limited on the duration of their program by wartime exigencies. The SFAS program may also soon feel pressure due to the mounting requirements for Special Forces soldiers in the War on Terrorism.

Introduction: A Brief History of the Office of Strategic Services

The summer of 1941, 11 July, saw the birth of the parent of the Office of Strategic Services (OSS), the Office of the Coordinator of Information (COI). President Franklin Roosevelt, frustrated with the lack of coordination among the agencies normally responsible for intelligence (the Department of State [DOS], the Federal Bureau of Investigation [FBI], the War Department's Military Intelligence Division [G-2][52] and the Office of Naval Intelligence [ONI]), he created a new agency directly under the White House.[53] Impressed with the vision and organizational

---

50   *elementalism:* a tendency to postulate a separation into independent entities or elements of things (such as mind and body, space and time) that can be only verbally so separated; Elementalistic testing can be conducted for the most part by technicians, eliminating the psychologist as observer, interpreter, diagnostician and valuator, simply speaking, eliminating subjectivity.

51   Organismic theories in psychology are a family of holistic psychological theories which tend to stress the organization, unity, and integration of human beings expressed through each individual's inherent growth or developmental tendency.

52   Military staff s have letter designations for the levels. S-level, for example S-2, is a brigade or a staff element of a colonel level command. G-level staff, for example G-2 is a general officer level command staff. S/G-1 is personnel; S/G-2 is intelligence; S/G-3 is operations; S/G-4 is logistics/supply; S/G-5 is future plans/planning; S/G-6 is communications.

53   www.cia.gov/cia/publications/oss/, *COI Came First.*

ability of Wall Street millionaire lawyer, William J. Donovan, a Medal of Honor winner in WWI, President Franklin picked him to "direct the ....excursion into espionage, sabotage, 'black' propaganda, guerrilla warfare and other 'un-American' subversive practices." Donovan, in a memorandum to the President, promised him "an international secret service staffed by young officers who were 'calculatingly reckless' with 'disciplined daring' and 'trained for aggressive action'."

The Coordinator of Information (COI) only survived due to the relationship Donovan had with the President. It was jealously undermined by the other traditional intelligence agencies. Even the support of the President did not fully protect the new agency. On 13 June 1942, the COI ceased to exist.[54] Half of the organization, the "white" propaganda division, was transferred to the newly formed Office of War Information and the rest of the organization was renamed the Office of Strategic Services and placed under the Joint Chiefs.

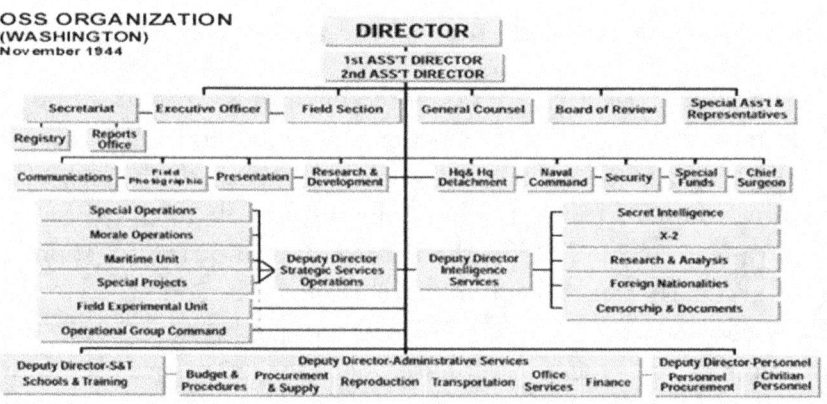

Even prior to the war, Donovan had close ties with the British Secret Intelligence Service and the OSS organizational structure was greatly influenced by this relationship. In its formative stages, the OSS owed its survival to the aid received from the British about operational training methods, clandestine communications, and espionage techniques. The British trained the first OSS operatives in secret.

---

54   www.cia.gov/cia/publications/oss/, *What was OSS?*

At the height of its operations, the OSS had approximately 13,000 men and women assigned. Of these, 9000 were military with one in every four an officer. About 4500 of these military and civilians were women[55], a few of which were operationally deployed behind enemy lines.

Donovan was exceptionally energetic, resourceful and aggressive. He was also unconventional and the OSS readily assumed his character. Effective action was the sole objective regardless of organizational detail, waste, or propriety of rank and position. Traditional military protocol was superfluous and insubordination rampant. This absence of a rigid hierarchy enabled an exceptional group of men and women to work with great effectiveness. The "OSS undertook and carried out more different types of enterprises calling for more varied skills than any other single organization of its size in the history of our country."[56] Unfortunately, this also led to cases of incompetence and corruption, which may have been one of the reasons Donovan endorsed the establishment of the assessment process in December 1943.

With the death of President Roosevelt in April 1945, Donovan and the OSS lost their greatest supporter. President Truman disliked Donovan, and regardless of the successes of the OSS, he felt no obligation to save it at the conclusion of the war. President Truman signed Executive Order 9621 on 20 September, which dissolved the OSS as of 1 October 1945.[57] Fortunately, parts of the OSS were retained as the "Strategic Services Unit" as a nucleus of a peacetime intelligence service. The SSU was later moved to the Central Intelligence Group until the National Security Act of 1947 formed the Central Intelligence Agency.[58]

A Brief History of the Army Special Forces

With the establishment of the CIA in 1947, the Joint Chiefs of Staff (JCS) passed what they considered the "murky UW pool of obscured depth,"[59]

---

55   www.cia.gov/cia/publications/oss/, *What was OSS?*

56   OSS Assessment Staff, *Assessment of Men: Selection of Personnel for the Office of Strategic Services.*

57   www.cia.gov/cia/publications/oss/, *An End and a Beginning.*

58   www.cia.gov/cia/publications/oss/, *An End and a Beginning.*

59   Bank, *From OSS to Green Berets: The Birth of Special Forces.* Copyright 1986 by Aaron Banks; published by Presidio Press.

the Unconventional Warfare mission to the new agency. However, in 1948, the Secretary of Defense revisited the issue. A subsequent study by the JCS concluded that responsibility for policy planning within the military for UW continue with JCS, and that the Army should be the prime operator, particularly for guerrilla warfare, in support of resistance/guerrilla groups.

For the next couple of years, progress languished and was focused on the possibility of a combined Ranger/Special Forces organization. In July 1951 the issue began to gel. The Far East commander disbanded his Ranger units and the Commander in Chief, Europe indicated that he had no need for Rangers in his theater. Both commanders stressed that Rangers were not capable of conducting guerrilla warfare because of racial and language barriers. The Army Field Forces (AEF) agreed and further stated that "all reference to Rangers be deleted because Special Forces would be involved in subversive activities....and ....should focus on the utilization of indigenous guerrilla groups...and that Special Forces be regarded and kept as a separate, distinct organization[60]."

Organizationally, the responsibility to develop the plan for Special Forces was placed under General Robert A. McClure of the G-3, Office of the Chief of Psychological Warfare. General McClure was a very vocal and persistent advocate of psychological operations, UW and Special Forces since the end of WWII. General McClure and his staff, including Aaron Bank[61], developed a concept and plan for establishing a consolidated PsyWar and SF training facility at Fort Bragg, North Carolina. On 27 March 1952, the chief of Staff, Army, General J. Lawton Collins, approved the center. Maybe technically, 1 May 1952 is the birthday of Special Forces which was the on-or-about date the Department of the Army directed as the establishment of the Psychological Warfare Center (which included a Special Forces Department).

---

60   Bank, 155.
61   As a lieutenant, Bank joined the OSS in the spring 1943. He is known as the 'Father of Special Forces." He served first on an OSS Operational Group (OG) of 30 men whose mission was to infiltrate enemy territory and join with existing guerrilla bands and support them in conducting guerrilla warfare. His is most famous for his activities on a Jedburgh team in Italy. The Jedburghs were 3-man teams, two officers and one enlisted radio operator. The Jedburghs infiltrated enemy territory to organize the guerrilla potential and conduct unconventional warfare, including guerrilla warfare.

According to Colonel Bank, General McClure directed that the organization of Special Forces be "an OSS type of organization from top to bottom; from command, control and logistics to field operating units[62]... with the mission to infiltrate by air, sea, or land deep into enemy-controlled territory and to stay, organize, equip, train, control, and direct the indigenous potential in the conduct of Special Forces Operations. Special Forces Operations were defined as: the organization of resistance movements and operation of their component networks, conduct of guerrilla warfare, field intelligence gathering, espionage, sabotage, subversion, and escape and evasion activities."[63]

Any mention of Ranger or commando operations was deleted and emphasis placed on the direct action (combat) role of the indigenous forces controlled by SF where the indigenous forces perform the action either covertly, clandestinely or overtly. Evolving from the OSS Operational Groups (OGs) (see Annex P: OSS Manuals from WWII) and the Jedburgh teams, two-15 man Special Forces "A" teams would relatively equal one OSS OG, while a split "A" team would roughly equal one Jedburgh team (usually three people). The organizational structure of companies and battalions was only a "sop to the traditionalists."[64]

The first Special Forces group formed was activated on 19 June 1952 and designated the 10th Special Forces Group (SFG) with Colonel Aaron Bank as its first commander. In November 1953, the 10th SFG was deployed to Bad Tolz, West Germany. At the same time, part of the 10th SFG was spun-off and established a new SFG at Fort Bragg, the 77th SFG. Continued growth included forming the 1st SFG on Okinawa, Japan in June 1957 and the 77th SFG being redesigned the 7th SFG on 6 June 1960.[65] The Green Beret became the official headgear of Special Forces on 21 September 1961 at the request of President Kennedy, a staunch friend and supporter of Special Forces.[66] This also coincided with the activation of the 5th SFG. In rapid succession, the 8th SFG was acti-

---

62   Bank, 158.
63   Bank, 163.
64   Bank, 160-1
65   Public Affairs Office (PAO) The John F. Kennedy Special Warfare Center and School (USAJFKSWCS)
      To Free the Oppressed; A Pocket history of U.S. Special Forces.
66   PAO USAJFKSWCS

vated on 1 April 1963, the 6th SFG on 1 May 1963 and the 3rd SFG on 5 December 1963.[67] The fourteen years involvement in the Viet Nam War from 1956 through 1972 was the height for Special Forces.

Following Viet Nam, Special Forces were victims of the post-war drawdown and saw the rapid deactivation of the 1st, 3rd, 6th and 8th SF Groups.[68] Only the 5th, 7th and 10th SFGs remained active. With the election of President Reagan in 1981 and his renewed emphasis on defense, Special Forces also benefited from this resurgence in defense. The 1st Special Operations Command was established at Fort Bragg on 1 October 1982 with a two-star general as its commander. The qualification course was made longer and harder and a major step was taken on 1 October 1984 when Special Forces was established as a separate career field for non-commissioned officers. Relatively soon thereafter, the warrant officer career field was established in 1985 and on 9 April 1987, a separate branch was established for officers.[69] Expansion of Special Forces continued with the reactivation of the 1st SFG in 1984 and the 3rd SFG on 20 June 1990.

Currently, all Army Special Forces are assigned under the U.S. Army Special Forces Command (USASFC) with its headquarters at Fort Bragg. Commanded by a two-star Special Forces general, the USASFC is a major subordinate command of the United States Army Special Operations Command (USASOC) which is assigned all Army Special Operations Forces (SOF), including both active and reserve Special Forces, Civil Affairs, Psychological Operations, Special Operations Aviation, Rangers and some select Special Mission Units. The USASOC is comprised of more than 46,000 active duty and reserve soldiers, with more than 10,000 of these being soldiers assigned to the five active and two reserve Special Forces Groups.

Following the events of 11 September 2001, emphasis on Special Forces has dramatically increased, enhanced by the Special-Forces-led victory over the Taliban in Afghanistan. In November 2002, Secretary of Defense Ronald Rumsfeld ordered an internal study by the Institute for

---

67   PAO USAJFKSWCS
68   PAO USAJFKSWCS
69   PAO USAJFKSWCS

Defense Analyses (IDA) to conduct a quick, but extensive study of special operations from a "blank sheet." The study recommends significant increases in Special Operations Forces, likely including Special Forces. This will only increase the challenge in selecting and assessing personnel for Special Forces.

The OSS Assessment Process

The OSS operated for the first couple of years by recruiting personnel through networking of known individuals and by teams of OSS recruiters. The caliber of the new personnel was entirely based on reputation and the assessment of the recruiters using whatever haphazard means they developed. Often the recruit responded to an advertisement or other notice announcing a search for volunteers with foreign language capabilities to be interviewed for special assignments. The selection consisted of an interview with an Army officer, a detailed compilation of personal history, verbally testing in a language and then, if deemed acceptable the final question: would the candidate volunteer to operate behind enemy lines in uniform or civilian clothes? An affirmative answer completed the selection process and the volunteer subsequently reported for training in one of the Operational Groups (OGs). While there were many very successful operators obtained in this process, there were all too many incidents where the training programs were carrying the brunt of bad recruitment.[70]

The genesis of the idea for an assessment process was broached in October 1943 using an example form the British War office Selection Board (WOSB). The WOSB has a program for testing officer candidates for the British Army. The process was run by an imaginative group of progressive psychiatrists and psychologists.[71] From this program came the idea of a social matrix mixing and the leaderless group concept. Donovan fully and eagerly embraced the concept and directed immediate implementation.

---

70   OSS Assessment Staff, *Assessment of Men: Selection of Personnel for the Office of Strategic Services.*
71   ibid.

Donovan's staff, as was typical, showed no less enthusiasm than he did and immediately embarked on the endeavor. The first assessment site was a country estate outside Washington in Fairfax, Virginia. This was "Station S." The estate had plenty of room and structures to set up the testing, both indoors and outside. The first candidates arrived in December 1943.[72]

The assessment staff was comprised entirely of psychiatrists, psychologists and a few support staff. There were no operational personnel in the assessment staff and none would be involved until just before the program closed in August 1945. After some initial adjustments, it was established that the optimal flow for the program at "S" was classes of eighteen candidates, six times per month for an average of 108 candidates per month.[73]

Due to the overwhelming requirement by late winter 1944, a new assessment unit was established in Washington proper. This unit, called "Station W," conducted a one-day assessment program more focused for the non-operator. Station "W" had a flow of approximately 200 candidates per month. Briefly, for about six months (June – December 1944), a west coast assessment unit in California, Station "WS" was temporarily established; however, it does not play a significant role.[74] Likewise, the overseas stations in Ceylon, China and India played a minor role and will not be further discussed.

The two main assessment units "S" and "W" accounted for 5,391 candidates assessed between December 1943 and August 1945. There were 2372 persons assessed at "S" and 3071 assessed at "W" (for those watching the total, 52 of the personnel were assessed twice.).[75]

The assessment staff's methodology was described by them as "the multiform organismic, or holistic, system of assessment." [76] The attempt was to arrive at a picture of the personality as a whole and the organization of the essential dynamic features of the individual, using this as a basis for understanding and predicting the individual's specific behavior.[77]

---

72   ibid.
73   OSS Assessment Staff, *Assessment of Men: Selection of Personnel for the Office of Strategic Services.*
74   ibid.
75   ibid.
76   ibid.
77   ibid.

The organismic[78] method of assessment is based on the fact that the highest order of effectiveness depends on two things: (1) the individual's ability to perceive and interpret properly the whole situation that confronts him, and (2) his ability to coordinate his acts and direct them in a proper sequence toward the proper objects in a way that a satisfying effect will be produced. Consequently, tasks and situations must be chosen which cannot be properly solved without organization, since the power to organize is the measurement desired. [79]

The organismic assessment method depends on the ability of the psychologist to observe the pattern and effectiveness of candidate behavior. This method requires two or three competent observers for each event and is thus expensive in time and qualified personnel. Accordingly, there were twelve psychiatrists and psychologists at "S" for each group of eighteen candidates, and furthermore, two or three of these assessors observed each individual during each situational event. Since no one event is sufficient for deductive analysis, the candidates were exposed to multiple and varied events of a similar type to those they would face in the field.[80]

This is markedly different and more complicated than the elementalistic approach to assessment. Elementalistic methods provide quantitative objective measures of relatively simple processes calling for accurate quantitative measurements of partial, isolated processes. Elementalistic testing can be conducted for the most part by technicians, eliminating the psychologist as observer, interpreter, diagnostician and valuator, simply speaking, eliminating subjectivity. Elementalistic methods can be administered and scored by almost anyone after a short training period using low salary staff members and is therefore cheap; presented to a large group at one time and is quick, i.e. mass testing; generally successful in identifying those entirely unqualified or with some definite defect; and eliminates the inherent errors of subjective judgment since subjective bias does not enter into the scoring.[81]

---

78   Organismic theories in psychology are a family of holistic psychological theories which tend to stress the organization, unity, and integration of human beings expressed through each individual's inherent growth or developmental tendency.

79   OSS Assessment Staff, *Assessment of Men: Selection of Personnel for the Office of Strategic Services*.

80   OSS Assessment Staff, *Assessment of Men: Selection of Personnel for the Office of Strategic Services*.

81   ibid.

Elementalistic methods are useful and have proven valid in certain cases. Organismic assessment should include elementalistic methods but add processes that require time and thought, i.e. supplementary procedures such as interviews, situational tests, etc, which make tentative interpretations of the facts gained and attempt to arrive at a plausible representation of the personality as a whole. This wealth of additional information allows the trained psychologist to improve the accuracy of mechanical predictions from test scores alone. Of course this depends on the competence of the psychiatrist or psychologist, the number and kinds of procedures used for obtaining additional facts, time allowed (length of the assessment), etc. This led to the conclusion that additional procedures such as an autobiography, interviews, situational tests, psychodrama, projections tests, etc., should be included in the assessment.[82]

It was significant that the "OSS assessment program recognized the necessity of relating all observations to each other, not in a mechanical way, but by an interpretive process aiming at the discovery of general patterns and action systems, and made this the guiding principle of all its operations."[83]

Three other key points of the OSS assessment program were the personality sketch, the personal history interview and the staff conference review at the end of assessment. "The personality sketch is a translation of the abstract formulation into everyday speech with the elimination of everything that is not relevant to the administrator's task of placement and management of personnel. The ideal personality sketch is one that pictures the candidate in action, performing work similar to that which he will be expected to do in the future. The sketch itself was the work of two assessors, thus each sketch corresponded to the conclusions of different minds."[84]

Of all the procedures implemented at "S", the Personal History Interview was, without a doubt, the single most important tool. Nothing has been found to replace the clinical interview in importance and usefulness. The staff at "S" found this to have contributed more heavily than any other

---

82   ibid.
83   ibid.
84   ibid.

procedure to the final rating of all the personality variables described later in the paper.[85]

The staff conference at the end of assessment is where all the assessors review each candidate, update and agree on each personality sketch and agree on any recommendations. This conference keys on group discussion as critical since the judgments of the majority are, in the long run, more valid than judgments of any one individual, assuming that the abilities of the members are relatively equal.[86] No one "senior officer" dominated the findings or had any overriding final say. The majority opinion prevailed.

The chief overall purpose of the OSS assessment staff was to eliminate the unfit, using sufficiently reliable predictions. The assessment of men they saw as the scientific art of arriving at sufficient conclusions from insufficient data.[87] The task the assessment staff faced was described in a typical message from the field:

"The organization has been recruiting too many men, civilian or military, who have intelligence and sometimes the necessary mechanical training but who lack common sense, know nothing about working with men or how to look after the welfare and the morale of men under them. We simply must have men who can shoulder responsibility and use initiative with common sense. Simply because a man has intelligence does not qualify him for this type of work"[88]

The assessment staff was expected to judge the suitability of each recruit for a selected assignment, nothing more. This proved impossible. The assessment staff could not obtain adequate job descriptions and even if they had, the classes, even when only eighteen personnel, were comprised of personnel going to such a variety of positions and skill sets that no one station could possibly assess all. Additionally, this mostly did not matter, since most of the candidates ended up going to assignments different from the one for which they were recruited. Obviously, this was an exigency of wartime need. Therefore, the staff decided at the start to judge each candidate

---

85 OSS Assessment Staff, *Assessment of Men: Selection of Personnel for the Office of Strategic Services.*
86 ibid.
87 ibid.
88 ibid.

in relation to a set of general qualifications that were applicable to most OSS overseas assignments.[89] These were fused, ultimately, into ten major variables basic to the needs of the OSS as shown in the table below:

Ten Major Variables[90]	
1) Motivation for Assignment	War morale, interest in proposed job
2) Energy and Initiative	Activity level, zest, effort, initiative
3) Effective Intelligence	Ability to select strategic goals and the most efficient means of attaining them; quick practical thought-resourceful, originality, good judgment
4) Emotional Stability	Ability to govern disturbing emotions, steadiness, endurance under pressure, snafu tolerance, freedom from neurotic tendencies
5) Social Relations	Ability to get along well with other people, good will, team play, tact, no disturbing prejudices, no annoying traits
6) Leadership	Social initiative, ability to evoke cooperation, organizing and administering ability, acceptance of responsibility
7) Security	Ability to keep secrets; caution, discretion, ability to bluff and to mislead
8) Physical Ability	Agility, daring, ruggedness, stamina
9) Observing and Reporting	Ability to observe and to remember accurately significant facts and their relations to evaluate information, to report succinctly
10) Propaganda Skills	Ability to apperceive the psychological vulnerabilities of the enemy; to devise subversive techniques of one sort or another; to speak, write, or draw persuasively

89   ibid.
90   ibid

For rating these variables, the staff found that the four-point scale below was the most useful for nonprofessional members of the organization. The assessment staff, however, as professionals, preferred a six-point scale.

Four (4) Point Rating Scale[91]			
1	2	3	4
Inferior	Low Average	High Average	Superior
Unsatisfactory	Satisfactory	Very Satisfactory	Outstanding

At "S", in order to reveal and evaluate the strength of the above variables, the assessment staff organized the assessment to follow three fundamental, yet critical steps:

(1) "Plant the assessment procedures within a social matrix composed of staff and candidates."[92] The staff and the candidates living together under the same roof for the entire period of assessment, giving the assessment the "flavor of a house party," accomplished this. The candidates were thus unknowingly under constant assessment.

(2) "Select several different types of procedure and several procedures of the same type for estimating the strength of each variable." Some of the tools used included: the interview; informal observations; individual task situations (Construction Test in which the candidate had to direct two recalcitrant assistants in helping him construct a wooden structure within a given time frame; Recruiting Test in which the candidate had to interview a person applying for a position in a secret organization; Improvisions where two candidates had to deal with each other in a face-to-face situation.); group task situations; projection tests; and sociometric questionnaire (like a peer evaluation).[93]

(3) "Include in the program a number of situational tests in which the candidate is required to function at the same level of integration and under somewhat similar conditions as he will be expected to function

---

91   OSS Assessment Staff, *Assessment of Men: Selection of Personnel for the Office of Strategic Services*.
92   ibid.
93   ibid.

under in the field."[94] For example, a person who scores well on a written test about mechanical functions may not be able to perform hands-on mechanical functions in the field. Therefore, a combination of elemental and organismic testing will reveal the strength of the variables.

Whereas the assessment at "S" was in a comfortable social matrix environment, the one-day assessment at "W" was just the opposite. Whereas the students at "S" arrived together in a truck wearing sterile fatigues and were warmly received, the candidates at "W" reported on their own in their own clothing. No attempt was made at "W" to make the candidate feel comfortable; in fact the opposite was true. While the men changed into sterile fatigues at "W," little attempt was made to hide the differences in rank.[95]

The procedures at "W," by necessity, were fast and furious. As at "S," the candidates were briefed on security and given a "student" name and warned not to reveal their real name or background to another candidate or anyone not associated with the assessment. First a Personal History form was filled out, followed by a P-S Experience Blank, the Physical Symptoms Inventory, the Work Conditions Survey and the progressive Matrices Test. They were then given a schedule to follow for the day.[96]

Following their interview and lunch, the candidates began situational testing. The Ball and Spiral test was used to study group structure and attitudes and was a stress situation. The Bridge test was the only test at "W" that looked at mechanical skills of the candidates. Interestingly, for the women, a Filing Test was designed. The test provided observations on Effective Intelligence, Social Relations, Leadership, and Energy and Initiative. Following these events, the group was divided into two groups and given 30 minutes to organize and prepare to present a briefing. The last test was a sociometric test which resembles a peer rating type test. After this test, the candidates were debriefed, exit interviews conducted and the candidates dismissed. The assessors then finalized their draft observations and held a conference of the entire staff, similar to "S."[97]

94   ibid.
95   OSS Assessment Staff, *Assessment of Men: Selection of Personnel for the Office of Strategic Services.*
96   ibid.
97   ibid.

The OSS assessment process ran for twenty months from December 1943 through August 1945. During that time, they assessed 5,391 candidates with a selection rate of 75%. [98] Of the selectees, the failure rate in the field was estimated to only be 3-5%.[99] Twelve trained, experienced and competent psychiatrists and psychologists conducted the assessment at "S," where 2372 candidates were selected for field operations in a three and a half day program.[100]

The profile of the candidates was far more cosmopolitan than the average American. Approximately one out of four candidates spoke a foreign language. About half of the candidates at "S" and "W" had been outside the United States before joining the OSS, which is significant for the 1940s. The pool was predominantly young, white, native-born, educated males. While "W" had a fair representation of female, the "S" population was almost all male. Generally, the candidates were in the upper socio-economic status.[101]

The Special Forces Assessment Process

Concern over the selection and assessment of Special Forces soldiers dates back almost to the inception of Special Forces. In 1954, the George Washington University Human Resources Research Office, operating under contract to the Department of the Army, conducted a study titled *Factors Related To The Effectiveness Of Special Forces Personnel.*[102] According to the stated purpose of the study, this "research was designed to identify differences between the background characteristics, personality traits, interests, and attitudes of effective and ineffective Special Forces personnel, as a first step in the development of techniques for screening volunteers for Special Forces training."

Another study directed by General William Yarborough when he was the commander of the U.S. Army Special Warfare Center was reported

---

98   ibid.
99   ibid.
100 ibid.
101 ibid.
102 Abelson, *Factors Related To The Effectiveness Of Special Forces Personnel,*

in the U.S. Army Human Factors Research & Development 11th Annual Conference report dated October 1965. The title of the study was *Psychological Factors in Selection of Special Forces Officers* and the purpose was to "determine those qualities in an officer which will enable him to perform his special warfare mission to a maximum degree."[103]

The report that was the stimulus for the start of the current Special Forces Selection and Assessment process was published in December 1987 by the Training Research Laboratory of the Army Research Institute (ARI) Field Unit at Fort Benning, Georgia. The study, chartered by the commander, USAJFKSWCS, was based on two issues; first, the attrition in the Special Forces Qualification Course (SFQC) was around 50% and, second, the cost of putting a student through the SFQC was estimated at close to $250,000.[104] Adding to this problem, attendance in the SFQC required a Permanent Change of Station (PCS) move for the student (and family). The attrition from the course was "dumping" a large number of unprogrammed personnel into the Fort Bragg and 18th Airborne Corps replacement center. This was causing havoc with the Army's personnel system.

The key conclusion of the report that set the groundwork for Special Forces Assessment and Selection (SFAS) stated:

"Individuals successfully meeting or exceeding the pre-selection process standards would then be eligible for the Selection Phase at the Special Warfare Center, which for all practical purposes, would be the new Phase I (pre-selection-assessment) of the qualification course. This phase would take place at Fort Bragg (on temporary duty-TDY- orders if practical)...."[105]

In the summer of 1988, the Army implemented the gist of the recommendation of the above referenced ARI study. The newly established SFAS was to be a 21-day TDY assessment and selection program intended to reduce the attrition in the SFQC to no more than 10%. The idea was to absorb 90% of the attrition in a TDY status. SFAS does significantly

---

103   Medland, *Psychological Factors in Selection of Special Forces Officers*, 147.
104   Thompson, *Special Forces Qualification Course: Exploratory Research for Selection and Development*, 1.
105   Thompson, 13.

reduce attrition in the SFQC, but has never achieved the goal of only a subsequent 10% attrition in the SFQC. [106] One example is as shown by the ARI analysis of SFAS candidates in the SF pipeline 1992-1993. Of 2,673 SFAS candidates in 1992-1993, only 36% or 969 successfully completed SFAS and started the qualification course (SFQC). Of these 967, only 72% or 703 soldiers graduated SFQC.[107] This was a 26.3% overall selection rate.

SFAS was designed to determine the level at which candidates demonstrated the basic traits of: physical fitness; motivation; intelligence; responsibility; stability; trustworthiness; sociability; and leadership. The mental, learning and personality tests were: Defense Language Aptitude Battery (DLAB); Audio Perception Battery; Wonderlic Personality Indicator Test; Jackson Personality Test; and the Minnesota Multifaceted Personality Inventory (MMPI) Test. Field/Situation Tests included physical fitness tests; swimming tests; runs of various lengths; obstacle course; tactical movements; log drills; and problem-solving events. These tests and events were mostly conducted in a leaderless environment without any announced standards.[108] The candidates were only told to do the best they could and, when the event was concluded, they received no feedback. The environment was very "stoic."[109]

The first ten days was individual assessment and the candidates were not permitted to voluntarily withdraw until this phase was complete. The second phase of eleven days assessed leadership and ability to function as a team. Two selections boards were held, the first after the first ten days and the final board at the end of SFAS. This board was comprised of the active duty assessors and chain of command, chaired by a senior officer. The assessors were active duty Special Forces soldiers selected for this purpose and provided assessment training from subject matter experts from TRADOC's Cadet Command. ARI provided behavioral psychologists only to assist by observing the cadre. The initial nine courses averaged

---

106 Personal experience of the author who was the Action Officer in HQDA, Pentagon DCSOPS, charged with coordinating, monitoring and reporting the Chief of Staff, Army on the SFAS program from 1988 through 1989. In addition, the author continued to be involved as the Chief of Staff, USAJFKSWCS, the DCSOPS, USASOC and as the Assistant Commandant, USAJFKSWCS.

107 ARI Special Report 33, October 1997, 8.

108 Velky, *Special Warfare: SFAS,* 14.

109 ARI Special Report 33, October 1997, 35.

190 candidates observed by approximately 40 assessors for an approximate ratio of one assessor for six candidates. Of course, with the attrition after the first ten days this ratio improved.[110]

Improvements and changes to the SFAS program have continued over the years. Pull-ups were added to the assessment events in 1992 for an assessment of upper body strength. Physical fitness and the Army Physical Fitness Test (APFT) scores have proved to be strongly related to selection.[111] In 1993, a new, structured, video-based assessor-training program was introduced. Study had found that there was inconsistency in assessor subjective evaluations, which substantially improved with the new training program.[112] Additionally, Peer Ratings, properly administered, is a good tool for judging important personality and interpersonal characteristics. Recognizing this, the SFAS Peer rating forms and instructions were significantly improved in 1995 and automated in 1997.[113]

A theme of Special Forces selection is that the process is a continuous one throughout the training and is not just limited to SFAS.[114] The first screening is with the recruiters, a series of pre-screening tests combined with the entry-level standards. These entry-level standards have changed and been modified over time with changing philosophies of the leadership. For example, originally candidates had to score a 110 on the General Technical (GT) part of the Armed Services Vocational Aptitude Battery (ASVAB). In 1996 this was waived to 100 in order to widen the pool potential candidates. Whereas candidates once had to complete a 50-meter swim prior to attending SFAS, this was moved to the end of the SFQC in 1996 as graduation criteria.[115] It was determined that this was not a critical safety factor and that candidates could be taught to swim.

There have been numerous attempts to develop and refine pre-screening tests and procedures for SFAS. Valid prescreening reduces the number of personnel that need to be recruited to achieve the SFQC graduates

110 Velky, 14.
111 ARI Special Report 33, October 1997, 22.
112 ARI Special Report 33, October 1997,.30.
113 ARI Special Report 33, October 1997, 34-35.
114 Diemer and Joyce, "Special Forces Entry-Level Training: Vision for the Future," *Special Warfare,* Winter 1999, 3.
115 ARI Special Report 33,October 1997, 13-14.

needed to sustain the force. Equally important is the reduced cost in dollars, manpower and facilities. An ARI study published in May 1999[116] recommended a Rating Sheet for recruiters to use in developing an Order of Merit list of potential candidates for SFAS (see chart below):

Order of Merit Chart[117]			
Assignment of Points			
1 Point	2 Points	3 Points	Total
GT<112	GT=113 to 120	GT>120	
APFT<228	APFT = 228 to 245	APFT > 245	
Time in Service > 3yrs	Time in Service = 3yrs	Time in Service < 3yrs	
Airborne = No		Airborne = Yes	
Decision Rules			Sum Total
1st priority (Top Recruit): Sum total = 9 to 12 points			
2nd priority (Moderate Recruit): Sum total = 8 points			
3rd priority (Provide counseling/delay entry): Sum total = 4 to 7 points			

While this data was helpful, it also became fairly irrelevant. The pool of potential personnel and the limited numbers of volunteers permit only the minimal prescreening. Recruiters are given recruiting goals and their performance is evaluated on their achieving those recruiting goals. The recruiters are held accountable only for input, not for the numbers that eventually graduate SFQC. For example, a Special Operations Proponency Office (SOPO) decision briefing to the Commanding General, USAJFKSWCS in the spring of 1999 recommended that recruiters be tasked with a recruiting goal of 1500 personnel for SFAS in FY00. The previous number was 1200 and the recruiters were constantly having difficulty even filling those numbers.

---

116 Zazanis, et.al. Prescreening Methods for Special Forces Assessment and Selection, May 1999, 14-17.
117 Zazanis, et.al., A-1.

Where recruiting is the first screening of building a Special Forces soldier, SFAS is the second screening, albeit the most intense. It is in SFAS where it is hoped most of the remaining attrition will occur. According to the ARI Technical Report 1094 dated May 1999, data analyzed from 1990-1996 supports this position. ARI found that during this seven year time period, only 36% of the personnel who started SFAS were successful in entering SFQC.[118]

Two studies by ARI, "Special Forces Selection and Training: Meeting the Needs of the Force in 2020," [119] in 1999 and "The SF Pipeline Review: Voices from the Field,"[120] in 2000 identified the critical Special Forces performance attributes. The chart below outlines these attributes and skills.

Critical Attributes		
Physical Fitness	Physical Fitness	Ruck-marching, strength, and endurance
	Swimming	
Cognitive	General Cognitive Ability	Understanding, remembering and applying information
	Judgment/ Planning	Making sound decisions
	Adaptability	Thinking on your feet, coping with unexpected problems
	Creativity	Finding new ways of solving problems
	Basic Math	Adding, subtracting, multiplying and dividing
	Language	Speaking a foreign language well
	Perceptual Ability	Attentive to and observant of surrounding

---

118 Zazanis, et.al., 3.
119 Zazanis, et.al. "Special Forces Selection and Training: Meeting the Needs of the Force in 2020,"*Special Warfare,* Summer 1999, 22.
120 Zazanis, et.al. "The SF Pipeline Review: Voices From the Field," *Special Warfare,* Fall 2000, 6.

Personality/ Interpersonal	Cognitive Flexibility	Comfortable with uncertainty
	Cultural Adaptability	Modifying own style in new culture
	Stress Tolerance	Remaining level-headed under stress
	Team Player/ Dependability	Supporting the team effort
	Autonomy	Comfortable working alone
	Initiative/ Perseverance	Self-motivated, giving 100% effort
	Moral Courage	Displaying integrity/honesty in actions
	Maturity	Displaying appropriate behavior for a situation
Communications	Oral Communications	Presenting verbal information clearly
	Written Communication	Writing materials clearly
	Nonverbal Communication	Interpreting/using nonverbal behaviors accurately

The studies concluded that while SFAS provides a high degree of assessment of physical fitness attributes and a moderate level of most cognitive and personality attributes, it provided only a low level of assessment of communication and cultural adaptability attributes. The second study found that the most reported deficiencies where maturity, interpersonal skills, initiative/perseverance, self-discipline, adaptability and judgment/planning. The deficiencies are directly related to the low levels of assessment of these attributes in SFAS.[121]

---

121 Zazanis, et.al. "The SF Pipeline Review: Voices From the Field," *Special Warfare,* Fall 2000, 6.

The SFAS that was implemented in 2002 was a fundamental change from the original SFAS and incorporates processes and procedures that addressed many of the deficiencies identified by the various ARI studies. The SFAS is still a TDY event. Gone are the "stoic" assessors. The SFAS cadre now teaches, coaches and mentors candidates while assessing their trainability and suitability. A student company is now operational with trainer/advisor/counselors or TACs. This is probably the greatest strength of the revised process. These TACs keep and mentor the same pool of candidates not only through the SFAS, but also throughout the entire SFQC.[122] This provides for long-term assessment that is so critical in addressing the deficiencies identified in the earlier ARI studies.

The new student company has another key innovation in the establishment of the Special Operations Preparation and Conditioning Course (SOPC). Run by both active duty and National Guard SF NCOs, the SOPC has two phases. The first phase concentrates on physical training, swimming and land navigation to prepare candidates for Phase I SFAS. The second phase focuses on the same areas, but adds small-unit tactics to help students with the remaining phases of SFQC.

This reorganization in both structure and in thought now formalizes the assessment process as a long term, multi-phase process that extends the duration of a candidate's tenure in the training pipeline which can be up to two years in length. Chapter 8, *Training and Preparation*, outlines the new system.

Comparison

Using trained professional psychologists and psychiatrists as assessors in an interactive social matrix environment, the OSS assessment process focused on small classes of eighteen recruits with up to a 3:1 ratio of assessors to assessed. Great importance was placed on making the candidates comfortable and relaxed between events, while subjecting them to

---

122 Clark, Skinner, and Tertychny. "The SFQC Metamorphosis: Changes in the SF Training Pipeline," *Special Warfare*, Winter 2002, 2.

intense mental stress during situational tests. The OSS assessment staff depended almost entirely on a clinical approach to assessment.

Decidedly different, the SFAS process uses experienced Special Forces soldiers who attend an Assessor Training Course as assessors. A small staff of trained professional psychologists and psychiatrists assist the Special Forces assessors, but the assessment decisions reside with the active duty chain of command and leadership. While getting away from the stoic, non-interactive assessor approach, the SFAS assessor nevertheless works with large classes (up to 300 recruits) at an average ratio of 1:15 assessor to assessed. Fortunately, the candidate now has a tactical/ advisor/ counselor (TAC) who follows and mentors him through the entire four phases of the now combined SFAS and SFQC. The great advantage is one learned by the OSS assessment staff that an extended time is needed to properly assess character and behavioral attributes.

The OSS assessors were limited on the duration of their program by wartime exigencies. The SFAS program may also soon feel pressure due to the mounting requirements for Special Forces soldiers and the increasing attrition due to the operational tempo and the destructive policies of the current administrations social experimentation.

The possibility that trimming the conventional forces would create a smaller pool from which Special Forces could recruit, in both the short and long run, may be a very good thing. In the past twenty-five years, SF has recruited heavily from the active-duty forces of the Army in particular. On a roller coaster up-and-down ride, for the most part, this has been fairly dictatorial to conventional unit commanders and units throughout the Army to allow this "cherry picking" of their personnel to occur; so therefore, there are many key leaders from sergeant majors to commanders who were not pleased at having to lose some of their best personnel to SF recruiters.

However, the real key point is that for the past twenty-five years, those who have volunteered to come to Special Forces have had to attend the selection and assessment phase which has varied in length from three weeks, give or take a few days, with an average attrition rate of anywhere between 50%, but more likely approaching 70% of those who volunteer.

The question to pose is of the 70% that are not selected or have chosen to "voluntarily withdraw," how many of these are still on active duty? And if they are on active duty, they are probably senior in rank, either sergeants major or colonels, or generals; therefore, they are in positions of influence. And, given human nature for what it is, it is seriously doubtful that they blame themselves for not being selected into Special Forces. The likelihood is they blame the selection process as being unfair, "gatekeeping," or if they had withdrawn, it was because they were being unfairly targeted, harassed or otherwise; therefore, these personnel are not favorably inclined towards Special Forces. Regardless, there is significant animosity between the conventional force and Special Forces.

A type of selection more in line with what the OSS did in World War II might be more appropriate for the future. Focus recruiting on the civilian population, in areas of language expertise that is desired, using an abbreviated initial selection model. One way would be the three- to four-day assessment that the OSS conducted. But follow that with a requirement for the person to enlist in the infantry, go through basic training, then on to advanced individual training (AIT), and then be assigned to a Special Forces ODA. While on the ODA, to the point of even being over strength, have him go through a two-year probation at which time the ODA then decides if they're SF material or not. If acceptable, they go to SFQC. If not, they can either leave the military or they can go back to another branch of the Army. This type of selection would solve several problems. First, it would virtually eliminate one of the causes for animosity. Secondly, it would not be dependent upon the size of the regular Army force structure for recruiting. Third, it would provide for an automatic language capability in targeted languages.

8

Training and Preparation

First, there is training… then there is training…as my friend Colonel Jack Braham says when he quotes an unknown author:

> *"Amateurs train until they get it right.*
> *Professionals train until they can't get it wrong."*

The formal Special Forces training is laid out below which consists of four phases:

1. assessment and selection,

2. followed by the qualification course phases,

3. which is then followed by assignments to a unit

4. and then advanced skills training.

The final and real culmination of training for a Special Forces soldier falls under the category of live environmental training. What does this mean? That's when Special Forces conduct the various training events and exercise overseas in countries with host nation counterparts. This is the training environment in which the Special Forces soldier hones his skill set. And nothing in the formal training system fully prepares anyone for the actual face-to-face live environment where you have to work *through, with and by* indigenous populations and your indigenous military counterparts.

In these overseas live environment training events, the difference between Special Forces and other military elements that train with host nation forces, is that the Special Forces teams not only trained with their counterparts, they live 24/7 with them during the entire time they are deployed overseas. This is where the ethnographic knowledge and the trust is developed that is invaluable if and when there is a conflict event requiring cooperation and understanding between nations.

Special Forces prepare for operations primarily by conducting training, operations and persistent engagement with nations that are important to U.S. national security strategy. In other words, SF helps to strengthen our friends and helps influence those with whom we wish to be friends. Likewise, this sends a notice to other nations and groups that may not have friendly intentions toward the United States. Concurrently, this engagement empowers cultural awareness and understanding, provides access adjacent to denied areas of interest, and establishes lasting personal relationships. Some examples of these operations are internal defense and development (IDAD), foreign internal defense (FID) operations, counterinsurgency (COIN) operations, foreign humanitarian assistance (FHA) operations, foreign disaster relief (DR) operations, peacekeeping operations (PKO), humanitarian demining assistance, stability operations, security force assistance (SFA), counter-drug (CD) operational support and security assistance (SA) programs.[123]

The above-mentioned peacetime operations must continue during conflict as an economy of force effort, both within the operational and strategic area of operation (AOR) and around the globe maintaining continuous engagement and enhancing regional stability.

Formal Training

Special Forces training, in fact, begins long before the individual ever volunteers for Special Forces. Special Forces is not an acquisition organization. In other words, unlike the infantry, artillery, engineers, or other specialties in the Army, Special Forces recruits from these specialties only

---

123 All these terms have been defined and discussed in previous chapters.

after the individual has completed their initial training and specialty qualification. And even then, the individuals must attend initial phase of the Special Forces Qualification Course which is the Assessment and Selection Phase (Chapter 7). This phase consists of approximately three weeks of intense 24-hour a day assessment before they are selected for the formal Special Forces training.

Special Forces Eligibility (Up-to-date as of April 2014)

The following criteria is required for all applicants (officers and enlisted):

1. Must be an active duty male soldier.

2. Must be U.S. citizen (not waiverable).

3. Must be airborne qualified or volunteer for airborne training.

4. Must be able to swim 50-meters wearing boots and battle dress uniform (BDU) prior to beginning the Special Forces Qualification Course. All soldiers will be given a swim assessment during SFAS to determine whether he has the aptitude to learn to swim.

5. Must score a minimum of 229 points on the Army Physical Fitness Test (APFT), with no less than 60 points on any event, using the standards for age group 17-21.

6. Must be able to meet medical fitness standards as outlined in AR 40-501.

7. Must be eligible for a "SECRET" security clearance (security clearance is not required to attend SFAS).

8. No soldier, regardless of Military Occupational Specialty or basic branch will be recruited if he is unable to reclassify from his current MOS or basic branch into CMF 18.

9. Must not be currently serving in a restricted MOS or branch.

Additional criteria exclusive to enlisted applicants:

1. Enlisted applicants must be in the pay grade of E-4 to E-7. Successful completion of SFAS is a prerequisite to the SFQC.

2. Must be a high school graduate or have a general equivalency diploma (GED).

3. Must have a general technical (GT) score of 100 or higher.

4. Stabilization of current drill sergeants and detailed recruiters will not be broken.

5. Specialists, corporals, and sergeants who successfully complete SFAS will normally have their Retention Control Point waived to attend the SFQC. Upon successful completion of SFQC, they will be allowed continued service. Staff sergeants approaching their RCP will not be allowed to apply. Each sergeant first class (SFC) must have no more than twelve years time in service and nine months time in grade when applying for SFAS and must be either airborne or ranger qualified. SFCs must also be able to PCS to the SFQC within six months of selection from SFAS.

6. Soldiers on assignment will not be allowed to attend SFAS without their branch's prior approval. Soldiers on orders to a short tour area will be allowed to attend SFAS if a deferment is not required. These individuals will be scheduled for the next available SFQC after their DEROS (date eligible for return from overseas). Soldiers who volunteer for SFAS prior to receiving assignment notification will be deferred to allow SFAS attendance. For SFAS graduates, assignment to the SFQC will take precedence over any assignment conflict.

7. OCONUS-based soldiers may attend SFAS in a TDY and return status anytime during their tour. Upon successful completion of SFAS, soldiers will be scheduled for the next available SFQC provided they have completed at least two-thirds of their overseas assignment obligation and have received PERSCOM (US Army

Personnel Support Command) approval for curtailment of the remainder of their overseas tour obligation. Soldiers serving on a short tour will not have their assignment curtailed.

8. CONUS-based soldiers may attend SFAS in a TDY and return status anytime during their tour. Upon successful completion of SFAS, soldiers will be scheduled to attend the SFQC, ensuring that they will have completed at least one-year time on station prior to PCS.

9. Must have a minimum of twenty-four months remaining Time in Service (TIS) upon completion of the SFQC.

Additional criteria exclusive to Officer applicants:

1. Have at least a secret security clearance prior to final packet approval and meet eligibility criteria for Top Secret clearance.

2. Have completed the Officer Basic Course and have been successful in your branch assignments prior to application for Special Forces.

3. Have a Defense Language Aptitude Battery (DLAB) Score of 85 or higher or a Defense Language Proficiency Test (DLPT) of a minimum of 1/1 reading and listening score.

4. Have a minimum of 36 months remaining time in service upon completion of Special Forces Detachment Officer Qualification Course (SFDOQC).

All applicants must not:

1. Be barred to reenlistment or be under suspension of favorable personnel action.

2. Have been convicted by court-martial or have disciplinary action noted in their official military personnel fiche under the provisions of the Uniform Code of Military Justice (Article 15). This provision can only be waived by the commanding general,

United States Army Special Warfare Center and School on a case-by-case basis.

3. Have been terminated from SF, ranger, or airborne duty, unless termination was due to extreme family problems.

4. Have thirty days or more lost time under USC 972 within current or preceding enlistment.

There are now two ways for soldiers to volunteer to attend SFAS:

- As an existing soldier in the Army or Army National Guard with the enlisted rank of E-4 (corporal/specialist) or higher, and for officers the rank of O-2 (1st lieutenant) promotable to O-3 (captain), or existing O-3s.
- The other path is that of direct entry, referred to as Initial Accession or IA. Here an individual who has no prior military service or who has previously separated from military service is given the opportunity to attend SFAS. Both the Active Duty and National Guard components offer Special Forces Initial Accession programs. The Active Duty program is referred to as the "18X Program" because of the Initial Entry Code that appears on the assignment orders. These soldiers will attend Infantry One Station Unit Training (OSUT, the combination of Basic Combat Training and Advanced Individual Training), Airborne School, and a preparation course to help prepare them for SFAS. This program is commonly referred to as the "X-Ray Program," derived from "18X." The candidates in this program are known as "X-Rays."

Special Forces Assessment and Selection (SFAS)

This program is physically and mentally demanding. To accomplish physical-related goals set by SFAS, applicants must be in good physical condition upon arrival at Fort Bragg, N.C. Soldiers attending the SFAS program will perform physical tasks that will require them to climb obstacles (by use of a rope) 20 to 30 feet high, swim while in uniform, and travel great distances cross-country while carrying a rucksack with a minimum of 50 pounds. The SFAS program requires upper and lower body strength and physical endurance to accomplish daily physical-oriented goals on a continuous basis for twenty-four days.

The Special Forces soldier trains on a regular basis over the course of their entire career. The initial formal training program for entry into Special Forces is divided into phases collectively known as the Special Forces Qualification Course (SFQC) or, informally, the "Q Course." The length of the Q Course changes depending on the applicant's primary job field within Special Forces and their assigned foreign language capability but will usually last between 56 to 95 weeks. Entry into the United States Army Special Forces begins with Assessment and Selection (SFAS). Getting "selected" at SFAS will enable a candidate to continue on to the next phases of the Special Forces Qualification Course. If a candidate successfully completes these next phases he will graduate as a Special Forces soldier and will generally be assigned to a 12-man Operational Detachment Alpha (ODA), commonly known as an "A team."

The Army Research Institute (ARI) has been able to closely correlate performance on the APFT and a 4-mile rucksack march with success in SFAS. During fiscal year (FY) 89 and FY 90 ARI evaluated the cumulative APFT score (17 to 21 age group standard) with the percent of candidates who started SFAS and who passed the course. The average PT score for SFAS graduates is 250. The average PT results are depicted below:

APFT Score	Percent Passing Course
206-225	31
226-250	42
251-275	57
276 or higher	78

ARI evaluated the ability of SFAS students to perform a 4-mile ruckmarch in battle dress uniform (BDU), boots, M-16, load bearing equipment, and a 45-pound rucksack. The overall average 4-mile ruckmarch time for graduates is 61 minutes. The less time to complete a 4-mile ruckmarch, the better the percent who passed the course. The average PT results are depicted below:

Ruckmarch Time (Min)	Percent Passing Course
54 and less	81
55-64	63
65-74	34
75-84	10

Special Forces Qualification Course (SFQC) and Special Forces Detachment Officer Qualification Course (SFDOQC)

General. The Career Management Field (CMF) 18 is subdivided into five accession Military Occupational Specialties (MOSs):

- 18A, Detachment Commander
- 18B, SF Weapons Sergeant
- 18C, SF Engineer Sergeant
- 18D, SF Medical Sergeant
- 18E, SF Communications Sergeant.

Each SF volunteer receives extensive training in a specialty, which prepares him for his future assignment in a SF unit. SF units are designed to operate either unilaterally or in support of and combined with native military and paramilitary forces. Levels of employment for Special Operations forces include advising and assisting host governments, involvement in continental United States-based training, and direct participation in combat operations.

Purpose. The SFQC/SFDOQC teaches and develops the skills necessary for effective utilization of the SF soldier. Duties in CMF eighteen primarily involve participation in Special Operations interrelated fields of unconventional warfare. These include foreign internal defense and direct action missions as part of a small operations team or detachment. Duties at other levels involve command, control, and support functions. Frequently, duties require regional orientation, to include foreign language training and in-country experience. The SF places emphasis not only on unconventional tactics, but also knowledge of nations in waterborne, desert, jungle, mountain, or arctic operations.

Training. After successful completion of SFAS, officers who have not already attended their Advanced Course will attend either the Infantry or Armor Career Captain's Course. For the enlisted soldier, the SFQC is currently divided into three phases: Individual Skills, MOS Qualification, and Collective Training. The enlisted applicants SFQC training will be scheduled upon successful completion of SFAS.

Written by: Training Developers of Training Development Division 1, DOTD, USAJFKSWCS

Soldiers selected to attend the SFQC will PCS to Fort Bragg, N.C. where they will begin the rigorous training of the SFQC for 52-94 weeks. The course focuses on core tactical competencies, MOS skills, survival, language and cultural skills. Upon completion of the SFQC, Soldiers join the Special Forces brotherhood, earn the right to wear the Special Forces tab and don the highly coveted Green Beret.

SFQC Phase 1 - Course Orientation and History [6weeks]
Course Number: 2E-F253/011-F95 *Clearance:* Interim Secret
Class Size: 180 *Iterations:* 8 per year *Course Duration:* 6 weeks

The SF Orientation Course is an introduction to Special Forces and falls under the auspices of the 4th Battalion, 1st SWTG (Airborne). The SFOC is designed to orient the student to the standards of the entire SFQC as well as to the standards and expectations of the 1st SWTG (Airborne) commander. The course is comprised of seven weeks of classroom instruction on the history and lineage of the SF Regiment (1 week) Student G's in Robin Sage (2 weeks), SF command and control, duties and responsibilities of each MOS, overview of the SF core missions and methods of instruction (2 weeks), Basic Airborne Refresher, airborne operations, introduction to the SF attributes (1 week), and Cultural training (1 week). The students are introduced to the concepts of small-unit tactics and conducts refresher training on land navigation.

SFQC Phase II, Small Unit Tactics (SUT) [13 weeks]

Course Number: 2E-F254/011-F96 *Clearance:* Secret

Class Size: 180 *Iterations:* 8 per year *Course Duration:* 13 weeks

Prerequisites: Successful completion of the Special Forces Orientation Course.

The Special Forces Small Unit Tactics is the second phase in the qualification course. The 13-week program provides soldiers in the SFQC the apprentice-level tactical combat skills required to successfully operate on an SFOD-A.

Students will master the following tactical skills: advanced marksmanship; small-unit tactics; mounted operations; Special Forces common tasks; urban operations; mission analysis; Advanced Special Operations Level 1; sensitive site exploitation; military decision making process.

At the end of Phase 2, Soldiers will enroll in SERE Level C, To better meet the demands of the current operating environment, Company C, 1st Battalion, 1st Special Warfare Training Group, has implemented significant changes to resistance training in the Survival, Evasion, Resistance and Escape Course, or SERE, to increase the intellectual quality of training and to replicate the complexities of the contemporary operating environment, or COE.

In the future, detention is likely to be of two types: governmental, in which diplomatic relations will be either limited or non-existent; and non-governmental, which can be carried out by a host of potential irregular adversaries. To better replicate the COE, SERE's resistance training lab, or RTL, now includes governmental and nongovernmental detention scenarios across the spectrum of captivity. SERE's Pineland scenario, which serves as the vehicle for resistance training, has been rewritten to include peacetime governmental and nongovernmental hostage detention.

To address the intellectual quality of training, SERE has fully implemented a single-skill-set resistance model, the directed communications model, or DCM, into resistance academics and the RTL evaluation. Soldiers now receive 110 hours of training in negotiation and dilemmas that requires them to apply the DCM's experience-based technique of problem-solving and learning. The goal is to help the student find a practical solution, not necessarily a perfect one. That adaptive approach to ill-structured problem environments allows instructors to tailor the training to the students' capabilities. The training develops skills that will transfer not only to other phases of training but also into the soldier's career — the skills required to negotiate a hostage-detention scenario are essentially the same as those needed to influence a tribal elder in Afghanistan.

Graduates of SERE can apply their survival skills either during evasion or in captivity. They can produce and execute a plan that applies evasion techniques and incorporates the doctrine of personnel recovery. Soldiers can also assess their captivity environment not only to identify the opportunity and means of escape but also to create a POW/detainee/hostage action plan for resisting exploitation and surviving to return with honor.

SFQC Phase III, MOS Training

Course Number: 2E-18A, 011-18B30-C45, 011-18C30-C45, 011-18E30-C45, 011-18D30-C45

Clearance: Secret *Class Size:* ~35 each MOS *Iterations:* 8 per year

Course Duration: 14 Weeks (18B, 18C, 18D), 16 WEEKS (18E)

Prerequisites: Successful completion of the Special Forces Orientation Course, Small Unit Tactics and SERE training.

Each soldier going through the Special Forces Qualification Course is assigned to one of the five occupational specialties: Detachment Commander, or 18A; Weapons Sergeant, or 18B; Engineer Sergeant, or 18C; Special Forces Medical Sergeant, or 18D; and Communications Sergeant, or 18E.

Special Forces Officer (18A)

The Special Forces officer is the team leader of an Operational Detachment Alpha (ODA), a highly trained 12-man team that is deployed in rapid-response situations. The officer organizes the mission, outfits the team and debriefs them on the mission objective.

>   Active/Reserve: Active Duty
>   Officer/Enlisted: Officer
>   Restrictions: Closed to Women

18A - Special Forces Detachment Commander:
Course Number: 2E-F253/011-F95 *Course Duration:* 14 weeks

Over the past year, Company A, 1st Battalion, 1st Special Warfare Training Group, has made changes to its instruction that are larger and more significant than any in its history. Dedicated to teaching critical skill sets and developing leadership capacities in future SF officers (18A), Co. A continues to refine its ability to train SF officer candidates to operate effectively in complex, dynamic environments and to become adaptive problem solvers.

During the officers' military occupational specialty, or MOS, training phase (Phase IV), the company's small-group instructors, or SGIs, and field team work together to give students fourteen weeks of training in tasks identified by the most recent critical task selection board. Focusing on skill sets related to unconventional warfare, or UW, Phase IV training modules include SF doctrine; special-operations mission planning; cross-cultural communication and negotiations; MOS cross-training; and UW, counterinsurgency and foreign internal defense, or FID. Instruction also includes tactical airborne operations and three field-training exercises that focus on developing the students' ability to conduct SF missions across the spectrum of conflict. To complete Phase IV, students must demonstrate the level of proficiency required for them to perform successfully as SF detachment commanders.

Recent changes to the Special Forces Qualification Course, or SFQC, have enhanced the training environment and increased the 18A students' understanding of SF missions. The SFQCs 18A training exercises are now entirely nested within the "Pineland" strategic training scenario. The current training environment allows 18A students to plan and conduct FID missions in a permissive environment and UW operations in an uncertain or hostile environment. The company has also designed and implemented a FID training exercise, conducted as part of the FID module of instruction, which replicates a joint combined exchange training mission in the Republic of Pineland and develops students' understanding and ability to conduct combined operations with partner-nation forces.

Whether students are working with partner-nation forces from the Republic of Pineland or resistance forces in the People's Republic of Pineland, they learn and apply skill sets that are critical for success in the SFQC's "Robin Sage" culmination exercise and as an SF detachment commander. Throughout Phase IV, the 18A students gain knowledge, understanding and proficiency of SF leader skills through the instruction and mentoring from their SGIs. The SGIs dedicate countless hours of coaching, teaching and mentoring to every aspiring SF captain, and the quality of training is unparalleled.

In addition to providing SF-qualification training, Co. A also teaches the Detachment Leaders course, a new initiative designed to provide follow-on, advanced resident training to newly qualified SF captains as they transition from the 1st SWTG to the operational SF groups. The Detachment Leaders course, which taught its first iteration in January, is designed to expand students' base of knowledge and give them exposure to the contemporary operational environment.

The course delivers focused training on SF-specific topics from SGIs, guest speakers and Army special-operations personnel, using operational vignettes from SF detachments and video teleconferences with forward-deployed units. Students also gain a better understanding of the joint, interagency, intergovernmental and multinational environment; SF persistent-engagement missions; and combat operations of joint special operations. Although the initial iterations of the course were focused on recent SF officer graduates, the course is now listed in the Army Training Requirements and Resources System and is open to SF warrant officers and SF NCOs who have been selected to serve as detachment operations.

Special Forces Weapons Sergeant (18B)

Special Forces weapons sergeants are the weapons specialists. They're capable of operating and maintaining a wide variety of U.S., allied and other foreign weaponry.

> Active/Reserve: Active Duty
> Officer/Enlisted: Enlisted
> Restrictions: Closed to Women

18B - Weapons Sergeant:
Course Number: 2E-F253/011-F95 *Course Duration:* 14 weeks

Weapons sergeants have a familiarization with weapons systems found throughout the world. They gain extensive knowledge about various types of U.S. and foreign small arms, submachine guns, machine guns, grenade launchers, forward-observer procedures and directs fires and in-direct-fire weapons (mortars).

They learn the capabilities and characteristics of U.S. and foreign air defense and anti-tank weapons systems, tactical training and range fire as well as how to teach marksmanship and the employment of weapons to others. Weapons sergeants employ conventional and unconventional tactics and techniques as tactical mission leaders. They can recruit, organize, train and advise or command indigenous combat forces up to company size.

Special Forces Engineer Sergeant (18C)

Special Forces engineer sergeants are specialists across a wide range of disciplines, from demolitions and constructions of field fortifications to topographic survey techniques.

> Active/Reserve: Active Duty
> Officer/Enlisted: Enlisted
> Restrictions: Closed to Women

18C - Engineer Sergeant:
Course Number: 2E-F253/011-F95 *Course Duration:* 14 weeks

Engineer sergeants are experts in the planning, design and construction of buildings, demolition, mine warfare, special purpose munitions and explosives, counter booby trap and unexploded ordinances clearance operations and improvised munitions and explosives. The construction module requires soldiers to learn to read blueprints as well as design, and to construct a theater-of-operations building, as well as field fortifications to be used as fire bases while deployed on an SFODA. Special Forces engineers are taught basic to advanced demolition skills that will enable them to destroy targets in non-electric and electric firing systems, with U.S., foreign and civilian demolition components.

Engineer sergeants plan, supervise, lead, perform and instruct all aspects of combat engineering, demolition operations and theater-of operations construction engineering in either English or their target language. They can recruit, organize, train and advise or command indigenous combat forces up to company size.

Special Forces Medical Sergeant (18D)

Special Forces medical sergeants are considered to be the finest first-response/trauma medical technicians in the world. Though they're primarily trained with an emphasis on trauma medicine, they also have a working knowledge of dentistry, veterinary care, public sanitation, water quality and optometry.

Active/Reserve: Active Duty
Officer/Enlisted: Enlisted
Restrictions: Closed to Women

18D - Medical Sergeant:
Course Number: 2E-F253/011-F95 *Course Duration:* 14 weeks

Medical sergeants specialize in trauma management, infectious diseases, cardiac life support and surgical procedures, with a basic understanding of veterinary and dental medicine. Both general health care and emergency health care are stressed in training.

Medical sergeants provide emergency, routine and long-term medical care for detachment members and associated allied members and host-nation personnel. They establish field medical facilities to support unconventional warfare operations, provide veterinary care, and prepare the medical portion of area studies, brief backs and operation plans and orders.

Soldiers selected for MOS 18D attend 250 days of advanced medical training. Additionally, they spend two months of the year on a trauma rotation in hospital emergency rooms. The medical-training phase includes a nationally accredited emergency medical technician paramedic program. They can recruit, organize, train and advise or command indigenous combat forces up to company size.

Special Forces Communications Sergeant (18E)

Special Forces communications sergeants can operate every kind of communications gear, from encrypted satellite communications systems to old-style high-frequency Morse key systems.

Active/Reserve: Active Duty
Officer/Enlisted: Enlisted
Restrictions: Closed to Women

18E - Communications Sergeant:
Course Number: 2E-F253/011-F95 *Course Duration:* 16 weeks

The Special Forces communications sergeant has to learn U.S. communication systems as well as those systems found throughout the world. He must incorporate this information and technology into his communications planning, and teach it to the other members of his ODA. Communications sergeants have a thorough grounding in communication basics, communications procedures, computer technology; assembly and systems applications.

They must understand communication theory – how to install, operate and maintain FM, AM, HF, VHF and UHF radio systems They must be able to make communications in voice to data, and to read voice and data radio nets by utilizing computer systems and networks.

Communications sergeants are experts in sending and receiving critical messages that link the SFODA with its command and control elements. They are familiar with antenna theory, radio wave propagation and how to teach it to others. Communications sergeants prepare the communications portion of area studies, brief backs and operation plans and orders. They can recruit, organize, train and advise or command indigenous combat forces up to company size.

SFQC Phase IV, Unconventional Warfare CULEX[124] (Phase 5)

Course Number: 2E-F255/011-F97 *Clearance:* Secret

Class Size: 144 *Iterations:* 8 per year *Course Duration:* 4 weeks

Prerequisites: Successful completion of the Special Forces Orientation Course, Small Unit Tactics and Survival, Evasion, Resistance and Escape training and military occupational specialty training.

Robin Sage, for more than 40 years the world's best collective training event for preparing Soldiers for unconventional warfare, or UW, has trained every soldier currently in Special Forces. But changes made to keep pace with current operations have produced a Robin Sage unlike the one many of its alumni remember.

The 14-day exercise, taught by the cadre of Company D, 1st Battalion, 1st Special Warfare Training Group, is the culmination exercise of Phase V of the Special Forces Qualification Course, or SFQC. Although Robin Sage continues to represent each entry-level SF Soldier's formative UW experience before he joins an SF group, Co. D. has made significant advances in the methods used to provide the training. One of the things to change has been Phase V's program of instruction, or POI. The POI has been changed to increase small-group instruction, provide entry-level education on the fundamentals of insurgency and

---

124 Culmination Exercise (CULEX)

UW, and enhance or add contemporary UW topics. Examples include a 100-percent increase in training in subversion and sabotage and a new entry-level class on targeting in UW.

Led by the cadre, students conduct a case study of the fundamentals of insurgency, culminating with a discussion of key points of insurgencies in China, Algeria and Cuba. Co. D also ties all the small-group instruction and practical exercises together into a UW case study that includes viewing and discussing the movie "Defiance," which depicts resistance to Nazi occupation of Belarus during World War II. The movie provides a real-world example that captures students' attention and serves as a springboard for discussion and interaction prior to the students' receipt of their warning order for the UW operation in Pineland. The training in the fundamentals of insurgency, the UW case study and the leveraging of students' language skills allow the cadre to introduce more complex scenarios with a better balance of lethal and non-lethal operations across urban and rural environments.

By this fall, other changes will be implemented to expand students' knowledge of UW. Before students begin the SFQC, they will take five UW classes (fundamentals of UW, underground, auxiliary, guerrilla tactics and operations) via distance learning. That basic instruction will be reinforced throughout the course by the cadre and the instructors of the student SF detachments. At the end of Phase IV, students will take a comprehensive exam to test their UW knowledge. Those who fail will not enter Phase V, because they will not have the basic UW knowledge that will be necessary for success.

Throughout Phase V, the cadre team sergeant, or CTS, and his student SF detachment remain the focal point of training. The CTS is responsible for the development of his civilian hosted area — the physical and human infrastructure necessary for simulating UW operations in denied territory. Most importantly, the CTS serves as the small-group instructor for his student detachment, providing the appropriate blend of coaching, teaching, training and mentoring through face-to-face interaction with students and through "in-role" feedback during the Pineland scenario. Each CTS brings the experience, knowledge and familiarity with current tactics, techniques and procedures that allow him to make subtle changes in the scenarios in order to provide realistic training that is crucial to each student's success. CTSs are selected for their UW operational experience, and their combined experience gives Co. D one of the highest concentrations of real-world UW experience in the SF Regiment.

While the fundamentals of UW haven't changed much over the last forty years, UW training has evolved in order to remain relevant. Even though the dominant features of Robin Sage and Pineland remain rucksacks, muddy boots and a focus on UW in denied territory, Co. D has made significant changes in what and how students are trained, based on the experience of the cadre team sergeants and the needs of the SF groups and the 21st-century operating environment.

SFQC Phase V, Language and Culture

Course Number: 2E-F253/011-F95 *Clearance:* Secret *Course Duration:* 24 weeks

Class Size: varies *Iterations:* per year

Prerequisites: Successful completion of the first four phases of the SFQC

Soldiers receive Basic Special Operations Language Training in the language assigned to them at the completion of Special Forces Assessment and Selection. Languages are broken into two categories based on their degree of difficulty. Soldiers who are assigned a Category I or II language will be enrolled in an eighteen-week language program, while soldiers who are assigned a Category III or IV language will attend twenty-four weeks of language training.

Students receive instruction in three basic language skills: speaking, participatory listening and reading (limited). The following areas of emphasis are covered during the training: overview of physical and social systems, economics, politics and security, infrastructure and technology information, culture and regional studies. Language instruction focuses on functional application geared toward mission-related tasks, enhanced rapport building techniques, cultural mitigation strategies, interpreting and control of interpreter methods. Also during Phase 2, a progressive PT program is started in order to prepare for Phase 3.

To successfully complete Phase 2, soldiers must achieve a minimum of 1/1 Listening and Speaking as measured by the two-skill Oral Proficiency Interview (OPI).

The language course in which the soldier is selected to attend will most likely reflect the SF Group in which he will be assigned. Example language course lengths are in the following table.

6 Months		
ARABIC	KOREAN	POLISH
RUSSIAN	CZECH	TAGALOG
PERSIAN	THAI	SERBO CROAT
4 Months		
SPANISH	PORTUGUESE	FRENCH

Category I/II: French, Indoensian-Bahasa and Spanish

Category III/V: Arabic, Chinese-Mandarin, Czech, Dari, Hungarian, Korean, Pashto, Persian-Farsi, Polish, Russian., Tagalog, Thai, Turkish and Urdu.

SFQC Phase VI, Graduation

The final stage is comprised of one week of out-processing, the Regimental First Formation where students don their "Green Berets" for the first time, and the graduation ceremony.

The Special Forces training requires a commitment of one (1) (2 years for 18Ds) of intensive coursework based on the soldier's military specialty training. A soldier is awarded the "Green beret" and the Special Forces Tab at the end of all the course of training. Admission into the Special Forces Regiment begins the day before graduation to meet the leaders of the SF units they will be assigned to. They are officially welcomed into the regiment the day after at the graduation ceremony which is a combination of the Regimental First Formation and graduation at the Civic Center. They are awarded their certificate of graduation, the Special Forces Tab, their Green Beret and the coveted Yarborough knife at this ceremony.

Advanced Skills Training

Following is the list of advanced skills training courses available for Special Forces at the United States Army John F. Kennedy Special Warfare Center and School (USAJFKSWCS), Fort Bragg North Carolina this list was taken from the USAJFKSWCS Academic Handbook for Academic Year 2013 – 2014

Detachment Leaders Course

Course Number: 2E-F270/011-F109 *Clearance:* Interim Top Secret *Location:* Fort Bragg

Class Size: 40 *Iterations:* 8 per year *Course Duration:* 2 weeks

Prerequisites: The course is open to Special Forces-18A officers, 180As and CMFeighteen NCOs selected for the position of operational detachment operations sergeant positions.

Scope: The Detachment Leader's Course provides a professional forum for subject-matter experts and senior ARSOF / JIIM[125] leaders to address ARSOF-specific topics and develop a common understanding of the contemporary operational environment.

Course Description: The post-SFQC Detachment Commander Course conducted by A/1/1 SWTG(A) provides advanced resident training to expand the newly qualified Special Forces captains' base of knowledge as they transition from 1st Special Warfare Training Group(A) to the

---

125 JIIM: Joint, Interagency, Intergovernmental, and Multinational

operational groups. The course focuses on ARSOF senior leader insights and guidance; advanced instruction in ASO; interagency partnerships and education; the U.S. Army Special Operations Command and the U.S. Army Special Forces Command operational, logistical and intelligence functions; operational lessons learned and updates from deployed ARSOF units.

The course establishes the foundation for a Special Forces officers' continuing education process.

Special Forces Combat Diver Qualification Course (CDQC)

Course Number: 2E-SI/ASI4W/011-ASIW7 *Clearance:* Secret

Class Size: 45 *Iterations:* 5 per year *Course Duration:* 6 weeks

Prerequisites: Must be a male United States Special Operations Command soldier assigned or on orders to an authorized combat-diver position. Must successfully complete the following IAW AR 611-75 Management of Army Divers, paragraph 2-18: meet the medical fitness standards IAW AR 40-501 Standards of Medical Fitness, paragraph 5-9, with the examination completed within twenty-four months prior to the start date of the scheduled SFCDQC and ensure that DD Forms 2808 (Report of Medical Examination) and 2807-1 (Report of Medical History) are sent to the CG, USAJFKSWCS ATTN: AOJK-OP (G3) Fort Bragg, NC 28310-9610.

Must pass a physical training test with a minimum of: 52 pushups; 62 sit ups; 7 forward grip pull ups; a two-mile run time of no greater than 14 minutes 54 seconds; a 500-meter open-water swim in BDUs using a side or breast stroke; must pass a five-mile run within 40 minutes. Student must present a memorandum signed by the first O-5 in his chain of command which states that he passed all requirements. This memorandum must be dated within six months of the start date of the scheduled SFCDQC. Successful completion of the PT requirements will be verified in writing by the individual's unit commander. Must pass an oxygen intolerance/hyperbaric chamber pressure equalization test (given during the first day of the course) in accordance with the requirements contained in AR 40-501, Chapter 5, paragraph 5-9w. Any variation from the above standards require a waiver from the commanding general, USAJFKSWCS.

Course Description: Combat diver closed-circuit diving operations. Combat swimmer techniques, dangerous marine life, specialized physical conditioning for combat divers, cardiopulmonary resuscitation, buddy rescue and life-saving techniques, the dive reporting system; waterborne infiltration operations, waterproofing and bundle rigging; tides and currents, pool and tower training; emergency assent procedures and decompression, open-circuit diving; closed-circuit diving; altitude diving, closed circuit underwater navigation, underwater search operations, dive equipment and maintenance, diving physics; physiology and injuries; U.S. Navy diving tables; small-boat operations; surface infiltration; submarine operations, helocast operations, kayak operations, Special Operations Combat Expendable Platform airborne infiltration and a course culmination situational-training exercise.

Special Forces Combat Diving Supervisor Course (CDSC)

Course Number: 2E-F65/011-ASIS6 *Clearance:* Secret

Class Size: 21 *Iterations:* 2 per year *Course Duration:* 3 weeks

Prerequisites: Must be a graduate of the Special Forces Combat Diver Qualification course or Basic Underwater Demolition/SEAL course in the grade of E-6 or above. Must possess a current Special Forces diving physical examination in accordance with the requirements of AR 40-501 Standards of Medical Fitness, Chapter 5, paragraph 5-9 completed within twenty-four months of course completion date. Must report with medical records and originals of the physical examination documents on the day of course in-processing. Must pass a physical-fitness test, conducted in accordance with the provisions of FM 21-20 Physical Fitness training consisting of a minimum of: 52 push-ups, 62 sit-ups within a two-minute period and completion of a two-mile run within 14 minutes, 54 seconds or less (all age groups) (AR 611-75 Management of Army Divers, Chapter 2, paragraph 2-19b). Must report with a certification of the successful completion of the physical-fitness test signed by a commander in the grade of lieutenant colonel or higher. Any variation from the above standards requires a waiver from the CG, SWCS NLT 45 days prior to the class start date.

Course Description: Plan and supervise Combat Diving Operations (day and night); diving operations planning and briefing, tides and currents; nautical charts and navigation, submarine operations; diving operations; pre-dive and post-dive inspection, Diving Equipment; Dive logs and reporting system, medical aspects of diving; diving physiology, diving injuries, hyperbaric chamber operations; high-pressure air and oxygen use and safety, diving physics; open- and closed-circuit diving, U.S. Navy dive tables, altitude diving and a course culmination situational training exercise.

Special Forces Combat Diving Medical Technician (CDMT)

Course Number: 011-ASIQ5 *Clearance:* Secret

Class Size: 30 *Iterations:* two per year *Course Duration: three* weeks

Prerequisites: Students must be male, active- or reserve-component Department of Defense enlisted personnel. They must be qualified SF or Ranger medics who have graduated from the Special Operations Combat Medic Course, U.S. Navy SEAL corpsmen, U.S. Air Force Para-Rescue medics or other DoD medical personnel assigned to or on orders for duty as SOF medics. Candidates not on dive status must pass an initial SFCDQC physical examination completed not more than twenty-four months before the start date of the scheduled SFDMTC, IAW AR 40-501, Paragraphs 5-9 and 8-14a(7). Candidates on dive status must have a current SFCDQC physical examination completed not more than 36 months before the start date of the SFDMTC, IAW AR 40-501, Paragraphs 5-9 and 8-14a(7). All candidates must report to in-processing with their medical records and original DD Forms 2808 and 2807-1. They must have passed an Army Physical Fitness Test within six months of the course completion date and administered IAW the provisions of TC 3-22.20 and they must have scored at least 70 percent in each event according to the 17-21-year-old standards, regardless of their age

[AR 611-75, Paragraph 2-18d(2)]. They must pass a swim test consisting of swimming 300 meters using any stroke [AR 611-75, Paragraph 2-18D(3)]. Students must report for in-processing with a certification that they have passed the AFPT and swim tests signed by their unit commander. Students must pass an oxygen intolerance/hyperbaric chamber pressure equalization test on the first day of the course, in accordance with the requirements of AR 40-501, Chapter five and Paragraph 5-9W.

Course Description: Medical planning for diving operations; diving physiology: altitude diving; diving physics; diving physiology, neurological assessment, dangerous marine life; U.S. Navy Dive Treatment tables, Stress in diving, differential diagnosis of diving accidents and injuries, decompression theory and sickness, hyperbaric chamber operations; hyperbaric oxygen theory, air purity standards and a Diving Medical Technician course culmination situational training exercise - medical actions.

Military Free-Fall Parachutist Course (MFFPC)

Course Number: 2E-SI4X/ASI4X/011-ASIW8 Clearance: Secret

Class Size: 54 *Iterations:* nineteen per year *Course Duration:* three weeks

Prerequisites: Active component or reserve component SOF commissioned officers (LT-CPT), warrant officers (WO1-CW3) or enlisted personnel (PFC-MSG). Other commissioned officers, warrant officers or enlisted personnel of the active or reserve components, selected DoD civilian personnel or allied personnel who have been nominated for attendance through their chain of command. Applicants must be qualified military static-line parachutists and not weigh more than 240 pounds; must have a current Class III flight physical examination IAW AR 40-501 dated within two years of course completion date; must report with complete medical records including a current Physiological Training Record, High-Altitude Parachutist Initial (HAP INT) (AF Form 1274; AF Form 702, Navy Form 1550/28-NP-6 card; or USAAMC[126] AA Form 484). Any variation from the above standards requires a waiver from the CG, USAJFKSWCS.

---

126 US Army Aeromedical Center

Course Description: Military Free-Fall (MFF) ground training: packing of the Ram Air Parachute System (RAPPS) main parachute, parachute donning procedures, emergency procedures and aircraft procedures/jump commands; body stabilization in the vertical wind tunnel. MFF operations: aircraft procedures, emergency procedures, body stabilization and how to exit an aircraft from the door or ramp using dive or poised exit positions. Rigging of weapons, combat equipment, night vision goggles and the use of portable oxygen equipment. MFF parachute operations consist of MFF parachute jumps from altitudes of 9,500 to 25,000 feet with and without weapons, combat equipment, NVGs and supplemental oxygen system in day and night conditions.

Military Free Fall Jumpmaster Course (MFFJM)

Course Number: 2E-F56/011-F15 *Clearance:* Secret

Class Size: 30 *Iterations:* nine per year *Course Duration:* five weeks three days

Prerequisites: Active- or reserve-component commissioned officers, warrant officers, noncommissioned officers and enlisted personnel of the United States military services, selected students of foreign allied countries and DoD personnel who are assigned to, or will be assigned to, a military free-fall position. Must have completed a SOCOM-recognized static-line jumpmaster course and a SOCOM recognized Military Free Fall Parachutist course. Must have a current Class III flight examination IAW AR 40-501 dated within five years of course completion date if the soldier is presently on military free-fall status/orders. Must have a current Physiological Training Record, High-Altitude Parachutist Initial. (AF Form 1274; AF Form 702; Navy Form 1550/28-NP-6 card; or USAAMC AA Form 484). Personnel cannot exceed 240 pounds. Must have served as a military free-fall parachutist for a minimum of one year and completed a minimum of 50 military free-fall jumps. Must be current Military Free-Fall Parachutist Level III IAW USASOC 350-2, 27 September 01. Any variation from the above standards requires a waiver from the Commanding General, SWCS.

Course Description: MFFJM training focuses on Jumpmaster Personnel Inspection, emergency procedures, oxygen equipment, wind-drift calculations, jump commands, aircraft procedures, techniques of spotting, ram-air personnel parachute packing and rigging, advanced high-altitude, high-opening infiltration skills, computer-guided and compass-driven navigation, night-vision goggles rigging and emergency procedures, nonstandard combat equipment and weapon rigging, grouping and canopy flight into unmarked/blacked-out drop zones and rigging, loading and deployment of GPS-guided bundles. Each student will plan and execute several night, 02, HAHO operations at altitudes up to 25,000 feet MSL in complete blackout conditions utilizing NVGs and navigate onto unfamiliar/unmarked drop zones.

Advanced Military Free Fall Course (CAMFF)

Course Number: 011-F66 *Clearance:* Secret

Class Size: Seven *Iterations:* four per year *Course Duration:* nine weeks

Prerequisites: Active component commissioned officers, non-commissioned officers and warrant officers who are current MFF jumpers and qualified military free-fall jumpmasters, upon successful completion of MFFIC, all Army NCOs will be available for future assignment as MFF instructors at B Co, 2d Bn, 1st SWTG (A), Yuma Proving Grounds, Arizona. Must possess a current Class III physical examination IAW AR 40-502 dated within five years of course completions date. Must also possess a current Physiological Training Card (AF Form 1274; AF Form 702; Navy Form 1550/28-NP-6 card; or USAAMC (AA) Form 484). Must meet height and weight standards as outlined in AR 600-9, or service equivalent. Personnel cannot exceed 240 pounds. Must have served as a military free-fall jumpmaster for a minimum of one year and completed a minimum of 100 free-fall parachute jumps. Must havenine months remaining in service upon graduation. Personnel reporting to training who do not meet all of the prerequisites will not be admitted to the course. Any variation from the above standards requires a request for exceptions in writing from the soldier's battalion commander through the group commander, to the commanding general, USAJFKSWCS.

Course Description:

Military Free-Fall ground training: students learn advance free fall techniques in the vertical wind tunnel, by conducting drills that replicate instructor to student free-fall operations.

Military Free-Fall Air Operations (Yuma Proving Ground, Ariz.): Students revalidate their competency with the MC-4 parachute system before transitioning to the Instructor-Certified Ram-Air Parachute System (ICRAPS); (Non-Standard Military Free-Fall parachute system). Transition training consists of packing the main parachute, donning the parachute system, conducting jumpmaster personnel inspections and performing emergency procedures using the parachute system. Additionally, students receive refresher training on aircraft procedures, drop-zone operations and rigging external equipment before the start of airborne operations.

Special Forces Intelligence Sergeant Course (SFISC)

Course Number: 011-18F40 *Clearance:* TS-SCI

Class Size: Fifty *Iterations:* three per year *Course Duration:* fourteen weeks

Prerequisites: Active- or National Guard- component U.S. Army Special Forces enlisted personnel (CMF 18) in the rank of staff sergeant through sergeant first class, with a minimum of two years operational detachment-alpha or operational detachment-bravo time, who have a validated mission need or have been nominated by their chain of command are allowed to attend to the Special Forces Intelligence Sergeants Course. Any variation from the above standards requires a waiver from the commanding general, SWCS. Must be a U.S. citizen. All students must pass the Army Physical Fitness test during the course IAW FM 21-22 and the SFISC Student Evaluation and Grading Criteria. Students will be graded IAW their age group and must meet or exceed 70 percent in each event. Any student on profile is required to bring a copy of their profile (temporary or permanent).

All students must meet height and weight IAW AR600-9 Army Weight Control Program. All students attending this course must have a finalized top secret clearance and be read-on the following caveats: SI/TK/G/H and have a PKI emailed to their SOCRATES[127] account on JWICS[128].

Course Description:

Fort Bragg Module: Conventional and unconventional intelligence collection and processing; irregular warfare analytics; critical thinking structured analysis, information operations; force protection, threat vulnerability assessment, evasion and recovery planning; analytical skills training/emerging analytic techniques; intelligence cycle; intelligence preparation of the environment; intelligence architecture; photography; digital intelligence systems, biometrics, forensics, digital-media exploitation; joint, conventional and Special Forces targeting, targeting exercise (individual/network).

National Capital Region Module (Wash, D.C.): Interagency operations, Students will develop an understanding of the strategic intelligence operations of national agencies/SOF integration. Students will conduct analyst exchanges with national intelligence agencies in preparation of a real-world intelligence packet briefed to a VIP.

Advanced Special Operations Techniques Course (ASOTC)

Course Number: 2E-F141/011-F27 *Clearance:* Secret

Class Size: Twenty-four *Iterations:* twelve per year *Course Duration:* fourteen weeks

Prerequisites: Must be a graduate of one of the following courses IAW USSOCOM Directive 525.5 Advanced Special Operations.

Must possess a secret security clearance with the ability to obtain a top-secret clearance with sensitive compartmented information access and have U.S. citizenship. Must be an E6-E8, W1-W3 or O2-O4. Must have a minimum

---

127 SOCRATES: Special Operations Command Research, Analysis, and Threat Evaluation System
128 JWICS: Joint Worldwide Intelligence Communications System

of two years of SOF experience at the tactical level. Upon enrollment must have a remaining service obligation of two years (non-waiverable). Upon graduation (non-waiverable) will incur an additional two-year service obligation and must serve a four-year utilization tour in a SOF billet that requires ASOT Level 3 qualification validated by USSOCOM J3X.

Course Description: Special operations; mission planning; advanced special operations; interagency operations; unconventional warfare practical exercise; culmination exercise and graduation.

Advanced Special Operations Managers Course (ASOMC)

Course Number: 2E-F 272/011-F111 *Clearance:* TS-SCI

Class Size: Sixteen *Iterations:* six per year *Course Duration:* four weeks

Prerequisites: Students must be graduates of course 2E-F141/011-F27 the Advanced Special Operations Techniques course (Level 3). (c) Has a minimum of three years operational experience as a Level 3 operative. (d) Has a pay grade of E7-E9, W2-W5, 04-05 or GS12-GS15. (e) Possess a top-secret security clearance with sensitive compartmented information access. Those individuals without a verified clearance will not be admitted to the course. (f) Any variation from the above prerequisites requires a waiver approved by the commander, SWCS.

Course Description: Classified.

Operator Technical Surveillance Course (OTSC)

Course Number: 2E-F259/011-F99A *Clearance:* Secret

Class Size: Twenty-four *Iterations:* three per year *Course Duration:* nine weeks

Prerequisites: Must be in the grade of E6-E7, W1-W3 and O3. Must have at a minimum one year SOF experience at the tactical level. Must possess at a minimum a current secret-security clearance. Individuals without a verified clearance will not be admitted to the course. Individual must be assigned to USASOC, JSOC or MARSOC.

Course Description: The Operator Technical Surveillance course is designed to qualify selected SOF personnel in the concepts, responsibilities, functions and procedures associated with technical-support operations for SOF missions across the spectrum of operations. The OTSC graduate will possess an intermediate-level skill set with knowledge required to effectively conduct technical-support operations that will provide a force multiplier for SOF commanders. The course instructs SOF operators in the use and exploitation of tactical assets for intelligence, surveillance and reconnaissance; and target development using advanced digital photography and video equipment.

Advanced Technical Surveillance Course (ATSC)

Course Number: 2E-F259/011-F99B *Clearance:* Secret

Class Size: Twenty-four *Iterations:* three per year *Course Duration:* four weeks

Prerequisites: Must be in the grade of E6-E7, W1-W3 and O3. Must have at a minimum one year SOF experience at the tactical level. Must possess at a minimum a current secret-security clearance. Individuals without a verified clearance will not be admitted to the course. Individual must be assigned to USASOC, JSOC or MARSOC. Must be a graduate of the OTSC.

Course Description: The Advance Technical Surveillance course is designed to qualify selected SOF personnel in the concepts, responsibilities, functions and procedures associated with technical-support operations for SOF missions across the spectrum of operations. The ATSC graduate will possess an advanced-level skill set with knowledge required to effectively conduct technical support operations that will provide a force multiplier for SOF commanders. The course instructs SOF operators in the use and exploitation of tactical assets for intelligence, surveillance and reconnaissance. Students are also trained in target development using advanced digital photography and video equipment.

Special Operations Analytics and Intelligence Course (SOAIC)

Course Number: 2E-F284/011-F117 *Clearance:* TS-SCI

Class Size: Twenty *Iterations:* five *Course Duration:* five weeks

Prerequisites: None

Course Description: Train and educate select Green Berets, SOF enablers and interagency personnel to access, analyze and fuse intelligence data up to the top-secret/sensitive compartmented information level to provide specialized intelligence support to the full range of SOF missions. This course will run in the National Capitol Region.

Special Forces Network Development Course (NDC)

Course Number: 2E-F271/011-F110 *Clearance:* TS-SCI

Class Size: Twenty *Iterations:* four per year *Course Duration:* three weeks

Prerequisites: (a) Must be an active- or reserve-component Special Forces qualified officer (18A) O3-O5, warrant officer (180A) W3-W5, or senior enlisted (18 series) E7-E9. (b) Must have a minimum two years SOF experience at the tactical level. (c) Must possess a top-secret security clearance with sensitive compartmented information access. The 1st SWTG (A) S2 will verify all clearances. Those individuals without a verified clearance will not be admitted to the course. (d) Must be Achilles Dagger qualified. (e) Any variation from the above standards requires a waiver from the CG, SWCS.

Course Description: Train and educate SOF personnel to design, develop, assess, vet, protect and expand complex indigenous networks. The course prepares SOF personnel for analyzing regional cultural and social environments; assessing individuals for participation in activities in support of Phase I and II U.S.-sponsored resistance objectives; vetting, protecting and expanding both resilient and enduring networks through traditional and modern methodologies.

Unconventional Warfare Operational Design Course (UWODC)

Course Number: 2E-F269/011-F108 Clearance: TS-SCI

Class Size: Twenty *Iterations:* six *Course Duration:* four weeks

Prerequisites: (a) This course is open to all personnel who have been selected by their chain of command for attendance. (b) Ideally, students should have a minimum of two years SOF experience and be a qualified officer in the grade of O3-O5, warrant officer W2-W5 or senior enlisted E7-E9. (c) Students must possess a minimum current secret-security clearance. The 1st SWTG (A) S-2 will verify all clearances. Those individuals without a verified clearance will not be admitted to the course. (d) Any variation of the above standards requires a waiver from CG, SWCS.

Course Description: Train and educate SOF and interagency personnel in the art of comprehensive UW planning through design. The course prepares SOF and interagency personnel for analyzing, assessing and developing a potential regional resistance and surrogate element in support of PE/UW[129] activities as an operational or contingency alternative for GCC's, U.S. ambassadors and strategic decision-makers; able to understand, implement and articulate the unique requirements at the operational and strategic level to plan, develop and enable resistance/insurgent element; participates in operational and strategic campaign design and planning as an SME to guide and facilitate, theater-level PE/UW plans.

SOF Digital Targeting Training (STTE)

Course Number: TBD Clearance: TS-SCI

Annual Attendance: 225 *Iterations:* Modular *Course Duration:* one to five weeks

Prerequisites: All students attending this course must have a finalized top-secret security clearance with SCI access

---

129 PE/UW: Preparation of the Environment/Unconventional Warfare

Course Description: Qualify SOT-As[130], select joint SOF and other selected personnel to conduct advanced digital-targeting operations in support of the full range of special operations through the employment of wireless and digital technology.

SOF Site Exploitation, Technical Exploitation Course (SOFSE TEC)

Course Number: 2E-F262/011-F102 *Clearance:* Secret

Class Size: Sixteen *Iterations:* ten per year *Course Duration:* three weeks

Prerequisites: Active- and reserve-component enlisted personnel in the grade of E1 though E8, warrant officer WO1 through WO3, officers O1 through O3 who are assigned to a SOF unit and government civilians who have a valid mission need and who have been nominated by their chain of command for attendance. The target audience for the TEC is composed of SOF operators, interagency partners, personnel in military intelligence, interrogators and soldiers assigned to chemical or explosive-ordnance disposal units detailed to assist in SOFSE.

Course Description: Instruction on advanced battlefield forensics; on-site presumptive identification of trace and residue; detection, capture and transfer of latent prints without dusting; conducting imaging, storing and exploiting large volumes of digital media; employment of ballistic imaging devices; employment of credibility assessment tools; conducting advanced document digitization and gist; and conducting advanced cell-phone exploitation. Enables soldiers to conduct specialized SOFSE activities that are beyond the capabilities of the SOFSE advanced operator. TEC students will learn to operate within a SOFSE facility designed to further exploit sensitive-site materials and detainees who have been removed from the objective; perform basic and advanced operator tasks to enable them to assist SOFSE advanced operators on-target. Provides training in advanced battlefield forensics; on-site presumptive identification of trace and residue; detection, capture and transfer of latent

---

130 SOT-A: Special Operations Team-Alpha - conducts signals intelligence-electronic warfare in support of Special Operations elements

prints with or without dusting; imaging, storing and exploitation of large volumes of digital media; employment of ballistic imaging devices; and advanced document digitization. Graduates receive PDSI D5H.

SOF Sensitive Site Exploitation Operator Advanced Course (SOFSE OAC)

Course Number: 2E-F258/011-F98 *Clearance:* Secret

Class Size: Twenty-four *Iterations:* ten per year *Course Duration:* three weeks

Prerequisites: Active- and reserve-component enlisted personnel in the grade of E1 though E8, warrant officer WO1 through WO3, officers O1 through O3 who are assigned to a SOF unit and government civilians who have a valid mission need and who have been nominated by their chain of command for attendance.

Course Description: Special Operations Forces Site Exploitation team organization and responsibilities, planning, interagency collaboration, biometrics, forensics and documents and media exploitation, improvised explosive devices exploitation, tactical questioning and detainee-handling procedures.

Exploitation Analysis Center - Organic (EAC-O)

Course Number: 2E-F261/011-F101 *Clearance:* Secret

Class Size: Six *Iterations:* ten per year *Course Duration:* three weeks

Prerequisites: Active- and reserve-component enlisted personnel in the grade of E1 though E8, warrant officer WO1 through WO3, officers O1 through O3 who are assigned to a SOF unit and government civilians who have a valid mission need and who have been nominated by their chain of command for attendance.

Course Description: EAC-O technician roles/responsibilities; site exploitation materials collection and submissions techniques; digital photography; tool markings; impressions; firearms comparison; post-blast investigation; and analyzing drugs, explosives and chemicals using the gas chromatograph/mass spectrometer technology.

Special Forces Physical Surveillance Course (SFPSC) (Build Phase) New!

Course Number: 2E-F285/011-F188 *Clearance:* Secret

Class Size: Twenty-two *Iterations:* four per year *Course Duration:* eight weeks

Prerequisites: Must be in the grade of E6-E7, W1-W3 or O3. Individual must have at a minimum one-year SOF experience at the tactical level. Individual must possess at a minimum a current secret-security clearance. Individual must be assigned to USASOC, JSOC or MARSOC with an operational requirement for this capability as seen by their command without a verified clearance will not be admitted to the course.

Scope: Train and select SF, joint SOF and other selected personnel to conduct multi-modal non-technical personal- and target surveillance operations in support of the full range of special operations.

Special Forces Sniper Course (SFSC)

Course Number: 2E-F67/011-ASIW3 *Clearance:* Secret

Class Size: Forty *Iterations:* four per year *Course Duration:* eight weeks

Prerequisites: Army active component or reserve component Special Forces or Ranger qualified commissioned officers, lieutenant through captain; warrant officers 180A and enlisted personnel, E4-E8, assigned to or on orders to a Special Forces detachment or Ranger company; and selected Department of Defense personnel. Must have in their possession at class in-processing: a memorandum from their security manager verifying their secret-security clearance dated not earlier than thirty days prior to the start date; and a periodic health assessment and psychological evaluation that were administered within twelve months of the class start date. Must be on jump status with current hazardous duty orders. Must pass an entrance examination. The examination will be a diagnostic shoot consisting of shooting five groupings. Each grouping will consist of shooting five rounds at twenty-five meters from the prone supported position with the current service rifle using iron sites. Three of the five groups must have all five rounds in an area equal to or less than one and a quarter inch in diameter to pass the shooting evaluation. Must not possess a medical profile that would prohibit participation in training and must not be taking any medications that may affect reflexes or judgment. Vision must be correctable to 20/20 in each eye. Any variation from the above standards requires a waiver from the CG, USAJFKSWCS.

Course Description: Marksmanship, rural field craft, technical-surveillance equipment, alternate sniper weapon systems and practical application. Trains selected special-operations forces personnel in Level 1 special-operations sniper skills and operational procedures that are necessary for them to engage selected targets with precision fire from concealed positions at ranges and under conditions that are not possible for the conventionally trained sniper in support of all SOF missions across the operational continuum.

Special Forces Advanced Reconnaissance Target Analysis Exploitation Techniques Course (SFARTAETC)

Course Number: 2E-F133/011-F46 *Clearance:* Secret

Class Size: Fifty-two *Iterations:* four per year *Course Duration:* eight weeks

Prerequisites: Active component SF enlisted personnel (CMF 18) in the rank of sergeant to master sergeant (no foreign).

Course Description: Provides specialized and comprehensive instruction and training in the tactics and techniques needed by combatant commander in-extremis forces to accomplish assigned missions, to enhance the common skill readiness level of currently designated CIF personnel and to provide a basic entry-level program for personnel assigned to theater CIFs.

Special Forces Senior Mountaineering Course (Level-2)

Course Number: 2E-F273/011-F112 *Clearance:* Secret

Class Size: Twenty-two *Iterations:* three per year *Course Duration:* six weeks

Prerequisites: Must be assigned to an active duty or National Guard Special Forces Group and must be in the MOS of eighteen series, be physically fit (scored no less than 270 in age group on APFT). Must have mountaineering experience, be on a mountain team and certified as a basic (Level 3) mountaineer. Must pass the Special Forces physical exam IAW paragraph 5-3, Chapter 5, AR 40-501, within one year of class date and must report with an SF physical (which is annotated in MEDPROS[131]).

Course Description: Tactical mountain operations, field-craft training, animal packing, maintaining mountaineering equipment, selecting appropriate mountaineering equipment, high alpine medical considerations, medical emergencies, trauma emergencies, weather forecasting, belay climbers, construct improvised climbing equipment, casualty extraction, moving non-trained personnel over vertical obstacles, conducting mountain operations at night, equipment hauling, three-man party climbs with lead climbing and graded practical exercises. The Senior Mountaineering Course (Level-2) is rock- and alpine-focused on training and educating select SF Soldiers in all Level-2 Mountaineering Skill Sets. Graduates will have the ability to serve as their unit's subject-matter experts in tactical military operations in mountainous terrain, lead untrained and indigenous forces over mountainous terrain, conduct pack-animal operations and have the ability to certify Basic Mountaineers (Level 3) for attendance to the Senior Mountaineering course.

Special Forces Master Mountaineering Course (Level-1)

Course Number: 2E-F274/011-F113 *Clearance:* Secret

Class Size: Twenty-two *Iterations:* one per year *Course Duration:* four weeks

---

131 MEDPROS: Medical Protection System: designed to track immunization, medical readiness, and deployability data for the Army

Prerequisites: Must be assigned to an active duty or National Guard Special Forces Group in the MOS of eighteen series or be assigned to a USSOCOM unit or other federal agency and meet the USSOCOM SOF baseline interoperable mountaineering training standards IAW USSOCOM Manual 350-34. Must be physically fit (scored no less than 270 in age group on APFT). Must have mountaineering experience and be a graduate of the USAJFKSWCS Senior Mountaineering Course. Must pass the Special Forces physical exam IAW paragraph 5-3, Chapter 5, AR 40-501, within one year of class date and must report with an SF physical (which is annotated in MEDPROS).

Course Description: Tactical mountain operations in a winter environment, field-craft training, maintaining mountaineering equipment, selecting appropriate alpine mountaineering equipment, high-altitude medical considerations, cold-weather medical evacuation techniques, weather forecasting, belay climbers, construct improvised-climbing equipment, avalanche rescue, snowpack analysis, winter guiding techniques, moving non-trained personnel over winter alpine terrain, alpine bivouac, winter tactical considerations, a tactical culmination exercise.

The Master Mountaineering course (Level-1) is a winter-alpine mountaineering course focused on training and educating select SF soldiers in all Level-1 Mountaineering skill sets. Graduates will have the ability to serve as their unit's SME on cold weather, high-altitude, advanced-mountaineering operations, lead untrained and indigenous forces over mountainous terrain in winter conditions, conduct avalanche and deliberate vertical-rescue operations and have the ability to serve as a battalion or group master trainer for mountaineering.

9

Special Operations Forces (SOF)

Special Operations Forces, i.e. the ever popular abbreviation, SOF, hosts a plethora of units and organizations and elements for not only the Army but also the Air Force, Navy and Marines. Special Forces is only one, but Special Forces, in numbers of people, makes up about 70+% of all SOF.

Special Operations Forces (SOF) are defined as:

> **Special Operations:** *[Joint Publication (JP) 1-02, "Department of Defense (DOD) Dictionary of Military and Associated Terms 8 November 2010 as amended through 15 April 2012.]* Operations requiring unique modes of employment, tactical techniques, equipment and training often conducted in hostile, denied, or politically sensitive environments and characterized by one or more of the following: time sensitive, clandestine, low visibility, conducted with and/or through indigenous forces, requiring regional expertise, and/or a high degree of risk. Also called **SO.** (JP 3-05)

The below excerpt from the National Defense University Library describes the legislation that founded United States Special Operations Command (USSOCOM).

The Goldwater-Nichols Department of Defense Reorganization Act of 1986[132], sponsored by Senator Barry Goldwater and Representative Bill Nichols, caused a major defense reorganization, the most significant since the National Security Act of 1947. Operational authority was centralized through the Chairman of the Joint Chiefs as opposed to the service chiefs. The chairman was designated as the principal military advisor to the president, National Security Council and Secretary of Defense. The act established the position of vice-chairman and streamlined the operational chain of command from the president to the secretary of defense to the unified commanders.

Since 1986, Goldwater-Nichols has made tremendous changes in the way DOD operates-joint operations are the norm-Arabian Gulf, Zaire, Haiti, and Bosnia. Implementation of the act is an ongoing project with Joint Vision 2010 (1996) and Joint Vision 2020 (2000). Both documents emphasize that to be the most effective force we must be fully joint: intellectually, operationally, organizationally, doctrinally, and technically. The joint force, because of its flexibility and responsiveness, will remain the key to operational success in the future.

Specifically for SOF, the Goldwater-Nichols Department of Defense Reorganization Act of 1986 stated:

SEC. 212. INITIAL REVIEW OF COMBATANT COMMANDS

(a) MATTERS To BE CONSIDERED.—The first review of the missions, responsibilities (including geographic boundaries), and force structure of the unified and specified combatant commands under section 161(b) of title 10, United States Code, as added by section 211 of this Act, shall include consideration of the following:

---

132 Goldwater-Nichols Department of Defense Reorganization Act of 1986; 100 STAT. 992;   PUBLIC LAW 99-433—OCT. 1, 1986; 99th Congress

(1) .....

(2) Creation of a unified combatant command for special operations missions which would combine the special operations missions, responsibilities, and forces of the armed forces.

However; it was the *National Defense Authorization Act for Fiscal Year 1987*[133] (Known as the Nunn-Cohen Amendment) that formally established U.S. Special Operations Command and assigned forces. SOF are specifically identified in Title 10, United States Code (USC), Section 167 as:

(i) IDENTIFICATION OF SPECIAL OPERATIONS FORCES.—(1) Subject to paragraph (2), for the purposes of this section special operations forces are those forces of the armed forces that—

(A) are identified as core forces or as augmenting forces in the Joint Chiefs of Staff Joint Strategic Capabilities Plan, Annex E[134], dated December 17,1985;

(B) are described in the Terms of Reference and Conceptual Operations Plan for the Joint Special Operations Command, as in effect on April 1, 1986; or

C) are designated as special operations forces by the Secretary of Defense.

(2) The Secretary of Defense, after consulting with the Chairman of the Joint Chiefs of Staff and the commander of the special operations command, may direct that any force included within the description in paragraph (1)(A) or (1)(B) shall not be considered as a special operations force for the purposes of this section.

---

133 National Defense Authorization Act for Fiscal Year 1987; 100 STAT. 3816 PUBLIC LAW 99-661—NOV. 14, 1986; Public Law 99-66; 99th Congress
134 Annex E of the joint strategic capabilities plan is a classified document.

In accordance with his prerogatives under the identification of Special Operations Forces, the Secretary of Defense did not immediately assign all the currently assigned organizations to the new command.

Below are excerpts from *The 20th Anniversary edition of the USSOCOM History: 1987-2007;* USSOCOM History and Research Office:

> On 15 October 1987, Secretary Weinberger assigned all Army and Air Force Active and Reserve Component PSYOP and CA units to USSOCOM. General Stiner pushed through an initiative that the Secretary of Defense approved in March 1993, designating PSYOP and CA as SOF. This decision enabled USSOCOM to command and control these units in peacetime as well, which greatly improved the command's ability to fund, train, equip, and organize these forces.
>
> Created by the Navy on 16 April 1987, the NAVSPECWARCOM only had the Naval Special Warfare Center (the training command) assigned to it. Naval Special Warfare Groups I and II (and their SEALs and Special Boat Units) were not assigned because the Navy argued that these organizations and their forces belonged to the Pacific and Atlantic fleets, respectively, and therefore not available for assignment to USSOCOM. On 23 October 1987, Secretary Weinberger ruled in favor of USSOCOM. Accordingly, operational control of the SEALs, Special Boat Units, and NSW groups passed to NAVSPECWARCOM on 1 March 1988, and that command assumed administrative control for these units on 1 October 1988.
>
> The USSOCOM most recent component—the Marine Corps Forces, Special Operations Command (MARSOC) was established on 4 February 2006. Headquartered at Camp Lejeune, N.C., the Marine Corps component of USSOCOM started with approximately 1,400 Marines, sailors, and civilian employees and was commanded by a U.S. Marine Corps two-star general. MARSOC includes five subordinate commands: The Foreign Military Training Unit (FMTU), two Marine Special Operations

battalions, the Marine Special Operations Support Group, and the Marine Special Operations School. MARSOC was projected to grow to about 2,500 by FY 2010.

Likewise, on 14 November 2006, using the same justification, the Deputy Secretary of Defense reassigned U.S. Army reserve component civil affairs and psychological operations units from USSOCOM to U.S. Joint Forces Command. This was an incongruent flip-flop and now, the debate has gone full circle and DOD is exploring the return of these reserve forces to USSOCOM.

The below charts show the current broad organization of US SOF as of 2014. In the past twenty-five years SOF has undergone a great deal of change and modernization. This change has been accelerated with past 10+ years of war in Afghanistan and Iraq. The bulk of the SOF force and with the bulk of the missions in the Army Special Forces.

USASOC, as the Army component of USSOCOM, as the bulk of the forces in the command and, as indicated above, continues its evolution of organizational change. However, there is little change where the boots meet the ground.

U.S. Army Special Operations Command (~29,000)	U.S. Army John F. Kennedy Special Warfare Center and School <ul><li>1st Special Warfare Training Group</li><li>Special Warfare Education Group</li><li>Special Warfare Medical Group</li><li>Special Forces Want Officer Institute</li><li>David K. Thuma Non-commissioned Officer Academy</li><li>Capabilities Development And Integration Directorate</li></ul>

U.S. Army Special Warfare Command
- 1st Special Forces Group
- 3rd Special Forces Group
- 5th Special Forces Group
- 7th Special Forces Group
- 10th Special Forces Group
- 19th Special Forces Group
- 20th Special Forces Group
- Military Information Support Operations Command
  - 4th Military Information Support Group
    - 6th Military Information Support Bn
    - 7th Military Information Support Bn
    - 8th Military Information Support Bn
  - 8th Military Information Support Group (Provisional)
    - 1st Military Information Support Bn
    - 5th Military Information Support Bn
    - 9th Military Information Support Bn
  - 3rd Military Information Support Bn
- 528th Sustainment Brigade
  - ARSOF Support Operations Teams
  - Special Operations Resuscitation Teams
  - ARSOF Liaison Elements
  - Medical Level II Teams
  - 112th Special Operation Signal Battalion
- 95th Civil Affairs Brigade
  - 91st Civil Affairs Battalion
  - 92nd Civil Affairs Battalion
  - 96th Civil Affairs Battalion
  - 97th Civil Affairs Battalion
  - 98th Civil Affairs Battalion

	75th Ranger Regiment ▪ 1st Ranger Battalion ▪ 2nd Ranger Battalion ▪ 3rd Ranger Battalion ▪ Special Troops Battalion

	U.S. Army Special Operations Aviation Command
	▪ 1/60 Special Operations Aviation Regiment
	   ○ 1st Special Operations Aviation Battalion
	   ○ 2nd Special Operations Aviation Battalion
	   ○ 3rd Special Operations Aviation Battalion
	   ○ 4th Special Operations Aviation Battalion
	▪ Special Operations Training Battalion

Navy's Special Warfare Command, as the Navy component of USSOCOM, also continues its evolution. Some of the more significant changes have been deep inland missions that the SEALs have conducted as a part of the wars in Afghanistan and Iraq. These missions are a departure from the traditional sea-based role of the SEALs, with the best-known being the Pakistan raid to kill Osama bin Laden.

U.S. Navy Special Operations Command (~8,800)	U.S. Navy Special Warfare Command
	Naval Special Warfare Center
	Development Group
	Naval Special Warfare Group 1 ■ SEAL Teams 1 ■ SEAL Teams 3 ■ SEAL Teams 5 ■ SEAL Teams 7
	Naval Special Warfare Group 2 ■ SEAL Teams 2 ■ SEAL Teams 4 ■ SEAL Teams 8 ■ SEAL Teams 10
	Naval Special Warfare Group 3 ■ SEAL Delivery Vehicle Unit 1 ■ SEAL Delivery Vehicle Unit 2
	Naval Special Warfare Group 4 ■ Special Boat Team 12 ■ Special Boat Team 20 ■ Special Boat Team 22
	Naval Special Warfare Group 10
	Naval Special Warfare Group 11 ■ SEAL Teams 17 ■ SEAL Teams 18

AFSOC, as the air component of USSOCOM, has its major evolution being the acquisition of the CV 22 tilt rotor aircraft. The 6th SOS was activated 1 April 1994 as a FID/UW Squadron. The 6th SOS focus is on advising and training foreign aviation forces. The 6th SOS brings a special capability to FID/UW in that they worked with Special Forces to train indigenous populations to develop their own capability. The establishment of the 6th SOS as a FID/UW organization is probably the single greatest contribution provided by AFSOC to the FID/UW mission sets.

Air Force Special Operations Command (~18,000)	27 Special Operations Wing
	1st Special Operations Wing ■ 6th Special Operations Squadron (FID/UW)
	24th Special Operations Wing
	Air Force Special Operations Air Warfare Center
	352nd Special Operations Group
	353rd Special Operations Group
	919th Special Operations Wing
	193rd Special Operations Wing
	209th Civil Engineer Squadron
	227th Special Operations Flight
	280th Combat Communication Squadron

MARSOC, as the Marine component of USSOCOM, is the latest addition to the SOF force structure. The Marines successfully fought being included in the original force structure of USSOCOM in 1986. However, as the MFP 11 funding increased for SOF, and in order to edge out some of that funding, the Marine Corps began calling their amphibious units afloat, the Marine Expeditionary Units, "Special Operations Capable" or MEU(SOC).

U.S. Marine Corps Forces Special Operations Command (~3,000)	Marine Special Operations School
	Marine Special Operations Support Group
	Marine Special Operations Regiment
	1st Marine Special Operations Battalion
	2nd Marine Special Operations Battalion
	3rd Marine Special Operations Battalion

10

SOF Core Activities

According to *Joint Pub 3-05 (18 April 2011)*, SOF has eleven (11) core activities.

Rarely do any of these tasks stand alone. All of the other core activities can, and in some cases, must support unconventional warfare. UW incorporates all the other core activities by having them conducted *through, with or by* the indigenous population; however, UW, while providing a venue for the conduct of the other activities, is never in a supporting role to any of the other core activities with the possible exception of counter-insurgency operations (author's opinion).

Unconventional warfare requires external support in order to be successful. Since COIN is conducted to prevent an insurgent takeover of a friendly entity, the insurgent likely will have an external sponsor. It is this external sponsor that becomes the target of a UW campaign. Conducting UW in the insurgent's sponsoring nation-state may contribute to the defeat of the insurgency by regime change in the sponsoring state, thus terminating support to the insurgency in the friendly nation.

Each core mission is complex in and of itself. Any SOF unit attempting to be expert in all eleven core activities must experience a dilution of effort and resources, thus prohibiting competence in some of the missions, if not in all. Consider counter-terrorism (CT), special reconnaissance (SR) and direct action (DA). Special Forces units usually approach these as stand-alone missions and train to execute them in a unilateral manner. Each mission then receives repetitive training time, consuming significant resources. Second, the three missions of counter-terrorism, special reconnaissance and direct action are missions other SOF and conventional forces also have as missions. Some of these other SOF units are better trained, organized and resourced than are the Special Forces Groups to conduct these missions. Therefore let them have the lead in these missions. These are not *through, with and by* missions if conducted unilaterally, so SF should only focus on these missions with the point of view on how to conduct them *through, with and by* indigenous partners. SF duplication of missions that other SOF are better suited to conduct is duplication we can ill afford.

Core Activities

(1) **Unconventional Warfare (UW)** 2012 (JP 3-05) 8 November 2010 (as amended through 15 April 2012) The latest official publication, — Activities conducted to enable a resistance movement or insurgency to coerce, disrupt, or overthrow a government or occupying power by operating through or with an underground, auxiliary, and guerrilla force in a denied area. Also called UW.

(2) **Direct Action (DA)** Short-duration strikes and other small-scale offensive actions conducted as a special operation in hostile, denied, or diplomatically sensitive environments and which employ specialized military capabilities to seize, destroy, capture, exploit, recover, or damage designated targets. Also called DA. (JP 3-05 April 2011)

(3) **Special Reconnaissance (SR)** Reconnaissance and surveillance actions conducted as a special operation in hostile, denied, or politically sensitive environments to collect or verify information of strategic or operational significance, employing military capabilities not normally found in conventional forces. Also called SR. (JP 3-05 April 2011)

(4) **Foreign Internal Defense (FID)** Participation by civilian and military agencies of a government in any of the action programs taken by another government or other designated organization to free and protect

its society from subversion, lawlessness, insurgency, terrorism, and other threats to its security. (JP 3-22)

This definition focuses U.S. Government efforts in support of a friendly nation that asks for U.S. help during internal crises and instability. The words "to free and protect" imply there is some level of crisis. FID programs, therefore, will only be implemented when a nation is experiencing internal security challenges or instability. The focus of FID assistance is to help the host nation address the drivers of conflict and the cause(s) of instability. This certainly requires interagency leading the effort to help resolve the root causes.

Further explanation posits FID is civil and military assistance that helps a country respond to a threat that it cannot handle on its own. FID consists of three categories of programs: FID Indirect Support, FID Direct Support, and FID Combat Operations. FID indirect support provides equipment or training support in order to enhance the host nation's (HN) ability to conduct its own operations. FID direct support involves U.S. forces actually conducting operations in support of the HN. In FID combat operations, the U.S. military may be required to conduct operations directly in the place of HN forces, particularly if HN security force capacity is still being developed. This was the case in Afghanistan, Iraq and Vietnam as examples.

U.S. Army doctrine states that FID and COIN occur as part of Irregular Warfare. Doctrine also recognizes indirect and direct support within FID. Indirect support to FID works to build host nation self-sufficiency. This is where the interagency and the non-military U.S. departments have the lead. Direct support involves U.S. forces military and/or law enforcement agencies directly assisting the host nation's civilian populace or military forces.[135]

(5) **Counter-terrorism (CT)** Actions taken directly against terrorist networks and indirectly to influence and render global and regional environments inhospitable to terrorist networks. (JP 3-26). Special Force's

---

135 Source: *White Paper: The Doctrinal Nesting of Joint and U.S. Army Terminology;* U.S. Army Peacekeeping and Stability Operations Institute; U. S. Army War College; 10 March 2011.

role in CT is (or should be) to work *through, with, and by* friendly indigenous organizations (military or paramilitary) to attack terrorists. Unilateral attacks of terrorists and terrorist organizations is the realm of other SOF and conventional forces.

(6) **Counter-proliferation of Weapons of Mass Destruction (CP)** Those actions taken to defeat the threat and/or use of weapons of mass destruction against the United States, our forces, friends, allies, and partners. Also called **CP.** (JP 1-02, April 2012) See also non-proliferation. (JP 3-40). Like CT, SF's role in CP is (or should be) to work *through, with, and by* friendly indigenous organizations (military or paramilitary) primarily using HUMINT to locate and identify the threat. If deniability is desired, SF might arrange a kinetic solution through or by indigenous partners or through a third party using surrogates. Unilateral solutions are the realm of other SOF and conventional forces.

(7) **Civil Affairs Operations (CAO)** The activities of a commander that establish, maintain, influence, or exploit relations between military forces, governmental and non-governmental civilian organizations and authorities, and the civilian populace in a friendly, neutral, or hostile operational area in order to facilitate military operations, to consolidate and achieve operational U.S. objectives. Civil-military operations may include performance by military forces of activities and functions normally the responsibility of the local, regional, or national government. These activities may occur prior to, during, or subsequent to other military actions. They may also occur, if directed, in the absence of other military operations. Civil-military operations may be performed by designated civil affairs, by other military forces, or by a combination of civil affairs and other forces. Also called CMO. (JP 1-02. SOURCE: JP 3-57) (JP 3-05 April 2011)

The below excerpt from part of my after action report on the Haiti mission in 1994- 95 is a prime example of a combination of CAO/CMO, FID, SFA, SA, PSYOP/MISO, and IO. I called this mix unconventional operations (UO). This was a true *through, with and by* operation; however, the *through, with and by* was as much *through, with and by* the people as it was *through, with and by* the Haitian government or the remnants of the Haitian military.

> Never totaling more than 1,200 personnel (including support personnel), which comprised only 5% of the total U.S. force package, the Special Forces controlled 95% of the land mass and 80% of the population in Haiti...

> ....In each AOR, the SF were the only authority. There were no police, and the Haitian military was effectively disassembled. The town mayors, many of them Cedras appointees, had fled; the legal system was not operational; lawyers and judges were corrupt and many had fled; the prison system was atrocious; there was no border control; no port control; the electrical system was inoperative; the water system was destroyed. In short, the SF had to organize a complete political, legal, civil, and administrative infrastructure in 95% of Haiti. Again, the success of this operation depended not on prior UO focused training, but on the quality of the Special Forces soldiers.

(8) **Psychological Operations (PSYOP)** (now called **MISO**[136])(JP 1-02, 8 November 2010, as amended through 15 April 2012) Planned operations to convey selected information and indicators to foreign audiences to influence their emotions, motives, objective reasoning, and ultimately the behavior of foreign governments, organizations, groups, and individuals in a manner favorable to the originator's objectives. Also called MISO. (JP 3-13.2)

MISO are the dissemination of truthful information to foreign audiences in support of U.S. policy and national objectives. Used during peacetime, contingencies and declared war, these activities are not forms of force, but are force multipliers that use non-violent means in often violent environments. Persuading rather than compelling physically, they rely on logic, fear, desire or other mental factors to promote specific emotions, attitudes or behaviors. The ultimate objective of U.S. Military Information Support Operations is to convince enemy, neutral, and friendly nations

---

136   MISO: Military Information Support Operations

and forces to take action favorable to the U.S. and its allies (MISO website).

(9) **Information Operations (IO)** The integrated employment, during military operations, of information-related capabilities in concert with other lines of operation to influence, disrupt, corrupt, or usurp the decision-making of adversaries and potential adversaries while protecting our own. Also called IO. See also computer network operations; electronic warfare; military deception; operations security; military information support operations. (SecDef Memo 12401-10)(JP 1-02 April 2012)

(10) **Security Force Assistance (SFA)** The Department of Defense activities that contribute to unified action by the U.S. Government to support the development of the capacity and capability of foreign security forces and their supporting institutions. (JP 3-22)

SFA encompasses DOD activities that support security cooperation (SC)[137], some elements of SA and FID and can occur during irregular warfare (IW). SFA can incorporate elements of SC, SA and FID. The definition in FM 3-07 is a little different and defines SFA as "the unified action to generate, employ, and sustain local, host-nation, or regional security forces in support of a legitimate authority." Elements of SA and FID could occur separate from SFA and there can be FID activities that are not SFA. SFA is not an operation in itself, but are activities conducted across the spectrum of conflict or in any of the operational themes that supports unified action.

In most situations involving this assistance, there is relatively little weight on offensive and defensive operations from a U.S. perspective. However, when U.S. forces accompany Foreign Security Forces (FSF) in combat, the weight of offensive and defensive operations will change to address the situation and align with the FSF efforts as already laid out. SFA is not just a stability activity, although it is a key contributor to the primary stability tasks of establishing civil security and civil control. This assistance

---

137 security cooperation (SC) — All Department of Defense interactions with foreign defense establishments to build defense relationships that promote specific U.S. security interests, develop allied and friendly military capabilities for self-defense and multinational operations, and provide US forces with peacetime and contingency access to a host nation.

could focus on improving the FSF of a host nation that is currently under no immediate threat, on paramilitary forces to counter an insurgency, or on advising FSF in major combat operations against an external threat.

Although Joint doctrine recognizes that SFA has a relationship to COIN and that SFA is integral to successful FID, COIN and stability, it does not establish a clear relationship among these terms. SFA is discussed in JP 3-22, Foreign Internal Defense, and JP 3-24, Counterinsurgency, as DOD activities supporting FSF. U.S. Army doctrine uses the same Joint definition and recognizes that SFA can occur across all operational themes and across the spectrum of conflict. JP 3-22 also states, "Both FID and SFA are subsets of SC. Neither FID nor SFA are subsets of each other." By using joint definitions, however, SFA nests within SA, SC and FID and supports FID though FID Direct and Indirect Support.[138]

(11) **Counterinsurgency (COIN)** Comprehensive civilian and military efforts taken to defeat an insurgency and to address any core grievances. (JP 1-02)

Joint doctrine recognizes that in supporting IDAD through FID, the military is normally focused on Counterinsurgency (COIN). As part of FID, COIN involves activity taken by a government to defeat insurgency to reestablish the host nation government's legitimacy.

Accordingly, following this logic, an insurgency can occur anytime and anyplace where there is a governing authority; therefore COIN can also occur anytime and anyplace, as long as there is a governing authority to defend its legitimacy. U.S. military forces can conduct COIN operations in support of a host nation or when no host nation governance exists. Such was the case of Afghanistan in 2001.

COIN in support of a host nation can occur through any category of FID, whether separately or simultaneously. As stated above, FID consists of three categories of programs: FID Indirect Support, FID Direct Support, and FID Combat Operations. The White Paper in the footnote below states that COIN can also occur outside FID programs when only

---

138 Source: *White Paper: The Doctrinal Nesting of Joint and U.S. Army Terminology*; U.S. Army Peacekeeping and Stability Operations Institute; U. S. Army War College; 10 March 2011.

supporting a military governing authority. This means we could provide COIN support to a foreign military dictatorship against an insurgency trying to overthrow the dictatorship. I am having some difficulty with this moral and ethical dilemma.

Based on these explanations, COIN can occur as a part of irregular warfare, but is not an element of FID since it can occur with or without a host nation or civilian-coalition governance.

11

Conclusions

- The core purpose of Special Forces is to accomplish Special Operations activities *through, with or by* indigenous populations. No unilateral activities.
- UW is the primary SF activity and it is only conducted *through, with or by* the indigenous population for the purpose of regime change.
- Unconventional warfare's only purpose is political victory.
- The military must understand and accept that UW is not a military operation, it is political.
- Unconventional warfare is political warfare conducted *through, with and by* indigenous populations to achieve a legitimate political solution and prevents the exposure of U.S. military except for those Special Forces soldiers that must be on the ground supporting, advising, directing the indigenous population effort.
- UW is total war to the indigenous population involved. Anything short of regime change will result in the genocide or enslavement of those involved in the UW effort against the regime.
- In UW, regime change is only the first phase. Victory is when the supported population has established a viable, safe, secure, functioning representative government.
- If we do not have the political leadership with the political will to pursue the continuation of the UW campaign for as long as it

may take, it is morally bankrupt to even begin a UW campaign.

- There is a moral and ethical imperative to unconventional warfare.
- The required premise for UW is ubiquitous, persistent, continuous engagement.
- Internal defense and development/foreign internal defense/counterinsurgency operations all must be interagency-led operations that must be planned for and be put into effect simultaneous with any unconventional warfare operation.
- Regional orientation and focus is imperative for Special Forces.
- Persistent and continuous forward presence/stationing is imperative for Special Forces
- UW is generational war and there is little room for cultural errors.
- Every move must be culturally integrated.
- Special Forces units must remain focused on their area of responsibility.
- Without this regional focus there is no viable *"through, with and by"* with indigenous populations that will support national objectives in a timely manner.
- Interagency coordination and collaboration remains problematic.
- The definition of Special Forces is very definitive.

The primary activities for Army Special Forces are UW and IDAD (FID and COIN). It is clear that unilateral DA, SR and CT are activities for Special Forces only *in-extremis*[139] conditions or only *through, with or by* indigenous personnel. Clearly, other SOF or conventional force elements are more appropriately tasked for these unilateral missions. UW and IDAD (FID and COIN) require intense focus and can be conducted only *through, with or by* the indigenous population if there is any hope or expectation of legitimacy of the action with the host population. Diversion of training time and resources to missions more properly performed by other elements dilutes and diminishes Special Forces primary capabilities.

---

139 Oxford Dictionary of the U.S. Military: *in-extremis*: term used to describe a situation of such exceptional urgency that immediate action must be taken to minimize imminent loss of life or catastrophic degradation of the political or military situation

"One enduring reason for the difficulty we have in balancing SOF direct and indirect approaches is lack of respect for how difficult the indirect approach is. Training foreign forces is not difficult. Working with foreign forces to achieve security objectives shared by their government and ours in ways that are consistent with U.S. interests and values is extremely hard. There has been a tendency for conventional force commanders to assume their forces can relieve SOF of its indirect activities, particularly training and working with foreign forces. Worse, some SOF commanders have agreed and shunned such missions in favor of direct action. When this happens, **both types of forces are saying they do not believe working "by, with and through" host nation forces requires special skills, which is incorrect**" (*emphasis added*). *(Testimony on Special Operations Forces, 11 July 2012, Christopher J. Lamb, Distinguished Research Fellow Center for Strategic Research, Institute for National Strategic Studies, National Defense University, House Committee on Armed Services Subcommittee on Emerging Threats and Capabilities)*

"So I think that what we need to start looking at, when I look at this list, is direct action, special reconnaissance, security force assistance, unconventional warfare, foreign internal defense, civil operations, operations, counter-terrorism, military information support operations, counter-proliferation of weapons of mass destruction, and information operations, I get exhausted just reading that list. And, you know, one thing that we're not talking about here, we still have this thing out there called sequestration.[140] So we really need to start looking at how do we take and narrowly focus these missions, because as one of the things we say in the military, **if everything's a priority, nothing's a priority. And so how do you properly train people on this litany of ten or so different tasks? You know, they're not going to be able to do it very well.**(*emphasis added*)" *Representative Allen B. West, R-FLA; CQ CONGRESSIONAL TRANSCRIPTS, Congressional Hearings; House Armed Services Subcommittee on Emerging Threats and Capabilities Holds Hearing on the Future of Special Operations Forces; July 11, 2012.*

---

140 In U.S. law, a procedure by which an automatic spending cut is triggered, introduced to the federal budget... most recently implemented in the Budget Control Act of 2011

Most importantly, keep the Special Forces units involved and engaged with indigenous populations outside the United States to open "windows" and help provide insight into ambiguous areas. This will assist with regional stability. The strength of Special Forces is in their cultural and regional focus.

To accomplish this, significantly increase priority for unconventional warfare and UW education and training. Ensure regional orientation and funding to sustain persistent, continuous presence in their respective regions. Give the active and National Guard Special Forces battalions clear areas (regions) of responsibility that remain fixed. It takes years and decades to cultivate an area and inculcate regional expertise. Special Forces cannot change language and region every few years and be expected to develop any significant degree of expertise or understanding of a region or to achieve cultural knowledge, credibility, legitimacy and trust of the indigenous population. Likewise, Special Forces cannot be uprooted from their area of regional focus and arbitrarily thrown into the conflict of the moment.

These regions must be carefully selected based on world dynamics and not based on current force structure. This means identify the regions and allocate (vice apportion) the units, then determine the headquarters structure at SF Group level. This will mean that different regions will have different mixes and numbers of allocated battalions and units.

Another key related issue is to up-rank SF; make group commanders brigadier generals (0-7s); battalion commanders' colonels (0-6s); Operational Detachment-B (ODB) commanders' lieutenant colonels (0-5s) and Operational Detachment-A (ODA) commanders' majors (0-4s). In operations involving SF, the actual number of personnel needed is relatively small, yet the requirement usually calls for an O-6. Likewise, ODBs as Advanced Operational Bases (AOBs) or Special Operations Command and Control Elements (SOCCEs) require higher ranking personnel. Furthermore, every non-commissioned officer (NCO) position on an ODA should be authorized up to E-8, which allows for retention of personnel and experience.

Increase SF manning of the major headquarters to reflect the percentage size of the force. Currently, of the personnel assigned to HQ USSOCOM, only a small percentage of these are SF qualified. It is not surprising that there is little attention on UW.

The real key to all the above is the command and control relationship. Special Forces are the force that is selected, assessed, trained, organized and equipped to globally engage on a continuous basis indigenous populations. SF is the only force that lives with, eats with, works with, and immerses long term (decades and for generations) in the culture of indigenous populations. Special Forces is the only U.S. entity that learns about and understands the cultural, political, economic and military environments of the indigenous population. At least, this is the proper use of Special Forces even if this is not fully happening now.

Therefore, in any area, the ground must be "owned," both metaphorically and operationally, by the SF element. No other element should enter that operational space without the knowledge of and coordination with the appropriate SF element. The actual SF operational element on the ground, be it a group, battalion, ODB or ODA, answers to the American Ambassador and should be his interagency coordinator for any and all activities, peace or war.

This is generational war and there is little room for cultural error. Every move must be culturally integrated. This is the salient issue. Of course, this opens the most controversial door of any operation or activity – command and control. Certainly a case can be made that any element that enters the SF element area, regardless of reason, is under the Command and Control (C2) of that SF element. It does not matter if it is a conventional military formation or JSOC or the CIA. The SF element "owns" the ground because they have been there, or should have been there, for years/decades. They are the only U.S. entity that truly understands the environment. The real solution to this situation is the reorganization and reactivation of the Office for Strategic Services, as a separate Cabinet – level organization comprised of Special Forces and the CIA.

The United States Army John F. Kennedy Special Warfare Center & School (USAJFKSWCS) is a world-class Army SOF training institution. The USAJFKSWCS has served with distinction the training needs of Army SOF (ARSOF) and the Department of Defense under different names and organizational structures in response to varying security requirements of the Cold War and post-Cold War.

If *tribal* memory and sentiment are to be relied upon, the Center's signature period came under its designation as the U.S. Army Special Warfare Center. Through its Military Advisory and Training Assistance (MATA) course(s), the school prepared literally thousands of officers and NCOs from all the Services, other government agencies and from many allied nations for advisory duty in Viet Nam during the 1960s. After the U.S. withdrawal from Viet Nam, our military all but erased advisory concepts and doctrine from its operational repertoire, especially when linked to counter insurgency efforts.

The new USA JFK Special Warfare Center and School, however, and the Special Forces operational groups, sustained the 'guerilla POI' and critical military advisory skills that ultimately turned the tide against a rebel takeover in El Salvador, and that ultimately pushed the Taliban out of Afghanistan *by, with and through* the Northern Alliance. These unconventional operations represent the majority of the few bright spots in U.S. security operations since the end of World War II.

In light of this infrequently-publicized distinction, and with a clear opportunity and need to nurture its demonstrated unconventional operations heritage, the USA JFK SWCS must make yet another transition in its journey to maturity. This time it must transcend into a world-class center of unconventional operations and advisory education and training, a center of knowledge and innovation to serve the security needs of America and her allies in the 21st century.

USAJFKSWCS should offer Special Forces and other ARSOF professionals, and selected interagency counterparts, an educational and training framework that permits professional educational growth beginning at the entry (tactical) level through the strategic levels of unconventional and advisory operational art, combining academic inquiry with field application.

Degree-granting programs, certifications and occupational specialties, both civilian and military, offered in-house, on-line and in collaboration with an array of academic institutions (MIT, Harvard, University of Wales, Johns Hopkins, Brown, Columbia, National Defense University, etc.) will produce well-rounded tactical, operational and strategic thinkers prepared to conceptualize, plan and apply the elements of national power (diplomacy, information, military, economic) to achieve country or regional security conditions that will produce the prosperity and freedoms that characterize stable states. MIT and the University of Wales offered tailored doctoral programs for Special Forces officers. This program would have tailored for each particular enrollee a specific program tailored to their job requirements, monitored by full professors from MIT and Wales, online, that would be completed in 2 to 2 ½ years. This was offered in 2011 and much to my chagrin, was totally rebuffed without investigation by the commander, USAJFKSWCS.

The school should be led and staffed by distinguished academic, military and administrative persons, who engage in conceptual and doctrinal development, experiment with and examine concepts and force configuration excursions, and who will teach and mentor emerging leaders as they track through their professional education programs over the course of their unconventional warfare and operational careers.

Additionally, USAJFKSWCS could be the National and International Center for Academic and Professional Excellence for Unconventional Warfare, sponsoring and hosting seminars, forums, conferences and war games. USAJFKSWCS could be the National Integration Center for Unconventional Operations and The Interagency Process.

The school could offer the regional and functional commands, as well as other government agencies, a venue for examining lessons learned, for developing remedial approaches, and to formulating mid-and long-term strategies to achieving national security objectives in a forum that brings together proven operators from across the interagency. The school could serve to centrally shape, manage and over-watch the doctrine, organization, training, material, leadership, personnel and facilities (DOTML-PF) sustainment programs of ARSOF, and of those forces in support of unconventional warfare.

The advantages of this enterprise effort are obvious. The United States gains regional experts with on-the-ground experience, able to help obviate Huntington's "jungle-like world of multiple dangers, hidden traps, unpleasant surprises and moral ambiguities." Additionally, this provides for mutual trust and understanding through personal and sustained contact with regional personalities. This is easily the most important outcome of the long-term regional orientation.

In most of the developing nations, personal relationships are the key to trust and understanding. SF can develop these relationships and facilitate the critical interface between coalition forces in a conflict. SF, sufficiently resourced, can maintain a persistent forward presence that can reassure nervous nations and increase regional stability. Furthermore, in the event of an incident or even conflict, these elements then provide a ready source of first-hand regional expertise.

UW and IDAD (FID and COIN) provide the most realistic option for the uncertain future. The incredible expenditure of national treasure, both in the lives of our sons and daughters and in the tax burden on our citizens, does not have to be repeated short of a global conflict. Although not risk free nor free, Special Forces, conducting UW and IDAD (FID and COIN), fully supported by the other SOF elements, the conventional forces and the full range of interagency participants, with patience and understanding of the generational aspects of unconventional operations, can foster democracy and enhance the probability of legitimate, sustainable results.

Annex A: Case Examples

The below listed case examples highlight the problem with the United States not having a committed strategy that transcends elections and new administrations. Of course, the valid argument is that elections have consequences and reflect the changing will of the people. This is true. However, this does not excuse the politicians and the media from clearly representing the moral and ethical obligations of the nation. Of course, this could have an impact on electability and self-serving politicians will never attempt to place such a moral obligation in front of an electorate. I continue to believe that, if properly and honestly informed, the American people are better than this. These examples, unfortunately, show our failure as a nation to be moral and ethical. I pray in the future we will do better.

Title	Page
Major Jim Gant and Afghanistan	131
Lawrence of Arabia in World War II	134
Special Forces with the Montagnards in Vietnam	136
Captain Douglas A. Livermore's article *"Broken Valor"*	143
The Non-Burman Ethnic Peoples in Burma (Myanmar)	150

Case Example of Major Jim Gant

Major Jim Gant truly understood UW and "through, with and by" and he lived it …and was crucified by the U.S. Army and abandoned by the SF leadership (who bowed to the conventional military and political regime) for being successful because these leadership entities were "politically correct" and were either professionally compromised or intellectually unable to support substance over form…they insisted on having omelets without breaking any eggs. Of course, UW and what it takes to be successful remains misunderstood by many, if not most. Gant and some others did understand, and paid for it and were sacrificed on the altar of political correctness. My definition of "political correctness" is moral cowardice. Reflectively, many just don't recognize that "slippery slope."

'American Spartan' by Ann Scott Tyson, about Maj. Jim Gant's mission in Afghanistan

By Bing West, Published: March 28 2014 (reprinted by permission of the author)

Bing West, a former assistant secretary of defense and combat Marine grunt, is the author of the classic about advisers in Vietnam, "The Village," and five books about the wars in Iraq and Afghanistan.

Wearing jeans, a jacket and a baseball cap, the full-bearded man looked at the apprehensive young soldiers fresh from Kansas. In a few hours, he would lead them into an Afghan village where they would live and fight for a year. He wanted to motivate them.

"Who am I? I am a warrior," Special Forces Maj. Jim Gant said by way of introduction. "If you want to kill, you must be willing to die. I am willing to do both. …"

"I love my men as I love my own children. … What you are going to do is not okay. It's not fun, it's not safe, it's highly stressful. I do not expect all of you to make it home."

Welcome to "American Spartan," the "Catch-22" of the Afghanistan war, a mixture of romanticism, fantasy and hard-core dedication. Gant is a real-life character. The author, Ann Scott Tyson, a former Washington Post reporter, is his wife. She has woven together four tales: an over-the-top adventure, a delusional military strategy, a love story and a failure of organizational leadership.

First, the sheer adventure. Gant is a mountain man, circa 1840. He is Jeremiah Johnson, living in the wrong century. Despite his heavy drinking, volcanic mood swings and numerous wounds, he survived more than 40 months of combat. In 2003 and again in 2011, he and a dozen Special Forces soldiers lived in a mountain village in eastern Afghanistan, adjacent to the Pakistan border. When I visited that village, both the elders and the soldiers from the 1st Battalion of the 32nd Infantry told tales about Gant's exploits. He captured one insurgent after a two-day chase. Another time, he drove into the center of the deadly Korengal Valley and fought his way out.

Adopted by a Pashtun tribe, Gant's team, called the Spartans, set up an intelligence net, with drop points for agents to hide letters for team members. The tribesmen led the Spartans into the mountains, pointing out paths the Taliban fighters used and hamlets that sheltered them. In a dozen clandestine operations, not once was a hide site compromised. Inside the village, the Spartans played volleyball, provided medical supplies and wrote to their families to collect enough money to build a girls' school. Reacting immediately to tip-offs, they kept the Taliban off balance and prevented al-Qaeda terrorists from returning to a 10-mile swath of eastern Afghanistan. A remarkable small-unit accomplishment, but tiny compared with the 1,500-mile border along the Pakistani sanctuary.

Second, the delusional strategy. Gant's deep affection for Pashtun tribal ways came to the attention of the top command. Four-star Generals. Stanley McChrystal in 2009, David Petraeus in 2010, and John Allen in 2011 fervently believed that nation-building was a military objective, despite President Obama's disbelief in the mission and the treachery of Afghan President Hamid Karzai. So the generals tapped Gant in 2011 to demonstrate that Special Forces teams could train tribesmen to defend their villages.

When Gant succeeded in one village, Petraeus asked him how to connect such village militias to the serpentine government in Kabul. Gant responded, "It cannot be done." Our best and brightest generals were pursuing an impossible strategy, having taken the wrong lesson from Iraq. There, seeking protection against both Sunni Islamists and the Shiite government in Baghdad, in 2006-2007 the Sunni tribes came over to the American side.

In Afghanistan, however, the 10 million members of the Pashtun tribes never came over to the American side. In Iraq, one religious sect fought the other; in Afghanistan, it was one sub-tribe against another. Gant's village rejected the Taliban. But ten miles up the road, the villagers of Ganjgal, loyal to the Taliban, ambushed Afghan soldiers in a battle that resulted in two Medals of Honor. Our generals dispersed a few hundred platoons and teams like Gant's among 5,000 villages in 400 districts, hoping to knit together fractious Pashtun tribes from the bottom up. The arithmetic did not add up. There were too few American units. In any case, Karzai was sabotaging the effort, preferring to rule by cronyism.

Third, the love story. Gant took his private war to a legendary level. After he and reporter Ann Scott Tyson fell in love, she sneaked into the Pashtun village to live with him and his team. Don't try to count how many journalism and military rules the two of them broke. By way of partial redemption, Tyson has a sharp and sentimental eye. Read this book to savor the rich, candid details of love between a man and a woman, between Afghan and American comrades in battle, and between two cultures. Her incisive description of Pashtun ways explains why generals such as Petraeus believed that our military could build a nation.

For a year, Tyson lived in the village, her presence known by word of mouth to the Taliban, to many American soldiers and to thousands of Pashtuns. Obviously, our intelligence system is not designed to track tribal dynamics at the district level. Thus we cannot predict the multitude of accommodations among Afghan soldiers, the Taliban and the tribes that will occur once we depart.

Fourth, the failure of organizational leadership. The higher command had no inkling of Tyson's presence and Gant's unorthodox methods. Tyson depicts the colonels above Gant as paper-shufflers who never stayed overnight in a village. Gant's men were devoted to him, the enemy was fearful, and the Pashtun community was obedient. Our generals compared him to Lawrence of Arabia, the ascetic English officer who fought alongside Saudi tribesmen.

But by bringing Tyson into the village, he ran terrible risks for his team. Had she been pinned down in a firefight, every soldier would have rushed forward to save her. Gant was not betrayed, as the book's subtitle suggests; he went too far.

Eventually, the high command terminated Gant's career and those of two other superb Special Forces officers who agreed with his values: Matt Golsteyn and Dan McKone. We Americans admire our Green Berets because men like Gant, Golsteyn and McKone live among the tribes and challenge our Islamist enemies to do battle over basic ideals. Their seniors should mentor them and direct their enthusiastic efforts. Regrettably, the Special Forces command did not address the lack of leadership by the colonels who failed to guide junior leaders such as Gant and his comrades.

Army and Marine grunts tried; they toiled without complaint at their Sisyphean task. They fought and died for the Afghans, but they couldn't substitute for the lack of Afghan leadership. At one point, Gant told his team: "We will never win in Afghanistan. ... It gives us a place to go and be warriors."

Many — probably most — of our grunts hold that view; they are our guardians, regardless of the folly of the mission. They fight because they are warriors, not because naive generals believe that American soldiers can persuade Afghan tribes to fight for a punk government.

One general wrote that Gant lived in "a fantasy world." That is true. But the generals placed him there without providing mature leadership to guide him. The combination of the warrior spirit and a fabulist strategy created this tale of daffy devotion. According to his wife, "Jim had become more Pashtun than the Pashtuns." He tried to be the leader the Pashtuns didn't have.

Our overall strategy failed because we lacked sufficient control over the feckless Afghan leaders we placed in power. It's a wonder the exuberant Gant didn't lead a coup attempt against Karzai. Fortunately, his excessive risk-taking and unbridled devotion did not end in tragedy.

"Catch-22" was a satirical novel, sprinkled with gritty vignettes of real combat during World War II. "American Spartan" is the real-life story of living a fantasy, sprinkled with allusions to an impossibly ambitious strategy.

Case Example of T. E. Lawrence of Arabia.

Lawrence of Arabia

Thomas Edward (T.E.) Lawrence is best known for the work he did in the Middle East during World War I. Lawrence gained great status with the Arabs. Lawrence certainly was not an imposing figure. He stood barely 5'5" and almost did not get into the British Army.

To set the stage, Lawrence was a very good student and at Oxford University he graduated with high honors. A very inquisitive individual, from 1911-14 he joined an archeology expedition to excavate a 2400 year old B.C.E. site in Syria known as Carchemish or Karkemish[141]. He found that he had a natural affinity with the Arab people whom he met and he learned their language, customs and history.

When war (World War I) was declared in August 1914, Lawrence tried to join the army but was initially turned down because he was too short. The minimum height was five feet five inches, and as Lawrence was just at 5' 5", he was initially refused. He was persistent and eventually joined the intelligence branch of the British general staff. His knowledge of Arabic and Arabs was fairly unique and led to an assignment in Egypt where he served in the Arab Bureau at the main British headquarters. Very independent and unpretentious, he carelessly ignored the British Army protocol for smartness of uniform and was seen as an able but unkempt junior officer.

On the battlefront, the British military campaign in the Middle East had not started well and on the 5th of June 1916, the Arab Revolt, also known as the Arab Awakening, started. The purpose of the revolt was Arab independence from the Ottoman Turks and to create a unified Arab state from the Mediterranean to the Gulf of Aden and the Arabian Sea. The revolt had some initial successes, but soon lost its original impetus. With the Turks as a common enemy, the Arabs and the British

---

141 Carchemish also spelled Karkemish was an important ancient capital which at times was independent but also having been part of the Mitanni, Hittite and Neo Assyrian Empires, and is located on what is now the frontier between Turkey and Syria.

and French made an alliance with Grand Sherif Hussein, ruler of the Hejaz and Guardian of the Holy City of Mecca. In October 1916, the British investigated the revolt and one of these investigating officers was Lawrence.

Lawrence was sent to meet the Amir Feisal, the son of Grand Sherif Hussein. Feisal and Lawrence developed an immediate rapport. Feisal's men were keen fighters but were very ill-disciplined. Lawrence saw their potential but also realized that Feisal's men had no chance of capturing their target, Medina. The Turks controlled the rail line and would always have the opportunity to supply Medina. Lawrence believed that Feisal's best chance lay in guerilla warfare against the rail line but away from Medina. Lawrence did not want to destroy the Medina to Damascus line as it would be needed by the allies. His goal was to harass the Turks along the route so that they would have to use more and more troops to guard it.

As Allenby[142] had hoped, more and more Arab tribesmen joined the revolt as it became more successful. Allenby was quite happy for Lawrence to wear Arab dress - something other British officers could not tolerate. Eventually, Feisal and the Arabs entered Damascus in triumph and he and Lawrence took charge of civil and military order for several weeks. At the end of October, 1918, an armistice was concluded with the Turks.

Lawrence lived among those Arabs who fought the Turks. He lived the life of a Bedouin, always doing more than those with whom he fought - riding his camel further, pushing his body harder. He ate what they ate which led to a number of debilitating stomach ailments. But by doing this, he earned the respect of those who fought with him.

Lawrence and Feisal had a force of 3,000 Arabs that tied down 50,000 Turks who could not help their comrades against Allenby. The Turkish High Command also spread their forces (150,000 men in total) thinly across the region making the British campaign that much easier.

---

142 Field Marshal Edmund Allenby, 1st Viscount Allenby, commander of the Egyptian Expeditionary Force.

"To the student of war, the whole Arab campaign provides a remarkable illustration of the extraordinary results which can be achieved by mobile guerilla tactics. For the Arabs detained tens of thousands of regular Turkish troops with a force barely capable of engaging a brigade of infantry in a pitched battle." Lieutenant-General Sir John Bagot Glubb (KCB, CMG, DSO, OBE, MC (16 April 1897, Preston, Lancashire – 17 March 1986), known as Glubb Pasha, was a British soldier, scholar and author, who led and trained Transjordan's Arab Legion between 1939 and 1956 as its commanding general)

Alas, once more, those who earned the victory had it hijacked. The British and French reneged on their promise of Arab independence and divided up the geography in accordance with the 1916 Sykes-Picot Agreement and the Balfour Declaration of 1917 to the detriment of the Arab allies. Lawrence always felt he had failed and betrayed the Arabs because of this deceit.

In 1935 Lawrence crashed his motor bike and died. He was 45 years old.

Lawrence was one of the first "modern" era military officers to embrace *"through, with, and by."* Fortunately, Allenby supported him. Although this was an overt operation, the British kept pictures of him out of circulation which provided cover for him so that the Turks did not know what he looked like even though they had a bounty on his head.

Seven Pillars of Wisdom provides a classic study of unconventional warfare. You can trace all seven phases (see Annex K: UW Briefing). You can also see that the insurgents did not survive their victory.

Case Example of Special Forces and the Montagnards

The Montagnards

From Raleigh Bailey, *The Montagnards: Their History and Culture.* (Washington, D.C.: Center for Applied Linguistics, 2002). Used with permission.

The first group of Montagnard refugees were mostly men who had fought with the Americans in Vietnam, but there were a few women and children in the group as well. The refugees were resettled in Raleigh, Greensboro, and Charlotte, North Carolina, because of the number of Special Forces veterans living in the area[143], the supportive business climate with numerous entry-level job opportunities, and a terrain and climate similar to what the refugees had known in their home environment. To ease the impact of resettlement, the refugees were divided into three groups, roughly by tribe, with each group resettled in one city. Beginning in 1987, the population began to grow slowly as additional Montagnards were resettled in the state. Most arrived through family reunification and the Orderly Departure Program. Some were resettled through special initiatives, such as the program for reeducation camp detainees, developed through negotiations between the U.S. and Vietnamese governments. A few others came through a special Amerasian project that included

---

143 Special Forces Major (Retired) Mike Linnane, my good friend, was instrumental in the initiation and success of this resettlement program and is personally responsible for the program's success in the Greensboro area.

Montagnard youth whose mothers were Montagnard and whose fathers were American.

In December 1992, a group of 402 Montagnards were found by a UN force responsible for the Cambodian border provinces of Mondolkiri and Ratanakiri. Given the choice to return to Vietnam or be interviewed for resettlement in the United States, the group chose resettlement. They were processed and resettled with very little advance notice in the three North Carolina cities. The group included 269 males, 24 females, and 80 children.

Through the 1990s, the Montagnard population in the United States continued to grow as new family members arrived and more reeducation camp detainees were released by the Vietnamese government. A few families settled in other states, notably California, Florida, Massachusetts, Rhode Island, and Washington, but by far North Carolina was the preferred choice for the Montagnards. By 2000, the Montagnard population in North Carolina had grown to around 3,000, with almost 2,000 in the Greensboro area, 700 in the Charlotte area, and 400 in the Raleigh area. North Carolina had become host to the largest Montagnard community outside of Vietnam.

In February 2001, Montagnards in Vietnam's Central Highlands staged demonstrations relating to their freedom to worship at local Montagnard churches. The government's harsh response caused nearly 1,000 villagers to flee into Cambodia, where they sought sanctuary in the jungle highlands. The Vietnamese pursued the villagers into Cambodia, attacking them and forcing some to return to Vietnam. The United Nations High Commission for Refugees granted refugee status to the remaining villagers, most of whom did not want to be repatriated.

In the summer of 2002, close to 900 Montagnard villagers were resettled as refugees in the three North Carolina resettlement sites of Raleigh, Greensboro, and Charlotte, as well as in a new resettlement site, New Bern. The new population of Montagnards, like previous groups, is predominantly male, many of them having left wives and children behind in their haste to escape and with the expectation that they could return to their villages. A few intact families are being resettled.

How have the Montagnard newcomers fared? For the most part, those who came before 1986 adjusted quite well given their backgrounds — war injuries, a decade without health care, and little or no formal education — and given the absence of an established Montagnard community in the United States into which they could integrate. Their traditional friendliness, openness, strong work ethic, humility, and religious beliefs have served them well in their adjustment to the United States. The Montagnards rarely complain about their conditions or problems, and their humility and stoicism have impressed many Americans.

Among those who came between 1986 and 2000, able-bodied adults found jobs within a few months and families moved toward a low-income level of self sufficiency. Montagnard language churches were formed and some people joined mainstream churches. A group of recognized Montagnard leaders, representing the three cities and various tribal groups organized a mutual assistance association, the Montagnard Dega Association to help with resettlement, maintain cultural traditions, and assist with communication.

The adjustment process has been more difficult for the 2002 arrivals. This group had relatively little overseas cultural orientation to prepare them for life in the United States, and they bring with them a great deal of confusion and fear of persecution. Many did not plan to come as refugees; some had been misled into believing that they were coming to the United States to be part of a resistance movement. Moreover, the 2002 arrivals do not have political or family ties with the existing Montagnard communities in the United States since they come from villages and tribes that were not part of the earlier resistance movement.

The Fate of the Montagnards...

Posted By Blackfive • *www.**blackfive**.net/main/2008/07/the-**fate**-of-the.
html; www.**blackfive**.net/main/2008/07/page/2/*[144]*

[July 30, 2008]

Here's a story about the fate of the Montagnards...and how a few retired
Special Forces soldiers helped them:

Veterans Assist Indigenous Survivors

Story by Pfc. Benjamin Watson Posted on 07.30.2008 at 11:46AM

In 1986, several hundred natives of Vietnam, called either DeGas or
Montagnards, and their families, were relocated to the United States as
refugees. In the latter part of 1992, close to 400 additional DeGas were
granted asylum in the United States and were resettled in North Carolina,
particularly in Greensboro, Raleigh, Charlotte and Asheboro. Were it not
for the involvement of retired U.S. Army Special Forces soldiers, it is
unlikely that the Montagnard people would have ever gotten to the U.S.

When the leaders of the Montagnards were brought to the U.S., they
were asked where they wanted to settle, according to retired U.S. Army
Special Forces Master Sgt. George Clark, who today is President of Save
The Montagnard People, Inc. The Montagnards were offered land in
Florida and Louisiana, but were uninterested. The Montagnards reply,
said Clark, was that "'we've got to be close to the Special Forces. They
grew up with us, we grew up with them.' That's why they're in North
Carolina."

In 1975 there were seven million Montagnards living, said Clark. Today
there are approximately 600,000. "I got involved with these folks way
back in the sixties," said Clark, "I spent a lot of time with them in
Vietnam. I stayed with them from '67 through '70. April Fool's Day
1970, I got made a fool of: I found out what an [AK-47 rifle] felt like.

---

144   Any email(s) sent to Blackfive@gmail.com will be considered in the public domain with free use granted
      for publication in any media or form.

When I got shot up, Montagnards jumped on my body to keep me from taking any more hits…How do you pay that back?"

"The Montagnards do not forget how the Americans helped them," said retired Major General Khambang Sibounheuang, a former Royal Laotian Army commando, and himself a Montagnard from Laos. Sibounheuang addressed Montagnard languages—which vary according to region — as well as Montagnard history and family dynamics, before getting into the tragic fate DeGas face still today. "They're a very unique people, much like the Native Americans," said Clark. "These are small population people that originally came from the Polynesian Islands. They're from Mayo-Polynesia. They're not Oriental people. They were sea-farers, they lived in the flatlands. They got driven to the high country."

A number of factors contribute to the ongoing plight of the Montagnard population. Chief among these is the Vietnamese government's position that the Montagnard's Christian way of life represents a threat to national unity. Because the Vietnamese government prohibits open expression of political dissent, and because the practice of Christianity is categorized as dissent, there are few outlets for Montagnard grievances. Additionally, according the U.S. State Department, there are few lawyers in Vietnam and trial procedures are rudimentary at best. "If you ask the Montagnards, they say, 'We just want peace. We just want to co-exist,'" said Clark. They want to live in their own villages, raise their own chickens and eat their own food. That's all they're asking for, Clark said.

Seated behind a desk in a small room in downtown Greensboro, N.C., is a calm and not entirely tall man with dark, combed hair who was born in the Central Highlands of Vietnam. He is a man who chooses his words with obvious care, a middle-aged man who spends much time feeling out each thought in his native tongue before spelling them out in English. He is Y Siu Hlong, and he is among the earliest of Montagnards to set foot on American soil in 1986.

His people— a native cluster of minority tribes collectively called the Montagnards, or Degas — had by this time been attempting to evade ethnic cleansing for eleven years. "When I first arrived at the airport," said Hlong about coming to the U.S. with the help of Americans in Thailand in the eighties, "I was crying. I didn't know how life in the United States was going to be, and what kind of food we're going to eat. We thought, 'In the United States we won't have bamboo shoots, we won't have rice, we won't have anything. Maybe we'll just eat bread,'" he says with a kind of sadness to his laughter afterwards.

Upon arriving in the states with the assistance of former U.S. Army Special Forces Soldiers, Hlong wasted no time doing his part to assist in the broader Montagnard cause. In 1986, Hlong began work with the Montagnard/Dega Association, Inc., in downtown Greensboro. "We think back to our brothers and sisters still left behind in the jungle" because, he explains, many stayed behind to continue defending their land after time and again being brutally oppressed by nationalist military forces in the region. Today, he is the executive director and caseworker coordinator for the Montagnard/Dega Association, Inc.

Hlong stands up and pulls a box down off the shelf. It overflows with faxes his office has received in response to the many relocation requests he plays a role in submitting to the United Nations. It is the process of relocating Montagnards that seems to weigh most heavily on Hlong's mind today. What makes this process difficult is that each Montagnard tribe's dialect is different from the others — there is no one Montagnard tongue. Therefore, Hlong says, finding the correct translator for each applicant can make or break the process of relocating Degas from Vietnam, Laos or Cambodia to the U.S. All of the faxes are rejection notifications. He pulls one off the top and puts on his glasses and inspects the pages closely. "This guy was put in jail for five years in a camp in Dak Lak province. But the way [translators] wrote it up here is different... All these people were put in jail. That's why they escaped to Cambodia, where many of them remain still today," he said and added, "often, these refugees will wait an interminably long period of time — many until death — in conditions of temporary shelter and unstable food supply simply for a chance to be reunited with the Degas who have been delivered before them."

It is a sobering job Hlong has. But for him, like former Royal Laotian Army Commando Major General Khambang Sibounheuang, it is something that has to be done. General K.B., as he is called, is an exuberant and expansive third-generation Montagnard who assisted U.S. forces in what has since been called the Shadow War in Laos during the sixties and early seventies.

Sibounheuang met the American who would guide him to the U.S. while helping dig up four, 750-pound live bombs, some buried twenty feet in the Laotian mud and dirt. The Americans he met were in the country as part of the United States Agency for Internal Development's Rural Development Program, providing aid to devastated cities such as Phalane, Laos, Sibounheuang explained. It was this group of USAID workers that was able to get Sibounheuang out of the country in late 1975. Because by 1974, soldiers of the former Royal Laotian Army, Sibounheuang among them, found that their lives were in certain danger.

"We really had nowhere to go. We didn't know that the following year the U.S. would allow Laotians who could prove they worked with the American government to immigrate to the United States. Back in 1974, we couldn't conceive of being allowed to go to America. Our only choice was to stay, or flee to Thailand." And Thailand is the point where Sibounheuang and his wife, with the help of USAID worker, John Tucker, boarded a Boeing 747 for America.

The jet was huge, says Sibounheuang. "I couldn't take my eyes off it. Once inside, it was like another world. It seemed fitting that such a large and comfortable aircraft should take us to America." Their destination: Murfreesboro, Tennessee. John had picked Tennessee, explains Sibounheuang, because his hometown was Tullahoma, Tennessee, and because he said the climate and geography reminded him of Laos.

Sibounheuang, like Hlong, got right to the business of helping fellow Laotians and Montagnards still struggling in the jungles and refugee camps. He sent money he had saved while working in Tennessee as a patrol security officer to Thailand to assist in the cause. Today, Sibounheuang heads the International Relief Center, Inc., a foundation based out of Nashville, whose mission it is to build and improve schools and clinics in Laos and Cambodia.

Many Royal Laotian officers, says Sibounheuang, fled the cities of Laos in the mid-seventies to either Thailand or to take part in a guerrilla movement in the mountains. Some spent years waiting in refugee camps before being allowed to immigrate to a safer place than Laos. Thousands of refugees, non-officers and civilians are still waiting in Thai refugee camps still today, says Sibounheuang.

Shortly after the events of Sept. 11, a battalion of former soldiers originally from the Central Highlands of Vietnam, Laos and Cambodia, volunteered for the U.S. military engagement in Afghanistan. They wanted no pay. All they asked was for transportation to the region, ammunition and one final condition: that their battalion takes the place of an equal number of American soldiers. The request was declined, according to Sam Todaro, who is on the Board of Directors for Save the Montagnard People, Inc., an organization established to save and assist Montagnards living today.

This gesture, explained Sam, is emblematic of the loyalty and worth of the Montagnard people, a people who nowadays live and work for the most part in North Carolina. "These former U.S. allies add value economically, culturally and socially to our state," said Pat Priest, director of the Lutheran Family Services in the Carolinas refugee resettlement program. "In fact, we have been constantly amazed at their ability to gain self-sufficiency sooner than most other groups of refugees." Their strong work ethic has been a boon to many local businesses.

"I have the privilege of working with about fifty Montagnards every day," wrote R. Michael Nussbaum, president of Southern Foods in Greensboro, N.C. "They are such wonderful people...hard working, polite, happy and so very dedicated to what they do." Take H'Juel Ya, for example. H'Juel, 19, was born in the Cambodian jungle to parents who had, by the time of her birth, spent 15 years setting up and tearing down camp along the Central Highlands of Vietnam and Cambodia. Many Montagnards had little choice but to remain, essentially, on the run for their lives in an effort to evade capture and placement in reeducation camps, or prisons. With a price of one unit of gold on their heads when captured by local national armed forces, Montagnards were then, and remain today, a sought after commodity.

But H'Juel, like Clark, knows Montagnards are much more than simply a sum of money. H'Juel Ya volunteers her available afternoons to working with Y'Siu Hlong's Montagnard/Dega Association, Inc., in Greensboro, N.C. When not volunteering with the Montagnard community, H'Juel works part-time as a waitress and full-time attending college in Greensboro. Her intention is to major in international business affairs, with a minor in Spanish. "At the age of 40," she said, "I'd like to be a business owner." When asked what kind of business she would like to own, H'Juel said owning an innovative restaurant is something she could see herself enjoying. For H'Juel, however, age 40 won't be getting here any time soon.

In the meantime, she assists Y'Siu's organization with events such as last month's Montagnard forum at Moon Hall Conference center on May 15. H'Juel translated aloud a Montagnard declaration written and voiced initially in the native language by Y'Siu Hlong. Y'Siu was among the Montagnards who volunteered to assist U.S. forces in Afghanistan in 2001. "There are 177 Montagnards in uniform today," said Clark. "Out of a population of 600,000 [Montagnards worldwide], that's one of the biggest percentages of any ethnic group serving in the U.S. armed forces. According to Clark, there are 27 Montagnards in Iraq right now fighting. Four of them are on their third tour.

"They're good enough to fight for us," he said, "beside our brother soldiers and marines. Aren't they good enough for us to save their families?" There's nothing quite like seeing Montagnard children arrive in the U.S., confessed Clark. "Imagine a child that's never had a Christmas present, never seen a television, never heard of air-conditioning or seen a refrigerator. And you come in and introduce them to all that at one time."

Broken Faith: How Failures to Honor Commitments with Past Indigenous Allies Threatens Future Combat Operations

By Captain Douglas A. Livermore

(Reprinted with the author's permission)

In the second half of the 20th Century the United States military has been increasingly reliant upon indigenous forces to fight its wars. With a relatively small standing army, the U.S. has been forced to field fewer numbers of its own troops, requiring that the majority of responsibility be placed on local personnel. Understandably, this places considerable risk on these indigenous allies, who are left to deal with the repercussions when U.S. forces eventually leave their country. And, as the masters of combat operations waged "by, with, and through" indigenous forces, U.S. Army Special Forces have always found themselves at the forefront of these operations. Be it working with tribal warriors deep in some unforgiving jungle or kicking down doors with local commando forces in some Central Asian city, Special Forces invariably form close bonds with these indigenous troops. Unfortunately, the U.S., as a whole, has often failed to keep faith with its local allies once its troops have redeployed, and these brave comrades have paid the price. This has been the case when the U.S. withdrew its combat troops from Vietnam, Iraq, and soon, Afghanistan. Informed by these shameful examples from the past, it is imperative that we make every effort to support our indigenous allies so as to ensure our future successes.

U.S. Army Special Forces forged a particularly close association with the Montagnard people of the Vietnamese Central Highlands. This group, also known as the "Degar" people, had historically been discriminated against by the more numerous, urban dwelling ethnic groups of Vietnam. The Montagnards were actually a group of many tribes rather than a singular ethnic group. Even among the Montagnards, there are significant linguistic and cultural differences, though most tribes shared far more in common with each other than with other Vietnamese groups. Tribes would frequently migrate once the soil and game in a particular area was depleted, though tribes usually remained in their own regions.

Montagnard religion was primarily animist, though each tribe usually had a designated "god" and health concerns were addressed by a tribal sha-man ("medicine man"). The Montagnards were originally forced out of the more fertile coastal lowlands of southern Vietnam by invading groups from Cambodia prior to the ninth century A.D, moving into the iso-lated and rugged Central Highlands. In the Highlands, the Montagnards practiced relatively primitive forms of agriculture and hunting, and their society clung fervently to its beliefs and cultural identity. As a result, most Vietnamese referred to the Montagnards as *moi*, a pejorative term mean-ing "savage".

The Degar derived their more common name, *Montagnards*, from the colonial French. By the time the French colonized Vietnam and solidi-fied their claims in the late nineteenth century, the Montagnards had truly come into their own as "the mountain people" in French. While the Montagnards were generally shunned during times of peace, their presence in the strategic Central Highlands often made them valuable allies during conflicts. The *Viet Minh,* led by the charismatic Ho Chi Minh, had vehemently opposed foreign occupation of Vietnam since before the Japanese presence during World War II. During WWII, the *Viet Minh* minimally resisted the Japanese, preferring instead to marshal its forces to attack other resistance groups and to eventually fight the French. Members of the U.S. Office of Strategic Services, precursor of both the Central Intelligence Agency and U.S. Army Special Forces, had deployed a team to join up with Ho Chi Minh in 1945. Operational effects were extremely limited and the U.S. failed to respond to any of Ho Chi Minh's requests for international recognition of Vietnam's inde-pendence following WWII. During the subsequent French Indochina War, both the *Viet Minh* and French courted the Montagnards and tribal forces fought bravely on both sides of the conflict. French troops and their allies desperately opposed the *Viet Minh* but were ultimately unable to stem the tide of the popular, indigenous insurgency.

France ceded its claim to Indochina after the crushing defeat of its forces in 1954 at Dien Bien Phu, and the subsequent Geneva Convention parti-tioned Vietnam into a Communist North Vietnam and a Western-aligned South Vietnam. While France agreed on a general election to be held in

1956 which would decide upon the reunification of Vietnam, neither the U.S. nor the South Vietnamese military regime of Ngo Dinh Diem agreed to those terms. The Geneva Convention established the dividing line between the two countries at the 17th Parallel, and each side settled in for a protracted conflict. *Viet Minh* elements that found themselves south of the border were rebranded as *Viet Cong* but continued guerrilla warfare operations against the military regime in its new capital, Saigon. Western fears were that the Communist, who were incredibly popular in most parts of Vietnam given their recent victory over the French, would continue to strengthen relations with the Soviet Union and China. U.S. foreign policy was, therefore, heavily influenced by the "domino theory" that held that much of Southeast Asia would be "lost" to Communism if South Vietnam was allowed to fall.

Almost immediately, the Americans recognized the importance of mobilizing disaffected minority groups, such as the Montagnards, to defend South Vietnam from Communist aggression emanating out of Hanoi, the new capital of North Vietnam. However, the South Vietnamese were far less enthusiastic about any effort to engage with or enable the Montagnard people. The Diem government largely ignored the Montagnards and the Central Highlands, blocking participation by the Montagnards in the government and supporting the encroachment of ethnic Vietnamese into Montagnard tribal lands starting in 1954. Some 80,000 Vietnamese refugees from North Vietnam were resettled in the Central Highlands, and the Saigon government made no concessions to the Montagnards who were displaced.

Tensions simmered until 1958, when a peaceful Montagnard protest was attacked by authorities, resulting in several casualties. Diem's government ordered the seizure of crossbows and spears from the Montagnards, a move that only further angered them and increased disillusionment. U.S. advisors continued to push Saigon to be more inclusive with the Montagnards and organize them to resist *Viet Cong* incursions into the Central Highlands. As a completely ungoverned space, the South Vietnamese government had no idea what was actually happening in the Central Highlands, though U.S. intelligence made it abundantly clear that the Communists were bombarding the Montagnards with propaganda and

U.S. SPECIAL FORCES
DEPLOYMENT
1 June 1963

O   A detachments
●   B detachments
★   Special Forces Headquarters

25   0   100 MILES
25   0   100 KILOMETERS

undertaking efforts to win them over to the cause of Vietnamese unification under Communist control.

In 1961, the South Vietnamese finally agreed to allow U.S. Army Special Forces advisors, with their South Vietnamese Special Forces counterparts, to approach the elders of the Rhade tribe of the village of Buon Enao in Darlac Province of the Central Highlands. The Rhade tribe was one of the largest and most influential members of the Montagnard community, and the U.S. military mission hoped that they could be convinced to participate in a village defense program that it had pushed the South Vietnamese to form as a counter to the increasingly-successful *Viet Cong* campaign. The Rhade elders, when approached by American Special Forces troops offering weapons, equipment, training, and support facilities, agreed to join the fight against Communist aggression. This first project, known as the "Buon Enao Experiment", proved wildly successful, as the expansion of the program throughout Darlac Province resulted in the province being declared "secure" by the end of 1962. At that time, there were some 43,000 Montagnards in village defense groups and another 18,000 capable of conducting air mobile offensive operations outside the province.

Once initiated, the program rapidly expanded, with Special Forces detachments establishing village defense units across South Vietnam. The 5th Special Forces Group (Airborne) took primary responsibility for the mission, deploying upwards of a reinforced battalion to provide detachments and command and control capabilities. While it would not come to be known as the Civilian Irregular Defense Group (CIDG) for some time, these early efforts to wrest control of the isolated villages of the Central Highlands bear many similarities to the later Village Stability Operations (VSO) that were implemented later in our conflict in Afghanistan. As the CIDG program spread across South Vietnam, it attracted many other minority groups, though the Montagnards would continue to comprise the largest contributors to the program.

Despite a history of discrimination, the Montagnards eagerly joined forces with the U.S. to resist North Vietnamese Army and Viet Cong incursions into their tribal lands, and committed their entire society to the American objectives in Vietnam. Many Special Forces A-Teams lived, trained, and fought directly alongside their Montagnard counterparts deep in the Vietnamese jungle. Renowned for their skill and ferocity in battle, the Montagnards proved instrumental in countering the Viet Cong and North Vietnamese Army in South Vietnam. Unlike as was the case with many other indigenous units with whom Special Forces partnered in Vietnam, the Montagnards could always be relied upon to stand alongside American troops. Even during the early campaigns, when supplies were minimal and arms antiquated, the Montagnards showed themselves to be a force to be reckoned with.

Originally, the Montagnards were armed with surplus M1 carbines, M3 "Grease Guns," and other supplies left over from WWII and Korea. However, these weapons were a vast improvement over the crossbows and spears the Montagnards had traditionally been armed with prior to partnering with the U.S. U.S. Special Forces teams, augmented by South Vietnamese Special Forces, undertook progressively more advanced training with the Montagnards. Starting with basic marksmanship, Montagnards were also trained in raids, ambush, counter-ambush, first aid, and a host of other advanced combat skills that exponentially increased their combat effectiveness. The SF experience with the Montagnards and CIDGs in Vietnam serves as a perfect case study of just how impactful Special Forces can be as a "force multiplier" when operating "by, with, and through" dedicated indigenous forces. The SF teams lived in the villages and worked directly alongside their Montagnard comrades, cementing the bonds of respect and friendship that would endure past the end of the war.

Most CIDGs operated in close proximity to their villages, giving them a marked advantage in resisting *Viet Cong* and NVA forces as they attempted to pass through these areas. However, after 1964, CIDGs shifted focus from purely defensive purposes to a more offensive mindset. Operations were conducted farther afield as Montagnard groups provided mobile strike forces across the country. Led by Special Forces teams, CIDGs participated in several such operations launched across the border into neighboring Laos and Cambodia to attack the "Ho Chi Minh Trail" and support zones upon which most Communist forces operating in South Vietnam were so dependent. In addition to fighting directly alongside the Montagnards on the frontlines, U.S. Special Forces advisors also provided critical support with firepower (artillery and air support), medical evacuation and care, and other specialized capabilities that the Montagnards did not internally possess. In many ways, the CIDG, and specifically the Montagnards, proved far more effective allies than the conventional South Vietnamese troops in fighting the Communist forces. On several occasions, Montagnards bravely fought alongside Special Forces teams while South Vietnamese Army troops either broke and ran or failed to show up on the battlefield.

The CIDG program continued to make significant security gains throughout the 1960s, right up until the program was turned over to South Vietnamese military oversight. Efforts to turn over CIDG/Montagnard units to South Vietnamese Special Forces control began in earnest 1968, but the South Vietnamese quickly showed themselves to be unable and unwilling to continue supporting the program. On paper, the South Vietnamese assumed command and control of nearly all of the CIDGs by 1970, but the reality on the ground was that the U.S. Special Forces teams continued to provide the vast majority of support. The 5th Special Forces Group (Airborne) redeployed its last elements from Vietnam by the end of 1971, leaving the Montagnard units completely under the control of South Vietnamese Special Forces. Many of the CIDGs withered and disappeared due to a lack of supplies, weapons, ammunition, and competent South Vietnamese Special Forces advisors. Most of the security gains for which the U.S. and Montagnards had sacrificed so bravely were lost as the *Viet Cong* and NVA surged across South Vietnam toward final victory. While many of the difficulties associated could be traced back to South Vietnamese materiel and manpower short-ages, it was also clear that lingering discrimination and distrust of the Montagnards played a large role.

When the U.S. withdrew its troops, many Montagnards were left be-hind without any assistance and at the mercy of the victorious North Vietnamese. Hundreds of thousands of Montagnards fled across the bor-der into neighboring Cambodia and Laos to escape reprisals. Widespread reports of land confiscation, executions, rapes, mutilations, and other horrendous atrocities committed against the Montagnards resulted in international condemnation of the victorious Communist regime. Even today, reports of atrocities committed against Montagnards still concern international human rights groups. Efforts by Special Forces leaders to convince the U.S. government to intervene were largely ignored and the U.S. only resettled some two thousand of the refugees. The majority of these refugees were relocated to North Carolina, where they remain with the support of many former Special Forces Soldiers. The most well-known of these groups is "Save the Montagnard People" in Ashboro, North Carolina. The wholesale slaughter of the Montagnards remains as a particularly dark epilogue that stains the U.S. involvement in Vietnam. From a population of approximately two million before the war, there are only an estimated 600,000 to 800,000 Montagnards left in the world. Many Montagnards and U.S. Vietnam War veterans continue to bitterly hold the U.S. government responsible for failing to save more of the Montagnards.

Similarly, the U.S. has largely failed to provide adequate assistance to both Iraqi or Afghan interpreters and other support personnel during this closing phase of the Global War on Terror. Brave Afghans and Iraqis, who risked everything to help the Americans rebuild their respective coun-tries, face the direst of consequences. Some estimates hold that as many as 100,000 Iraqis aided the Americans in their efforts to first invade and then rebuild Iraq, while estimates of Afghans far exceed those numbers. From my own experiences, I came to rely on several brave Iraqis and Afghans, primarily as interpreters, that made it possible for us to conduct operations during highly sensitive counterinsurgency efforts. The U.S entered into both Iraq and Afghanistan with little preparation, ramping up rapidly and invading with few interpreters or other cultural experts. There was a distinct lack of capable interpreters during each of my combat deployments, but the few indigenous personnel who answered the call were brave men whom I could always trust with my life. In addition to enduring the same hardships that my men and I did, they also paid the same sacrifices as we. We lost a number of brave interpreters and other local allies during our combat operations. They were amazing human beings and we honored them each as we did the loss of Americans.

Even before the last U.S. combat troops withdrew from Iraq, unsettling reports of death threats against interpreters and other support personnel were commonplace. Several interpreters and their families were targeted by both Sunni and Shia terrorist groups, who saw any assistance given to the Americans as treasonous. In Afghanistan, interpreters and other support personnel are constantly targeted for assassination by the Taliban and other groups. This is why nearly all interpreters who operated with Americans wore masks and used pseudonyms to protect themselves. Despite these efforts, terrorist groups still managed to discover their identities and multiple reports attest to the brutal extremes to which these people would go to exact what they saw as justifiable vengeance. In many cases, interpreters were betrayed or killed in horrific ways by members of their own families.

Unfortunately, when operations began to wind down in Iraq, few concessions were made to help these brave men and women relocate to the safer locations. While the U.S. Department of State did create special programs for granting of visas to former U.S. allies, the systems proved so byzantine and non-intuitive that few Iraqis were able to navigate the processes to obtain visas for them and their families. Many Iraqis were required to apply as "refugees," an impossible task given that refugees could only apply for visas from outside their country of origin. Few Iraqis or their families could legally travel outside Iraq as the majority of their passports and other official papers dated from the Saddam regime and were therefore void. Moreover, the average wait times for the State Department to conduct its required background checks could take years, a period of time that few Iraqis could afford. When the State Department unceremoniously closed its program in 2010, only a few thousand visas had been granted while tens of thousands remained in backlog.

The vast majority of U.S. troops will withdraw from Afghanistan at the end of this year. The Taliban have already made it abundantly clear that they will continue to punish Afghans who aided the Coalition over the last thirteen years. Even more so than in Iraq, the Taliban have shown themselves to be particularly adept at hunting down and killing those Afghans who have helped the Coalition forces. Either through random targeting using ambushes along routes to Coalition bases, or through more personalized killings in the villages where these comrades live. This propensity for vengeance has caused a panicked rush of applications for visas by Afghans terrified for the lives of their families and themselves. Unfortunately, the State Department has seemed wholly incapable and unwilling to deal with the increased demand for emergency visas. There is every indication that the next few years will see another bloodbath as former U.S. supporters are slaughtered for having the courage to stand with the Americans.

The recent rise in sectarian violence that accompanied the emergence of the Islamic State in Iraq and the Levant (ISIL) renewed the threat against former U.S. allies in Iraq. A recent spike in killings against former interpreters and other support personnel has renewed the debate on what the U.S. should to do aid former comrades still in danger. At the moment, the State Department has indicated no special considerations for those who previously aided the U.S. and who may be at greater risk. Many neighboring countries have either closed their borders with Iraq or greatly restricted movement in order to quell the spread of ISIL fighters. This current situation in Iraq has every indication of becoming another stain upon America's honor, assuming that we continue to make no effort to keep faith with our former Iraqi allies who have already sacrificed so much to aid our efforts.

Particularly for Special Forces, who nearly always rely on indigenous forces to achieve our objectives, it is imperative that the U.S. endeavor to "keep faith" with our local allies. Whether this is by providing adequate protections in their own countries or mechanisms for relocating them and their families to safety, it is necessary that these eventualities be explored prior to a crisis occurring. If nothing is done to rectify these past and emerging failures, there is the very real danger that, in future conflicts, our Special Forces soldiers will be hard-pressed to find men and women willing to trust us with their very lives. Without that level of trust and faith, it is impossible to build the bonds of camaraderie necessary to fight effectively side by side. The reputation of our country, and by extension our ability to achieve our national objectives "by, with, and through" indigenous partners, is very much in jeopardy.

About the Author

 Douglas A. Livermore is a Special Forces officer with extensive leadership and operational planning experience obtained over a decade of military service in both the Infantry and Special Forces. In addition to multiple combat deployments to both Iraq and Afghanistan, Doug has engaged in several sensitive contingency operations in Mali, the Democratic Republic of Congo, the Central African Republic, Uganda, and Djibouti. He is a distinguished graduate of the Special Forces Detachment Officer Qualification Course as well as the Special Forces Unconventional Warfare Operational Design Course. In addition to holding degrees in Military History and Military Arts and Sciences from the U.S. Military Academy at West Point, his experiences have provided him unique and detailed insights into the areas of unconventional/guerrilla warfare, counterinsurgency, counterterrorism, and international stability operations. The opinions and positions stated here are his alone and do not represent the views or policies of the Government of the United States or any of its agencies.

Non-Burman Ethnic Peoples of Burma

The case of the ethnic people who steadfastly fought and died with Americans and British allies in the Burmese jungles fighting the Japanese in World War II have not only been abandoned by us, but our government is today engaging the Myanmar Government and the very same bloodline of Burmese power brokers and puppets who were allied with Japanese invaders. The post-World War II Burmese-dominated government and the entrenched ruling military class of Burmese generals have been pursuing the systemic oppression, marginalization, exploitation and ultimate genocide of the non-Burman ethnic peoples of Burma. This is solely for personal financial gain by dominating ethnics' natural resource-rich ancestral homelands. Many armed ethnic minorities who have been holding the line for Democracy in Burma for decades, have been subsequently and substantially neglected by the U.S. Government. As background, the below article was published in America's Future, Volume 52, November/ December 2010. Reprinted by permission of the author.

Our Forgotten Allies Stand in the Gap by Colonel (Retired) Tim Heinemann[145] (reprinted with permission)

We scarcely suspect that America's old hill tribe allies from World War II today stand staunchly in the path China's expansionism. Intent on securing direct access to the Indian Ocean – a centuries-long aim – China regards Burma as its front door to world markets, natural resources and enduring economic prosperity. Ethnic freedom fighters in Burma today, whose forefathers fought at the sides of Yanks and Brits long ago, wage a decades-long resistance against Burma's brutal military dictatorship. They threaten China's desire to dominate Burma, securing unfettered access to Indian Ocean, natural resources of Africa and European markets.

With America focusing on Southwest Asia, China grabs strategic terrain everywhere. In Burma, China pours in billions to dictator, General Than Shwe, who systematically rapes Burma's human and natural resources – a scorched earth campaign with over 3500 ethnic villages destroyed, over

---

145 Colonel Tim Heinemann is a retired Special Forces officer who founded and operates a non-profit organization, Worldwide Impact Now (WIN), that helps indigenous peoples in Burma (Myanmar) and Africa. He is the foremost expert on the non-Burman ethnic groups in Burma.

470,000 internally displaced persons and 800,000 forced laborers as casualties, because ethnic lands are rich in natural resources.

Congressman Dana Rohrbacher's National Review article of 24 Sept is telling:

> *"I recently returned from the Thai-Burmese border, where I consulted with members of the Burmese democracy movement. I was deeply impressed with not only their courage, but also their commitment to a decentralized, denuclearized, democratic Burma. The freedom-loving people of the region want to be our allies against an evil enemy, as they were in the fight against the Japanese in World War II. The American government has treated them as pariahs.*
>
> *A few Americans — missionaries, former members of the Special Forces, and a sprinkling of adventurers — are there on the border as volunteers. Reminiscent of the Flying Tigers before Pearl Harbor, though not as well equipped, this ragtag contingent of American idealists help as best they can, though often facing hostility from elements in our own government. They are doing what my father used to call "the Lord's work" — literally as well as figuratively.*
>
> *Our government did not support brave anti-Taliban forces in Afghanistan, like Commander Massoud, until after we had been attacked on 9/11. Had we done so, the attack might not have happened. So there is a cost to a policy of ignoring those struggling against tyrannical and/or fanatical forces, as in Afghanistan — and in Burma. When America supports those brave souls fighting for their freedom against despicable tyrants, we are not only doing the right thing by them, we are invariably bolstering the safety of our own country."*

The pity is that most Americans have no idea our old buddies fight on, ever in hope of America as their champion. These gallant defenders of their people now face down the Burmese dictator in a last stand as China pours on resources to hasten their doom.

Tim Heinemann, a retired Special Forces colonel, is the founder of the humanitarian non-profit organization, Worldwide Impact Now (WIN), based in St Louis. He and his wife organize other American volunteers in support of pro-democracy movements and ethnic minorities of Burma. Refer to one of their websites: www.burmaincrisis.org

Update: Since 2011, the Government of Myanmar has self-proclaimed that it is "reformed". The international community has generally bought this "overnight enlightenment" story line, while side-stepping the issue of six decades of crimes against humanity, war crimes and human rights abuses perpetrated against ethnics by the Burmese government and it generals. This is no different from failing to conduct the Nuremburg War Crimes Trials after World War II. Amazingly, the Burmese generals, who today remain ever immune from prosecution, are guaranteed 25% of all Parliamentary seats and they also substantially control the economic base using the Burmese Army as their enforcement arm. In this context, the international community now sees Myanmar / Burma as its business cash cow and humanitarian cause célèbre. In so doing, it has violated the first imperative of aid and development to "first do no harm to the people." Today, the new KFC restaurant opening in Rangoon gets more press than does Burmese Hind Gunships[146] attacking the Kachin[147] just to the north. The Myanmar Government now leverages 'internationals' favor, finances and resources to control aid and development in ethnic zones. This further entrenches Burmese elites in power, while concurrently marginalizing ethnics already suffering from decades of dictatorship and oppression. The much-touted on-going ceasefire negotiations mask sophisticated Burmese pressure tactics, coercion and corruption taking place in the shadows. Internationals revel at the prospect of peace, while ethnics on the frontier well understand Burmese intent as meaning "no resistance to Burmanization of all ethnics" in the enduring spirit of "One Voice-One Ethnicity-One Religion."

Bottom line. Either out of misplaced consideration for the illegitimate Burmese central government or intentional duplicity, the U.S. Government has inexcusably dithered for decades on the issue of

---

146 The Hind is a Russian made attack helicopter, known as the "flying tank." It is almost invulnerable from ground fire and devastating to the lightly armed ethnic fighters.

147 The Kachin people are a group of ethnic groups who largely inhabit the Kachin Hills in northern Burma's Kachin State and neighboring areas of China and India. More than ninety nine percent of the Kachin people identify themselves as Christians.

backing the non-Burman pro-democracy ethnic groups, whose World War II war record alone merits our unqualified support. The larger issue likely is the U.S. was, and still is, afraid of mischief-making at China's front door. Reality in the eyes of the watching world? No courage by the world's defender of freedom to stand with like-minded mates. The U.S. Government's general favor of central governments-in-power is dangerously bereft of a moral rudder in an era in which it should be the leader in "humanity matters." Credible and durable super power stature worthy of allies in the young 21st century will either come from taking moral stands in obscure places like Burma or deteriorate and dissolve by demonstrating a lack of moral fiber or loyalty to friends. The U.S. Government's conspicuous lack of courage here should cause introspection by Americans as to what we really stand for today.

Annex B: Core Values & Truths

SF Core Values

Army SOF Attributes

Army Values

SOF Truths

SOF Imperatives

SF Core Competencies

SF Creed (Original)

SF Creed (USASOC "PC" Version)

<u>Special Forces Core Values</u> (FM 3-05.20, June 2001)

Warrior Ethos. Special Forces is a fraternity of warriors, the ultimate professionals in conducting special operations when the cause of freedom is challenged. The SF warrior tradition originates from SF's early roles in unconventional warfare and is exemplified by the SF Motto, "De Oppresso Liber."

Professionalism. Special Forces soldiers provide the nation with a broad range of capabilities to address challenges to our national security and national interests. SF soldiers interface with high-level military commanders, country-teams, ambassadors and heads of state. Through their actions and their range of technical and tactical skills. SF soldiers serve worldwide as operational and strategic assets.

Innovation. Special Forces soldiers ~are creative and inventive in accomplishing their missions. Through the judicious application of conventional and unconventional problem-solving, they solve problems imaginatively, developing the right solutions outside the constraints of institutional norms.

Versatility. Special Forces soldiers adapt quickly to rapidly changing environments, consistently operating and. easily transitioning across the entire spectrum of conflict, from, peace to war. SF is truly a capability-based organization providing the widest range of capabilities to accomplish assigned missions.

Cohesion. The cohesion within an SF detachment enables it to withstand the most violent shocks and stresses of combat and to perform its duties' under demanding circumstances, without definitive guidance, while accomplishing· the commander's intent.

Character. SF soldiers understand the operational environment. They can be trusted to do the right thing and never to quit. SF soldiers recognize the political implications inherent in their missions. Knowing the cost of failure, they succeed against all odds.

Cultural Awareness. SF soldiers use interpersonal skills to work with all foreign cultures, gaining the trust, confidence and cooperation of the people by winning their hearts and minds. SF soldiers have a situational awareness that enables them to deploy Worldwide and accomplish their missions in ambiguous and complex situations.

SF Core Attributes (FM 3-18 Special Forces Operations, 28 May 2014)

Integrity	Is trustworthy and honest; acts with honor and unwavering adherence to ethical standards.
Courage	Acts on own convictions despite consequences; is willing to sacrifice for a larger cause; is not paralyzed by fear of failure.
Perseverance	Works toward an end; has commitment; possesses physical or mental resolve; is motivated; gives effort to the cause; does not quit.
Personal Responsibility	Is self-motivated and an autonomous self-starter; anticipates tasks and acts accordingly; takes accountability for own actions.
Professionalism	Is a standard-bearer for the regiment; has a professional image, to include a level of maturity and judgment mixed with confidence and humility; forms sound opinions and makes own decisions; stands behind own sensible decisions based on own experiences.
Adaptability	Has the ability to maintain composure while responding to or adjusting own thinking and actions to fit a changing environment; possesses the ability to think and solve problems in unconventional ways; has the ability to recognize, understand, and navigate within multiple social networks; has the ability to proactively shape the environment or circumstances in anticipation of desired outcomes.
Team Player	Is able to work on a team for a greater purpose than self; is dependable and loyal; works selflessly with a sense of duty; respects others and recognizes diversity.
Capability	Has physical fitness, to include strength and agility; has operational knowledge; is able to plan and communicate effectively.

Army Values

The Seven Army Values

Loyalty: Bear true faith and allegiance to the U.S. Constitution, the Army, and other soldiers.

Be loyal to the nation and its heritage.

Duty: Fulfill your obligations. Accept responsibility for your own actions and those entrusted to your care.

Find opportunities to improve oneself for the good of the group.

Selfless Service: Put the welfare of the nation, the Army, and your subordinates before your own. Selfless service leads to organizational teamwork and encompasses discipline, self-control and faith in the system.

Respect: Rely upon the golden rule. How we consider others reflects upon each of us, both personally and as a professional organization.

Honor: Live up to all the Army values

Integrity: Do what is right, legally and morally. Be willing to do what is right even when no one is looking. It is our "moral compass"—an inner voice.

Personal Courage: Our ability to face fear, danger, or adversity, both physical and moral courage.

SOF Truths (USSOCOM Version SOF Fact Book 2014) "SOF Truths,"

U.S. Army Special Operations Command

Humans are more important than Hardware.

Quality is better than Quantity.

Special Operations Forces cannot be mass produced.

Competent Special Operations Forces cannot be created after emergencies occur.

Most Special Operations require non-SOF support

SOF Imperatives (Army Doctrine Publication (ADP) 3-05: Special Operations dtd 31 August 2012)

- Understand the operational environment
- Recognize political implications
- Facilitate interagency activities
- Engage the threat discriminately
- Consider long-term effects
- Ensure legitimacy and credibility of Special Operations
- Anticipate and control psychological effects
- Apply capabilities indirectly
- Develop multiple options
- Ensure long-term sustainment
- Provide sufficient intelligence
- Balance security and synchronization

SF Core Competencies (FM 3-05.20, June 2001)

SF possesses distinguishing core competencies, many derived from the UW mission. These competencies have evolved over the years due to changing mission requirements and focus by the geographic CINCs to dictate the needs of SF training. These SF core competencies, discussed below, make SF the force of choice for complex, difficult, high-risk, and politically sensitive missions.

Warfighting

SF soldiers are the epitome of the professional soldier. From hand-to-hand combat to the maneuver tactics of conventional forces, SF soldiers are expert warriors and masters of the profession of arms. The SFODA is fully versed in light infantry TTP up to and including the battalion level. SF soldiers are experts at integration of fire and maneuver skills. Their patrolling skills—carried out in unilateral, combined, or joint operations— include all aspects of combat patrolling. SF soldiers are tactically competent and have advanced training in operations, intelligence, medical skills, engineering, communications, and heavy and light weapons. They also have a working knowledge of the employment of PSYOP and Civil Affairs (CA).

Training

SF soldiers are masters in the art and science of training. They are fully competent to assess unit and individual requirements, develop and implement programs to address identified needs, and evaluate the results of those programs. Most important, these assessments, programs, and evaluations are focused on the actual mission needs of the force to be trained.

Physical Fitness

SF soldiers maintain a high level of fitness. This level of fitness directly correlates to the SF soldier's combative skills, which he adopts as a discipline and as a means of self-defense.

Intercultural Communications

Since its activation, SF has focused on developing and employing foreign forces and other assets, such as international organizations, in support of U.S. policy objectives. As a result, SF has recognized the ability to influence foreign audiences by managing the content and flow of information through effective intercultural communications as fundamental to mission success. Beginning with the SFQC, SF soldiers are trained and educated in these complex communications skills. SF competency in intercultural communications rests on four pillars: interpersonal skills, nonverbal skills, language proficiency, and area and cultural orientation.

Interpersonal Skills

Interpersonal skills are critical to SF operations. They require the ability to listen with understanding, the ability to maintain an open mind, and the sensitivity to observe and grasp the essential components of a given situation. SF soldiers combine the ability to overcome ethnocentricity and to treat foreigners as equals, while also communicating and teaching across intercultural barriers. SF soldiers use their interpersonal skills to get the desired action from a foreign counterpart.

Nonverbal Skills

Over half of human communication is nonverbal. Understanding gestures and behavior can be very difficult when they also have an intercultural dimension. When gestures, behavior, and language are complementary, the complete picture evolves. Some nonverbal forms of communication are demeaning, derogatory, or even inflammatory. These gestures vary from culture to culture. Nonverbal communication requires an understanding of the gestures applicable to each culture. The SF soldier's regional orientation permits him to focus on the nonverbal "vocabulary" of a specific region and to train to be sensitive to nonverbal communication.

Language Proficiency

Language proficiency is a key element in intercultural communications. Each prospective SF soldier is tested for language aptitude. To be qualified in his MOS, each SF soldier must attend language school. This schooling is, however, just a start point. SF soldiers continue to improve their language skills through unit-sponsored training, repeated deployments into the region of orientation, and self-study. As a result, each SFOD possesses personnel with varying degrees of proficiency in one or more foreign languages.

Area and Cultural Orientation

SF units are regionally oriented to ensure they have the resident skills and cultural understanding necessary to communicate with and influence their foreign counterparts. Regional orientation permits SF soldiers to develop a thorough understanding of the cultural and religious history and the social, political, and economic dynamics of given population groups. This understanding of the operational area extends to the physical factors of geography and climate within the specified region. These physical factors influence not only the attitudes, beliefs, and behavior of the indigenous populace but also the actual conduct of military operations. Formal training and cultural immersion during repeated deployments are the vehicles for developing this orientation and understanding. One aspect of such area and cultural orientation is that it promotes and nurtures a strong set of personal and professional relationships formed over the years between SF soldiers and their military and civilian counterparts in the target region. These relationships are often key to mission success.

Problem Solving

The nature of UW and other SF missions often defies templated or "schoolhouse" solutions. A hallmark of the SF soldier is the ability to analyze a situation, then adapt and apply U.S. doctrine, TTP, equipment, and methods in a culturally sensitive and appropriate manner to resolve difficult issues in non-standard situations.

Clandestine Infiltration And Exfiltration

SF maintains proficiency in a wide variety of low-visibility and clandestine infiltration and exfiltration techniques. Although SF is a ground-oriented force, it is competent in air, sea, and land infiltration and exfiltration methods using both military and civilian modes of transportation. These techniques are not limited to doctrinal and routinely practiced methods. They also include mission-specific, improvised techniques. This competency permits SF to operate in places that other forces consider to be denied areas.

Interagency, Joint, Combined, and Multinational Operations

SF has unique capabilities to fill the operational void between civilian dominated or civilian-led activities and military operations. They work with foreign militaries that often are involved in functions or activities that are the exclusive function of civilian agencies in the United States positions SF to assist with interagency programs in foreign nations. Because SF routinely operates as part of a joint SOF team, within a joint SOF command structure, it is well prepared to facilitate joint operations among any combinations of force types. SF possesses the unique ability to enable combined operations. From its UW origins, SF maintains the full range of skills, organization, and training to integrate foreign forces, regular or irregular, into a combined operation effectively.

Political Awareness

Sometimes referred to as "warrior-diplomats," SF soldiers maintain a keen appreciation of the political aspects of their operational environment. They must understand U.S. policies, goals, and objectives and be able to articulate them in a manner that convinces their foreign counterparts to support them. Similarly, they must understand the political context within which their counterparts operate.

Austere or Hostile Environments

SF has developed the ability to operate for extended periods in hostile, remote, and austere environments with little or no external support. SF's ability to operate in these environments provides one of the means to maintain low visibility during SF operations.

Advanced Technology

The complex, one-of-a-kind nature of assigned missions has driven SF to develop procedures for adapting military and civilian technology in innovative ways. Coupled with non-standard procurement procedures, this competency permits SF to apply creative solutions to mission requirements. This skill has also enabled SF to perform well in the rapidly evolving IO mission area.

The Special Forces Creed (Original)

I am an American Special Forces soldier. A professional!
I will do all that my nation requires of me.
I am a volunteer, knowing well the hazards of my profession.
I serve with the memory of those who have gone before me:
    Roger's Rangers, Francis Marion, Mosby's Rangers,
    the first Special Service Forces and Ranger Battalions
    of World War II, the Airborne Ranger Companies of Korea.
I pledge to uphold the honor and integrity
    of all I am - in all I do.
I am a professional soldier.
I will teach and fight wherever my nation requires.
I will strive always, to excel in every art and artifice of war.
I know that I will be called upon to perform tasks
    in isolation, far from familiar faces and voices,
    with the help and guidance of my God.
I will keep my mind and body clean, alert and strong,
    for this is my debt to those who depend upon me.
I will not fail those with whom I serve.
I will not bring shame upon myself or the forces.
I will maintain myself, my arms, and my equipment
    in an immaculate state as befits a Special Forces soldier.
I will never surrender though I be the last.
If I am taken, I pray that I may have the strength
    to spit upon my enemy.
My goal is to succeed in any mission
    - and live to succeed again.
I am a member of my nation's chosen soldiery.
God grant that I may not be found wanting,
    that I will not fail this sacred trust.

"De Oppresso Liber"

Special Forces Creed (USASOC "PC" Version)

I am an American Special Forces Soldier!
I will do all that my nation requires of me.
I am a volunteer, knowing well the hazards of my profession.
I serve with the memory of those who have gone before me.
I pledge to uphold the honor and integrity of their legacy in all that I am - in all that I do.
I am a warrior.
I will teach and fight whenever and wherever my nation requires.
I will strive always to excel in every art and artifice of war.
I know that I will be called upon to perform tasks
in isolation, far from familiar faces and voices.
With the help and guidance of my faith, I will conquer my fears and succeed.
I will keep my mind and body clean, alert and strong.
I will maintain my arms and equipment in an immaculate state befitting a Special Forces Soldier,
for this is my debt to those who depend upon me.
I will not fail those with whom I serve.
I will not bring shame upon myself or Special Forces.
I will never leave a fallen comrade.
I will never surrender though I am the last.
If I am taken, I pray that I have the strength to defy my enemy.
I am a member of my nation's chosen soldiery,
I serve quietly, not seeking recognition or accolades.
My goal is to succeed in my mission - and live to succeed again.

De Oppresso Liber

Annex C: 1994 Unconventional Operations Forces War College Paper

The origin of this article is my U.S. Army War College Study Project, dated 15 April 1993, Carlisle Barracks, PA. This War College paper is the origin of the term *through, with and by* which is now used ubiquitously when discussing Special Forces and unconventional warfare. This article is an abbreviated version published in *Special Warfare Magazine,* PB 80-94-4, October 1994, Vol. 7, No. 4.

SPECIAL FORCES AS UNCONVENTIONAL OPERATIONS FORCES

By Colonel Mark D. Boyatt
15 April 1993

The purpose of this paper is to clarify the roles and missions of United States Army Special Forces. The term Unconventional Operations (UO) vice Special Operations (SO)[148] will be introduced, defined and ex-plained. The paper will explain why Army Special Forces (SF) are the

---

148 Special Operations (DOD): [Joint Pub 1-02]: Operations conducted by specially trained, equipped, and organized DOD forces against strategic or tactical targets in pursuit of national military, political, eco-nomic, or psychological objectives. These operations may be conducted during periods of peace or hostili-ties. They may support conventional operations, or they may be prosecuted independently when the use of conventional forces is either inappropriate or infeasible.

principle UO force and articulate why the UO mission is critical. Most importantly, it will show why the numbered active duty Special Forces Groups (SFGs) should primarily focus on this mission and not be diverted to missions duplicated by other Special Operations Forces (SOF) or General Purpose Forces.

UNCONVENTIONAL OPERATIONS

SOF has become a popular term for a broad array of very diverse forces and organizations. The essence of SOF, the elements that contribute most significantly over the long term to the U.S. national security strategy *in terms of the numbers of active missions and their effect on national security objectives*, are the Army Special Forces conducting unconventional operations as defined in this paper. Current doctrine does not identify these unconventional operations forces as specific, distinct forces. Furthermore, there is not a published definition of unconventional operations (UO) in Joint PUB 1-02, **Department of Defense Dictionary of Military and Associated Terms**. This paper provides a proposed definition for unconventional operations and identifies principal unconventional operations forces (UOF). Proposed definition for Unconventional Operations:

> **Unconventional operations are low visibility, economy of force and economy of resources operations. Unconventional operations are unique in that relatively small operational elements work in a combined environment and accomplish their missions *through, with and by indigenous personnel*. This environment is usually political sensitive, frequently requiring close cooperation with Department of State and other non-DoD agencies in remote locations across the operational continuum.**

During peacetime, UO primarily consist of operations with nations that are important to U.S. national security strategy. Some examples of these operations are foreign internal defense operations, humanitarian assistance operations, peace-keeping operations, demining operations, nation building operations, counter-drug assistance and security assistance programs. During conflict or war, UO are primarily unconventional warfare operations. Examples of unconventional warfare operations are guerrilla warfare, evasion and escape, subversion, sabotage and other operations of a low visibility, covert or clandestine nature.

The above-mentioned peacetime operations may continue during conflict as an economy of force effort, either within the operational and strategic area of operation (AOR) or in adjacent AORs. An example of the synergistic effect of this strategy is found in the experiences in the Arabian Gulf Conflict of 1991. While some U.S. Army Special Forces contributed to the effectiveness of coalition warfare in the AOR, other Special Forces elements conducted economy of force missions in Turkey, Africa, South/ Central America and the Pacific and Asia, enhancing regional stability.

Unconventional operations provide a low-risk political option with the potential of high levels of political return.

Conducted without fanfare, unconventional operations usually attract little, if any, media coverage.

UNCONVENTIONAL OPERATIONS FORCES

This paper introduces Unconventional Operations Forces (UOF) as a new term. UOF are those United States Special Operations Forces (SOF) that are unique in their capability to conduct a wide range of unconventional operations, as opposed to those SOF elements whose SO missions are more narrow and specialized.

These unconventional roles consist primarily of teaching, training and organizing military, paramilitary or other indigenous elements in the conduct of foreign internal defense operations, unconventional warfare, humanitarian assistance, peacekeeping, demining, nation building, counter-drug assistance, etc. These efforts focus on nations and populations that are important to U.S. national security strategy. Best defined as forces principally organized and trained to accomplish their mission *through, with or by indigenous personnel*, UOF are unique. The only SOF specifically organized, trained and equipped to conduct these missions in this manner are the numbered Army Special Forces Groups.

ROLES AND MISSIONS

According to *Joint Pub 3-05*, SOF have five principal missions and six collateral special operations activities.

I. Principal Missions

> (1) Unconventional Warfare (UW)
> (2) Direct Action (DA)
> (3) Special Reconnaissance (SR)
> (4) Foreign Internal Defense (FID)
> (5) Counter-terrorism (CT)

II. Collateral Special Operations Activities

> (1) Security Assistance (SA)
> (2) Humanitarian Assistance (HA)
> (3) Anti-terrorism and Other Security Activities
> (4) Counter-narcotics (CN)
> (5) Personnel Recovery
> (6) Special Activities

Several of these missions are, in reality, subsets of others. The introduction of unconventional operations precipitates combining several of these missions. By adding unconventional operations, the principal missions shrink to three, with several subsets. The following proposed changes better organize and clarify the SOF missions into functional areas.

I. Proposed Principal Missions
> (1) Unconventional Operations (UO)
>> - Unconventional Warfare (UW)
>> - Foreign Internal Defense (FID)
>>> -- Security Assistance (SA)
>>> -- Humanitarian Assistance (HA)
>>> -- Counter-Narcotics (CN)

    (2) Direct Action (DA)
            - Counter-Terrorism (CT)
            - Personnel Recovery

    (3) Special Reconnaissance (SR)

II.   Proposed Collateral Special Operations Activities

        (1) Special Activities
        (2) Anti-terrorism and Other Security Activities

The proposed changes categorize UW and FID as the primary elements of UO. Security assistance naturally becomes a subset of FID, as does humanitarian assistance. Personnel recovery becomes a subset of DA. Humanitarian assistance and counter-narcotics are shown as subsets of foreign internal defense. This realignment of mission categories simplifies the training focus for units.

The following chart shows the SOF elements and their primary missions under current doctrinal publications. Chart 1 shows only the five principal mission areas--UW, FID, DA, SR, and CT.

SOF Missions

Type Unit*	Primary
Army	
Special Forces	UW,FID,DA,SR,CT
Rangers	DA,CT
SO Aviation	DA,SR and Support all operations
Navy	
SEALS	DA,SR,CT,FID,UW**
SBU	Support all operations
SDVT	Support all operations
Air Force	
Fixed-wing	Support all operations
Rotary-wing	Support all operations

SO Weather	Support all operations
Special Tactics	Support all operations
Special Ops ***	FID,UW
Special Msn Units	DA,SR,CT,FID,UW

* USMC MEU(SOC) is not listed because this is not a core SOF element.

** Although the SEALs have UW as a mission, their definition is more like DA. They see UW as strikes/raids behind enemy lines unlike Army SF. Army SF practice UW in the traditional sense of working with indigenous elements in a denied area.

*** The 6th Special Operations Sqd. recently formed has no organic aircraft and is focused on training indigenous personnel in the use of their own aircraft

Much of the understanding of Special Forces' (SF) missions is limited to a relatively narrow view. Whereas, by doctrine, Special Forces has five primary missions--unconventional warfare (UW), foreign internal defense (FID), special reconnaissance (SR), direct action (DA), counter-terrorism (CT)--most attention and resourcing focuses on three missions: counter-terrorism, direct action and special reconnaissance operations.

First, attempting to address five missions results in a dilution of effort and resources. Consider DA, SR, and CT. Units usually approach these as stand-alone missions and train to execute them in a unilateral manner. Each mission then receives repetitive training time, consuming significant resources. Second, the three missions of counter-terrorism, special reconnaissance and direct action are missions other SOF or general purpose forces also have as missions. Some of these other SOF units are better trained, organized and resourced than are the numbered Special Forces Groups to conduct these missions. This is duplication we can ill afford in these times of shrinking budgets.

Without a doubt, counter-terrorism must keep its high priority due to its political sensitivity, but should be a subset of direct action. The probability that CT forces will be needed may have increased with the uncertainty facing the changing world. While some people believe terrorism is decreasing, history suggests this is unlikely.[149] Regardless, terrorism is still a politically sensitive area. However, once again, there are other elements focused on this mission. The numbered Special Forces Groups should not be so tasked. *[This means that we should either get out of the CIF business…which is probably not possible…but we can rescope the self-invented mission of trying to duplicate the National Force mission and get the mission back into the tasked mission of in-extremis mode vs. the surgical mode. This requires much less resourcing and permits the rotation of the CIF mission this each year to a different SF Company size unit……vice the perpetuation of a prima donna unit which is not focused on the core SF mission of UW/UO.]*

Unilateral direct action and special reconnaissance operations, since the late '70s, have received priority attention as Special Forces' missions. These are high visibility, immediate gratification missions, well within the comfort zone, and easily identified with by most people, most importantly the conventional Army. The numbered Special Forces Groups can and do conduct these operations.

They do so by sacrificing expertise and competence in unconventional operations. Again, other units and some General Purpose Force elements receive specific resourcing to train, equip and organize for these missions. To consider the numbered Special Forces Group assets for **unilateral** DA and SR should be a last choice. Only if other units or general purpose forces are inappropriate or unavailable should the numbered Special Forces Groups receive DA or SR tasking--rather than being considered first. Numbered Special Forces Groups best conduct these missions ***through, with or by indigenous assets***.

The following chart shows the SOF elements and their *proposed* primary missions. The introduction of UO as a mission category--along with DA and SR--focuses the missions

---

149 Walter Laqueur, first in his monumental works Guerrilla, 1976 and Terrorism, 1977, and again in his update to Terrorism, his book, The Age of Terrorism, 1987, makes the point that terrorism is a tactic to effect political change and has been used over the centuries by disaffected and politically impotent segments of society. Terrorism is a tactic closely associated with insurgencies and guerrilla warfare. As political phenomenon, they are not mutually exclusive of each other. The future, reflected in the post Cold War realities, suggests insurgency and terrorism will occur with increasing regularity.

functionally. This chart shows only the proposed primary missions and not secondary, subordinate or collateral missions.

Proposed SOF Missions

Type Unit	Primary
Army	
Special Forces	UO
Rangers	DA
SO Aviation	DA,SR and Support all operations
Navy*	
SEALS	DA,SR
SBU	Support all operations
SDVT	Support all operations
Air Force*	
Fixed-wing	Support all operations
Rotary-wing	Support all operations
SO Weather	Support all operations
Special Tactics	Support all operations
Special Ops	UO**
Special Msn Units*	DA,SR

* Elements of these SOF organizations, on occasion, conduct FID, a portion of UO.

** The 6th SOS conducts part, but not the full range of UW

Army Special Forces' ability to conduct the broad range of unconventional operations described earlier in the paper is unique in the U.S. military. Certainly, other SOF elements and, on occasion, elements of the General Purpose Force execute portions of unconventional operations. However, only the numbered Special Forces groups, by virtue of their organization, training, equipment and orientation, are capable of covering the complete UO spectrum.

The uniqueness of unconventional operations lies in its cultural aspects. These cultural aspects apply equally to the requirements of teaching or the conduct of military operations. To conduct effective unconventional operations requires a detailed knowledge and understanding of the host nation's culture and, most importantly, a unique attitude. Two key elements of effective UO are language training and area studies. These are basic elements of a numbered Special Forces Group's training. Unfortunately, when one of the numbered Special Forces units focuses on a non-unconventional operations mission in response to a tasking, these are the first areas to suffer. To achieve adequate proficiency in these cultural aspects requires regional focus and intensive training. Additionally, the conduct of UW or FID requires integrated proficiency in DA and SR. These areas are not ignored. They are only approached with a different training focus and attitude. The uniqueness of unconventional operations, as explained earlier, is in executing these missions in a combined environment, ***through, with or by indigenous personnel.***

Why care about focusing the SF mission on UO? Why not leave the missions as now assigned--UW, FID, DA, SR, CT? The reasons are clarity of purpose and resources.

Too often many people confuse enthusiasm for competence. They also believe the potential to conduct a given mission equals the capability to execute it competently. This business requires a professional approach that appreciates the full extent of the missions' requirements and recognize limitations.

The prime resource is time. Currently, many of the numbered SF units (battalions and teams) have too much focus on DA, SR, or CT.[150] Accordingly, much of their training time is spent perfecting their *unilateral* capabilities in these areas. They spend very little time on the UO aspects. By so narrowly focusing on the DA, SR, or CT missions, these elements have degraded their ability to be truly effective in the more complex activities of UO. They cannot make the transition without significant effort and time or they must accept increased risk. Likewise, units effectively trained in UO will not be able to transition rapidly to

---

150   The 7th SFG is probably an exception to this generality. Of all the Special Forces Groups, the 7th SFG is most oriented to UO.

effective *unilateral* DA, SR or CT. These, too, are complicated missions requiring intensive training.

Critics can point out a shortfall in the capability of the overall conventional force resulting from this proposal to delete special reconnaissance as a unilateral mission for the numbered SF Groups. This shortfall is in human intelligence (HUMINT) forward of the corps fire coordination line (FCL). Many conventional Army commanders expect Special Forces to fill this role and this attitude is reinforced through misrepresentation of SF in the Army's Combat Training Center (CTC) program and the Battle Command Training Program (BCTP). Unilateral SR by Special Forces is an easy solution to their problem.

If there are no other options, Special Forces may have to do this; however, this should not assume nor require Special Forces to act unilaterally. Unconventional Operations Forces should be required by the regional combatant commanders to routinely conduct peacetime, pre-conflict missions in their assigned regions, with the specific task of cultivating relationships with the objective of identifying the capability, availability and potential of indigenous assets.

An effective and efficient way of conducting HUMINT collection (operational intelligence and defensive source operations [ASOT], not foreign intelligence collection) is through indigenous assets trained by the UOF. These assets might conduct missions alone or be organized, trained, equipped and led by UOF. Unilateral collection by SF is the method of last, and most ineffective and inefficient, choice.

UO is a complex field that requires dedicated attention and training to achieve and maintain proficiency. To dilute and divert the efforts and resources of the numbered Special Forces Groups to *unilateral* CT, DA and SR as primary missions severely degrades the ability of these groups to address adequately the UO role. The ***unilateral*** CT, DA and SR missions are better conducted by other SOF units or the General Purpose Force elements so focused.

Unfortunately, the SOF community, DoD and Congress seem fixated on the unilateral CT, DA and SR missions. These are highly visible missions and receive most of the attention and resourcing. Resourcing training for unconventional operations missions is a very low priority. A prime reason for this is that UO training is difficult to conduct, time intensive and expensive. Also, it is difficult to measure, validate and certify. It is easy and cheap in resources (time) to measure, validate and certify DA and SR training.

Many people seem to have forgotten that "routine and not so glamorous" unconventional operations in fact contribute most to U.S. national security strategy in terms of the numbers of missions conducted and their effect on national security objectives.[151]

Unconventional Operations Forces have a significant, if not leading, role to play in implementing national security efforts. Indications are the world of 2000 and beyond will probably be much more unstable than the one of the '90s. The control and relatively enforced stability of the bipolar world of the '70s and '80s has given way to a growing concern by numerous nations about their national security.

The stage is set for increasing regional instability. The role that the U.S. is to play in this unstable environment is unclear. One "means" that is available, though in need of significant attention, is through unconventional operations. UO, prudently and judiciously executed, can provide for regional stability through low-level U.S. presence. This presence can act as a brake on regional ambitions, demonstrate U.S. interest, possibly mitigate the spread of Weapons of Mass Destruction (WMD) and augment the counter-proliferation strategy.

---

151 Special Forces elements have been training with their counterparts in many nations around the globe for many years. Through their presence in these countries, relationships and contacts have been established that have had far reaching effects. In many of these countries, the military counterparts with whom Special Forces have worked have eventually risen to various positions of power--in some cases even Head-of-State. These relationships have led to regional stability in some cases and access to critical facilities in others. In almost all cases, SF is viewed in these countries as informal ambassadors of the U.S. and positive examples of democracy. The leverage gained in negotiations with foreign governments over our national security goals and objectives often staggers the imagination of the casual observer. For example, if one accepts that one of our goals in Liberia was to gain and maintain the trust and confidence of its leader, President Doe, then the efforts of a single Special Forces sergeant met and exceeded expectations. There are other operations, usually classified, where Special Forces soldiers' accomplishments far exceeded anything thought possible in terms of the long term positive impact on U.S./allied relations.

Nations that see or benefit from these unconventional operations may become more convinced and assured of U.S. interest in and concern for a given region. This presence can foster diplomacy, whereas absence may foster conflict. Nations or regions that perceive themselves adrift from or outside the sphere of concern of the world's only super-power, may feel compelled to pursue their own independent means of national security. This can exacerbate regional arms races, possible proliferation of weapons of mass destruction and regional instability.

U.S. foreign policy remains in transition. Our current foreign policy seems to be reactive vs. proactive. This is not surprising. At best, it is difficult to anticipate world and regional events. Samuel Huntington[152] describes it thus:

> All in all, the emerging world is likely to lack the clarity and stability of the Cold War and to be a more jungle-like world of multiple dangers, hidden traps, unpleasant surprises and moral ambiguities.

Unconventional operations can provide a window through which this "jungle-like world" can be viewed with greater clarity. This is the arena, the regionally focused arena, within which unconventional operations forces thrive and can, if properly and timely employed, provide a unique option in executing the national security strategy of the U.S.

RECOMMENDATIONS

First, codify in doctrine the terms unconventional operations (UO) and unconventional operational forces (UOF). As a distinct element of SOF, recognize UOF as key implementers of national security strategy.

Secondly, the primary mission for active component numbered Army Special Forces Groups must be unconventional operations. Either eliminate or clearly state DA, SR and CT as duplicative, subordinate missions for the numbered Special Forces Groups. Clearly indicate that other SOF

---

152 Samuel Huntington is an Eaton Professor of the Science of Government and Director of the John M. Olin Institute of Strategic Studies at the Center for International Affairs at Harvard University.

or general purpose force elements are more appropriately tasked for these missions. Unconventional operations require intense focus. Diversion of training time and resources to missions performed by other elements is a duplication.

Finally, and most important, keep the numbered Special Forces Groups' units involved outside the United States to open these "windows" and help provide insight into these ambiguous areas. This will assist with regional stability. To adequately do this will require change to the current structure, funding and employment of the SF battalions. The strength of Special Forces is in their cultural and regional focus. We must capitalize upon this strength.

To accomplish this, significantly increase funding and priority for unconventional operations and UO training. Ensure regional orientation and funding for the UOF to operate as much as possible in their respective regions. Give the fifteen active and six National Guard Special Forces battalions clear areas (regions) of responsibility that remain fixed. In takes a long time, sometimes years, to cultivate an area and inculcate regional expertise in a unit. An Unconventional Operations Force cannot change its language and region every few years and be expected to develop any significant degree of expertise or understanding of a region.

These regions must be carefully selected based on world dynamics and not based on current force structure. This means identify the regions and allocate (vice apportion) the battalions, then determine the headquarters structure at SF Group level. This may mean that different regions will have different mixes and numbers of allocated battalions. Concurrently, make the SF battalions more organizationally independent, even at the expense of the SF Group support structure.

The current SF Group headquarters structure will probably require modification. Some structure should be moved to the battalions. Conversely, no matter how much the battalions' structure increases, the SF Group must have assets available to augment or weight a battalion in a given scenario. Another consideration is to move the Group headquarters into the theaters and make them the Army component headquarters for the

CINC's Special Operations Commands. The focus of UOF activity will be the battalion, not the SF Group.

The advantages of this are obvious. The United States gains regional experts with on-the-ground experience, able to help obviate Huntington's "jungle-like world of multiple dangers, hidden traps, unpleasant surprises and moral ambiguities." Additionally, this provides for mutual trust and understanding through personal and sustained contact with regional personalities. This can easily be the most important outcome of the long-term regional orientation. In most of the developing nations, personal relationships are the key to trust and understanding. UOF can develop these relationships and facilitate the critical interface between coalition forces in a conflict as in DESERT SHIELD/STORM. UOF, sufficiently resourced, can maintain a forward presence that can reassure nervous nations and increase regional stability. Furthermore, in the event of an incident or even conflict, these elements then provide a ready source of first-hand regional expertise.

Unconventional operations provide a realistic option for the uncertain future. Unconventional operations forces, focused and resourced, can provide a low risk option for the future as U.S. foreign policy continues to evolve. However, significant attention and resources must be focused on these unconventional operations forces. These unconventional operations forces can, and most likely will, play an increasingly active role around the world, especially during the next 10-30 years of global transition.

Annex D: Evolution of Unconventional Warfare Definition

This Annex tracks the historical evolution of the definition and context of Unconventional Warfare. There is no attempt to try to identify every possible reference, anecdotal or official. The following 43 (+/-) references will lay out an accurate, if not exact, picture of the evolution of the definition of unconventional warfare as per United States doctrine.

We will start after World War II and the Korean War and after the 1947 National Security Act which reorganized the military and the Department of Defense.

****

(1951) Army Field Manual 31-20 Organization and Conduct of Guerrilla Warfare October dated 1 February 1951

At the time of this publication, no "Special Forces" organization existed within the U.S. military.

On the 27th of March 1952, the Chief of Staff of the Army, Gen. Collins, gave his approval for the establishment of a Psychological Warfare and Special Forces Center at Fort Bragg North Carolina. On 29 May 1952 the Chief of Army Field Forces at Fort Monroe, Virginia, formally announced the activation of the Psychological Warfare Center at Fort Bragg. The 10th Special Forces Group was a subordinate unit of the Psychological Warfare School at Fort Bragg.[153] The first Special Forces Group, the 10th SFG, was activated at Fort Bragg, NC on 19 June 1952 with Colonel Aaron Banks as its commander.[154]

Likewise, unconventional warfare was not yet a term in use. But having just come out of the Second World War, there was an understanding of the role of politics. In the first chapter of FM 31-21, in the first section, the role of the then un-named interagency process was recognized:

c. The organization and exploitation of guerilla forces often touch upon spheres and policies outside those of the military establishment. When this occurs, the application of the principles in this manual will be coordinated with the affected agencies and departments of the national government.

The first mention of "special forces operations" occurs on page ten and continues the discussion of the political aspects, which today should be the purview of the interagency process:

c.(2) Coordination with other types of special forces operations and to avoid duplication, conflict, and omission of effort.

d. The promotion and direction of guerilla warfare cannot be carried on effectively as an activity of any one general staff section.

e. The political and postwar aspects of guerilla operations must be considered as well as the immediate military aspects.

---

153 Alfred H. Paddock, Jr. *U.S. Army Special Warfare: Its Origins.* 2002. University Press of Kansas. Pages 139 – 141.
154 Aaron Bank, Col. USA. *From OSS to the Green Berets: The Birth of Special Forces.* 1986. Presidio Press. Page 171.

The Field Manual (FM) discusses how to organize guerrilla forces and outlines three phases:

- *In the first phase of organization, individuals band together under local leadership.*
- *In the second phase of organization, the number and size of units increase.*
- *During the third phase of organization, unified command is established over certain areas.*

In the section on Responsibility: *the responsibility for fostering, supporting, and exploiting guerilla forces before and during hostilities is a national one. These operations are conducted by a national agency.*

Part 2 of the manual is titled: Theater Organization and Operations--Chapter 5: Theater Special Forces Command. This part of the manual made the visionary statement that:

> *"In future wars, the organization and conduct of guerrilla warfare in the enemy's rear areas, and other types of special forces operations may be expected to receive even greater emphasis than during World War II. As a result, such operations must no longer be considered as unusual or exceptional and must be accepted as a normal feature of military operations. This makes it essential that the theater organization contain adequate provisions for the conduct of special forces operations."*

They follow this with a *Section 22. Special Forces Operations* which states:

> *"These may be broadly defined as operations conducted for a military purpose in enemy controlled territory beyond the combat zone. In addition to the organization and direction of guerilla forces as described in this manual, these operations may include any or all of the following:*

- *Dissemination of propaganda*

- *The infiltration or organization of agents within the enemy's spheres of influence*
- *Subversive activities*
- *Commando operations*
- *Organization and operation of special intelligence nets*
- *Recovery of escaped allied prisoners of war and downed aircrews*

The theater organizational chart clearly had the Theater Special Forces Command on an equal par with the other Services:

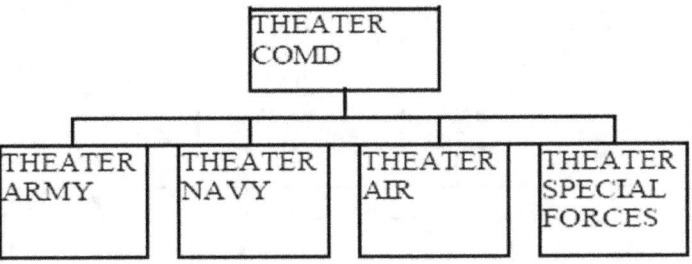

Figure 1. Theater special forces command organized on the same level as theater army, navy, and air

Under *"Responsibilities: the Theater Special Forces commander is responsible to the theater commander for the training, administration, and employment of special forces personnel and units. He is responsible to the theater commander for the conduct of special forces operations and the coordination of those operations with the theater army, navy, air, and organize joint task forces."*

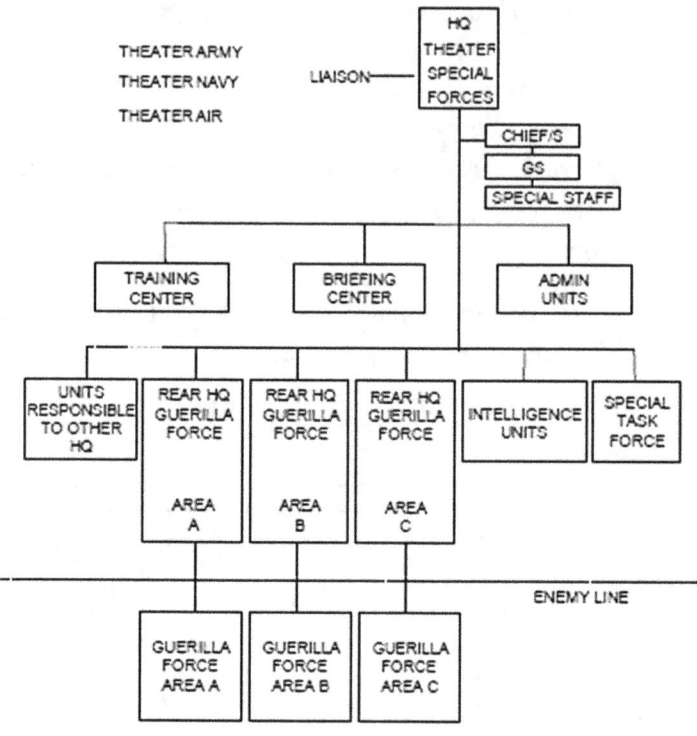

Figure 2. Typical Organization of theater special forces command

Also stated is: *"Controlled guerrilla forces operating in enemy controlled territory are the major subordinate commands of the theater Special Forces."*

Under section 38. Basic Policies. *"Political, economic, and military factors all directly affect special forces operations and are considered in planning and executing operations."* This was the recognition of the yet-to-be-named interagency process.

The manual also lays out six operational phases which line up with the current seven phases of unconventional warfare (see Annex K):

1) *Psychological preparation*
2) *Initial contact*
3) *Infiltration of operational groups*

4) *Organization and partial supply*
5) *Logistical buildup*
6) *Exploitation*

Note: *Operational Groups-These are composed of specially qualified military personnel, in uniform, organized, trained, and equipped to operate as teams within enemy territory. The size and composition of an operational group varies with the mission it is assigned. The underlying mission is usually to organize existing guerilla forces or resistance groups into a guerilla force under a unified command, capable of conducting strategically and tactical operations against the enemy in coordination with theater operation (see Annex P: OSS Manuals from WWII).*

The manual lays out an understanding of guerrilla operations that far exceeds current day understanding of the role guerrilla/insurgent forces can play in the operational area. In the section under exploitation after D-Day, the manual lays out the extremely valuable services guerrilla forces can provide to conventional U.S./coalition forces. Some are:

- *Intelligence and information for behind enemy lines*
- *Seizure of key facilities in the enemy's rear*
- *Rescuing prisoners of war*
- *Providing guides and interpreters*
- *Providing flank protection, both tactical and strategic*
- *Manning assigned sectors for regular combat particularly in extreme terrain such as mountain or jungle*
- *Mopping up and securing bypassed areas and cut off enemy units*
- *Population control*
- *Providing protection for key installations such as bridges, supply depots, lines of communications*

During the invasion of Iraq during Operation Iraqi Freedom (OIF), neither conventional nor the special operations commanders adequately planned for victory. There was no viable effort made to address the above listed items prior to the invasion. As a result, when the U.S./coalition forces declared "victory," they were totally unprepared for the insurgency that erupted.

****

(1955 May) Army Field Manual Army Field Manual 31-21 Guerrilla Warfare dated May (23 March) 1955 (Supersedes 1951 Army Field Manual 31-21, 5 October 1951)

This manual had the first doctrinal definition of unconventional warfare:

> *Unconventional Warfare. Unconventional warfare operations are conducted in time of war behind enemy lines by predominantly indigenous personnel responsible in varying degrees to friendly control or direction in furtherance of military and political objectives. It consists of the interrelated fields of guerrilla warfare, evasion and escape, and subversion against hostile states (resistance).*

As the first doctrine published after the official formation of Special Forces, it clarifies that clandestine operations, along with other skill sets, were essential in support of guerrilla operations. It also states "in time of war" and WWII was the last time we had a declared war. The writers certainly did not envision the "non-war" world of conflict of today. This FM also introduced a detailed model for supporting guerillas.

> *Each operational team has the capability of organizing and developing a guerrilla force. This guerrilla force has the following inherent capabilities*
>
> > *(1) To conduct guerrilla warfare in support of conventional military operations.*
> > *(2) To augment the execution of theater policies in the conduct of political, economic, sociological, and psychological operations.*

(3) To conduct clandestine operations. These operations include intelligence, security, evasion and escape, and sabotage, as they become essential for supporting the conduct of guerrilla operations.
(4) To conduct raider type operations.
(5) To conduct such other related operations as directed

This Field Manual (FM) mirrors how to organize guerrilla forces and follows the same three phases as the 1951 manual:

- *In the first phase of organization, individuals band together under local leadership.*
- *In the second phase of organization, the number and size of units increase.*
- *During the third phase of organization, centralized command is established over defined areas.*

Again this manual describes the utility of guerilla units after link-up with conventional forces:

- Flank protection
- Conventional combat
- Mop up by-passed areas
- Control of civilian population

The importance of the interagency is indirectly referred to in section *64. Role of Sponsoring and Sponsored Powers.*

a. When a sponsoring power, usually in conjunction with an appropriate government-in-exile, has completed the exploitation of a guerrilla force, it may release the force to the provisional government or, government-in-exile having primary nationalistic interest,
b. Under this provisional government falls the responsibility for physical, psychological, and administrative demobilization of such a guerrilla force.

There is no reference to Special Forces in this manual.

****

(1955 August) Army Field Manual 31-20 U.S. Army Special Forces Group (Airborne) dated 10 August 1955 (Supersedes Army Field Manual 31-20, 1 February 1951)

This is the first Field Manual (FM) specifically for Special Forces and was a classified document until declassified May 3, 1976.

> Under Purpose and Scope *"the manual also discusses the phases of development, organization, support, and direction of guerrilla forces, consisting primarily of indigenous peoples and a minimum number of participating United States personnel and, equipment."*

The definition of guerrilla warfare was:

> *Guerrilla Warfare: Comprises operations conducted generally in enemy held territory by predominantly indigenous forces organized on a quasi-military or military basis, with or without the support of sponsoring power, for the purpose of reducing the combat effectiveness, logistical support capability, industrial capability, and morale of an enemy nation by inflicting damage and casualties.*

This second definition of unconventional warfare was much shorter:

> *Unconventional Warfare: Consists of the interrelated fields of guerrilla warfare, escape and evasion, and subversion against hostile states.*

Under Characteristics of the Special Forces Group, *"the group is a cellular type unit employed at theater level. It operates initially within the Army forces of the theater to conduct guerrilla operation."* In this section, the term *JUWTF – joint unconventional warfare task force* is introduced.

The manual states that each *"cellular operational team"* has *"the capability of organizing and developing a guerrilla force"* with the inherent qualities of:

(1) To conduct guerrilla warfare in support of conventional military operations

(2) capitalize augment the execution of theater policies in the conduct of political, economic, sociological, and psychological operations.

(3) To conduct clandestine operations. These include intelligence, security, evasion and escape, and sabotage.

(4) To conduct raider type operations

(5) To conduct such other related operations as directed

The lowest level operational detachment was the team FA (Functional A) what we know today as the A-Team (or Special Forces Operational Detachment - A --SFODA). The mission was to organize a guerrilla regiment. The Team FB mission was to organize the district command of two or more guerrilla regiments. The Team FC mission was to organize a larger district and deal with guerrilla leaders. The Team FD mission was to organize an area command of two or more district commands.

Mission: the primary mission of special forces units for guerrilla operations is to infiltrate operational detachments by air, sea, or land to designated areas within the enemy's sphere of influence....

a) *To develop, support; organize, train, and exploit indigenous guerrilla potential already generated or to be generated in support of conventional military operations and the national military objectives.*

b) *To provide appropriate specialists and advisors to assist in achieving the above on a coordinated basis.*

c) *To perform such other missions that may be directed by the area commander, or that may be inherent in or essential to the primary mission of guerrilla warfare.*

Several things are interesting about this very first mission of Special Forces. First, the mission is fully focused on guerrillas and guerrilla warfare. Second, it states that Special Forces can *generate guerrilla potential* whereas the current UW doctrine clearly says that Special Forces do not build a resistance. Maybe this is not in conflict. If a resistance exists, then Special Forces can generate guerrilla potential from this existing resistance. This is not generating a resistance, just capitalizing on it.

In chapter 4, the manual also points out the organization of the teams, operational teams. It states that *"the operational teams are identified by using letter combinations that indicate the relative operational levels after deployment."*

One can begin to see where the numerical designation of Special Forces detachments evolve with the "D" detachment being the group headquarters while the "C" is battalion level and the "B" is company level with the "A" being the smallest operational detachment level.

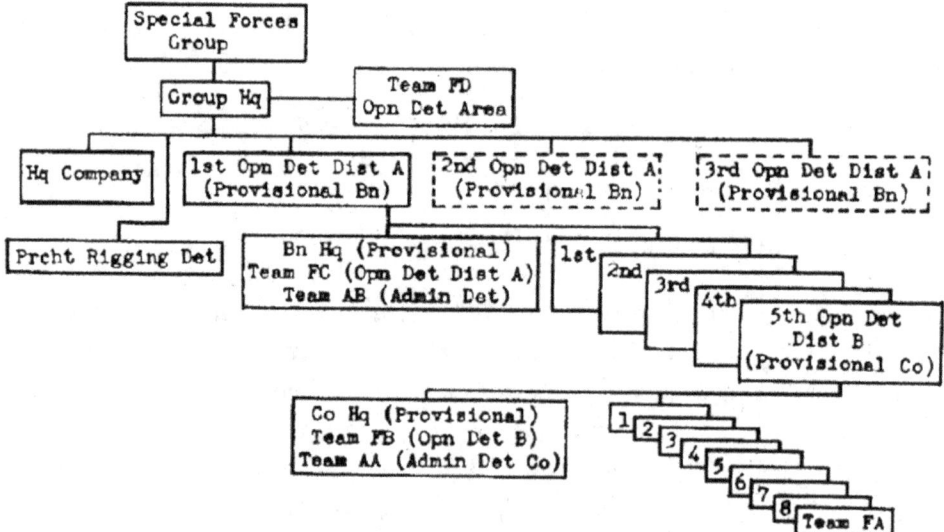

Figure 5. Nontactical organization of the special forces group.

This FM introduces seven (7) phases of the development of guerrilla forces:

a. *Phase 1 – psychological preparation*
b. *Phase 2 – initial contact with resistant elements*
   (Footnote in the FM states that phase 1 and 2 should be conducted prior to D-Day by governmental organizations other than Special Forces. However, if these phases have not been accomplished prior to D-Day, phases 1, 2 and 3 will be carried out simultaneously by special forces operational teams - this was the situation in Afghanistan in October 2001)
c. *Phase 3 – infiltration of special forces operational teams*
d. *Phase 4 – military organization of guerrilla forces*
e. *Phase 5 – buildup of guerrilla forces*
f. *Phase 6 – military exploitation of guerrilla forces.* This not only included combat missions but also acting as guides and interpreters, provide flank protection, mop up by-passed areas, act as security troops, and assist the military government or civil affairs.
g. *Phase 7 – administrative (The FM defines this as further utilization or demobilization of the guerrilla forces)*

****

(1958 May) Army Field Manual 31-21 Guerrilla Warfare and Special Forces Operations dated 8 May 1958 (Supersedes Army Field Manual 31-20, 10 August 1955, and Army Field Manual 31-21, 23 March 1955)

It is in this FM that we see an interesting addition in *Purpose and Scope - the material presented herein is applicable to both atomic and monotonic warfare.*

Special Forces in fact had an atomic role known as Project Greenlight with certain teams known as "Greenlight" teams. I know...in 1976, I was briefly a Greenlight team leader. The Greenlight mission did not exist when this manual was written.

During the Cold War, we actually did have man-portable nuclear devices. They weighed around 90 pounds with container. The weapons maximum capability was less than one kiloton. These were known as "backpack nukes." The weapon was officially retired in 1989, when it was declared obsolete.

This manual does not provide a definition for unconventional warfare. In the section "*Explanation of Terms*" guerrilla warfare is explained as a part of unconventional warfare.

> *"Guerilla warfare comprises that part of unconventional warfare which is conducted by relatively small groups employing offensive tactics to reduce enemy combat effectiveness, industrial capacity, and morale. Guerilla operations are normally conducted in enemy-controlled territory by units organized on a military basis. It must be emphasized that unconventional warfare is an activity which, in addition to guerilla warfare, includes evasion and escape and subversion against hostile states."*

Chapter 4: Mission of Special Forces.

Mission:

a. *The primary mission of special forces units is to develop, organize, equip, train, support, and control guerrilla forces and to conduct guerrilla warfare in support of conventional military operations.*

b. *Secondary missions of special forces units are —*

1) *Engage in psychological warfare, intelligence, escape and evasion, and subversion against hostile states (resistance).*

2) *Provide appropriate specialists and advisors to assist in accomplishing the above missions on a coordinated basis.*

3) *Perform such other missions as may be directed by the theater commander.*

Found in 21. Concept: b.(3) *On or immediately after D-day special forces teams are infiltrated into an area of operations where guerrilla potential exists. This potential may be either organized or unorganized.*

The Special Forces Group follows the same basic organization as the previous manual.

36. Command Structure: a. Depending on the size of the area and the extent of planned operations, a team FA, FB, FC, or FD is the command and control team for all unconventional warfare operations within the area.

****

(1961) Army Field Manual 31-21 Guerrilla Warfare and Special Forces Operations dated 29 September 1961 (Supersedes Army Field Manual 31-21, 8 May 1958)

This third definition of unconventional warfare now combines elements of the definitions of UW and GW from the earlier works.

Glossary of Terms:

Unconventional Warfare. The three interrelated fields of guerrilla warfare, evasion and escape, and subversion. (JCS Pub 1).

Unconventional Warfare Forces. Forces who engage in unconventional warfare. For the purposes of this manual, UW forces include both U.S. forces (special forces detachments) and the sponsored resistance force (guerrillas, auxiliaries and the underground). Often used interchangeably with the area command.

While the above was the approved joint definition per JCS Pub 1, Chapter 1 provided an expanded definition for UW and a delineation of responsibilities.

Chapter 1. Section 2. Definition of Unconventional Warfare

Unconventional warfare consists of the interrelated fields of guerrilla warfare, evasion and escape, and subversion against hostile states (resistance). Unconventional warfare operations are conducted in enemy or enemy controlled territory by predominantly indigenous personnel usually supported and directed in varying degrees by an external source.

Chapter 1. Section 3. Delineation of Responsibilities for Unconventional Warfare

a. *The responsibility for certain activities has been delegated to the service having primary concern. Guerrilla warfare is the responsibility of the United States Army.*

b. *Within certain designated geographic areas – called guerrilla warfare operational areas – the United States Army is responsible for the conduct of all three interrelated fields of activity as they affect guerrilla warfare operations.*

c. *The military operations of resistance movements are customarily supported and accompanied by political and economic activities – both overt and clandestine – of individuals and groups integrated, or acting in conjunction with guerrillas. The several types of activities are interlocking. The term unconventional warfare is used in this manual to denote all of the United States Army's associated responsibilities in the conduct of guerrilla warfare. The term guerrilla warfare is used to denote the primary overt military activities of the guerrilla forces.*

Chapter 2. Section 5. Guerrilla warfare: guerrilla warfare comprises combat operations conducted in enemy-held ter-

ritory by predominantly indigenous forces on a military or paramilitary basis to reduce the combat effectiveness, industrial capacity, and morale of the enemy. Guerrilla operations are conducted by relatively small groups employing offensive tactics. Guerrilla warfare supports other military operations.

Note: "The importance of the term "inter-related" cannot be overstated here. The term UW was used to portray a construct larger that the individual subordinate topics that comprised its whole. Other branches of the military and other government agencies shared responsibility for various components of the UW discipline. The Army was focused (over focused) on the more familiar guerrilla portion of this topic while remaining relatively uninterested in the subversion portion.

During this period, DoD and the CIA were competing for ownership of this role. The delineation broke out with the CIA assuming primacy for the peacetime resistance while the Army would assume control in wartime. While advocates of Special Forces understood that this division of labor along peacetime and wartime (underground forces and guerrilla forces or by overt and clandestine means) would not work, the military showed little interest beyond the commando-style operations, that they were now equating as guerrilla warfare.

The release of the 1961 FM 31-21, Guerrilla Warfare and Special Forces Operations, seems to have made a point to state that UW consists of the interrelated fields, insinuating that they should not be conducted in isolated or more accurately by different organizations. It then goes on to state that although the Army has responsibility for GW, in certain theaters the Army will remain prepared to assume control of all interrelated activities." - (comment by then LTC Mark Grdovic, SF)

In Chapter 1. Section 7. Special Forces Operations states:

> *The value of coordinating guerrilla activities with conventional military operations and the need for peacetime planning and training by the potential sponsor have been recognized by the United States. The unit organized and trained to implement the Army's responsibilities in directing guerrilla operations is the Airborne Special Forces Group. Special forces units may be called upon to operate behind a general, limited or cold war.*

In Chapter 1, Section 8 "Capabilities and Limitations" the opening paragraph states:

> a. *...Special forces directed guerrilla units (called UW forces) conduct operations...."*
>
> *(1) Missions in support of theater commander. These missions include—*
>
> > *(a) Interdiction of lines of communications, key areas and military and industrial installations.*
> >
> > *(b) Psychological operations.*
> >
> > *(c) Special intelligence tasks such as target acquisition and damage assessment.*
> >
> > *(d) Evasion and escape operations.*
> >
> > *(e) Cover and deception operations.*
>
> *(2) Missions to support combat operations of tactical commanders. In addition to an intensification of the tasks listed in (1) above, UW forces execute missions to directly assist conventional forces engaged in combat operations.*
>
> *Such missions may include—*
>
> > *(a) Seizure of key terrain to facilitate airborne and amphibious operations.*

(b) Employment as a reconnaissance and security force.

(c) Seizure of key installations to prevent destruction by the enemy.

(d) Diversionary attacks against enemy forces to support cover and deception plans.

(e) Operations which isolate selected portions of the battle area, airborne objective area or beachhead.

(3) Missions conducted after juncture with friendly forces. In the event control of guerrilla units is retained by the United States, the following missions may be assigned:

(a) Reconnaissance and security missions.

(b) When properly trained and supported, conventional combat operations.

(c) Rear area security missions.

(d) Counter-guerrilla operations.

(e) Support of civil affairs operations.

Chapter 3 introduces the Joint Unconventional Warfare Task Force (JUWTF) and has it on a par with the theater service components.

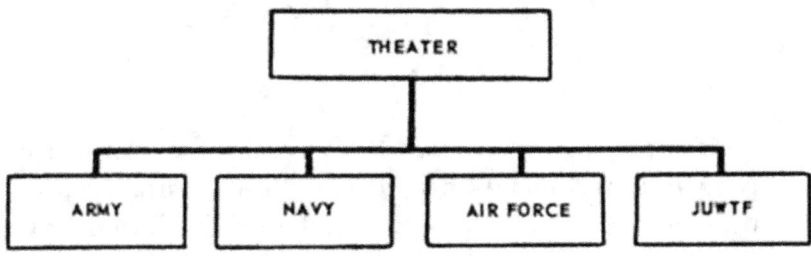

Figure 1. A theater organization.

The FM states that: *Initially, operational control of U.S. sponsored unconventional warfare forces is retained by the theater commander... exercised through the JUWTF...When guerrilla warfare operational areas fall under the area of influence of advancing tactical commands, operational control...is transferred through the theater army to the field army concern.*

Chapter 4: Airborne Special Forces Group: provides the following mission statement for Special Forces:

> *The mission of special forces is to develop, organize, equip, train, and direct indigenous forces in the conduct of guerrilla warfare. Special forces may also advise, train and assist indigenous forces in counterinsurgency operations.*

This SF FM also has the organization of the "Airborne Special Forces Group" as a headquarters and headquarters company and four Special Forces companies.

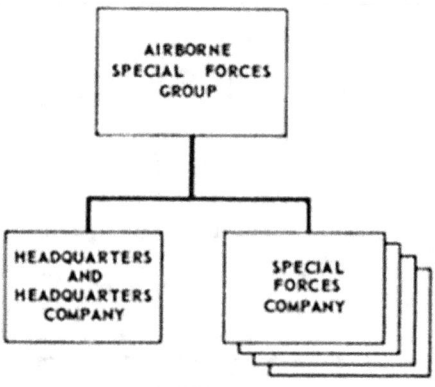

Figure 2. Airborne special forces group.

As is shown in the diagram below, each of the Special Forces companies is actually what we would call a battalion organization today. However, unlike today, the Op Det B (today's ODB) or company headquarters, did not have administrative and operational control of the Op Det A (today's ODAs). In this 1961 manual, all of the detachments were independently assigned directly to the headquarters of this company (battalion) organization. Not only were the three Op Det B organizations directly assigned to the company (battalion) headquarters but all twelve of the Op Det A's were also independently assigned directly to the (battalion) headquarters.

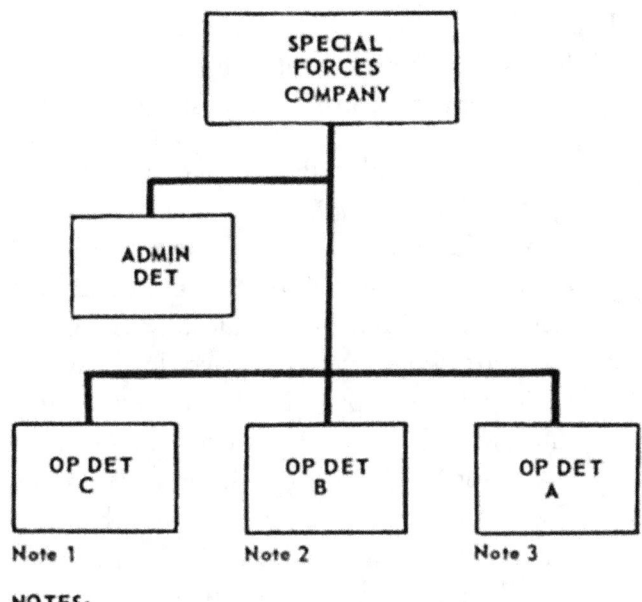

NOTES:
1. Op Det Comd is also Co Comd.
2. Three (3) per SF Co.
3. Twelve (12) per SF Co.

Figure 5. Special forces company.

On page 53, Section 44, states that *"A thorough knowledge of the enemy, terrain and resistance potential, coupled with an intimate understanding of the indigenous population within the operational areas, is essential to the success of unconventional warfare operations. Prior to deployment, special forces operational detachments complete detailed area studies..."*

On page 54, regional orientation is again emphasized by the following paragraph: Section 45 (2) *"In order to improve the chances for success in combat operations, the Special Forces detachment requires a greater degree of preparation in pre-deployment intelligence than Army units of battle group or comparable size. It is desirable for the detachment to acquire this intelligence background well in advance of operations by intensive area study of pre-designated regions of the world."*

This ability to acquire the regional intelligence as stated above, reinforces the importance of regional focus, regional engagement, on a persistent and continuous basis forward stationed.

> "In many regards this appears to have been the Army Special Forces response to an unfavorable delineation of responsibilities by DoD and an effort to justify retaining the skills required for working with the whole of the resistance and not merely those with a guerrilla force. If the reader wonders why this wouldn't have been resolved, it's important to place this in context. As this debate was underway, the Bay of Pigs fiasco had occurred. The end result was DoD having no interest in arguing for ownership of these questionable operations beyond those of the quasi-familiar and quantifiable guerrilla warfare portion as well as the escalating crisis to (re)learn counterinsurgency as soon as possible." - LTC Mark Grdovic

****

(1965 June) Army Field Manual 31-21 Special Forces Operations dated 5 June 1965 (Supersedes Army Field Manual 31-21, 29 September 1961, including C 1, 4 September 1963)

In this 1965 manual, now the fourth distinct definition of unconventional warfare is as follows:

> *Unconventional warfare includes the three interrelated fields of guerrilla warfare, escape and evasion, and subversion. Unconventional warfare operations are conducted within enemy or enemy-controlled territory by predominantly indig-*

enous personnel, usually supported and directed in varying degrees by an external source.

Unconventional warfare forces- U.S. forces having an existing unconventional warfare capability consisting of Army special forces and such Navy, Air Force, and Marine units as are assigned for these operations.

The difference in the UW definition between this 1965 manual and the 1961 manual definition is only in the first sentence. This definition leaves out *"in hostile states."* In both definitions the second sentences are exactly the same. A significant change is in the definition of *unconventional warfare forces.* For the first time the other Services are mentioned.

Under Chapter 1. Section 5. "Responsibilities for the Conduct of Unconventional Warfare," it states : *a. "Responsibility for developmental action in each of the interrelated fields of unconventional warfare has been delegated to that department or agency of the U.S. government having primary concern. Guerrilla warfare is the responsibility of the U.S. Army,"* but in *para b. ...U.S. Army Special Forces must be prepared to assume responsibilities for all three interrelated fields.*

To further emphasize the importance of the interagency process even at this early stage of the development of UW doctrine, the last paragraph c. states that *"Guerrilla operations are customarily supported and accompanied by both overt and clandestine political and economic activities of individuals and groups integrated or acting in concert with established guerrilla forces. These types of activities are interlocking."*

As far as the organization of the Airborne Special Forces Group is concerned, it is the same as in the 1961 manual all except that there is a signal company and an aviation company added. (It's interesting to note that in these earlier manuals the SF organization was called Airborne Special Forces Group vice; today they are called Special Forces Groups (Airborne).

The organization of the Special Forces Company (today's battalion) remains the same as in 1961. The mission statement has three parts as follows:

1) *To plan and conduct unconventional warfare operations in areas not under friendly control.*
2) *To organize, equip, train, and direct indigenous forces in the conduct of guerrilla warfare.*
3) *To perform such other unconventional warfare missions as may be directed, or as may be inherent in or essential to the primary mission of conducting guerrilla warfare.*

As far as the aviation company of the airborne Special Forces group is concerned, it was formed to *"To provide aviation support for the airborne special forces group in unconventional warfare operations in limited or general war."* This aviation company had both fixed wing and rotary wing assets.

Chapter 6, Concept of Employment of Army Special Forces. Section 31. General., states *"U.S. Army Special Forces detachments consist of personnel cross-trained in basic and specialized military skills and organized into small multipurpose detachments. These detachments are tailored to provide training to guerrilla forces in functions of command, staff, operations, intelligence, weapons and tactics, communications, medical, and demolitions."*

Unlike what we see in today's Special Forces and for that matter, in Special Forces since at least the '70s, this manual clearly has the Detachments C (the Battalion headquarters or as it's called here, the company headquarters) established with the intent of being a deployed element into the GWOA. Since my introduction to Special Forces in the mid-'70s, I have never seen or even heard of a battalion headquarters training itself to be deployable into the operational area for the purpose of training guerrilla forces or indigenous forces on command and staff. This was always relegated down to the ODA. This obviously was counter to the intent, or at least the original intent, of the formation of Special Forces.

This manual establishes *the phases in development of guerrilla warfare as:*

1) *phase 1: psychological preparation*
2) *phase 2: initial contact*
3) *phase 3: infiltration*
4) *phase 4: organization*
5) *phase 5: build up*
6) *phase 6: combat employment*
7) *phase 7: demobilization*

This manual also describes the methodology used to determine how many guerrillas can be training employed by Special Forces operational detachment. The number will vary in accordance with the geographical location, the ethnic groups encountered, the general level of illiteracy, and their previous exposure to military training. In some areas a complete Special Forces detachment may be required to train and direct the force of 200 guerrillas (page 77) whereas in other areas Special Forces detachments may direct, advise, train, and support large guerrilla formations.

> *"The 1965 FM expands on the role of SF in COIN in a separate Part Three COIN. In the newly added Counterinsurgency chapter, the FM makes a point to distinguish UW from COIN."* - LTC Mark Grdovic

> Page 180: Chapter 11 (COIN) Section 103. Planning Considerations

> *c. Broad unconventional warfare doctrine does not apply to counterinsurgency situations. In unconventional warfare operations, the U.S.-sponsored guerrillas operate deep within enemy or enemy-dominated territory and are the insurgent elements. Their efforts are directed toward the delay and harassment of the enemy military force and are facilitated by inducing the local civilians to support the guerrilla effort. In counterinsurgency operations, U.S. supported forces are operating in a less*

restrictive operational environment with their efforts directed toward prevention or countering the insurgent movement by winning the support of the population, thus denying the insurgents this support and by combat action against the insurgent forces. However, selected UW tactics and techniques such as establishing intelligence nets and methods used to gain the support of the local population and combat techniques such as raids and ambushes may apply to counterinsurgency. These tactics and techniques may be used in advising indigenous military and paramilitary forces engaged in remote area operations to promote defense and internal security, border control and surveillance tasks.

Page 181: Chapter 11 (COIN) Section 104. Missions of Special Forces in COIN

b. Primary Missions. The COIN trained Special Forces Group may be effectively employed:

(2) To train, advise, and provide operational assistance to host country special-forces type units operating against insurgent elements within areas of the host country dominated by the insurgent.

(3) To act as advisors to indigenous special forces, provincial authorities, and tribal leaders in the recruitment, organization, equipping, training, and operational employment of host country tribal elements or ethnic minority groups.

****

(1965 December) Army Field Manual 31-20 Special Forces Operational Techniques dated 30 December 1965 (This manual together with Army Field Manual 31 – 20A, 30 December 1965, supersedes Army Field Manual 31 – 20, 16 October 1964, including C 1, 13 February 1962 and C 2, 19 July 1962)

This manual does not provide a definition for unconventional warfare either in the glossary or in the body of the document. However in, Chapter 5. Planning and Operations. Section 1. Unconventional Warfare. Paragraph 33. Command and Control. Sub-paragraph a. Unconventional Environment there is a discussion of guerrilla warfare and guerrilla warfare operational areas (GWOA).

> When the GWOA has been designated by the unified commander, any of the special forces operational detachments (A, B, or C) may be selected to infiltrate first.

> The terrain, enemy situation, complex political problems, or the ethnic groupings within a resistance movement may require two or more detachments to the infiltrated simultaneously.

> This manual primarily discusses counterinsurgency.

> Subparagraph 45. Application of UW Techniques.

> Unconventional warfare techniques, in establishing intelligence nets; evasion and escape mechanisms on a limited scale; the use of psychological methods to gain support of the local population; and raids, ambushes, and air operations all have application in counterinsurgency.

(1969 February) Army Field Manual 31-21 Special Forces Operations - U.S. Army Doctrine dated 14 February 1969 (Supersedes Army Field Manual 31-21, 3 June 1965—Note: the referenced manual is actually dated 5 June 1965)

This manual begins by laying out the role of the U.S. Army Special Forces. According to this manual:

> *Chapter 1. Section II. 1-4. General: The role of U.S. Army Special Forces is to contribute within their capability to the accomplishment of whatever missions and responsibilities are assigned to the U.S. Army. Within the framework of that*

*contribution, the U.S. Army Special Forces group is a mul-
tipurpose force which, by organization, flexible command
arrangement, tailored logistical and fiscal procedures, and
highly trained personnel, can address a variety of missions. As
the repository of expertise within the Army for unconventional warfare (UW), Special Forces must be constantly prepared
to assume missions of this nature during any intensity of conflict. Since the option for unconventional warfare is selective,
special forces are able to employ these highly trained assets,
and other appropriate and very missions which contribute to
the accomplishment of the overall mission of the Army.*

*Section III. Special Forces Mission and Capabilities. 1-6.
Mission:*

1) *Plan and conduct unconventional warfare operations*

2) *Plan, conduct, and support stability operations*

3) *Plan and conduct direct action missions which are pecu-
liar to Special Forces due to their organization, training,
equipment, and psychological preparation.*

The manual then continues on into "1-7. Capabilities" section
which talks about organizing for guerrilla warfare, escape and
evasion's operations, advise, train and assist non-U.S. military
are paramilitary forces, but most interestingly is the *"(3) conduct
other unconventional warfare missions, either unilaterally or in conjunction with resistance forces."*

This is the first place that I have seen in the doctrine manuals any
discussion about "unilateral unconventional warfare" and I am
not sure what that means.

The Capabilities section continues to discuss *deep penetration missions to attack strategic targets and/or collect intelligence; infiltrate/
exfiltrate by air, land, or sea; survive and operate in remote areas
and hostile environments for extended periods of time with minimal*

external direction in support; recover friendly personnel from remote or hostile areas; provide planning assistance and training to U.S. or allied forces or agencies. This is the first mention in any of these manuals for some of these items or capabilities in roles.

This is also the first place where direct action missions have been specifically outlined to be conducted within hostile or denied areas without the support of indigenous forces. This is the first definitive break from Special Forces conducting operations *through, with, or by* indigenous forces and conducting unilateral operations. Of course, when this manual was written, there were no other elite forces available to conduct these kinds of missions behind enemy lines, in strategic situations, with little or no support. This manual predates the organization of the Rangers, or Delta. The SEALs were not considered because this is an Army manual.

The glossary in the manual describes the direct action mission as per below:

> *Direct Action Mission—Overt or clandestine operations in hostile or denied areas which are conducted by U.S. UW forces, rather than by U.S. conventional forces or through U.S. direction of indigenous forces.*

FM 31-21 dated 29 September 1961 Guerrilla Warfare and Special Forces Operations defines *unconventional warfare forces* as forces who engage in unconventional warfare. For the purposes of this manual, UW forces include both U.S. forces (special forces detachments) and the sponsored resistance force (guerrillas, auxiliaries and the underground). Often used interchangeably with the area command.

FM 31-21 dated 5 June 1965 Special Forces Operations, which supersedes the 1961 manual, defines *unconventional warfare forces* as U.S. forces having an existing unconventional warfare capability consisting of Army special forces and such Navy, Air Force, and Marine units as are assigned for these operations.

As far as I am concerned, any unilateral mission flies in the face of the unique capability of Special Forces to conduct all operations *through, with, and by* indigenous populations. There are plenty of other forces capable of unilateral operations. If and when Special Forces conducts any type of unilateral operation, that is an indication of a failure to get the indigenous population to conduct that mission *through, with, or by*. If there's any point in time when a unilateral direct action mission is required in support of UW, it should be conducted at the request of Special Forces by those SOF specifically dedicated to direct action such as Delta, Rangers, SEALs, etc., or conventional forces such are the 82d Airborne or the USMC.

This 1969 manual is also where we see the change in terminology and organization of the Special Forces Group. In the other manuals, the organizations that were called companies are now called Special Forces Battalions and in each battalion there are three Special Forces companies. In each of the Special Forces Companies there are five Special Forces Operational Detachments.

As far as deployment and utilization is concerned, this manual still states that the battalion headquarters organization and the company headquarters organization can deploy on independent UW missions. Again I've never even seen a battalion headquarters trained to do this type of independent UW mission.

As far as the organization of the operational detachments within each of the companies, the manual differentiates between UW/stability operations and direct action missions. These detachments consist of fourteen personnel and can organize, equip, train, and direct or advise non-U.S. military or paramilitary forces up to and including a battalion-size force for sustained operations. This is also the first place that they have delineated the exact size of an organization that a Special Forces detachment is to be capable of training. Furthermore, the UW/stability detachment has a different organizational structure than the direct action detachment.

UW/stability detachment: commander; executive officer; detachment Sgt.; 2 intelligence specialists; 2 engineer sergeants; 2 medical specialists; 2 weapons specialists; 2 radio operators; one supply sergeant.

Direct action detachment: commander; 2 enlisted team leaders; 2 assistant team leaders; 2 medical specialists; 2 engineer sergeants; 4 radio operators; one radio operator's supervisor. This attachment is organized to operate as to 6-man teams directed by the commander with the radio supervisor for communications.

Concept of employment.

1) *General. The Special Forces operational detachment is the basic operational element of the Special Forces Group. It is employed in an operational role to serve as a nucleus for the organization, training, and development of indigenous guerrilla or paramilitary forces for the conduct of unconventional warfare or stability operations. The operational detachment may also be employed unilaterally as a force for the accomplishment of direct action missions. This element of the Special Forces Group is capable of conducting sustained operations with limited outside support while operating directly under the supervision of the SFOB.*

It was during this time frame that the Cold War was going hot and heavy. Yes, we were deeply involved and embedded in Vietnam, but the Cold War and the Russians were still the driver of the organization of all U.S. military entities. Unquestionably, the focus on Europe and the Russian threat, both conventional and nuclear, fostered a direct action, unilateral, mentality. This unilateral mentality still persists today.

This time frame also viewed direct action as including strategic reconnaissance which was seen as a Special Forces unilateral mission. I've always considered this special reconnaissance activity conducted unilaterally by SF as a serious misuse and, probably an arrogant dismissal of indigenous reconnaissance capabilities.

Using Special Forces in a unilateral special reconnaissance role; in other words hiding in a hole in the ground watching a road intersection, meant the only impact that team had was their line of sight. Whereas, a developed indigenous strategic reconnaissance capability could cover an entire country.

In Part Two: Unconventional Warfare, there is a description of unconventional warfare as follows. This is the fifth definition to-date:

> *Unconventional warfare consists of military, political, psychological, or economic actions of a covert, clandestine, or overt nature within areas under the actual or potential control or influence of a force or state whose interests and objectives are inimical to those of the United States. These actions are conducted unilaterally by United States resources, or in conjunction with indigenous assets, and avoid formal military confrontation.*

> *Concept: UW is conducted to exploit military, political, economic, or psychological vulnerabilities of the enemy. It is implemented by providing support and direct action to indigenous resistance forces where appropriate, or by unilateral operations of U.S. UW forces. Its conduct involves the application of guerrilla warfare and selected aspects of subversion, political warfare, economic warfare, and psychological operations in support of national objectives*

> *Unconventional warfare operations may be covert, clandestine, or overt in nature. Covert operations are conducted in such a manner as to conceal the identity of the sponsor, while clandestine operations place emphasis on concealment of the operation rather than the identity of the sponsor. Overt operations do not try to conceal either the operation or the identity of the sponsor.*

This manual further identifies UW forces not only as U.S. Army Special Forces but also as elements of the U.S. Navy, including

Underwater Demolition Teams (UDT) and Sea Air Land Teams (SEAL teams) plus selected reconnaissance elements of the Marine Corps. They also identify elements of the Air Force including Special Air Warfare units.

It is in this 1969 manual that the term GWOA is replaced with UWOA.

On page 2-1 in Chap 2, Section II, b.(3) Stability Operations. *The Special Forces group may be assigned to unified and specified commands for the support of stability operations. The group may operate as a separate organization or as a major element of a Special Action Force (SAF) (chap 10). Special Action Force (SAF)—The SAF is a specially trained, area-oriented, partially language-qualified, ready force, available to the commander of a unified command for the support of cold, limited, and general war operations. SAF organizations may vary in size and capabilities according to theater requirements.*

For more information on the Special Action Force see Annex O.

****

(1971) Army Field Manual 31-20 Special Forces Operational Techniques dated 12 February 1971 (Supersedes Army Field Manual 31-20, 30 December 1965)

This manual does not have a definition for unconventional warfare. It presents the operational techniques for special forces operations primarily in the unconventional warfare operating area UWOA).

Chapter 5. Organization and Development of the Unconventional Warfare Operational Area. Section I. 5-1. General. The organization of an unconventional warfare operational area (UWOA) involves early compartmentation of the command structure and the subsequent build-up of the resistance force. The detachments thorough knowledge, through extensive area studies of the operational area, provide political, social, economic, and military information of the area, and an understanding of the ethnic groupings, customs, taboos, religions, and other essential data that will affect the organization, command and control, selection of leaders, and disciplinary measures to be enforced within the resistance force.

This manual continues to bring out, indirectly, the importance of the interagency process and the political commitment required for unconventional warfare.

****

(1982) Book, *Special Warfare, The Origins of Psychological and Unconventional Warfare*, COL(R) Paddock

Pg 124
While Volckmann clearly advocated the use of indigenous personnel in GW, he apparently intended that a Ranger unit would support and direct these personnel, and not the OSS type of Special Forces organization that he ultimately played such an instrumental role in creating. His use of the words, "special forces operations," then was synonymous with OCPWs[155] understanding of special operations"; that is all types of behind the lines activities conducted for a military purpose, not just guerrilla warfare. Later he would be more specific in differentiating between Ranger and commando missions and those involving the organization and support of indigenous personnel in GW."

Pg 127-128
"Part of the confusion that marked this effort (defining the mission of the newly created SF) was of their own making. Their concept of Special Forces Operations for instance was an all-encompassing heading under which were grouped many kinds of activities – of which GW was one – whose

---

155   OCPW - the Office of the Chief of Psychological Warfare, U.S. Army. 1951 -1952 Brig. Gen. Robert A. McClure led the organization and formulated the plans for the creation of the 10th Special Forces Group.

only common denominator was that they were conducted within or behind enemy lines. But as time went on, the architects of SF found it necessary to point out the error, as they saw it, of linking the SF group and its component missions with the term SFO, on the assumption that the SF Group was a TO&E unit designed to conduct all such operations. Needless to say, this rather subtle distinction was lost on many."

Between 1955-1961 the term UW began to appear in the doctrine over GW. Guerilla warfare was explained as that part of UW for which the Army retains responsibility. In a 1957 article entitled *Unconventional Warfare, the Psychological Role of Special Forces*, LTG Yarborough used the term *Unconventional Warfare* to describe the wider resistance efforts, of which the guerrilla element is merely a part. He stated,

"The nature of the unconventional warfare structure must be understood in order to appreciate the importance of the psychological component. Guerrillas are the action element of the total unconventional warfare system but they do not comprise it entirely. Moreover, guerrilla will not appear as the first manifestation of a well-conceived and organized resistance movement."

****

1989 Joint Pub 1-02 (Formerly JCS Pub 1) Department of Defense Dictionary of Military and Associated Terms dated 1 December 1989 (Supersedes JCS Pub 1, 1 June 1987)

This is one of the first documentations since the Goldwater-Nichols Department of Defense Reorganization Act of 1986 and provides the sixth definition for UW. It also provides a NATO definition:

Unconventional warfare--(DOD) a broad spectrum of military and paramilitary operations conducted in enemy-held, enemy-controlled war politically sensitive territory. Unconventional warfare includes, but is not limited to, the interrelated fields of guerrilla warfare, evasion and escape, subversion, sabotage, and other operations of a low visibility, covert or clandestine nature. These interrelated aspects of unconventional warfare may be prosecuted singly or collectively by predominantly indigenous personnel, usually supported and directed in varying degrees by (an) external source(s) during all conditions of war or peace.

unconventional warfare--(NATO) general term used to describe operations conducted for military, political or economic purposes within an area occupied by the enemy and making use of the local inhabitants and resources.

Unconventional warfare forces--(DOD) U.S. forces having an existing unconventional warfare capability consisting of Army special forces and such Navy, Air Force, and Marine units as are assigned for these operations.

****

(1990) Army Field Manual 31-20 Doctrine for Special Forces Operations dated 20 April 1990 (Supersedes Army Field Manual 31-20, 30 September 1977)

In the preface, this manual describes itself as "the Special Forces (SF) principles manual.... It describes SF roles, missions, capabilities, organization, command and control, employment, and support across the operational continuum and at all levels of war... The authoritative foundation for SF subordinate doctrine, force design, materiel acquisition, professional education, and individual and collective training."

The glossary references JCS Pub 1-02 and repeats the previous sixth definition; however, on page 3-1(see below) the manual introduces the seventh distinct definition of unconventional warfare. Two separate definitions in the same manual is interesting.

> *Unconventional Warfare - A broad spectrum of military and paramilitary operations conducted in enemy-held, enemy-controlled, or politically sensitive territory. Unconventional warfare includes, but is not limited to, the interrelated fields of guerrilla warfare, evasion and escape, subversion, sabotage, and other operations of a low visibility, covert or clandestine nature. These interrelated aspects of un-conventional warfare may be prosecuted singly or collectively by predominantly indigenous personnel, usually supported and directed in varying degrees by (an) external sources(s) during all conditions of war or peace. (JCS Pub 1-02)*

This manual has a different version of unconventional warfare on page 3 – 1:

> *UW is a broad spectrum of military and paramilitary operations, normally of long duration, predominantly conducted by indigenous or surrogate forces who are organized, trained, equipped, supported, and directed in varying degrees by an external source. UW includes guerilla warfare (GW) and other direct offensive low-visibility, covert, or clandestine operations, as well as the indirect activities of subversion, sabotage, intelligence collection, and evasion and escape (E&E).*

This manual replaced the 1977 FM 31-20 which defined "Special Operations (SO)" as specifically Strategic Reconnaissance, Direct Action and Counter Terrorism. This 1990 version defines SO as below:

> *Special Operations - (DOD) Operations conducted by specially trained, equipped, and organized DOD forces against strategic or tactical targets in pursuit of national military, political, economic, or psychological objectives. These operations may be conducted during periods of peace or hostilities. They may support conventional operations, or they may be prosecuted independently when the use of conventional forces is either inappropriate or infeasible. (JCS Pub 1-02)*

Special Operations - *Actions conducted by specially or-*
ganized, trained and equipped military and paramilitary
forces to achieve military, political, economic, or psychologi-
cal objectives by non-conventional military means in hostile,
denied, or politically sensitive areas. They are conducted in
peace, conflict, and war, independently or in coordination
with operations of conventional forces. Politico-military
considerations frequently shape special operations, requiring
clandestine, covert, or low visibility techniques, and oversight
at the national level. Special operations differ from conven-
tional operations in degree of risk, operational techniques,
mode of employment, independence from friendly support,
and dependence on detailed operational intelligence and in-
digenous assets. (USCINCSOC)

Public law (10 U.S.C 167) states that SO activities include the following as far as they relate to SO:

- *Direct action (DA).*
- *Strategic reconnaissance, which the U.S. Special*
  Operations Command (U.S.SOCOM) has incor-
  porated into a broader activity called special recon-
  naissance (SR).
- *Unconventional warfare (UW).*
- *Foreign internal defense (FID).*
- *Civil affairs (CA).*
- *Psychological operations (PSYOP).*
- *Counterterrorism (CT).*
- *Humanitarian assistance (HA).*
- *Theater search and rescue (SAR).*
- *Such other activities as may be specified by the*
  National Command Authorities (NCA).

In the post-Vietnam era Special Forces saw a significant drawdown of forces along with the rest of the military. Additionally,
due to many various factors, the reputation of Special Forces and
in particular of UW, was basically at rock-bottom. With the new

legislation of the Goldwater – Nichols Act of 1986 and the subsequent Nunn-Cohen Amendment of 1987, of all of the mission sets of Special Operations, UW was of the absolute lowest priority. It basically remained in that lowest priority position until after the 9–11 terrorist attacks and the subsequent involvement in Iraq and Afghanistan. The excerpt from the manual below shows that pullback from unconventional warfare.

> *SF can conduct a UW mission to support an insurgency or other armed resistance organization. The United States may undertake long-term operations in support of selected resistance organizations that seek to oppose or overthrow foreign powers hostile to vital U.S. interests. When directed, SF units advise, train, and assist indigenous resistance organizations. These units use the same TTP they employ to conduct a wartime UW mission. Direct U.S. military involvement is rare and subject to legal and policy constraints. Indirect support from friendly territory will be the norm.*

Page 3–2 talks about UW as a protracted politico–military activity, which of course it is. UW is primarily politically and interagency driven. Contrary to the earlier manuals this one states specifically that SF units do not create resistance movements.

Also this manual introduces new organizations in terms such as Army special operations task force, joint special operations task force, forward operating bases, special operations command and control elements, special operations commands, theater special operations commands, theater Army special operations support commands, joints special operations area (this replaces the UWOA), etc.

It also talks about SF ODBs, SF ODAs and lists the functions and mission sets for these in significant detail.

It also discusses the joint environment and the fact that every operational headquarters above the SF Group level is a joint headquarters.

Finally in Chapter 9 the manual begins to address unconventional warfare. As a cover statement to the chapter it states "UW is the most challenging of all SF missions because it involves protracted operations with indigenous forces in denied territory. Building rapport with and adapting to the ways of an indigenous resistance organization require carefully planned and carefully executed actions...."

It is very gratifying to see that this manual recognizes the moral and ethical implications of unconventional warfare. Page 9-2 states succinctly the moral issue – *"The center of gravity in any resistance movement is the people's will to resist. The people bear the brunt of the established authority's retaliatory measures. While armed resistance may be low intensity conflict (LIC) from the U.S. perspective, it is total war for those who take up arms. Defeat means death or a life in exile."*

The seven phases of U.S. sponsored UW are:

1) *phase 1: psychological preparation*
2) *phase 2: initial contact*
3) *phase 3: infiltration*
4) *phase 4: organization*
5) *phase 5: build up*
6) *phase 6: combat employment*
7) *phase 7: demobilization*

Unconventional Warfare

Page 3-2: *UW is the military and paramilitary aspect of an insurgency or other armed resistance movement. Armed resistance provides UW with its environmental context. UW is thus a protracted politico-military activity. SF units do not create resistance movements. They provide advice, training, and assistance to indigenous resistance organizations already in existence. From the U.S. perspective, the intent is to develop and sustain those organizations and synchronize their activities to further U.S. national security objectives. When*

*conducted independently, the primary focus of UW is on po-
litico-military and psychological objectives. Military activity
represents the culmination of a successful effort to organize
and mobilize the civil population. When UW operations
support conventional military operations, the focus shifts to
primarily military objectives. However, the political and psychological implications remain. Regardless of whether UW
objectives are strategic or operational, the nature of resistance
and the fundamental UW doctrine, tactics, and techniques
remain unchanged. UW includes the following interrelated
activities: GW, E&E, subversion, and sabotage.*

*GW consists of military and paramilitary operations con-
ducted by irregular, predominantly indigenous forces in
enemy-held or hostile territory. It is the overt military aspect
of an insurgency or other armed resistance movement.*

*Subversion is an activity designed to undermine the mili-
tary, economic, psychological or political strength of a nation.
All elements of the resistance organization contribute to the
subversive effort, but the clandestine nature of subversion dictates that the underground perform the bulk of the activity.*

*Sabotage is an activity designed to injure or obstruct the
national defense of a country by willfully damaging or destroying any national defense or war materiel, premises, or
utilities, to include human and natural resources. Sabotage
may be the most effective or the only means of attacking specific targets beyond the capabilities of conventional weapons
systems. It is used to selectively disrupt, destroy, or neutralize
hostile capabilities with a minimum of manpower and materiel resources.*

*In UW, intelligence collection is designed to collect and re-
port information concerning the capabilities, intentions,
and activities of the established government, or occupying
power, and its external sponsors.*

Contemporary UW takes on new significance for several reasons. Historically, SF has focused on UW as an adjunct to general war. However, the new U.S. policy of supporting selected anti-communist resistance movements requires SF to focus on UW during conflicts short of war. Moreover, global urbanization dictates a shift in emphasis from rural GW to all aspects of clandestine resistance.

****

(1992) Joint Publication 3-05 Doctrine for Joint Special Operations dated 28 October 1992 (Supersedes Joint Test Pub 3-05, October 1990)

No change in the definition from 1990. Unconventional Warfare-- a broad spectrum of military and paramilitary operations conducted in enemy-held, enemy-controlled, or politically sensitive territory. Unconventional warfare includes, but is not limited to, the interrelated fields of guerrilla warfare, evasion and escape, subversion, sabotage, and other operations of a low visibility, covert or clandestine nature. These interrelated aspects of unconventional warfare may be prosecuted singly or collectively by predominantly indigenous personnel, usually supported and directed in varying degrees by (an) external source(s) during all conditions of war or peace.

Unconventional warfare

a. UW includes guerrilla warfare and other low visibility, covert, or clandestine operations, as well as subversion, sabotage, intelligence collection, and E&E.

(1) GW consists of military and paramilitary operations conducted by irregular, predominantly indigenous forces in enemy-held or hostile territory. It is the overt military aspect of an insurgency or other armed resistance movement. Guerrilla forces primarily employ raid and ambush tactics against enemy vulnerabilities. In the latter stages of a successful

insurgency, guerrilla forces may directly oppose selected, vulnerable enemy forces while avoiding enemy concentrations of strength.

(2) Subversion is an activity designed to undermine the military, economic, psychological, or political strength or morale of a regime or nation. All elements of the resistance organization contribute to the subversive effort, but the clandestine nature of subversion dictates that the underground elements perform the bulk of the activity.

(3) Sabotage is conducted from within the enemy's infrastructure in areas presumed to be safe from attack. It is designed to degrade or obstruct the war-making capability of a country by damaging, destroying, or diverting war material, facilities, utilities, and resources. Sabotage may be the most effective or only means of attacking Pacific targets that lie beyond the capabilities of conventional weapon systems. Sabotage selectively disrupts, destroys, or neutralizes hostile capabilities with a minimum expenditure of manpower and matériel. Once accomplished, these incursions can further result in the enemy spending excessive resources to guard against future attack.

(4) In UW, the intelligence function must collect, develop, and report information concerning the capabilities, intentions, and activities of the established government or occupying power and its external sponsors. In this context, intelligence activities have both offensive and defensive purposes and range well beyond military issues, including social, economic, and political information that may be used to identify threats, operational objectives, and necessary supporting operations.

(5) E&E is an activity that assists military personnel and other selected personnel to:

(a) move from an enemy-held, hostile, or sensitive area to areas under friendly control,

(b) avoid capture if unable to return to an area of friendly control,

(c) once captured, escape. SO (special operations) personnel often will work in concert with the JRCC (joint recovery co-ordination center) of the JFC (joint force commander) while operating in an E&E network.

****

(1994) Joint Publication 1-02 Department of Defense Dictionary of Military and Associated Terms dated 23 March 1994 (Supersedes JP 1-02, 1 December 1989)

This is now the eighth definition for UW.

UW -- a broad spectrum of military and paramilitary operations, normally of long duration, predominantly conducted by indigenous or surrogate forces who are organized, trained, equipped, supported, and directed in varying degrees by an external source. It includes guerrilla warfare and other direct offensive, low visibility, covert, or clandestine operations, as well as the indirect activities of subversion, sabotage, intelligence activities, and evasion and escape.

Unconventional Warfare Forces-- United States forces having existing unconventional warfare capability consisting of Army Special Forces and such Navy, Air Force, and Marine units as are assigned for these operations.

****

(1995) Joint Publication 3-0 Doctrine for Joint Operations dated 1 February 1995

No definition of UW. In fact, there is no mention of unconventional warfare. They did mention and provide a definition for the joint special operations area (JSOA).

****

(1997) Joint Doctrine Encyclopedia dated 16 July 1997

This document continues with the eighth definition first found in FM 31-20 dated 20 April 1990.

Pages 713-715
UNCONVENTIONAL WARFARE
A broad spectrum of military and paramilitary operations, normally of long duration, predominantly conducted by indigenous or surrogate forces who are organized, trained, equipped, supported, and directed in varying degrees by an external source. It includes guerrilla warfare and other direct offensive, low visibility, covert, or clandestine operations, as well as the indirect activities of subversion, sabotage, intelligence activities, and evasion and escape. Also called UW. JP 1-02

Unconventional warfare (UW) includes guerrilla warfare (GW) and other low visibility, covert, or clandestine operations, as well as subversion, sabotage, intelligence collection, and evasion and escape (E&E). GW consists of military and paramilitary operations conducted by irregular, predominantly indigenous forces in enemy-held or hostile territory. It is the overt military aspect of an insurgency or other armed resistance movement. Guerrilla forces primarily employ raid and ambush tactics against enemy vulnerabilities. In the latter stages of a successful insurgency, guerrilla forces may directly oppose selected, vulnerable enemy forces while avoiding enemy concentrations of strength.

Subversion is an activity designed to undermine the military, economic, psychological, or political strength or morale of a regime or nation. All elements of the resistance organization contribute to the subversive effort, but the clandestine nature of subversion dictates that the underground elements perform the bulk of the activity.

Sabotage is conducted from within the enemy's infrastructure in areas presumed to be safe from attack. It is designed to degrade or obstruct the war-making capability of a country by damaging, destroying, or diverting war material, facilities, utilities, and resources. Sabotage may be the most effective or only means of attacking specific targets that lie beyond the capabilities of conventional weapon systems. Sabotage selectively disrupts, destroys, or neutralizes hostile capabilities with a minimum expenditure of manpower and materiel. Once accomplished, these incursions can further result in the enemy spending excessive resources to guard against future attack.

In UW, the intelligence function must collect, develop, and report information concerning the capabilities, intentions, and activities of the established government or occupying power and its external sponsors. In this context, intelligence activities have both offensive and defensive purposes and range well beyond military issues, including social, economic, and political information that may be used to identify threats, operational objectives, and necessary supporting operations.

E&E is an activity that assists military personnel and other selected persons to:

- *move from an enemy-held, hostile, or sensitive area to areas under friendly control;*
- *avoid capture if unable to return to an area of friendly control;*
- *once captured, escape. Special operations personnel often will work in concert with the Joint Search and Rescue Center of the joint force commander (JFC) while operating in an E&E network.*

UW is the military and paramilitary aspect of an insurgency or other armed resistance movement and may often become a protracted politico-military activity. From the U.S. perspec-

tive, UW may be the conduct of indirect or proxy warfare against a hostile power for the purpose of achieving U.S. national interests in peacetime; UW may be employed when conventional military involvement is impractical or undesirable; or UW may be a complement to conventional operations in war. The focus of UW is primarily on existing or potential insurgent, secessionist, or other resistance movements. Special operations forces (SOF) provide advice, training, and assistance to existing indigenous resistance organizations. The intent of UW operations is to exploit a hostile power's political, military, economic, and psychological vulnerabilities by advising, assisting, and sustaining resistance forces to accomplish U.S. strategic or operational objectives.

When UW is conducted independently during military operations other than war or war, its primary focus is on political and psychological objectives. A successful effort to organize and mobilize a segment of the civilian population may culminate in military action. Strategic UW objectives may include the following:

- *undermining the domestic and international legitimacy of the target authority.*
- *Neutralizing the target authority's power and shifting that power to the resistance organization.*
- *Destroying the confidence and will of the target authority's leadership.*
- *Isolating the target authority from international diplomatic and material support while obtaining such support for the resistance organization.*
- *Obtaining the support or neutrality of the various segments of the society.*

When UW operations support conventional military operations, the focus shifts to primarily military objectives. However, the political and psychological implications remain. UW operations delay and disrupt hostile military activities, interdict lines of communications, deny the hostile power unrestricted use of key areas, divert the hostile power's attention and resources from the main battle area, and interdict hostile mortifying capabilities. Properly integrated and synchronized UW operations can extend the depth of air, sea, or ground battles, complement conventional military operations, and provide the joint force commander with the windows of opportunity needed to seize the initiative through offensive action.

UW may be conducted by all designated SOF but it is principally the responsibility of Army Special Forces. Augmentation other than SOF, assist and provide as the situation dictates by psychological operations and civil affairs units, as well as other selected conventional combat, combat support, and combat service support forces.

In the above it says that SOF provides advice, training, assistance, etc. However, UW is a political/interagency operation which means the indigenous population will receive advice and assistance from all elements of the U.S. government. This is particularly true in the establishment of the resistance government-in-exile, and the establishment of an entire governmental structure to take over when he UW campaign sees success. If the government-in-exile is already in existence, then the same applies that the interagency players will be working with these indigenous personnel to ensure they are prepared to take back over the reins of government at the conclusion of military action.

When UW is conducted independently during military operations other than war, its primary focus is on political and psychological objectives. A successful effort to organize and mobilize a segment of the civil population may culminate in military action. Strategic UW objectives may include the following:

- *Undermining the domestic and international legitimacy of the target authority.*

- *Neutralizing the target authority's power and shifting that power to the resistance organization.*
- *Destroying the confidence and will of the target authority's leadership.*
- *Isolating the target authority from international diplomatic and material support while obtaining such support for the resistance organization.*
- *Obtaining the support or neutrality of the various segments of the society.*

UW is never conducted independently. It is paramount that UW is integrated completely and totally with the political/interagency process. Additionally UW's primary focus is always political and establishing the legitimacy of the indigenous population's government-in-exile our shadow government. Additionally, UW is always strategic. UW's objectives are always strategic. Of course there are always operational and tactical ways to achieve the strategic objectives. In these operational and tactical means are not just military, but interagency."

When UW operations support conventional military operations, the focus shifts to primarily military objectives. However, the political and psychological implications remain. UW operations delay and disrupt hostile military activities, interdict lines of communications, deny the hostile power unrestricted use of key areas, divert the hostile power's attention and resources from the main battle area, and interdict hostile war-fighting capabilities. Properly integrated and synchronized UW operations can extend the depth of air, sea, or ground battles, complement conventional military operations, and provide the JFC with the windows of opportunity needed to seize the initiative through offensive action.

During war, SOF may directly support the resistance movement by infiltrating operational elements into denied or politically sensitive areas. They organize, train, equip, and advise or direct the indigenous resistance organization. In situations short of war, when direct U.S. military involvement is inappropriate or infeasible, SOF may instead provide indirect support from an external location.

UW may be conducted by all designated SOF, but it is principally the responsibility of Army Special Forces. Augmentation other than SOF, will usually be provided as the situation dictates by psychological operations and civil affairs units, as well as other selected conventional combat, combat support, and combat service support forces.

It is correct that UW may be conducted by all SOF; however, it is not just limited to SOF, but must include the entire political/ interagency process and, at times, allies and partners. Again, to be perfectly clear, SF is the only U.S. organization, interagency or otherwise, that has as their primary focused mission as unconventional warfare. To be perfectly frank, all the other organizations are UW tourists.

****

(1998) Joint Publication 3-05 Doctrine for Joint Special Operations dated 17 April 1998

There is no change in the definition since the 1994 FM 31-20.

Unconventional Warfare-- a broad spectrum of military and paramilitary operations, normally of long duration, predominantly conducted by indigenous or surrogate forces who are organized, trained, equipped, supported, and directed in varying degrees by an external source. It includes guerrilla warfare and other direct offensive, low visibility, covert, or clandestine operations, as well as the indirect activities of subversion, sabotage, intelligence activities, and evasion and escape.

****

(1999 June) Joint Publication 1-02 Department of Defense Dictionary of Military and Associated Terms dated 23 March 1994 (As Amended through 29 June 1999) (Supersedes Joint Pub 1-02, 1 December 1989)

There is no change in the definition since the 1994 JP 1-02.

Unconventional Warfare-- a broad spectrum of military and para-military operations, normally of long duration, predominantly conducted by indigenous or surrogate forces who are organized, trained, equipped, supported, and directed in varying degrees by an external source. It includes guerrilla warfare and other direct offensive, low visibility, covert, or clandestine operations, as well as the indirect activities of subversion, sabotage, intelligence activities, and evasion and escape.

Unconventional Warfare Forces-- United States forces having been existing unconventional warfare capability consisting of Army Special Forces and such Navy, Air Force, and Marine units as our assigned for these operations.

****

(1999 August) Army Field Manual 100-25 Doctrine for Army Special Operations Forces dated 1 August 1999 (This publication supersedes FM 100-25, 12 December 1991)

This now reflects the ninth definition for UW.

This manual covers the range of military operations from war through military operations other than war (MOOTW):

2-2. ***Unconventional Warfare.*** *... a broad spectrum of military and paramilitary operations, normally of long duration, predominantly conducted by indigenous or surrogate forces who are organized, trained, equipped, supported, and directed in varying degrees by an external source. UW includes guerrilla warfare and other direct offensive, low-visibility, covert, or clandestine operations, as well as the* *indirect activities of subversion, sabotage, intelligence activities, and unconventional assisted recovery (UAR).*

2-3. Winning the conventional land battle "remains the absolute priority" despite an acknowledgment that potential adversaries are likely to follow unconventional strategies (terrorism, insurgency, or guerrilla warfare) when faced with a complex, adaptive army. Military operations conducted in enemy-held, enemy-controlled, or politically sensitive territory make up UW that includes guerrilla warfare and support to an insurgency. Indigenous personnel carry out UW. External forces may support or direct these forces in varying degrees in the full range of military operations. The focus of UW is primarily on the success of existing or potential insurgent, secessionist, or other resistance movements. The United States may engage in UW in three ways: as part of a major theater war or lesser regional contingency, in support of a citizen or partisan defense intended as a deterrent, and as an effort to support an insurgency. SF provides advice and support as training and assistance to UW organizations. Experiences in Afghanistan and Nicaragua prove that support for an insurgency can be an effective way of putting indirect pressure on adversaries. The costs versus the benefits of using UW against states that support insurgencies against the United States and its allies must be carefully considered before employment.

This is a morally corrupt and perverse use of UW and Special Forces. As has been previously stated, the only objective of UW is regime change. The indigenous population is in a total war situation with the current regime. If we make the political decision to support the indigenous population and conduct UW, we inherit the moral obligation to sustain support to the indigenous effort until such time as regime change has been accomplished. To do otherwise relegates the indigenous participants, men women and children, in the UW campaign to genocide, imprisonment/slavery or exile.

****

(2001 April) Joint Publication 1-02 Department of Defense Dictionary of Military and Associated Terms dated 12 Apr 2001 (This reference was not located)

****

(2001 June) Army Field Manual 3-05.20 Special Forces Operations dated June 2001 (Supersedes Army Field Manual 31-20, 20 April 1990)

Unconventional Warfare-- a broad spectrum of military and para-military operations, normally of long duration, predominantly conducted by indigenous or surrogate forces who are organized, trained, equipped, supported, and directed in varying degrees by an external source. It includes guerrilla warfare and other direct offensive, low visibility, covert, or clandestine operations, as well as the indirect activities of subversion, sabotage, intelligence ac-tivities, and evasion and escape.

The above definition was the current JP 1-02 definition in effect at the time dating to the 1994 version of JP 1-02. The below extract from Chapter 2 - Special Forces Missions, expands on the JP 1-02 definition.

*2.1. UW is a broad spectrum of military and paramilitary opera-tions, predominantly conducted **through, with, or by** indigenous or surrogate forces organized, trained, equipped, supported, and di-rected in varying degrees by an external source. UW includes, but is not limited to, guerrilla warfare, subversion, sabotage, intelli-gence activities, and unconventional assisted recovery (UAR). When conducted independently, the primary focus of UW is on political – military and psychological objectives. UW includes the military and paramilitary aspects of resistance movements. UW military ac-tivity represents the culmination of a successful effort to organize and mobilize the civilian populace against a hostile government or an occupying power. From the U.S. perspective, the intent is to develop and sustain these supported resistance organizations and to synchro-nize their activities to further U.S. national security objectives. SF* *units do not create resistance movements. They advise, train, and assist indigenous resistance movements already in existence to conduct UW and, when required, accompany them into combat. When UW operations support conventional military operations, the focus shifts to primarily military objectives; however, the political and psychological implications remain.*

This appears to be the first time the words *"through, with or by"* are introduced into the definition…and the word "and" is replaced with "or."

In the following paragraphs the doctrine introduces a new aspect of UW; *serving as liaison elements to coalition partners.* Of note is paragraph 2-18 which explains that SF ODAs bring secure communications and GPS technology to the coalition partner.

> *2-17. Coalition support activities require the United States to assess, integrate, support, direct, and employ these forces rapidly. Without the benefit of formal treaty arrangements and the interoperability derived from agreements and combined training, working relationships must be established with these coalition forces to assess and integrate them into multinational operations. Because SF personnel are trained to work with surrogates and are oriented to work with forces indigenous to a variety of regions around the globe, the Army has turned to SF to perform this function. The UW skills and core competencies that permitted SF to integrate and influence the activities of resistance groups successfully have proved readily adaptable to such coalition forces. Those skills exercised by SF working with coalition forces also reinforce SF UW skills. Accustomed to operating with forces possessing distinct capabilities, unique mixes of equipment, specific cultures and military doctrines, and their own agenda, SF has achieved success in this new application of UW. The conventional coalition forces trained, organized, equipped, advised, and led in varying degrees by SF and U.S. allies represent the newest evolution in UW-related surrogate forces.*

2-18. SF units conducting UW as part of coalition support operations are task-organized as Special Forces liaison elements (SFLEs). These elements collocate with military forces of coalition partners and provide essential U.S. command, control, communications, computers, and intelligence (C4I) links to the coalition partners. They can assess, train, organize, equip, advise, and lead coalition forces according to the terms of the specific coalition and the operational situation. SFLEs advise their foreign counterparts on U.S. military intentions and capabilities. They can also provide training, secure communications among the force, and downlinks to global positioning systems. The SFLEs also confirm the situation on the ground, assist in fire support planning, and enable overall coordination between U.S. forces and their coalition partners. They facilitate multinational operations by military units not trained for interoperability with U.S. forces.

*2-19. In addition to the three broad categories of insurgents, partisans, and coalition forces, SF performing UW must work **with and through** independently operating insurgents and clandestine organizations. These organizations offer force-multiplying capabilities, particularly in support of specific UW activities, such as UAR. Personal reward or gain can motivate these groups to cooperate with U.S. and coalition operations.*

****

(2001 December) Joint Publication 3-05.1 21 Joint Tactics, Techniques, and Procedures for Joint Special Operations Task Force Operations dated 19 December 2001

unconventional warfare--a broad spectrum of military and paramilitary operations, normally of long duration, predominantly conducted by indigenous or surrogate forces who are organized, trained, equipped, supported, and directed in varying degrees by an external source. It includes guerrilla warfare and other direct offensive, low visibility, covert, or clandestine operations, as well as the indirect activities of subversion, sabotage, intelligence activities, and evasion and escape. Same definition as per JP 1-02 dated 23 March 1994.

****

(2003 April) Army Field Manual 3-05.201 Special Forces Unconventional Warfare Operations dated April 2003

Unconventional Warfare--a broad spectrum of military and paramilitary operations, normally of long duration, predominantly conducted by indigenous or surrogate forces who are organized, trained, equipped, supported, and directed in varying degrees by an external source. It includes guerrilla warfare and other direct offensive, low visibility, covert, or clandestine operations, as well as the indirect activities of subversion, sabotage, intelligence activities, and evasion and escape. Same definition as per JP 1-02 dated 23 March 1994.

UWOA-- unconventional warfare operating area

Unconventional Warfare Aspects

1-1. UW also includes interrelated aspects that may be prosecuted singly or collectively by predominantly indigenous or surrogate personnel. An external source usually supported as standard practice these personnel in varying degrees during all conditions of war or peace. The intent of U.S. UW operations is to exploit a hostile power's political, military, economic, and psychological vulnerability by developing and sustaining resistance forces to accomplish U.S. strategic objectives.

1-2. Regardless of whether UW objectives are strategic or operational, the nature of resistance and the fundamental tactics and techniques of UW operations remain unchanged. UW includes the following interrelated activities.

1-3. Guerrilla warfare consists of military and paramilitary operations conducted by irregular, predominantly indigenous forces against superior forces in enemy held or hostile territory. It is the overt aspect of an insurgency.

1-4. Sabotage is an act or acts with intent to injure or obstruct the national defense of a nation by willfully damaging or destroying any national defense or war material, premises, or utilities, including human and natural resources. It may also refer to actions taken to injure or obstruct the military capabilities of an occupying power. Sabotage may be the most effective or the only means of attacking specific targets beyond the capabilities of conventional weapon systems. Sabotage selectively disrupts, destroys, or neutralizes hostile capabilities with a minimum of manpower and material resources. SF conducts sabotage unilaterally through indigenous or surrogate personnel. Sabotage is also a form of effects-based targeting performed by SF personnel.

1-5. Subversion is any action designed to undermine the military, economic, psychological, or political strength or morale of a regime. All elements of the resistance organization contribute to the subversive effort, but the clandestine nature of subversion dictates that the underground will do the bulk of the activity. Subversion is a form of effects-based targeting on human terrain.

1-6. Effective SF targeting demands accurate, timely, and well-organized intelligence. SF personnel must develop good intelligence skills for overt collection, tactical reconnaissance, and the assembly of available intelligence for mission planning packets. Sound target analysis uses the criticality, accessibility, recuperability, vulnerability, effect, recognizability (CARVER) matrix; provides options to planners; satisfies statements of operational requirements (SOR); meets the commander's objectives; and reduces the risk to operators.

1.7. Intelligence activities assess areas of interest ranging from political and military personalities to the military capabilities of friendly and enemy forces. SF must conform intelligence activities ranging from developing information critical to planning and conducting operations, sustaining and protecting themselves and the UW force, to assessing the capabilities and intentions of indigenous and coalition forces. These activities may be unilateral war conducted through surrogates. SF intelligence activities may require coordination with other government agencies (OGAs) and may involve national level oversight.

1-8. Unconventional assisted recovery is a subset of non-unconventional assisted recovery (NAR) and it is conducted by special operations forces (SOF). UW forces conduct UAR operations to seek out, contact, authenticate, and support military and other selected personnel as they move from an enemy held, hostile, or sensitive area to areas under friendly control. UAR includes operating unconventional assisted-recovery mechanisms (UARMs) and unconventional assisted recovery teams (UARTs). The UARM refers to an entity, or group of entities, or organizations within the enemy-held territory that operate in a clandestine or covert manner to return designated personnel to friendly control and most often consists of the established indigenous or surrogate infrastructures. UARTs consist primarily of SOF personnel directed to service existing designated areas of recovery (DARs) or selected areas for evasion (SAFEs) to recover the evaders.

1-9. UW has taken on new significance for several reasons. Historically, SF units have focused on UW as a part of general. Now, the U.S. policy of supporting selected resistance movements requires SF to focus on UW during conflicts short of war. Also, global urbanization provides for a shift in emphasis from rural guerrilla warfare to all aspects of clandestine resistance including urban and border operations. Training and support for these operations may come from the joint special operations area (JSOA) or from an external training or support site. Some scenarios may dictate a traditional role reversal-the urban guerrilla may conduct most of the operations while supported by the rural guerrilla.

1-10. UW is the most challenging of SF missions because it involves protracted operations with the joint forces, allied forces, indigenous or surrogate forces, U.S. agencies, or elements of all of these entities. UW involves detailed, centralized planning and coordination from the SFODA through the Secretary of Defense, and ultimately, decentralized execution. UW requires proficiency in other SF principal missions (one internal defense, direct action, and special reconnaissance) since, once deployed, in a UW mission may include portions of those missions. Before the conduct of SF UW operations, a resistance potential should exist. SF personnel do not create this resistance potential. It is already present and has usually developed into a resistance movement or an organized effort by some portion of the civil population to resist the regime.

1-11. When UW operations support conventional military operations, the focus shifts to primarily military objectives. When a conventional force is committed and its area of interest bears the JSOA, resistance operations may expand to help tactical command. **In addition, there are times when the introduction of conventional forces does not take the main effort away from unconventional operations; in fact, conventional forces may support the unconventional forces.**

****

(2003 June) Joint Publication 1-02 Department of Defense Dictionary of Military and Associated Terms dated 12 April 2001 (As Amended Through 5 June 2003)

unconventional warfare-- a broad spectrum of military and paramilitary operations, normally of long duration, predominantly conducted by indigenous or surrogate forces who are organized, trained, equipped, supported, and directed in varying degrees by an external source. It includes guerrilla warfare and other direct offensive, low visibility, covert, or clandestine operations, as well as the indirect activities of subversion, sabotage, intelligence activities, and evasion and escape. Same definition as per JP 1-02 dated 23 March 1994.

unconventional warfare forces—U.S. forces having an existing unconventional warfare capability.

****

(2003 December) JP 3-05 Doctrine for Joint Special Operations dated 17 December 2003 *(This was the first definition change to through, with or by)*

unconventional warfare-- a broad spectrum of military and para-military operations, normally of long duration, predominantly conducted ***through, with, or by*** indigenous or surrogate forces who are organized, trained, equipped, supported, and direct it in varying degrees by an external source. It includes but is not limited to guerrilla warfare, subversion, sabotage, intelligence ac-tivities and unconventional assisted recovery.

****

(2006) Army Field Manual 3-05 Army Special Operations Forces dated 20 September 2006 (Supersedes FM 100-25, 1 August 1999)

The definition for UW has undergone numerous changes since the term was first used in the 1950s. Although struggles have occurred in defining the details surrounding UW op-erations, one concept has remained constant-- UW is a form of warfare that usually involves the cooperation of indige-nous or surrogate personnel and their resources, coupled with United States government (USG) assets, to defeat a State, an occupying force, or non-state actors.

JP 1-02 approaches the defining of UW in a "classic" sense. ARSOF broadens the definition by defining UW operations as "a broad range of military and/or paramilitary opera-tions and activities, normally of long duration, conducted through, with, or by indigenous or other simulated forces that are organized, trained, equipped, supported, and otherwise directed in varying degrees by an external source. UW operations can be conducted across the range of conflict against regular and irregular forces. These forces may or may not be State-sponsored." This expanded definition includes the use of surrogates and the implementation of UW operations against non-State actors.

UW "usually" involves indigenous parties or surrogates? It is impossible to conduct UW without the involvement of indigenous populations! Indigenous populations are required in order to conduct "through, with and by." Also, again, there is no mention of regime change.

****

(2007 September) Army Field Manual 3-05.201 (S/NF) Special Forces Unconventional Warfare (U) dated 28 September 2007

*UW: Operations conducted **by, with, or through** irregular forces in support of a resistance movement, an insurgency, or conventional military operations.*

****

(2007 October) Joint Publication 1-02 Department of Defense Dictionary of Military and Associated Terms dated 12 April 2001 (As Amended Through 17 October 2007)

provides the following definition:

Unconventional Warfare *– A broad spectrum of military and paramilitary operations, normally of long duration, predominantly conducted **through, with, or** by indigenous or surrogate forces who are organized, trained, equipped, supported, and directed in varying degrees by an external source. It includes, but is not limited to, guerrilla warfare, subversion, sabotage, intelligence activities, and unconventional assisted recovery.*

This is a good definition of unconventional warfare, but some changes need to be made. First, change the word "forces" to "populations" and, most importantly, add "for the purpose of regime change." UW is conducted by indigenous populations not just irregular forces and the only purpose of UW is regime change. Also, the word surrogate should be moved into the definition of guerrilla warfare. UW is conducted by an indigenous population whereas they may be supported by a surrogate force in the guerrilla warfare. UW is the total interrelated operations used by an indigenous population supported by the United States and the interagency process, which includes the military and Special Forces, to affect regime change. This is totally a political decision, requiring total interagency integration in every phase of the operation.

****

(2008 February) Army Field Manual 3-0 Army Operations dated 27 February 2008

unconventional warfare-- a broad spectrum of military and para-military operations, normally of long duration, predominantly conducted **through, with, or by** indigenous or surrogate forces who are organized, trained, equipped, supported, and directed in varying degrees by an external source. It includes, but is not limited to, guerrilla warfare, subversion, sabotage, intelligence activities, and unconventional assisted recovery.

unconventional warfare forces--no definition or mention.

****

(2008 September) Army Field Manual 3-05.130 dated 30 September 2008 Army Special Operations Forces Unconventional Warfare

1-8. The definition of UW has evolved over time. The initial doctrinal concept for the United States to conduct UW originated with the creation of the OSS during WWII. In that classic context, UW was generally defined in terms of guerrilla and covert operations in enemy-held or -influenced territory. **The first official Army definition that touched upon aspects of UW appeared in 1950 as "partisan warfare."** *In 1951, the Army's UW assets were consolidated under the Office of Psychological Warfare, and the Army published the first two field manuals for the conduct of SO (with an emphasis on UW). By 1955, the first historical manual that specifically linked Army SF to UW (FM 31-20, Special Forces Group) declared, "UW consists of the three interrelated fields of guerrilla warfare (GW), escape and evasion, and subversion against hostile states."*

1-10. The current definition of UW is as follows:

> *Operations conducted* **by, with, or through** *irregular forces in support of a resistance movement, an insurgency, or conventional military operations.*

> *This definition reflects two essential criteria: UW must be conducted by, with, or through surrogates; and such surrogates must be irregular forces. Moreover, this definition is consistent with the historical reasons that the United States has conducted UW. UW has been conducted in support of both an insurgency, such as the Contras in 1980s Nicaragua, and resistance movements to defeat an occupying power, such as the Mujahideen in 1980s Afghanistan. UW has also been conducted in support of pending or ongoing conventional military operations; for example, OSS/Jedburgh activities in France and OSS/Detachment 101 activities in the Pacific in WWII and, more recently, SF operations in Operation ENDURING FREEDOM (OEF)/Afghanistan in 2001 and Operation IRAQI FREEDOM (OIF)/Iraq in 2003. Finally and in keeping with the clandestine and/or covert nature of historical UW operations, it has involved the conduct of classified surrogate operations. Details of classified operations are in FM 3-05.20, (C) Special Forces Operations (U), and FM 3-05.201.*

Obviously, I disagree with the limiting terminology of irregular forces. Unconventional warfare is conducted by the affected indigenous populations, men, women and children. Many, if not most of these, are not irregular forces. These personnel comprise the underground and the auxiliary. In some cases the women and children may also be involved in the irregular forces, and be actual fighters, thereby irregular forces. Women and children are also involved in sabotage, subversion and assisting escape and evasion.

****

(2008 December) Department of Defense Directive 3000.07 Irregular Warfare dated 1 December 2008

Codifies Irregular Warfare as consisting of Counterinsurgency, Stability Operations, Foreign Internal Defense, Counterterrorism, and, importantly, Unconventional Warfare.

4. Policy. It is DOD policy to:

c. Conduct IW independently of, or in combination with, traditional warfare.

*(1) IW can include a variety of steady-state and surge DoD activities and operations: counterterrorism; **unconventional warfare**; foreign internal defense; counterinsurgency; and stability operations that, in the context of IW, involve establishing or re-establishing order in a fragile state.*

(2) While these activities may occur across the full range of military operations, the balance or primary focus of operations gives a campaign its predominant character.

e. Maintain capabilities and capacity so that the Department of Defense is as effective in IW as it is in traditional warfare in order to ensure that, when directed, the Department can:

(1) Identify and prevent or defeat irregular threats from state and non-state actors across operational areas and environments.

*(2) Extend U.S. reach into denied areas and uncertain environments by operating **with and through** indigenous foreign forces.*

h. Synchronize appropriate DOD IW related activities with the efforts of other U.S. government agencies, foreign security partners, and selected international organizations...

****

(2009 April) Conference 7-9 April 2009

*unconventional warfare — Activities conducted to enable a resistance movement or insurgency to coerce, disrupt, or overthrow a government or occupying power by operating **through or with** an underground, auxiliary, and guerrilla force in a denied area. Also called **UW.***

(This was a big break in the definition after a large effort by a UW Working Group comprised of 25 representatives USSOCOM, USASOC, USASFC, SWCS, NPS, JSOU and CAC SOF Cell. This effort rescinded and replaced the above definitions within SOF; but it took until 2012 to change JP 1-02)

****

(2009 October) Joint Publication 1-02 Department of Defense Dictionary of Military and Associated Terms dated 8 November 2001 (As Amended Through 31 October 2009)

unconventional warfare-- a broad spectrum of military and para-military operations, normally of long duration, predominantly conducted ***through, with, or by*** indigenous or surrogate forces who are organized, trained, equipped, supported, and directed in varying degrees by an external source. It includes, but is not limited to, guerrilla warfare, subversion, sabotage, intelligence activities, and unconventional assisted recovery.

unconventional warfare forces—U.S. forces having an existing unconventional warfare capability. *(This was the last definition of UW forces in JP 1-02.)*

****

(2011 January) Training Circular (TC) 18-01 Special Forces Unconventional Warfare dated 28 January 2011

From the text:

*The commander, United States Special Operations Command (USSOCOM), defines UW as activities conducted to enable a resistance movement or insurgency to coerce, disrupt, or overthrow a government or occupying power by operating **through or with** an underground, auxiliary, and guerrilla force in a denied area.*

Introduction to Unconventional Warfare

1-1. The intent of U.S. UW efforts is to exploit a hostile power's political, military, economic, and psychological vulnerabilities by developing and sustaining resistance forces to accomplish U.S. strategic objectives. Historically, the military concept for the employment of UW was primarily in support of resistance movements during general-war scenarios. While this concept remains valid, the operational environment since the end of World War II has increasingly required U.S. forces to conduct UW in scenarios short of general war (limited war).

1-2. Enabling a resistance movement or insurgency entails the development of an underground and guerrilla forces, as well as supporting auxiliaries for each of these elements. Resistance movements or insurgencies always have an underground element. The armed component of these groups is the guerrilla force and is only present if the resistance transitions to conflict. The combined effects of two interrelated lines of effort largely generate the end result of a UW campaign. The efforts are armed conflict and subversion. Forces conduct armed conflict, normally in the form of guerrilla warfare, against the security apparatus of the host nation (HN) or occupying military. Conflict also includes operations that attack and degrade enemy morale, organizational cohesion, and operational effectiveness and separate the enemy from the population. Over time, these attacks degrade the ability of the HN or occupying military to project military power and exert control over the population. Subversion undermines the power of the government or occupying element by portraying it as incapable of effective governance to the population.

****

(2011 January) Joint Publication 1-02 Department of Defense Dictionary of Military and Associated Terms dated 8 November 2010 (As Amended Through 31 January 2011)

unconventional warfare-- a broad spectrum of military and paramilitary operations, normally of long duration, predominantly conducted **through, with, or by** indigenous or surrogate forces who are organized, trained, equipped, supported, and directed in varying degrees by an external source. It includes, but is not limited to guerrilla warfare, subversion, sabotage, intelligence activities, and unconventional assisted recovery.

****

(2011 April) Joint Publication 3-05 Special Operations dated 18 April 2011

Chap II.e, pages II-9 and10 explains unconventional warfare as:

UW are those activities conducted to enable a resistance movement or insurgency to coerce, disrupt, or overthrow a *government or occupying power by operating **through or with** an underground, auxiliary, and guerrilla force in a denied area. The United States may engage in UW across the spectrum of armed conflict from major campaigns to limited contingency operations. The U.S. has conducted UW in support of insurgent movements attempting to overthrow an adversarial regime as well as in support of resistance movements to defeat occupying powers (e.g., the Nicaraguan Contras and the Afghan Mujahedeen). UW was also successfully used against the Taliban in the initial stages of Operation ENDURING FREEDOM in Afghanistan. UW can be an effective way of putting indirect and direct pressure on a hostile government or occupying power.*

(1) Military leaders must carefully consider the costs and benefits prior to making a recommendation to engage in UW. Properly coordinated and executed UW may help set conditions for international crisis resolution on terms favorable to the United States or allies without the need for an overt U.S. Conventional Force (CF) commitment.

(2) The conduct of UW can have a strategic military-politico utility that can alter the balance of power between sovereign states, and there is potentially significant political risk both at home and abroad. The paramilitary aspect of UW may place DOD in a supporting role to inter-organizational partners. The necessity to operate with a varying mix of clandestine/covert means and ways places a premium on operations security (OPSEC) and all-source intelligence. In UW, as in all conflict scenarios, U.S. military forces must closely coordinate their activities with inter-organizational partners to enable and safeguard sensitive operations.

(3) A joint force commander (JFC) typically tasks SOF to conduct the military aspect of UW. It will usually require support relationships with some interagency

partners and some Service components. A JFC and staff must be able to conduct/support UW operations simultaneously during both traditional warfare and/or IW.

(4) While each UW mission is unique, U.S.-sponsored UW generally includes seven phases: preparation, initial contact, infiltration, organization, build-up, employment, and transition. These phases may occur concurrently in some situations or may not be required in others. For example, a large established resistance movement may only require initial contact and build up of logistical support to begin UW activities, thereby bypassing the other earlier phases of preparation, infiltration, and organization. The phases also may occur out of sequence, with each receiving varying degrees of emphasis, such as when members of an indigenous irregular force are moved to another country to be trained, organized, and equipped before being infiltrated back into the designated operational area, either with or without U.S. SOF.

(5) Senior civilian leaders and JFCs should understand that UW operations require time to mature and reach maximum effectiveness, especially when all of the insurgent or resistance underground networks have to be established. (Joint Pub 3-05, Chap 11.e, pgII-9-10)

Again, as I have stated, the only objective of UW is regime change. The indigenous population is in a total war situation with the current regime. If we make the political decision to support the indigenous population and conduct UW, we inherit the moral obligation to sustain support to the indigenous effort until such time as regime change has been accomplished. To do otherwise relegates the indigenous participants--men, women, and children, in the UW campaign to genocide, imprisonment/slavery and/or exile. To say that UW is to coerce or disrupt is disingenuous and deceptive.

Paragraph (2) and (3) above talk to interagency operations; however, this in no way stresses the absolute dependence that UW has on interagency operations.

Paragraph (5) only scratches the surface of the effects that not having conducted long-term preparation for UW has on operations. Proper engagement in regional focus, regional engagement, ethnographic preparation, all contribute to the ability to reach a high degree of effectiveness very rapidly in a UW situation.

****

(2012 April) Joint Publication 1-02 Department of Defense Dictionary of Military and Associated Terms dated 8 November 2010 (As Amended Through 15 April 2012) *(This dropped the "by" from the definition)*

The latest official definition as of January 2015

> **Unconventional Warfare** — *Activities conducted to enable a resistance movement or insurgency to coerce, disrupt, or overthrow a government or occupying power by operating **through or with** an underground, auxiliary, and guerrilla force in a denied area. Also called **UW**.*

What follows is a broken record (for those who remember vinyl records). As I have stated previously, the only purpose of UW is regime change. For the U.S. to engage with an indigenous population in revolt in anything less than regime change is morally corrupt. The indigenous population is in a total war situation with the current regime. If we make the political decision to support the indigenous population and conduct UW, we inherit the moral obligation to sustain support to the indigenous effort until such time as regime change has been accomplished. To do otherwise relegates the indigenous participants, men women and children, in the UW campaign to possible genocide or, at best, exile, prosecution, oppression, slavery, and imprisonment.

****

(2012 August) Army Doctrine Publication 3-05 Special Operations dated 31 August 2012

unconventional warfare--activities conducted to enable a resistance movement or insurgency to coerce, disrupt or overthrow a government or occupying power by operating ***through or with*** an underground, auxiliary and guerrilla force in a denied area. - JP 1-02. Source JP 3-05

****

(2012 August) Army Doctrine Publication 3-05 Special Operations dated 31 August 2012

unconventional warfare-- activities conducted to enable a resistance movement or insurgency to coerce, disrupt, or overthrow a government or occupying power by operating ***through or with*** an underground, auxiliary, and guerrilla force in a denied area.

****

(2013 September) Army Techniques Publication (ATP) 3-05.1 Unconventional Warfare

unconventional warfare-- activities conducted to enable a resistance movement or insurgency to coerce, disrupt, or overthrow a government or occupying power by operating ***through or with*** an underground, auxiliary, and guerrilla force in a denied area.

****

(2014 July) Joint Publication 1-02 Department of Defense Dictionary of Military and Associated Terms dated 8 November 2010 (As Amended Through 16 July 2014)

unconventional warfare-- activities conducted to enable a resistance movement or insurgency to coerce, disrupt, or overthrow a government or occupying power by operating ***through or with*** an underground, auxiliary, and guerrilla force in a denied area.

****

(2014 July) Joint Publication 3-05 Special Operations dated 16 July 2014

unconventional warfare-- activities conducted to enable a resistance movement or insurgency to coerce, disrupt, or overthrow a government or occupying power by operating ***through or with*** an underground, auxiliary, and guerrilla force in a denied area.

****

(2014 August) Department of Defense Directive 3000.07 Irregular Warfare (IW) dated 28 August 2014 (Supersedes DODD 3000.07 Irregular Warfare dated 1 December 2008)

Basically the same as the 2008 version.

3. Policy. It is DOD policy that:

c. Conduct IW independently of, or in combination with, traditional warfare.

> *(1) IW can include anything relevant to the activity in operation such as counterterrorism; unconventional warfare; foreign internal defense; counterinsurgency; and stability operations that, in the context of IW, involve establishing or reestablishing order in a fragile state or territory.*

> *(2) While these activities, whether taken in sequence, in parallel, or in blended form, may occur across the full range of military operations, the balance or primary focus of operations gives a campaign its predominant character.*

e. Maintain capabilities and capacity so that the Department of Defense is as effective in IW as it is in traditional warfare in order to ensure that, when directed, the Department can:

(1) Identify and prevent or defeat irregular threats from state and non-state actors across operational areas and environments.

*(2) Extend U.S. reach into denied areas and uncertain environments by operating **with and through** indigenous foreign forces.*

h. Appropriate DOD IW-related activities will be integrated with the efforts of other U.S. government (USG) agencies, foreign security partners, and selected international organizations...

****

(2015) Joint Publication 1-02 Department of Defense Dictionary of Military and Associated Terms dated 8 November 2010 (As Amended Through 15 January 2015)

As of this writing, this is where we currently stay with the definition of UW, which has been unchanged since 2012. And this definition continues to be bankrupt.

unconventional warfare-- activities conducted to enable a resistance movement or insurgency to coerce, disrupt, or overthrow a government or occupying power by operating ***through or with*** an underground, auxiliary, and guerrilla force in a denied area.

Annex E: Interagency Process

Interagency, interagency, interagency! For those in the military, it is easy to be disgusted with the interagency process. It has no seeming discipline; no one is in charge; the discussions seem petty and more like bickering and whining than an effort to accomplish a mission. The interagency process is seen, for the most part, as a joke. Usually, the agencies that would make up this process don't even wish to participate. Then, when and if they do participate, it is with the strictest guidance to their representatives to ensure their agencies prerogatives are totally protected and enhanced, regardless of the cost to the success of the operation. By design, there is no single decision-maker in an interagency process (except the President).

Even when there is a lead agency designated, there is nothing to enforce the honest, selfless participation by the other agencies. For one entity to be in charge requires the other participants to yield some measure of control...and what are the incentives to do so? An overwhelming feeling to "do right;" to do "good?" Each entity involved already believes they have the answer to "right" and "good." To give in to another entity's "right" or "good" means giving up some control, which is then perceived as a lessening of the importance of their agency. Normally, if not always, anything that results from an interagency process is the result of meeting the lowest possible common denominator that can be agreed upon. The value of the interagency process is that everything gets put under a microscope. Usually this results in either no action (which may be the best action!), or a watered down solution that usually satisfies no one (again, probably a good thing).

The interagency process? I could never find a definitive definition, not that there is a shortage of writings, discussion, opinions and debate. The only agreement I found is that the interagency process is "broken" or needed improvement or needed "something." My opinion is that it works just fine... as long as you understand the way of our government.

> Designed to fail: The framers of the U.S. Constitution did not want an efficient government. They wanted a better government than that provided by the Articles of Confederation, but they feared for the future of liberty in any overly strong concentration of power. They thus deliberately and with intent set about to create a divided government, one in which power was both separate and shared in order to inhibit coordination. Thus, at the beginning and at the very core of the U.S. concept of government are deeply embedded obstacles to coordination that can only be overcome at a significant constitutional and therefore political price.[156]

During the 11 July 2012 House Armed Services Subcommittee on Emerging Threats and Capabilities Hearing on the Future of Special Operations Forces, Dr. Christopher J. Lamb, Distinguished Research Fellow, Institute for National Security Studies, Center for Strategic Research , National Defense University made the following observations about interagency collaboration:

> "Well, I think the main obstacle to interagency collaboration is the very structure of our system. We have built very powerful, functional departments and agencies. And this makes a lot of sense. It gives us a great reservoir of support in all the relevant elements of national power. So there's a lot of advantage to that.
>
> But if you compare those strengths against the cross- organizational collaborative constructs we have, they're all very weak. So

---

156 Affairs of State: The Interagency and National Security-2008; Editor: Gabriel Marcella; The Strategic Studies Institute, U.S. Army War College, Carlisle, PA

our ability to actually integrate those -- those functional capabilities to good effect is very poor. And to bring it down to earth and relate to my own personal experience, I've had some examples that I can attest to in this regard.

But if you're sent to serve on an interagency group, you immediately have a great tension. On the one hand, you're trying to represent your agency correctly and protect its organizational equities and its preferred position. On the other hand, you have the sense that you're supposed to help the whole group accomplish the mission well.

And this is a tension that the system does not send clear demand signals on. Many times, those of us who have worked in a bureaucracy will be sent to these kinds of groups with the overriding mandate to make sure that the organization's preferred position comes out in the end; or if not, to ensure that it's not sacrificed, which means that the thinking gets watered down, the products get watered down, et cetera; the clarity gets watered down, et cetera.

So my view of this is that absent some kind of intervention from Congress (I actually believe and have written on this subject) to give the president the authority to delegate his authority for integrating across the cabinet-level departments and agencies, we're going to continue to find that this capability is very, very fragile.

Again, I think SOF really has to be congratulated as one of the few elements in the national security system that have taken this requirement seriously. I think they backed into it, realizing that they weren't going to get actionable intelligence to go after the bad guys without interagency collaboration. They built that level of collaboration up.

They then looked at their operations and said, "We're still not getting strategic effect." They started bringing in other things like political talent and information operations talent. And they started performing at a much higher level, our special mission units.

And I think that is a great success. We need to do the same thing on the indirect side. But this is a pocket of expertise and success that is not replicated as a general rule across the system.

There are other big problems. We have a penchant for taking all of our complex national security missions and dividing responsibility up among different entities for them. So we'll have some of them work the policy; some of them work the planning component; some of them will work the actual operations; some of them will assess it. Nobody manages the mission end to end as a typical rule.

In all the cases I've studied where we've had so-called "black swans[157]" of interagency collaboration, those that have performed really well, they do find a way to manage the mission end to end. That's one of their distinguishing characteristics."

Interagency coordination and collaboration remains problematic. So why is this process so important to Unconventional Warfare and Special Forces?

Why? Because everything Special Forces does is strategic in context and therefore must have visibility, buy-in and political support and direction.

Why? Because committing a Special Forces Detachment can have the same impact and consequences as committing an Army division, a Marine expeditionary unit, the Navy aircraft carrier or an Air Force Air Wing.

Why? *"Through, with and by"* operations, prudently and judiciously executed, can provide for regional stability through low-level U.S. presence. This presence can act as a brake on regional ambitions, demonstrate U.S. interest, possibly mitigate the spread of Weapons

---

157 Black Swan: an event with the following three attributes: First, it is an *outlier*, as it lies outside the realm of regular expectations, because nothing in the past can convincingly point to its possibility. Second, it carries an extreme impact. Third, in spite of its outlier status, human nature makes us concoct explanations for its occurrence *after* the fact, making it explainable and predictable. Summarized: rarity, extreme impact, and retrospective (though not prospective) predictability.

of Mass Destruction (WMD) and augment the counter-proliferation strategy.

<u>Why?</u> Because Special Forces elements are low visibility, culturally and ethnographically aware, mature and educated, and provide high-impact results with an extremely small footprint in our relationships with other nations.

<u>Why?</u> Because there is a moral imperative to actions taken by the U.S. not only as it concerns our national treasure of blood and money but it also concerns the blood and treasure of those to whom we make commitments.

So, the interagency process is designed to fail. Of course, this is not true. However, according to U.S. Ambassador David Passage[158], who lectures and mentors the interagency process at various military institutions, when the interagency process

"…. comes unglued, …(it is) not because of interagency dysfunction: it's come unglued because of the inability of the President's top national security team to agree on what U.S. policy should be…"

---

158 AMBASSADOR DAVID PASSAGE is a 33-year veteran of the U.S. Foreign Service who retired from the State Department in September 1998. He served on the NSC under President George H.W. Bush and National Security Adviser Brent Scowcroft from 1988-89 (widely regarded by most government officials and academic observers as the Gold Standard for how the NSC and interagency process should work), as U.S. Ambassador to Botswana from 1990-93, and as Foreign Affairs Adviser to two commanders of the U.S. Special Operations Command *From 1993-96, at MacDill AFB, Florida.* He has had extensive experience with both Latin America and guerrilla insurgencies in various parts of the world. Ambassador Passage was political officer at the American embassy in Quito, Ecuador, during the mid-1970s and Deputy Chief of Mission/Charge d'Affaires at the American Embassy in El Salvador at the height of that country's civil war, from 1984 to 1986. Coincidentally, he spent six years as a youth in Colombia and was in Bogotá during the violent uprising in May 1948 which sparked a decade-long civil war known as *La Violencia.* At the beginning of his Foreign Service career, Ambassador Passage was a pacification program analyst at the U.S. military assistance command in Vietnam. He also served as an American negotiator during the extensive U.S. diplomatic effort in the 1980s to secure the withdrawal of Cuban forces from Africa, an end to Angola's and Mozambique's civil wars which were fanned by internal insurgencies; independence for Namibia, which was also being fought for by an internal insurgency; and the policy of "constructive engagement" with South Africa (which was under the threat of possible guerrilla warfare from black nationalist movements). At the end of his career, Ambassador Passage was Director of Andean Affairs at the State Department, with responsibility for the overall conduct of U.S. relations with Colombia, Venezuela, Ecuador, Peru, and Bolivia. *He is currently a lecturer and consultant in National Security Affairs and has written numerous articles on U.S. foreign and defense policy.*

"If the leaders aren't in agreement over a policy response, the interagency isn't going to solve that problem for them. If they ARE in agreement, the interagency will quickly fall in line.

"in the end, it's "leadership" that matters. Wiring diagrams and executive orders and legislation are all superfluous to the interagency process: if you have leadership, you don't need legislation and executive orders and wiring diagrams. If you DON'T have leadership, all the executive orders and legislation and wiring diagrams in the world aren't going to solve your problem."

Following are some extracts from The Strategic Studies Institute collection of papers, *Affairs of State: The Interagency and National Security*, assembled in 2008[159].

Interagency coordination is a much sought after objective. Most agency players recognize the need for and value of practicable coordination with other agencies and components. While a worthwhile goal in normal circumstances, complex contingencies and crisis situations make such coordination an imperative. What many such contingencies and crises have demonstrated, however, is that coordination is a concept often more honored in the breach than in practice. This reality has led to a corresponding effort to seek conceptual approaches that will improve the possibility of coordination and the development of institutional practices that will implement better interagency coordination.

The single largest reorganization of the national security architecture since the Constitution came with the National Security Act of 1947 creating the Department of Defense (DOD), the Central Intelligence Agency (CIA), and the National Security Council (NSC).

While recognizing the need for coordination, it is important to understand that there are some inherent limits to the ability to coordinate and a number of recurring, systemic obstacles that

---

159 Affairs of State: The Interagency and National Security-2008; Editor: Gabriel Marcella; The Strategic Studies Institute, U.S. Army War College, Carlisle, PA

make it difficult when it is not impossible. Coordination is an important goal, but it is an unnatural act and it is fraught with troubles that the act of coordination itself can create or make worse.

The interagency process includes many situations similar to playing the game of poker. There are "players" or actors with certain objectives. A player's resources, as well as opponent actions and objectives, drive the options or "strategies" the player will use to achieve his or her goals. The achievement of these objectives is defined by "payoffs" or rewards that players receive after completion of the game. Most importantly, there is the added aspect of information. The nature of the game may preclude revelation of any information during the encounter or only partial information, or information exposed only after a decision is made. Many times a player might have insight into some information because of his or her position, but may also be duped by false information or players trying to disavow certain positions on purpose.

There are three layers to the interagency process.

The most senior, regularly constituted interagency group is the Principals Committee (PC). The six principal presidential advisors responsible for dealing with national security are the Secretaries of State, Defense, and Treasury, the National Security Advisor, Director of National Intelligence, and CJCS.

Subordinate to the Principals Committee is the Deputies Committee (DC). As the senior sub-Cabinet interagency forum, the DC is responsible for directing the work of interagency working groups and ensuring that issues brought before the PC or the NSC have been properly analyzed and prepared for high-level deliberation. The DC is where the bulk of the government's policy decisions are made in preparation for the PC's review and the President's decision. Issues decided above the DC level either are very significant national security decisions, are very contentious, or both. In some circumstances (e.g., crisis situations), a significant portion of interagency policy development and coordination may be done at the DC level rather than at lower levels.

The DC is composed of the deputy or relevant undersecretary to the cabinet secretaries. The regular DC members include the Deputy Secretary of State or Under Secretary of State for Political Affairs, Under Secretary of the Treasury or Under Secretary of the Treasury for International Affairs, Deputy Secretary of Defense or Under Secretary of Defense for Policy, Deputy Attorney General, Deputy Director of the Office of Management and Budget, Deputy Director of National Intelligence (or the Director of the National Counterterrorism Center if counterterrorism issues are being considered), Vice Chairman of the Joint Chiefs of Staff (Vice CJCS), Deputy Chief of Staff to the President for Policy, Chief of Staff and National Security Advisor to the Vice President, Deputy Assistant to the President for Homeland Security Affairs, Deputy Assistant to the President for International Economics, and the Deputy National Security Advisor (who serves as its chair except when the Deputy Assistant to the President for International Economics chairs meetings dealing with international economic issues). When international economic issues are on the agenda, the DC's regular membership adds the Deputy Secretary of Commerce, a Deputy United States Trade Representative, and the Deputy Secretary of Agriculture.

Subordinate to the DC are a variety of interagency working groups called Policy Coordination Committees (PCCs). These interagency committees are composed of substantive experts and senior officials from the departments and agencies represented on the DC. Although bounded by how much control is exerted over policy issues by the PC and DC groups, PCCs historically were the main forum for interagency coordination. In the post-9/11 policy environment with more issues being worked at the PC and DC level, PCCs have had more coordination and implementation duties than policy development responsibilities.

After President Obama took office and signed his own Policy Planning Directive (executive order) on February 13, 2009 outlining how he wanted his national security policy-making process to work, they became "Interagency Policy Committees" (or IPCs).

The IPCs are organized around either regional or functional issues. Regional IPCs normally are headed by Assistant Secretaries of State while functional IPCs are headed by senior department officials or NSC Senior Directors.

Regional IPCs include:
- Europe and Eurasia
- Western Hemisphere
- East Asia
- South Asia
- Near East and North Africa
- Africa (State and NSC co-chair).

Functional IPCs included (the department responsible for chairing the committee is in parentheses):
- Arms Control (NSC)
- Biodefense (NSC and Homeland Security Council [HSC])
- CombatingTerrorism Information Strategy (NSC)
- Contingency Planning (NSC: Pol-Mil and Crisis planning)
- Counter-Terrorism Security Group (NSC)
- Defense Strategy, Force Structure, and Planning (Department of Defense [DoD])
- Democracy, Human Rights, and International Operations (NSC)
- Detainees (NSC)
- Global Environment (NSC and National Economic Council [NEC] co-chair)
- HIV-AIDS and Infectious Diseases (State and Health and Human Services [HHS])
- Information Sharing
- Intelligence and Counterintelligence (NSC)

- Interdiction (NSC)
- International Development and Humanitarian Assistance (State)
- International Drug Control Policy (NSC and Office of National Drug Control Policy)
- International Finance (Treasury)
- International Organized Crime (NSC)
- Maritime Security (NSC and HSC)
- Muslim World Outreach (NSC and State co-chair)
- Proliferation Strategy, Counterproliferation, and Homeland Defense (NSC)
- Reconstruction and Stabilization Operations (State)
- Records Access and Information Security (NSC)
- Space (NSC)
- Strategic Communication (NSC and State: international public diplomacy)
- Terrorist Finance (Treasury)
- Transnational Economic Issues (NEC).

Again drawing from Ambassador Passage:

> "...if interagency consensus can be achieved at the IPC level, then approval above that is more or less a bureaucratic formality. If there is fundamental disagreement at the IPC level, then issues move to the DC to resolve. If resolution can't be achieved at the DC level, then issues move to the PC level. And if there's still fundamental disagreement at the PC level, then it has to go to the President for a decision.

> Examples of the first would be responses to disasters such as hurricanes sweeping into the Caribbean/Central America or a tsunami in the Indian Ocean or a volcano blowing its stack in the Philippines: each member of the interagency process knows what's going to be required of his/her agency and getting a U.S. response cleared through the interagency is easy and mechanical and approval is then sought from the DC, PC and NSC.

If, however, the policy issue is more complicated and there is fundamental disagreement among departments/agencies (what should the U.S. do about Syria? About IS? About Afghanistan? About Somalia?), it gets bucked from the IPC to the DC. Sometimes, deputies can come to agreement...but sometime not... So if the IPCs and DC can't resolve an issue, it goes to the PC. And if there's fundamental disagreement [say between DOD and DOS], the issue is then going to have to be thrashed out with the President.

The Project on National Security Reform (PNSR) began with the more or less complete and total breakdown of the interagency process under George W. Bush. State and Defense weren't talking to each other and Rumsfeld regularly made end-runs around both Powell and NatSecAdv Condoleezza Rice, straight into the Oval Office, and President Bush -- absolutely oblivious to the disintegration of his national security apparatus -- regularly agreed with whoever had gotten to him most recently (typically Rumsfeld or Cheney, since Powell was very much a "team" player) -- until, beginning about 2008, when the dysfunction was so apparent that even he couldn't ignore it any longer and started stepping in, sometimes against Rumsfeld (ultimately firing him) and even Cheney.

The PNSR was fundamentally flawed in that cabinet departments have their own legislative basis and Congressional committees and their powerful chairmen aren't going to surrender their ability to summons Cabinet Secretaries to kowtow before them. Period.

Goldwater-Nichols dealt only with DOD, and primarily with the four uniformed military services. Only one committee (SASC in the Senate, HASC in the House), and if the two committee chairman (Barry Goldwater and Bill Nichols) agreed that something needed to be done, something was going to be done -- ergo the 1986 legislation forcing "jointness" upon the uniformed services and accompanying changes to the structure of DOD including the establishment of ASD/SOLIC -- Jim Locher, having been the intellectual author of Goldwater-Nichols since he was Staff Director of the SASC under Goldwater, becoming the first ASD/SOLIC.

With the election of Barack Obama and appointment of Hillary Clinton as SecState, Bob Gates as SecDef [continuing from the previous administration] and [Gen] Jim Jones as NatSecAdviser, the need for PNSR basically evaporated. There has been no talk about reviving it or of legislative remedies to interagency dysfunction since then."

BOTTOM LINE: The interagency process is not broken because there is nothing to break. The interagency process works and works very well but only if there is coherent leadership from the Executive Branch.

Annex F: DIMEFIL, PMESII, MIDLIFE, ASCOPE

All of the currently used tools for analyzing the Operating Environment (OE) (including DIME, DIMEFIL, MIDLIFE, ASCOPE, and PMESII), provide a wide variety of constructs for analyzing both friendly and adversary systems. Although all of these constructs may not be necessary in all environments, they provide a useful set of tools for the analyst to gain a greater understanding of the operational environment.

DIMEFIL (Diplomatic, Informational, Military, Economic, Financial, Intelligence, Law Enforcement). DIMEFIL is "physical." These provide the ways to apply the means to achieve the ends.

Field Manual (FM) 3-0, Operations, defines the "instruments of national power" as diplomatic, informational, military, and economic, normally referred to as the DIME.

Joint Publication (JP) 3-0, Joint Operations, uses the term "instruments of national power" to define strategy as "a prudent idea or set of ideas for employing the instruments of national power in a synchronized and integrated fashion to achieve theater, national, and/or multinational objectives."

Even though the military may be the primary instrument of national power during war-fighting, the other elements of the "DIME" are not excluded; in fact, they continue to be essential instruments in the strategy of conducting the war. At the operational and tactical levels, the other elements of the DIME continue to be essential for mission success. It may be common to see all of the different instruments of national power used as "logical *lines of operations* (LLOs) where each of the instruments has complementary tasks and subtasks to meet the overall strategic objectives. This is especially true when considering all of the actions that may be taken prior to the initiation of hostilities with "flexible deterrent operations," or FDOs. These FDOs may be derived from any of the instruments of the DIME such as *information operations* (the "I" in DIME") or *economic sanctions* (combining diplomatic and economic instruments of power).

The financial instrument of power is closely related to the economic instrument of power; there are, however, some important differences. The economic instrument of power concerns issues such as regional and bilateral trade, infrastructure development, and foreign investment. Examples of the use of the economic instrument of power might include enacting trade sanctions, enacting restrictions on technology transfers, and reducing security assistance programs. The financial instrument of power concerns issues such as the transfer of funds and banking. The NSCT states:

Financial systems are used by terrorist organizations as a fiscal sanctuary in which to store and transfer the funds that support their survival and operations. Terrorist organizations use a variety of financial systems, including formal banking, wire transfers, debit and other stored value cards, online value storage and value transfer systems, the informal 'hawala' system, and cash couriers.

The intelligence instrument of power relates to continuous operations to develop the situation and generate the intelligence that allows forces to take actions against adversaries. Having an understanding of the intelligence capabilities of the adversary, and his ability to develop the situation from his perspective, is also a critical element in understanding the operational environment. The NMSP-WOT describes the intelligence instrument of power as used by adversaries:

> Extremist networks require specific and detailed information to achieve their ends. They gather this information from open sources, human contacts (both witting and unwitting), reconnaissance and surveillance, and technical activities. Terrorists use the resulting intelligence to plan and execute operations, and secure what they need to operate and survive. The intelligence component of extremist networks includes countermeasures to protect against infiltration or attack. Terrorist entities perform counterintelligence, apply operational security measures, use denial and deception, and exercise great care in determining the loyalty and reliability of members, associates, active supporters and other affiliates.

The law enforcement instrument of power relates to legal means within the operational environment, such as the *Patriot Act* and United Nations Security Council Resolutions (UNSCRs). The NSCT specifically addresses <u>UNSCR</u> 1373, "which imposes binding obligations on all states to suppress and prevent *terrorist financing*, improve their border controls, enhance *information sharing* and law enforcement cooperation, suppress the recruitment of terrorists, and deny them sanctuary."

Law Enforcement is particularly important in *counterinsurgency* operations (COIN). FM 3-24, Counterinsurgency, addresses this important issue:

> The cornerstone of any COIN effort is establishing security for the civilian populace. Without a secure environment, no permanent reforms can be implemented and disorder spreads. To establish legitimacy, commanders transition security activities from combat operations to law enforcement as quickly as feasible. When insurgents are seen as criminals, they lose public support. Using a legal system established in line with local culture and practices to deal with such criminals enhances the host nation government's legitimacy.

PMESII (Political, Military, Economic, Social, Infrastructure and Information Systems) PMESII is "concepts"

Political — The government is a constitutional democracy.

-- Constitution is ratified.
-- Parliamentary elections have been held.
-- Parliament is meeting.

The government is stable.

-- Government is organized.
-- Local government elections have been held.
-- Provincial government elections have been held.
-- Elected politicians do not advocate the use of paramilitary force.

Iraqi government institutions are functioning.

-- Ministers have been appointed.
-- Government officials follow only government direction.
-- Bureaucracy is operating.

Justice is administered by constitutional law.

The government is able to provide for the basic needs of its citizens.

-- Regulations enable electrical production and purchase.
-- Regulations enable fuel production and purchase.
-- Regulations enable water production, treatment, and purchase.
-- Regulations enable sewage treatment.
-- Regulations enable market-based food distribution.
-- Regulations enable financial institutions to function domestically.
-- Regulations enable financial institutions to function internationally.

The government is at peace with its neighbors.

Military — The military is able to defend the nation state against organized external threats.

  --- Military is manned.
  --- Recruiting program is in place.
  --- Replacements are being recruited.
  --- A career progression track is in place.
  --- Military is equipped.
  --- Military is trained.
  --- Military is organized.
  --- Personnel are being paid.
  --- Functions to assign replacements are in place.
  --- Functions to evaluate/discipline personnel are in place.

The military and police are able to defend the nation state against organized internal threats.

  --- Police force is manned.
  --- Recruiting program is in place.
  --- Replacements are being recruited.
  --- A career progression track is in place.
  --- Police force is equipped.
  --- Police force is trained.
  --- Police force is organized.
  --- Personnel are being paid.
  --- Functions to assign replacements are in place.
  --- Functions to evaluate/discipline personnel are in place.

The military and police follow the instructions of the civilian government.

The military and police only take direction from the civilian government.

Economic— The economy provides basic needs: water, food, sewage, electricity, fuel.

  --- Markets and shops are open.
  --- Markets can purchase goods for resale.
  --- Business owners can live on market prices.

--- Fuel is available to purchase.
--- Electricity is available to population.
--- Water is available to population.
--- Sewage treatment is available to population.

The financial system is functioning.

--- Banks are open and functioning.
--- Sufficient cash reserves.
--- Ability to make loans.
--- The stock market is functioning.

Social— Sectarian violence does not exceed the capacity of the police and military.

Society views the government as "legitimate."

Society views Al Qaeda as "illegitimate."

Society views paramilitary force as illegitimate.

Infrastructure— The utility infrastructure is able to support basic needs.

--- Food supply is sufficient to meet population's needs.
--- Domestic food production
--- Food imports
--- Electrical power production capacity is sufficient to meet population's needs.
--- Domestic production capacity
--- Domestic distribution capacity
--- Import capacity
--- Fuel production capacity is sufficient to meet population's needs.
--- Domestic production capacity
--- Domestic distribution capacity
--- Import capacity
--- Water supply is sufficient to meet population's needs.
--- Wells and reservoirs
--- Treatment plants

--- Water distribution system.
--- Sewage treatment capacity is sufficient to meet population's needs.
--- Sewage treatment plants.
--- Sewer and drainage system.

The transportation infrastructure is able to support basic needs

--- Road and rail network
--- Roads
--- Railroads
--- Bridges
--- Road bridges
--- Rail bridges

Financial infrastructure functionally sufficient

--- Banking institutions have adequate facilities.
--- Physical security
--- Connectivity
--- Stock trading institutions have adequate facilities.
--- Physical facilities
--- Connectivity

Informational— The people are able to obtain information about the nation-state and region.

--- Radio, television, newspaper are functioning.
--- Access by local and foreign press.
--- Local and foreign press provides moderate or unbiased reporting.
--- Local and foreign press has access and freedom of movement.

Mechanism statement for "are functioning": 1) infers they were not functioning but have increased their capacity, so they now are functioning. Must identify a "begin" time; indefinite duration. 2) Also infers functioning media can/will do the job—if not true, may need IO, specifically PSYOPS.

MIDLIFE (Military, Intelligence, Diplomatic, Law Enforcement, Information, Finance, Economic)

Interim Field Manual <u>FMI</u> 3-07.22, Counterinsurgency Operations, used the acronym MIDLIFE to describe the same instruments of national power as the acronym DIMEFIL. FMI 3-07.22 expired on 1 October 2006 and was replaced by FM 3-24, but the acronym MIDLIFE still lives on, probably because it is easier to remember and to say. The interim manual described counterinsurgency as "an offensive approach involving all elements of national power" and "leaders must consider the roles of **military, intelligence, diplomatic, law enforcement, information, finance, and economic** elements (MIDLIFE) in counterinsurgency."

ASCOPE (Areas, Structures, Capabilities, Organizations, People, and Events)

FM 3-24 does address another acronym used to describe civil considerations--"how the manmade infrastructure, civilian institutions, and attitudes and activities of the civilian leaders, populations, and organizations within an area of operations (AO) influence the conduct of *military operations*

FM 3-24 also indicates the relationship between the concepts of DIME and ASCOPE:

> Civil considerations generally focus on the immediate impact of civilians on operations in progress. However, at higher levels, they also include larger, long-term diplomatic, informational, and economic issues. At the tactical level, civil considerations directly relate to key civilian areas, structures, capabilities, organizations, people, and events within the AO.

FM 6-0, Mission Command: Command and Control of Army Forces, provides the detailed definitions for the six components of ASCOPE:

* Areas. Key civilian areas are localities or aspects of the terrain within an AO that are not normally militarily significant. This characteristic approaches *terrain analysis* (OAKOC) from a civilian perspective.

Commanders analyze key civilian areas in terms of how they affect the missions of their individual forces as well as how military operations affect these areas.

* Structures. Existing structures can play many significant roles. Some--such as, bridges, communications towers, power plants, and dams--are traditional high-payoff targets. Others--such as, churches, mosques, national libraries, and hospitals--are cultural sites that international law or other agreements generally protect. Still others are facilities with practical applications--such as, jails, warehouses, television and radio stations, and print plants--that may be useful for military purposes. Some aspects of the civilian infrastructure, such as the location of toxic industrial materials, may influence operations.

* Capabilities. Commanders and staffs analyze capabilities from different levels. They view capabilities in terms of those required to save, sustain, or enhance life, in that priority. Capabilities can refer to the ability of local authorities and a populace with key functions or services, such as, public administration, public safety, *emergency services*, and food. Capabilities include those areas in which the populace may need help after combat operations, such as, *public works* and utilities, public health, economics, and commerce. Capabilities also refer to resources and services that can be contracted to support the military mission, such as interpreters, laundry services, construction materials, and equipment. The host nation or other nations might provide these resources and services.

* Organizations. Organizations are nonmilitary groups or institutions in the AO. They influence and interact with the populace, the force, and each other. They generally have a *hierarchical structure*, defined goals, established operations, fixed facilities or meeting places, and a means of financial or logistic support. Some organizations may be indigenous to the area. These may include church groups, fraternal organizations, patriotic or service organizations, labor unions, criminal organizations, and community watch groups. Other organizations may come from outside the AO. Examples of these include multinational corporations, United Nations agencies, U.S. governmental agencies, and nongovernmental organizations (NGOs), such as the International Red Cross.

* People. People is a general term used to describe non-military personnel encountered by military forces. The term includes all civilians within an AO as well as those outside the AO whose actions, opinions, or political influence can affect the mission. Individually or collectively, people can affect a military operation positively, negatively, or neutrally. In stability operations and support operations, Army forces work closely with civilians of all types.

* Events. Events are routine, cyclical, planned, or spontaneous activities that significantly affect organizations, people, and military operations. Examples include national and religious holidays, agricultural crop/livestock and market cycles, elections, civil disturbances, and celebrations. Other events are disasters from natural, manmade, or technological sources. These create civil hardship and require emergency responses. Examples of events precipitated by military forces include combat operations, deployments, redeployments, and paydays. Once significant events are determined, it is important to template the events and to analyze them for their political, economic, psychological, environmental, and legal implications.

Annex G: Generational Warfare

Executive Report
JSOU Second Annual Symposium
1-3 May 2007
Hurlburt Field, FL
Irregular Warfare: Strategic Utility of SOF

Colonel Mark Boyatt (USA, Ret.)—Validity of IW as a Model

As background information, Colonel Boyatt introduced four key documents and studies concerning IW: *2006 Quadrennial Defense Review* and *Quadrennial Defense Review Irregular Warfare Roadmap,* Joint Warfighting Center, USJFCOM; *Irregular Warfare Special Study,* 4 August 2006; and the USMC/USSOCOM *Multi-Service Concept for Irregular Warfare,* Version 2, 2 August 2006. For discussion purposes, he used the working definition that Mr. Ishimoto had shared from the IW Roadmap. From Colonel Boyatt's perspective, IW is not a model but rather an umbrella, an attitude, or a context of thinking. He believes that rather than require a definition, think of IW as a "basket" in which to put anything that is not "regular" and helps separate ideas/concepts. It includes a collection of "tools," which he defined as the ten aspects outlined in the USJFCOM IW Special Study. IW is essentially warfare for the "human terrain," and to be successful one has to be engaged for at least a generation, versus hours, days, or even years. Boyatt described it as *generational warfare*. The key is how one stays engaged—for example, for generations with 1-year rotations, the interagency process (which should not be led by DOD), or domestic popular support. His solution is depicted in Figure 1.

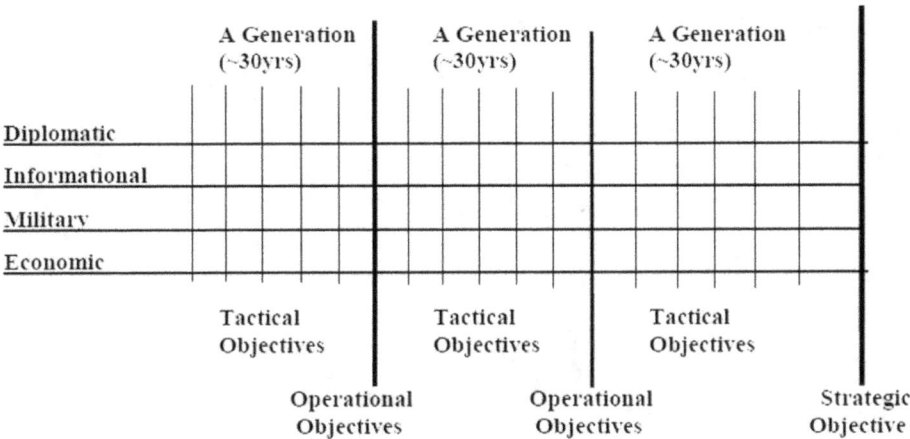

Each line has short-term, achievable, interagency coordinated goals geared to rotations of personnel (every unit/organization/commander/supervisor is given achievable goals). These goals are integrated steps in a long-term strategic campaign.

The strategic end state must be clearly defined. This end state should lead to a strategic campaign plan with a series of short-term, achievable, interagency agreed-upon tactical level goals. The tactical goals are geared to the rotations of units and individuals (including the interagency support mechanisms) that build over the course of years to achievable operational level goals. The operational goals ultimately support and finally achieve the desired strategic end state. Colonel Boyatt concluded that the strategic utility of SOF in IW lies in the understanding that IW is generational warfare and requires long-term continuous engagement, especially prior to conflict. Army Special Forces are selected, designed, organized, trained, and equipped for long duration engagement. The other elements of SOF provide on-call support with short duration or situational shaping engagements in support of Special Forces. The Special Forces mission is to accomplish goals and objectives *by, with, through* indigenous or surrogate elements in a manner that is perceived as legitimate and moral.

Executive Report: JSOU Second Annual Symposium; Irregular Warfare: Strategic Utility of SOF; 1-3 May 2007.

Annex H:
The Long War/Generational War

In 2007 MG(R) Sid Shachnow wrote and circulated an original paper per the title: **Special Forces - Adapting for the Long-War**. The draft document now titled "Special Forces – Generational Warfare" is based on the original document of the Veterans of Special Forces organization – www.veteransofspecialforces.org. As of 2014, the Veterans of Special Forces organization is inactive and dormant.

Special Forces - Adapting for the Long-War --Draft

-----Original Message-----
From: Sid Shachnow
To: LTG(R) Bill Tangney; COL(R) Mark Boyatt; Ed Mchale; MG(R) Jim Parker; MG(R) Ken Bowra; MG (R) Geoff Lambert; MG(R) Tom Csrnko; COL(R) Vavra, Glenn; MG(R) Harley Davis; COL(R) Glenn Harned; CSM(R) James Hargraves;COL James P. Nelson; MG(R) James Guest; COL(R) John H. Crerar; BG(R) Joseph B. DiBartolomeo; COL Joseph M Smith; MG(R) Leroy Suddath; Mark Beattie; COL Hector E. Pagan; Phil Kensinger; Remo Butler; BG Richard W. Mills; BG(R) Howard, Russell; COL Edwin Anderson
Sent: Thu, 16 Aug 2007 1:21 pm
Subject: Long War Paper (Draft #1)

This is our Veterans of Special Forces draft of our White Paper dealing with reorganization.

There is nothing original but would you look at it and let me have your thoughts? We would like to give a finalized paper to Admiral Olson before we meet him. If we can get it finalized in time I would like to send a copy to Gen. Wagner before we meet him on 22 August (2007). If you have received a previous email that made no sense, just ignore it. It got out by mistake. Thanks, Sid

****

Sid,

Well done. Two comments:

1. Page 5 recommend NOT calling Special Forces "Vanilla SOF." Address as Special Forces. Need to stay away from "Vanilla" and "White" SOF terms. Special Forces was and always will be Special Forces. Those other units can call themselves whatever they want, but they are not real SF.

2. Regional Orientation for SF Groups is a must, however, this has probably been another casualty of the ongoing GWOT in Iraq and Afghanistan, as SF Groups are engaged there, with the exception of 5th Group.

As you mentioned the QDR, attached is a good summary for you to review-some other possible points may be of value.

Also a good DoD briefing on "The Long War."

Sincerely,

****

MG (R) Shachnow
I wholeheartedly agree with the comments by you and MG (ret) _____.
It's a shame that every so often we must continue to relearn the same lessons. We won in El Salvador, Nicaragua, Honduras, and we slowed down the production, and exportation of narcotics from the Andean Ridge by doing it the old-fashioned way. The Kurds are our one bastion

of friendship thanks to the FID mission preformed by 10th SF Group after the 1st gulf war. We (SF) are now engaged in a great conflict to see if we can remain a viable asset in the war on terrorism. We have proven our mettle time and again but we never seem to create enough (Political Special Forces Officers) to get the prestige we are a community of warriors not politicians.

****

Sir: Bravo. For more than two decades I have been an advocate for the "SAF Asia[160]" structure so this is music to my ears. I do wish there might be a way to change the NG to reserve groups, which would make the White Paper's plan much easier to execute. I agree with the rank structure as you have outlined it....perhaps with the exception of SWC, which I still believe requires a MG. However, I anticipate a question you might be asked is, "what command opportunities will special forces colonels have to make them competitive for the SAF BG positions? Thanks for including me. v/r

****

Sid,

I read the paper with a great deal of interest and agree that a bold effort is the way.

Recommendations:
- The Special Forces Command should be a Four Star Command.
- The Theater Special Forces Commands should be Three Star Commands.
- The Special Forces Command should be a Direct Reporting Unit of the U.S. Army or a Uniformed Separate Service, organized using the U.S. Coast Guard as a model, outside DOD. Senior officers and NCOs from other branches (or services) should be prohibited from serving in key command and staff positions in the SF Commands.

---

160 See Annex O: Special Action Force

- Mulholland and other active duty SF Officers can be promoted or appointed to the key command and staff positions in the SF Command and its subordinate commands. All Brigade level commands should be GO commands (they operate around the world at very high levels). There are many great and capable SF Officers in the Special Forces Groups who can be promoted below the zone if need be.

- OGA representatives should be in their own sections under the G3 and should never hold key positions (such as the DOS Deputy Commander).

- All units in the command such as Aviation should have SF MOSs and should be administered and managed solely by the SF Command for training, education and promotions.

- In addition to the units you show, The SF Command should have an Operations Support Group with Light Infantry type units, to be used as SF Command deems necessary to support the FID missions worldwide, much like the Mobile Strike Forces that supported the 5th SFGA so successfully in RVN. Again, These SF Soldiers would have SF MOSs and would be ideal candidates to go to the SFODs after serving in the OGA.

- In the introduction of the White Paper I suggest that you again stress the difference in SF and SOF. Apparently, this cannot be explained enough.

Discussion:

- While these recommendations taken alone would seem draconian, when they are examined in light of Special Forces 50+ years of existence, Special Forces legacy on the battlefield working with, by, and through the indigenous people, and Special Forces unilateral capability in such organizations as SOG: running the Recon Teams, and the unequalled performance of the numbered SFGAs in OIF and OEF plus other places around the world serving under conventional senior officers who horn in on their successes and on many occasions badly misuse them, I believe it is time they are afforded an opportunity to be in charge of their own destiny.

- While the rank structure may at first glance seem excessive, we should be able to explain the levels of government (both U.S. and foreign), and the levels of theatre forces that SF must work with - Chiefs of Armies and rulers of other countries, as well as senior U.S. Combatant Commanders. I think we have all had the experience of finding that our counterparts in the Pentagon are all at least one rank higher than we.
- When thinking about these recommendations it should be kept in mind the number of tours the Special Forces Soldiers and Units have served and are serving multiple tours in OIF and OEF operating under JSOC or other JSOTGs while neglecting the JCET programs that in the long run will be many times more important than the direct action operations of SOF.
- Special Forces Soldiers and Officers have no peers historically or currently on the battlefields and in conflicts. They are unique and must be in charge of themselves without interference to be as successful as is necessary to win the GWOT or whatever it is being called today. It can be won with a long long-term operation in the villages and neighborhoods around the world. Surges and transient direct action mean very little in all of this.
- This concept for Special Forces should not be allowed to get bogged down in discussions with USSOCOM or USASOC but should be briefed to key Congressmen and their senior aides as the way to go by all of the former SF GO, SF Officers and SF NCOs. These folks should be urged to go to the operational areas and spend unchaperoned time with the SFODs so they can form their own opinions about SF.

Sid, I apologize for the length of these comments. I appreciate all that you and other members of VSF are trying to do for Special Forces, and hope that together we will be able to save this important part of our nation's defenses.

I think if we wait too long, or are not vigorous enough, we will not prevail.

****

Sid,

Thanks for the opportunity to review the paper.

Overall I think it is good. I agree in large part with many of the comments already provided, and I would like to just emphasize a few points.

I completely agree with the comments about Vanilla/White. Unless something has changed it is still U.S. Army Special Forces. I remain concerned that the regional focus for each group is not taken seriously, but strongly believe it must be preserved, especially after everyone else goes home and 5th and 10th Group are left to sort out Iraq and Afghanistan. (_____ makes a good point about relationships with the Kurds.)

_____ commented about Reserve Component SF. If there is some way to get/keep them involved, they can bring much needed political support that I believe will be required. I also think the SWC commander should be a two star with a BG AC.

Now, I do believe that _____ has hit the mark as far as a bold move. I believe his comments are what is truly needed to get our Army Special Forces out of the second fiddle mode. I don't think USASOC or USSOCOM will make the right thing happen for SF. They will continue to 'cherry pick' one or two SF folks to be three stars and keep the CINC job for the real DA operators. This does keep Army SF in its place.

All the very best,

****

Sir,

I like what I am reading in the White Paper and all the comments. I hope this is the start of a synergy that we can sustain. As far as my comments, I recognize up front that I will probably ruffle some feathers. Most everyone on your email list knows me and knows I have very strong, and sometimes, stubborn opinions. I do hope my comments provide some viable food for thought.

I agree with MG(R)___ that something fairly drastic has been required for a long time. On the other hand, we should not be too critical of our still-serving active duty brethren. All of you know better than I the situation of an active duty SF general officer. The very things we are discussing now were being discussed ever since the watered down and neutered Goldwater-Nichols/Nunn-Cohen legislation was put into effect (this was originally to be outside DoD as a National Special Operations Agency, but the Service chiefs, and others, including some is our own ranks, beat it back)... the organizational structure problems; the rank/grade structure deficits; the C2 relationships; the fact that "black velcro" dominated SOF; that "toys" were always more important than "boys"; that the SOF Truths make a good sound bite but policy does not follow; that we were being "sold out" to the conventional Army; that DA and the "Black world" dominated the resources, priority, policy, promotions (and still does) .... many of us saw this and were discussing these as-needed corrections while we were on active duty and, for the most part, we did very little ... we took a quiet middle of the road, survival approach. It also is obvious that the quiet, behind the scenes approach did not work either, and at best resulted in compromise and crumbs to satisfy the masses. We did not have very many Singlaubs. I am not convinced there is much to expect from the active duty leadership (at least not in the light of day). I agree with MG(R)___, the target should be Congress.

The core uniqueness of SF is "through, with and by." Basically, everything else is just icing on the cake... when a SF Soldier drops the hammer on his weapon, he is in mission failure because he was not able to get the indig to do this. Anything SF does "unilaterally," the conventional forces can do. It is just a matter of degree and with resourcing, anyone can do DA. Therefore, regional orientation is an absolute must – as most of you have stated. The rotation of SF in OIF and OEF is a travesty. The 5th Group flag should have been planted there for the duration – PCS or whatever – only individual replacements. NO OTHER GROUP should have rotated teams there. Why? First and most important is this broke the core "through, with and by" because it broke the critical relationships with the indig every rotation. Secondly, the rotation policy took the other SF Groups' focus away from their regions (i.e., the loss of JCETs as MG(R)___ pointed out and broken relationships in the other regions).

This is a global war ... not just an OIF/OEF war. This is generational war, not to be measured by time.

In my opinion, JSOC does not even match one SF Group in complexity, depth and breadth of missions, so, for parity, each SF Group should be a LTG ... okay, a reach. But those who remember the Unified Quest/ Joint & Army Wargames of 2001-2004 know we successfully war-gamed and exercised the TARSOC Concept (SF Groups looked a lot like the original SAFs and were commanded by BGs). These war games also exercised SF Group (TARSOC) C2 of vast regions with large conventional force structure subordinated to the SF ... I mean brigades (UAs they were called), air wings, navy ships, plus coalition forces. Of course all this is buried and none of it was discussed in the AARs to the 4-stars.

As MG(R)___ indirectly pointed out, the rank structure issue will not be significant if we can get out of DOD and reform the OSS. If we are to remain inside DOD, then the rank structure is critical and it is imperative we have equal status.

In the operational areas, the ground must be owned by the SF Group. No other element should enter that operational space without the knowledge of, coordination with, and approval of that SF Group ....liken the SF Group to an American Ambassador. Any element that enters the SF Group area, regardless, is under the C2 of that SF Group ...It does not matter if it is a conventional brigade combat team or the entire Delta force or the CIA...the SF Group owns the ground because they have been there, or should have been there, for years... this is a generational war and no room for fly-by cowboys...every move must be culturally integrated. This is the salient C2 issue...undoubtedly more rice bowls than we can count and we probably don't have much chance of breaking them all.

The most important overall issue is USAJFKSWCS. The School should be the number one priority of USASOC and all the schoolhouses should be the number one priority for USSOCOM.... ahead of JSOC and its units. For years I have heard commanders say that the schoolhouse is the top priority, but the money and manning never follows. It makes no difference what JSOC wants or what any JSOC unit wants, these requirements are automatically put about the cut line with only the most cursory justification. Not true for SF and certainly not true for the School. As an addendum, we may not have had the vision and plan to ask for the resources we should have. We may have been too willing to compromise.

The only focus of the School now, as I see it, is the immediate 5 meter target of producing SF Soldiers … everything else is compromised. The future is compromised. Where is the education? We have great training, but little education. The "Long War" will be won by education, not training … we are off focus.

Where is the plan for the future, except to keep pumping the SF pipeline and hoping enough get through to graduation … the old "throw enough on the wall and some will stick (check out the hundreds in holding, the ones with pending chapters, non-judicial and CM actions, cycling out and recycle/recycle/recycle). To its credit, the School is producing SF throughput, but is this methodology the best and worth the cost in human capital? Is there a better (not necessarily cheaper in dollars) way to do this?

However, the overall School priority picture may be coming clearer. DA SOF (Direct Action) does not need the School to fill its ranks. DA SOF does not need the School to educate its members. DA SOF does not need the School as a proponent of any of their units. Even though most operators in Delta are former SF (and I say former because they no longer are focused on through, with, and by), they don't **have** to have SF to man these organizations…. Aviators, infantry, etc. So it follows that an organization dominated by the DA side has little need for SWCS.

I believe the enhanced SAF concept[161] is the future base organization, regardless of whether or not we can ultimately be successful with a reborn OSS.

Many of the issues I have touched on have been better put forth by MG Shachnow in his Congressional testimony and by MG Guest in his editorial, "The Long Farewell."

V/R, Mark D. Boyatt, COL(R)

---

161 See Annex O: Special Action Force

****

(This document is based on an original document, *Special Forces - Adapting for the Long-War*, by the Veterans of Special Forces organization – www.veteransofspecialforces.org. MG(R) Sid Shachnow is the principal author with integrated comments by other SF veterans. This draft has been modified by COL(R) Mark D. Boyatt into this renamed version)

(Note by COL(R) Boyatt – It is now 2014. Our military is out of Iraq and drawing down rapidly in Afghanistan. I did not serve in either Iraq or Afghanistan. I did serve in peacetime South Korea where we said that we had one year of experience repeated 60+ times. From what I have observed and seen, it appears the same situation exists for Afghanistan --- one year of experience repeated 12+ times)

Draft – 4 January 2008
(Not officially approved by VSF nor was it ever released)
Special Forces - Adapting to Generational Warfare

Introduction

It has become axiomatic to say that our national security posture, and for that matter our national outlook, must change, given the 'new normal' we live in post-911. DoD has, with increasing resolve, sought to transform itself in light of that new reality while directing a land war in Afghanistan and Iraq in the face of massive internal and other governmental inertia. Much of the U.S. Government marches along with a 'business as usual' philosophy. Even after six years, as a nation, we still have not appropriately identified the situation. We debate this as a *Long War*, when, in reality, it is generational in character. The goal is to positively influence and affect the youngest generations and unborn generations as the only viable solution to stability. This requires stability and the integrated application of all the elements of national power; diplomatic, information, military, economic (DIME) through the interagency process. This effort will, like the Cold War, consume our time, our sons and daughters, and our national treasure as this century unfolds. More than ever, we in the military, and in particular within Army Special Forces (SF), need to engage in some open conversations on how we can best adapt and, in some cases, transform our unique assets to contribute to the winning of this Generational War.

This first Veterans of Special Forces (VSF) White Paper is intended to promote just such a dialogue. The Veterans of Special Forces (VSF) offers its time and views toward promoting this dialogue in a professional and constructive way. Your comments are invited.

Background and Discussion

Nothing about the special operations arena is ever simple. It is a vibrant, dynamic environment, one that is never short on issues. And never short on internal, and often emotional, disagreements on how to best address those issues.

In 2005, Commander, U.S. Special Operations Command (USCINCSOC), was tasked by Secretary of Defense to lead in formulating the joint effort against global radical terrorism. Over the past eighteen months, USSOCOM has developed an Irregular Warfare Joint Operating Concept (JOC) shaping the conduct of JFC (joint force command) operations through the 2014 – 2026 timeframe.

Concurrently, the Army and Marine Corps, in large measure as a result of increasing insurgent successes in Iraq and, to lesser degree in Afghanistan, published a new multi-service Counter Insurgency (COIN) manual, FM 3-24 / MCWP 3.33.5 (December 2006) that attempts to reorient ground forces to less kinetic and more holistic approaches to restoring stability to areas subject to insurgency. The notion of COIN as a viable concept of employment had been all but expunged by the Army leadership in the 1990s. FM 3-24 has taken the first step in resuscitating COIN, but much practical expertise had been lost over the decades, except where some SF groups practiced its principles in places like Central America and more recently in the Philippines.

High-Port and Cross-Over: After several years on the ground in Iraq, the United States military finds itself having to reassess its reliance on lethal force to achieve the security conditions that will permit the development of a viable Iraqi society--a society that neither threatens its regional neighbors, nor sustains radical jihadism. In the midst of the current operational *surge* in Iraq, we are now having to re-learn to apply the bullet, information, the medical aid kit and the drilling-rig in the right mix, in the right proportions and at the right times, much as we did successfully in Viet Nam in the 1960s and 70s (Note: We must stop being afraid of using the word *Viet Nam* when describing successes. It's OK. Really). But, now, we are increasingly to do so with forces whose DOTML-PF (doctrine, organization, training, material, leadership, personnel and facilities) were developed to support the application of lethal force on the fire and maneuver battlefield. Fortunately, we have a proven volunteer force that has weathered over four years of incredible adversity, and that has adapted through the exercise of character and tactical level leadership. Yet, those forces must ultimately be organized, employed and sustained by operating systems (e.g. C2, intelligence, and sustainment) far different from those we see today.

Shooters and Ombudsmen

The kinetic environment, with its commando élan, unique training, high-dollar equipment and weapons systems, finely honed decision-making processes, etc., has been pervasive. Lethal / surgical application of force provides immediate feedback, and when conducted well, provides immediate gratification. In the special operations world, it also tends toward the establishment of supporting organizations in pursuit of increasingly narrowly focused special operations missions. When viewed in light of the implications of a WMD strike against the U.S. or its friends by radical Jihadists, the focus is justified. When viewed in the context of generational warfare, the kinetic or direct action mission enjoys limited, albeit important, application.

On the flip side, we find Army Special Forces (SF) and their Civil Affairs (CA) and Psychological Operations (PSYOP) partners who operate in the broader diplomatic, informational, military and economic (DIME) arena, largely with an integrated but unglamorous approach, drawing little if any public scrutiny[162], applying lethal force when necessary, yet achieving through cultural and operational adaptation, communications skills, long-term vision and what the kinetic world refers to as application of 'soft skills' (a pejorative), resulting in the neutralization or elimination of grassroots insurgencies that could otherwise contribute to failed states and to the spread of radical jihadism. The performance of SF in El Salvador in the '80s, SF successes in collaboration with the Northern Alliance in Afghanistan, and more recently, SF successes in the Philippines bear witness to the validity of the more integrated and multi-disciplinary DIME approach to the long-term aims of U.S. security policy. Yet, these forces do not have the resourcing levels enjoyed by the more narrowly defined kinetic-focused forces.

Soldiers and Diplomats

The Quadrennial Defense Review 2006 (QDR 2006) underscored the need for greater interagency cooperation and collaboration in attempts to restore or sustain stability in an increasing number of failed and failing states. In parallel with that QDR was issuance of DoD Directive (DoDD 3000.05, Military Support for Stability, Security, Transition, and Reconstruction) and issuance of the DoS NSPD 44, Management of Interagency Efforts Concerning Reconstruction and Stabilization. Taken together and, if taken seriously, these documents begin to move the operational equation into the Special Forces area of expertise and influence.

JTF SWORD

USSOCOM directed USASOC to establish a deployable foundation for a JTF, to be designated JTF SWORD. The JTF SWORD was to be a no-growth (e.g. internal bill-payers) organization with the ultimate capability to command and control " ... joint SOF, conventional, and / or combined / partner nation forces in support of GWOT objectives at the operational level." It was envisioned that JTF SWORD would have the capability to conduct direct action (DA), unconventional warfare (UW),

---

162   Note: When Tier units are cited for achievement in operations it is good publicity. When SF units are cited, it is seen as running counter to USSOCOM's 'quiet warrior' philosophy.

and counter-terrorism (CT) missions. JTF SWORD appeared to weight its mission heavily on the kinetic end of the continuum of operations. Perhaps some balancing and restructuring of capabilities would make the JTF more effective in supporting Generational Warfare. What follows is some of VSF collective thought.

Rethinking the SF Group

The SF group has retained its basic structure that was developed during early '50s, with Europe-focused SF teams, some sprinkled with Lodge Act recruits … and with organic skill sets likely never to be duplicated again … to counter the Soviet threat to Europe in the early days of the Cold War. That structure has served the Nation well for over five decades. This flexible and adaptable organization, with the appropriate augmentation, is aptly suited for the integrated application of the inherently unique skills required to best address Generational Warfare. Today, each SF group is organized in nearly identical fashion. Each SF group must further adapt to its regional orientation, and the unique aspects of their respective operational environments. The 10th SFGA adapts in different ways to its region from that of the 7th SFGA to its region. Both become regionally 'street-smart'. And that is an invaluable posture to attain; one that cannot be readily duplicated if ever we lose it[163]. So, without abandoning those attributes so unique to the standing Special Forces group, we must look to leveraging those into an organization more readily conducive to the DIME-driven operational arena required for the conduct of operations in the 21st century.

The SAF[164]-like SF Group

The SAF (special action force) was a concept first envisioned in the 1960s to be employed within the context of internal defense and development (IDAD), primarily in Latin America and Southeast Asia. The concept saw the task organization of a SF group with the attached support assets

---

163 There is no standardized or programmatic approach evident to the attainment of, or of what constitutes, regional 'street-smarts' in the collective sense.

164 See Annex O: Special Action Force

required for a complex IDAD operational environment, where both lethal and constructive activities were envisioned. Foreign Internal Defense (FID) was the subset of IDAD that provided the focus of the SF Group-cum-SAF. Variants of the SAF were examined over the years, but the concept never achieved the level of legitimacy reserved for a joint operating concept or as joint doctrine. DoD avoided any discussion of concepts that addressed counterinsurgency.

Now is the time to address the new operational environment with an updated SF group, with organic interagency roles, and with command and control provided by an interagency Special Forces command and control, that begins to answer the operational requirements of Generational Warfare.

Attributes

With renewed and intensified interest in national security strategy as a function of the integration of diplomacy, information, military and economic (DIME) elements of national power, the key attributes of the organization envisioned for the SAF in this century are worth examining in light of:

- Adaptability: The organization must adapt to its operational environment; that is, to its diplomatic, information, military and economic environment. This demands a rethinking of the recruiting, training and professional education concept, providing the expertise to man the command.
- Unity of Effort: The organizational structure and the concept for its employment must be conducive to a unified effort from the contingency planning phase through employment and the sustainment of operations.
- Interagency: Rather than an ad hoc posting of whomever from other government agencies (OGA) is available at the moment, the commands' key positions are manned by the inter-agency leaders, with appropriate operational and support assets, and with appropriate authorities and responsibilities within the command, on a sustained basis. We recognize that as far as the interagency

is concerned, unity of command is not a goal that is achievable. However, it would appear that unity of effort is something on which we all could agree.

- Expandability: The SF group, in a deliberate and controlled fashion, can be expanded into a joint task force (JTF) to address conditions that present a threat to the stability of a region, or to carry out a functional role. These may range from natural disasters to major incursions by hostile nations, to the support of insurgency or counterinsurgency.

- Regional Presence and Engagement: SF groups do not rotate in whole or part outside their designated region of responsibility. In a contingency such as OIF, the regionally assigned SF group deploys for the duration and only does individual rotation of personnel. The "flags" do not rotate. The Special Forces UW Command, if not fully deployed into its target region, can sustain a major presence for years and decades in order to attain a level of 'regional street smarts' unattainable by any other means. Intimate, total emersion understanding forms the basis for intelligence development and realistic estimates of the DIME situations.

The Template

Some with some gray showing from under your berets … will recognize aspects of the structure of the SF groups outlined below from the days of the Special Action Force (SAF)[165]. While the below command and control structure and the SF Group has been updated, it draws from those original SAF notions, where appropriate.

Special Forces Unconventional Warfare Command: An Organizational Alternative for Generational Warfare

Our proposed Special Forces Unconventional Warfare Command would consist of a command and control headquarters drawn from the former

---

165 Some were designated as *Security Assistance Force* to better align with country or regional security strategies. See Annex O: Special Action Force.

U.S. Army Special Forces Command and Army Special Operations Command, It would be commanded by a three-star SF-qualified flag officer. The new Special Forces Command would be assigned a number of operational SF groups, PSYOP Group(s) and CA Bde(s), each organized for, and oriented to, a regional security strategy and trained and equipped to service regional requirements on a continuing basis. Each of these elements would be commanded by branch specific-qualified brigadier generals. The Special Forces Command with Title X authority, also has a Sustainment Command, commanded by a major general, responsible for resourcing and integrating DOTML-PF functions. Functions that are currently duplicated in USASOC would be streamlined and those dealing with institutional training would reside only in the Sustainment Command. JSOC would assume control of all units that it has a habitual relationship, like the Rangers, Aviation Regiment and others, however, Title X will be provided by the Sustainment Command. The Special Forces Unconventional Warfare Command is dedicated to continuing regional presence in support of regional strategies.

Key Aspects of the Special Forces Unconventional Warfare Command

The bill payers to form the Special Forces UW Command and the Sustainment Command would come from existing units and staff of the Army Special Operation Command. This could be a zero sum effort, but should have growth as required. The 96th CA Brigade and the 4th PSYOP Group would remain intact and subordinate to the Special Forces UW Command. Battalions of these organizations would be earmarked for direct support of respective Special Forces groups. regional orientation would be retained by these units and they would have a habitual direct support (DS) relationship with their respective SF groups similar to the relationship DS artillery battalions had with their supported maneuver brigades before the new BCT concept. In addition to those SOF units, the SF groups would have assigned supporting maneuver, maneuver support, service support and interagency elements tailored to the regional environment in which it operates. The SF groups form the basis for deployable Joint Expeditionary Task Forces. The command's institutional training and education requirements are sustained by the John F. Kennedy Special Warfare Center and School (SWCS). Commander of the Sustainment Command is also Commandant SWCS. The Sustainment command would have two one-star generals and an SES; one general officer for sustainment; one general officer for training; and the SES as the Provost of Education.

The SF Groups

The current SF Group would significantly increase in size. We envision an organization that is 3800 to 5500 strong. The operational groups, each commanded by a brigadier general, would have varying numbers of SF battalions, based on regional security requirements. Some of these battalions would be from the National Guard.

Civil Affairs and Information Operations capabilities would be provided to the SF Group on a habitual Direct Support basis by the 96th CA Brigade and the 4th PSYOP Group respectively.

An interagency core is embedded in the SF Group and expanded as necessary upon deployment.

Selected conventional maneuver, maneuver support, service support elements tailored to the appropriate regional environment would be aligned and attached for training and deployment.

JSOC elements would be on-call for supporting operational events as developed by the deployed SF Groups. No JSOC element or conventional force operates within the SF Group's regional area of responsibility without the knowledge of and coordination with the SF Group.

Designated SF National Guard battalions would be assigned to a SF Group and maintain a day-to-day operational relationship. We further envision that the Aviation and Engineers would be battalion-size units. The specific make up of other capabilities shown in the Group organization is subject to further study. The supported operational environment also drives the mix and depth of combat support and service support capabilities required to service a wide range of operational plans directing both UW and FID tasks. When Service maneuver, maneuver support and service support assets are not readily available, the Group maintains a contracting operations center to develop contracting estimates, develop courses of action for contract support, develop contract language that supports the operational plan, and integrates the right mix and type of contract support to sustain operations.

Figure 2 - Notional SF Group

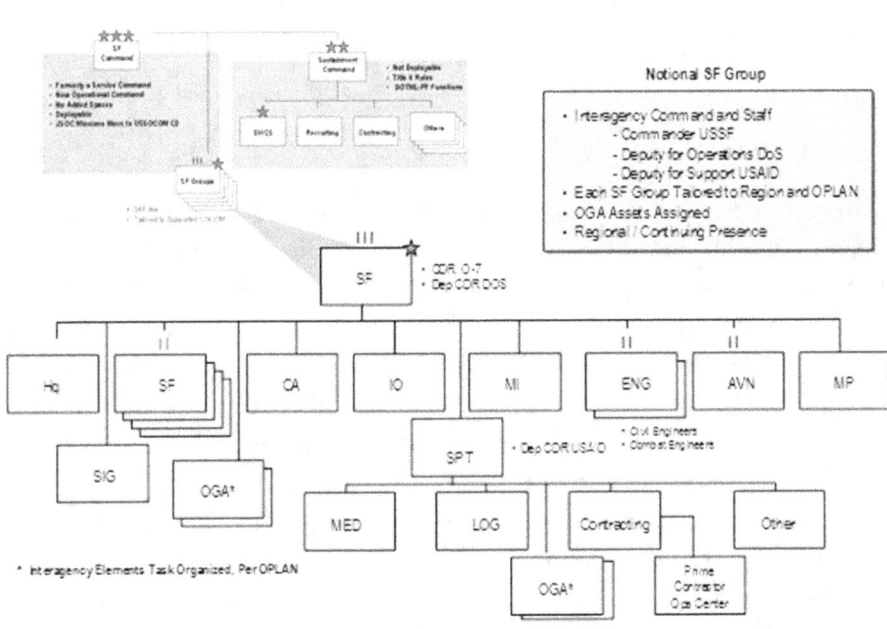

Figure 2 – Notional SF Group

The SF group is heavily reliant on its interagency composition to train, exercise and execute a full range of counter insurgency and irregular warfare requirements in support of regional commanders, or in support of the theater special operations command (SOC).

Of great importance is the SF group's mix of Department of State (DOS), USAID and CIA assets, as well as personnel assigned to key positions, along with attached advisors and liaison officers to the group headquarters.

A regionally-focused mix of interagency / OGA assets would be assigned to operational control of the SF Group. For the first time, the exercise of operational art on a day-to-day basis would be possible on an interagency basis. The desire to succeed and the major efforts of people of great good will from each of these government agencies would be key ingredients in making this organizational solution set workable. Special Forces, as part of the American Ambassador's Country Team, becomes the catalyst and coordination center for interagency operations.

When required, the SF Group would form a sub-unified command or form the nucleus of a JTF.

Resistance to Change

"There is nothing more difficult for success, nor more dangerous to handle, than to initiate a new order of things," said Machiavelli some five hundred plus years ago. The truth of this is forcibly brought home to those who attempted to put into effect a bold and significant organizational change. Reorganization can be a highly disruptive force. Need for change may be recognized only at the height of crises or in the depths of failure. However, change is inevitable. The challenge lies in the fact that SF has been successful and effective. Therein lays the danger that the urge to change and improve is diminished. Successful organizations and leaders tend to relax and contemplate their laurels. The factors that made the organization successful tend to become institutionalized. They are passed from one leader generation to the next intact and unquestioned, as part of the organizational culture. Over time, we tend to trade lean and effective concepts of employment for the comfortable embrace of dogma.

This reverence for the successful stereotype engenders a deep and enduring fear of changing the status quo, of leaving the certainty of the tried and proven for the experimental and hence dangerous innovation. Just as the pattern of success becomes a way of life, that success is accompanied by an abiding reluctance for institutional change. In this pattern lie the seeds of disaster. SF needs to make a clear and bold change in order to be effective in facing the challenges in the 21st Century. The timid will turn away from this proposal; the bold will study, critique, adapt and embrace this proposal as we commit to generational warfare.

****

The below is extracted from the **Executive Report: Joint Special Operations University (JSOU) Second Annual Symposium; 1-3 May 2007; Hurlburt Field, FL**

Irregular Warfare: Strategic Utility of SOF

Colonel Mark Boyatt (USA, Ret.)—Validity of IW as a Model

As background information, Colonel Boyatt introduced four key documents and studies concerning IW: *2006 Quadrennial Defense Review* and *Quadrennial Defense Review Irregular Warfare Roadmap,* Joint Warfighting Center, USJFCOM; *Irregular Warfare Special Study,* 4 August 2006; and the USMC/USSOCOM *Multi-Service Concept for Irregular Warfare,* Version 2, 2 August 2006. For discussion purposes, he used the working definition that Mr. Ishimoto had shared from the IW Roadmap. From Colonel Boyatt's perspective, IW is not a model but rather an umbrella, an attitude, or a context of thinking. He believes that rather than require a definition, think of IW as a "basket" in which to put anything that is not "regular" and helps separate ideas/concepts. It includes a collection of "tools," which he defined as the ten aspects outlined in the USJFCOM IW Special Study. IW is essentially warfare for the "human terrain," and to be successful one has to be engaged for at least a generation, vice hours, days, or even years. Boyatt described it as *generational warfare.* The key is how one stays engaged—for example, for generations with 1-year rotations, the interagency process (which should not be led by DOD), or domestic popular support. His solution is depicted in Figure 1.

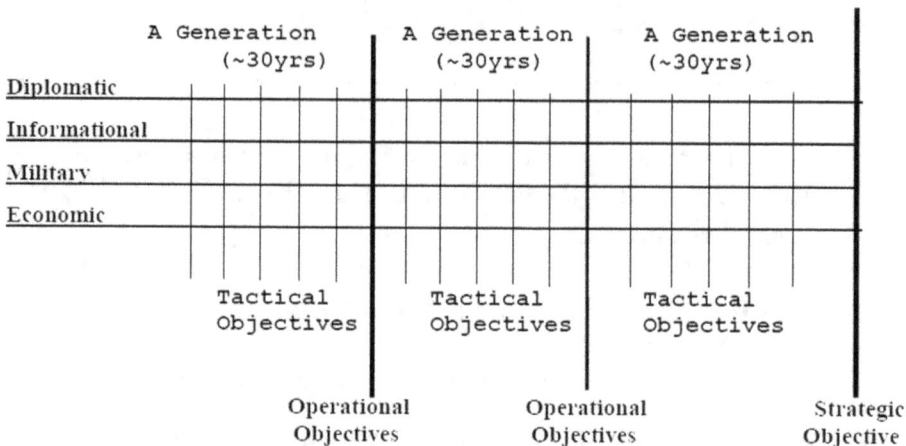

Each line has short-term, achievable, interagency coordinated goals geared to rotations of personnel (every unit/organization/commander/supervisor is given achievable goals). These goals are integrated steps in a long-term strategic campaign.

The strategic end state must be clearly defined. This end state should lead to a strategic campaign plan with a series of short-term, achievable, interagency agreed-upon tactical level goals. The tactical goals are geared to the rotations of units and individuals (including the interagency support mechanisms) that build over the course of years to achievable operational level goals. The operational goals ultimately support and finally achieve the desired strategic end state. Colonel Boyatt concluded that the strategic utility of SOF in IW lies in the understanding that IW is generational warfare and requires long-term continuous engagement, especially prior to conflict. Army Special Forces are selected, designed, organized, trained, and equipped for long duration engagement. The other elements of SOF provide on-call support with short duration or situational shaping engagements in support of Special Forces. The Special Forces mission is to accomplish goals and objectives *by, with, through* indigenous or surrogate elements in a manner that is perceived as legitimate and moral.

Annex I:
Unconventional Warfare Command

The Special Forces Unconventional Warfare Command would consist of a command and control headquarters, drawn from the former U.S. Army Special Forces Command and Army Special Operations Command, and would be commanded by a three-star SF-qualified flag officer. The new Special Forces Command would be assigned a number of operational SF groups, PSYOP Group(s) and CA Bde(s), each organized for, and oriented to, a regional security strategy and trained and equipped to service regional requirements on a continuing basis. Each of these elements would be commanded by branch-specific qualified general officers. The Special Forces UW Command with Title X authority also has a Sustainment Command, commanded by a general officer, responsible for resourcing and integrating DOTML-PF functions. Functions that are currently duplicated in USASOC would be streamlined and those dealing with institutional training would reside only in the Sustainment Command. JSOC would assume control of all units that it has a habitual relationship, like the Rangers, Aviation Regiment and others; however, Title X will be provided by the Sustainment Command. The Special Forces Unconventional Warfare Command is dedicated to continuing regional presence in support of regional strategies.

Key Aspects of the Special Forces Unconventional Warfare Command

The bill payers to form the Special Forces UW Command and the Sustainment Command would come from existing units and the staff of the Army Special Operation Command. This could be a zero sum effort, but should have growth as required. The 96th CA Brigade and the 4th PSYOP Group would remain intact and subordinate to the Special Forces UW Command. Battalions of these organizations would be earmarked for direct support of respective Special Forces groups. Regional orientation would be retained by these units and they would have a habitual direct support (DS) relationship with their respective SF Groups similar to the relationship DS artillery battalions had with their supported maneuver brigades before the new BCT concept. In addition to those SOF units, the SF groups would have assigned supporting maneuver, maneuver support, service support and interagency elements tailored to the regional environment in which it operates. The SF Groups form the basis for deployable Joint Task Forces. The command's institutional training and education requirements are sustained by the John F. Kennedy Special Warfare Center and School (SWCS). Commander of the Sustainment Command is also Commandant SWCS. The two-star Sustainment Command would have two one-star generals and an SES; one general officer for sustainment; one general officer for training; and the SES as the Provost of Education.

Aaron Banks Center for Advisory Leadership

The USA JFK Special Warfare Center and School (SWCS) has served with distinction providing the training needs of ARSOF and the Department of Defense under different names and organizational structures in response to varying security requirements of the Cold War and post-Cold War. If *tribal* memory and sentiment are to be relied upon, the Center's signature period came under its designation as the U.S. Army Special Warfare Center. Through its Military Advisory and Training Assistance (MATA) Course(s), the school prepared literally thousands of officers and NCOs from all the Services, other government agencies and from many allied nations for advisory duty in Viet Nam during the 1960s. After the U.S. withdrawal from Viet Nam, our military all but erased advisory concepts and doctrine from its operational repertoire, especially when linked to counter insurgency efforts, and by which its military leadership was so recently snake-bitten. The new USA JFK Special Warfare Center and School, however, and the Special Forces operational groups, sustained the guerrilla POI and military advisory skills that ultimately defeated a rebel insurgency and takeover in El Salvador, and that ultimately pushed the Taliban out of Afghanistan *by, with and through* the Northern Alliance. These unconventional operations represent the majority of the few bright spots in U.S. security operations since the end of World War II.

In light of this infrequently-publicized distinction, and with a clear opportunity and need to nurture its demonstrated unconventional operations heritage, the USA JFK SWCS must make yet another transition in its journey to maturity. This time it must become a world-class center of unconventional operations and advisory education and training, a center of knowledge and innovation to serve the security needs of America and her allies in the 21st century.

The *Aaron Banks Center for Advisory Leadership* will offer Special Forces and other ARSOF professionals, and selected interagency counterparts, an educational and training framework that permits professional educational growth beginning at the entry (tactical) level through the strategic levels of unconventional and advisory operational art. It will combine academic inquiry with field application. Degree-granting programs, certifications and occupational specialties, both civilian and military, offered in-house, on-line and in collaboration with an array of academic institutions (Johns Hopkins, MIT, UCLA, National Defense University, Harvard JFK School of Government, etc.) will produce well-rounded tactical, operational and strategic thinkers prepared to conceptualize, plan and apply the elements of national power (diplomacy, information, military, economic) to achieve country or regional security conditions that will produce the prosperity and freedoms that characterize stable states. The Center will be lead and staffed by distinguished academic, military and administrative persons, who will engage in conceptual and doctrinal development, experiment with and examine concepts and force configuration excursions, and who will teach and mentor emerging leaders as they track through their professional education programs over the course of their unconventional warfare and operational careers. The Center will offer the regional and functional commands, as well as other government agencies, a venue for examining lessons learned, for developing remedial approaches, and to formulating mid-and long-term strategies to achieving national security objectives in a forum that brings together proven operators from across the interagency. The Center will serve to centrally shape, manage and over-watch the doctrine, organization, training, material, leadership, personnel and facilities (DOTML-PF) sustainment programs of ARSOF, and of those forces in support of the Special Forces Unconventional Warfare Command. -- *Principal Author: LTC(R) Ken Benway*

Annex J: About the Author

MARK D. BOYATT, RETIRED U.S. ARMY SPECIAL FORCES COLONEL.

Colonel Boyatt is well known throughout the Special Operations community. In May 1976, he graduated first in his Special Forces Officers Qualification class as the Distinguished Honor Graduate and earned the Green Beret. Over a four-year period from 1976-1979, he has served as the commander of three different Special Forces Operational Detachments "A" in the 5th Special Forces Group (Airborne) --- a GREENLIGHT Special Atomic Demolition Team; a military freefall team; and was one of three BLUELIGHT counter-terrorist assault team leaders. He commanded the first Special Forces Mobile Training Team to Yemen in 1979. From December 1984-May 1987 he served as the S-3, 5th SFGA, then in the U.S. Army Special Operations Agency in the Pentagon until November 1989 when he assumed command of the 1st Battalion, 1st Special Forces Group forward deployed on Okinawa, Japan. From 1993-1994, he was the Chief of Staff of the United States Army John F. Kennedy Special Warfare Center and School (USAJFKSWCS). Subsequently, from 1994-1996, he was the Commander, 3rd Special Forces Group and commanded the Army Special Operations Task Force during Operation Uphold Democracy in Haiti 1994-1995. He then served as the Deputy Chief of Staff for Operations, G-3, for the United States Army Special Operations Command from 1996 - 1998 and then as the Deputy Commander and Assistant Commandant USAJFKSWCS from April 1998 until his retirement in January 2000. During his attendance to the Army War College at Carlisle, Pennsylvania 1992-1993, he published a thesis-level paper that originated the term "through, with and by, that continues to be referenced in the Special Operations community and joint doctrine.

FRANCIS MARK DOUGLAS BOYATT

Once upon a time, a long, long time ago, I was born. 17 September, 1948. I was named Francis after my grandfather on the Boyatt side, who was named after the Revolutionary war hero Francis Marion, the Swamp Fox. Mark came from my grandfather on the Ross side. Douglas came from the Scottish ancestry from my father's side.

I am a baby boomer... a brat ... a military brat. My dad fought in the Second World War. He went ashore on Utah Beach 13 August 1944 at Normandy as a member of the 191st Field Artillery Regiment of the Tennessee National Guard mobilized for the war. He participated with the unit in the breakout from Normandy, the relief of the Battle of the Bulge, and the crossing of the Rhine. They were at the first concentration camp liberated by the Americans. When he came home, he settled down in the Tennessee. He was from Scott County, just north of Knoxville, up on the Tennessee-Kentucky border.

My mother was born 24 April 1927 on the family farm along the river in Anderson County, Tennessee. Her family moved to another farm in Blount County, Tennessee just outside of Maryville, in the shadow of the Great Smokey Mountains, in 1936. My mother still lives in that same hand-made brick house. Both attended Maryville College where they met. Dad played on the football team, the Fighting Scots. Mom was a cheerleader.

They got married in the front yard of the house in 1947, December 24th, just before Christmas. The house was built around 1810-14 with handmade bricks. Expanded in 1911, it included at least four chimneys with eight fireplaces, about 5000 square feet, double front porches with big white pillars. Only two chimneys and four fireplaces remain usable today and then only if you put in a chimney insert. Over the years and during periods of time when we could not accompany my dad, we lived here with my grandparents. The farm consisted of about 250 acres, a large barn built in 1910 and many additional other structures with cattle and quarter horses. I spent many a day baling and putting up hay, building and repairing fences, milking cows, working in the slaughterhouse, mucking out stalls and spreading the manure, going to livestock auctions with my uncles and working in my uncles' country store, among other things. A great time for a kid. Priceless experiences.

Dad went back into the active military after I was born. He was a career noncommissioned officer…a sergeant. He left the military in 1968 while I was in college. He actually got a 100% disability military retirement, as he was diagnosed in 1962 with multiple sclerosis. He died in 2000, the year I retired from the military.

The military in those days was quite transit. We never stayed long in any one house. From the time that I was born until, well, I guess it was when I was about fourteen years old, we never lived in the same house continuously for more than three years. The first time we did was when we moved back to the farm and the house in Maryville (with my grandparents) in 1963, while my dad was assigned to Walter Reed Military Hospital for evaluation and treatment. That was the first time I lived in the same dwelling for more than three continuous years. I would live there about 3 ½ years until I left for college in 1966… the University of Tennessee, Knoxville, home of the Tennessee Volunteers…Go Big Orange! The next time that I lived in the same facility or same house for longer than that was 1994 in Fort Bragg housing. We lived there until I retired in January 2000.

So, therefore, I was a military brat. Pre-school we lived in Shirley, Massachusetts (Fort Devens), El Paso, Texas (Fort Bliss) and Fort Richardson, Alaska (after my parents pulled a mobile home from Tennessee across the U.S. and up the ALCAN Highway with a two ton truck -- we kids rode in the covered bed of the truck).

After returning from Alaska, we change schools more often than we change our underwear. I started the first grade when we were stationed at Fort Benning, Georgia. In the spring of the second grade, my Dad was assigned to Korea on an unaccompanied tour, and we moved back to Maryville, Tennessee. Here I finished out the second grade and spent the entire 3rd grade going to Alnwick Elementary, a country school just a couple miles down the road.

Then, after that, for the 4th and part of the 5th grades, we moved to Killeen, Texas (Fort Hood)- rode a open jeep up and down sand dunes; played baseball (I was the pitcher--we ended 2d after losing in the championship); hunted horned toads, rabbits and doves.

Next was a short move north to Lawton, Oklahoma and Fort Sill. Here I finished the 5th grade and most of the 6th grade - rode bikes; found soda bottles and collected the deposit; bowled; shot firecrackers; went dove and rabbit hunting; played football and made the all-star team; spent one night in the living room under a mattress as a tornado rolled by; saw a B-58 Hustler bomber explode in mid-air over Lawton.

From Fort Sill, Dad was then assigned to Germany. He left before we did, so we moved back to the farm in Tennessee where I finished out the 6th grade in Alnwick while we waited to travel overseas and link up with my dad. This entailed my mom driving all of us, my younger brother and my sister, the youngest of us all, to New York City to ship the Buick. After one or two nights in NYC, too huge to describe, we boarded the USS Patch, a troop ship, and made the seven day voyage to Bremerhaven, Germany.

The first year, we lived on the German economy in an apartment since my Dad was assigned to a U.S. Army detachment on the German Army post in Ingolstadt. Since there were no American schools here, I went to the 7th grade (my brother the 5th and my sister the 3rd grade) by correspondence from the University of Maryland. After a year, we moved to an American installation on the mountain above Wertheim am Main. I started the 8th grade at the small school there where the 8th grade and the 5th grade shared the same classroom with the principal on double (triple) duty as the teacher. That was quite interesting. Part way through the 8th grade, the "powers that be" found buses and sent us 8th graders on a 1 ½ hour one way bus ride everyday to the junior high school at Stuttgart Germany. It was during this school year, spring of 1962, that my Dad became visibly ill and we left Germany early to go back to Fort Benning, Georgia. This is where I started the 9th grade - junior high school- in Columbus Georgia.

In the spring of my 9th grade, my Dad was transferred to Walter Reed for treatment and for more evaluation. We moved back to the farm outside Maryville Tennessee where I then finished out high school -- played on the football team; Key Club; was mostly unknown but had fun-- graduating in 1966. From there, I went to the University of Tennessee, Knoxville. This is where I got involved in the ROTC program.

I was lucky. I never had to go through the confusion of what I was going to do with my life after I graduated from college. I have watched young people, including sons, nieces and nephews, struggle with what they're going to do once they graduate. This confusion also guides what subjects they take further along in college. I did not have to figure out what I going to be when I graduated. I didn't have any of those dilemmas. From age twelve I knew I was going to go into the military and that the military was going to be my career choice. So I never had any of the confusion that many of the college students of that time period had.

So I really got involved in the ROTC program and for the next five years (I was a fifth-year senior) spent most of my free time in ROTC pursuits. To graduate, I had to get an extension to stay in school and delay my commissioning. It seems that I had overlooked one 3-credit course that was only offered in the spring, so I had to remain in school for the extra year to complete my degree requirements, even though I had basically, completed ROTC.

I graduated and was commissioned on 6 June 1971 (adjusted to 10 June because we ROTC'ers could not have date of rank on West Pointers being commissioned that same summer).

But, while I was in ROTC, I immediately got involved in the extracurricular activities of the Tennessee Ranger company, a volunteer organization for those so inclined and it was a great adventure. As a small group of cadet volunteers (max of 50 or so) from the greater ROTC population (4500+ -- UT was a land grant college and either ROTC or Phys Ed was required), we did lots of training on our own and considered ourselves elite. We did training as a unit. We did physical training formations in the mornings before classes. We conducted our own field training exercises on weekends and holidays, including showing up to school a week early every year to conduct our own pre-school field exercise to train the new leaders. We checked out weapons (M1 rifles and M1919A6 machine guns), purchased our own blank adapters, and ran all over the countryside in East Tennessee. It was nothing to see a bunch of us walking down the side of road carrying machine guns and M1 rifles on the way to the local training area thanks to land use from a local farmer. Or in another place, a large expanse of rough terrain in the forested mountains around a series of quarries. This was all routine and there was absolutely no stigma attached to it. Nobody was around trying to holler about guns and weapons and the like. Plus East Tennessee is very conservative and a gun-oriented state. It still is today.

Anyway, I graduated from the University of Tennessee as a Distinguished Military Graduate (DMG) and therefore, got my choice of branch, which was infantry. Remember this was a difficult time for the nation. I was in ROTC during the heart of the Vietnam War and we all knew we were going to Vietnam as soon as we graduated. I went to Fort Benning, Georgia for Basic Officer's Course, Airborne School and Ranger School. However, the rules changed with the political situation. As it turned out, not a single person from our officer basic course was allowed to go to Vietnam. Every one of us were shipped to Germany and we all (or most anyway) went into mechanized infantry, 2d Battalion, 48th Infantry Regmt, 2d Brigade 3rd Armored Division, Gelnhausen, Federal Republic of Germany. So I spent the next 3+ years in Germany as the Vietnam War was winding down. This was a rough time for the Army. Lots of drugs; behavioral problems (witchcraft, etc); McNamara's 100,000; discipline issues; racial issues; reductions-in-force; draftees; etc.

As a new lieutenant, I had a mechanized infantry platoon – four M-113A1 armored personnel carriers (APCs). After about three months and upon completion of the platoon Operational Readiness Tests (which we passed – no small feat at that time), I got picked as the platoon leader of the newly organizing TOW missile antitank platoon for the battalion. The platoon, part of the Combat Support Company, had just turned in its 106mm recoilless rifles and received new TOW missiles and new APCs. Once fully formed and fully manned, the platoon had twelve APCs, each manned by four men, and two jeeps, one for the platoon sergeant and one for me, each with a driver, so a total of 52 people.

So, as the new equipment was arriving and to be "fair," the battalion commander required the three line companies to each give me fifteen men of their choice. I had no say in the decision and had to accept whomever was sent. You can well imagine that they pretty well cleaned their rosters of anybody they didn't want and I got them. During the time I was the platoon leader of the TOW platoon, a total of about 28 months, the entire population of the platoon turned over about three times and had nine different platoon sergeants. Probably no more than 30% of the soldiers left under honorable conditions. Most of them ended up being discharged from the Army under chapter action or going to jail. Even one of my platoon sergeants deserted.

So where is all this going? I'm trying to show how it all ended up with me in Army Special Forces. I came back from Germany in 1975 to attend the Infantry Officers Advanced Course (IOAC) at Fort Benning, Georgia. With the end of Vietnam and the reduction in force (RIF), the IOAC was undergoing an adjustment and reduction in course length. Originally a nine month course, my course was adjusted to eight months and subsequent courses were to be six months. We graduated from our course in December 1975 and, of course, that's when the students get their new assignments. It was during the course that I got promoted to captain.

Well, myself, along with nine other students, got selected and told we were going to Special Forces. This was because Special Forces had taken such a reduction in force after Vietnam that they were about down to about 50% officers in their line elements. Of course, even when I first went on active duty from ROTC, almost all the UT ROTC Rangers volunteered for airborne, Ranger, Special Forces. However, by this time I had three years of mechanized infantry under my belt, and now was firmly convinced that the future of the military was mechanized infantry. And that is not wrong. Special Forces are not the baseline force for our nation. Regardless, I did not want to go to Special Forces. I looked at that as being out of the mainstream. I was not really concerned about promotion, but about doing what I thought was going to be important in the military. Well, as it turned out, the personnel command that did the assignments could care less what I wanted to do. They were set in where they wanted me to go and that was it, the end. As I tried to change the assignment, I solicited help from two of my previous battalion commanders, both of whom later ended their military careers as generals, one with three stars and the other with two stars. They tried to change the mind of the assignments personnel to let me stay in a mechanized infantry assignment instead of a branch immaterial (as it was called) assignment to Special Forces; however, that didn't work out. They both got told to stay out of it. So in late December 1975, I signed into Fort Bragg and the 5th Special Forces Group.

Hello! Special Forces was not what I wanted to be; but, once I got involved it absolutely captivated me. So, subsequently, my entire military career other than a few side trips, have all been involved in some way with Special Forces. After I was a detachment commander for more than four years, I was then sent over to the 82nd Airborne Division to take over as a company commander of one of the infantry companies (Co C, 2/325 Parachute Infantry Regiment – PIR). I stayed in that company for thirteen months, was lucky enough to marry Nancy Eugenia Goodall on March 15, 1980 and then got assigned to Alaska. Again to take over an infantry company, Co A, 1st Bn, 60th Arctic Infantry Regiment, 172d Infantry Brigade.

I held that position for just about two years until I got assigned as the assistant inspector general for Alaska for my final six months there. I was selected off the alternate list in December 1982 to go to the Armed Forces Staff College at Norfolk as opposed to the Command and General

Staff College at Fort Leavenworth. It also was a big boon for me because it was all joint, and with Special Forces, basically, everything they do is joint. Then I spent a year unaccompanied in Korea after Armed Forces Staff College that punched both my joint specialty duty officer ticket and an overseas ticket. Plus I was guaranteed reassignment back to Fort Bragg and back to the 5th Special Forces Group.

When I got back to the 5th Special Forces Group in the late summer of 1984, I was assigned to the 1st Battalion, 5th Special Forces Group for about three months and spent the whole time in the field at the Oro Grande, New Mexico (Fort Bliss) training. As I got back from that, I was then moved to be the S-3 of the 5th Special Forces Group and I stayed in that position for the next twenty-seven months - until the summer of 1987. I was then assigned to the Office of Army Special Operations (ODSO), which then was renamed to the United States Army Special Operations Agency, in the basement of the Pentagon. I stayed there for 2 1/2 years, then was assigned to Okinawa to command the 1st Battalion, 1st Special Forces Group.

When I left there, I reunited with Nancy and the boys in Monterey, California to attend the Defense Language Institute (DLI) for Spanish. This was literally just a holding position until such time as I could go to the Army War College in Carlisle in the summer of 1992. From December 1991 until my class started, the Army had to find someplace to put me for about five months so it was Monterey and DLI. As a side note, Monterey, California, Pacific Grove and that whole environment at Fort Ord was the absolute worst experience we, as a family, ever had anywhere while in the military. Everything from the people, the post, the attitudes, the local people, the school system, everything about the place was the absolute worst I/we have ever experienced before or since.

After Carlisle I was then assigned back to Fort Bragg to the USA JFK Special Warfare Center and School as the Chief of Staff. This was a great experience until I could take command of the 3rd Special Forces Group in July 1994. While I was in the 3rd Special Forces Group we did the Haiti operation (Operation Uphold Democracy) in 1994-95. From that position I was then assigned in 1996 as the Deputy Chief of

Staff, Operations (G3), U.S. Army Special Operations Command at Fort Bragg and stayed in that position until April 1998 when I became the Assistant Commandant and the Deputy Commander, USA JFK Special Warfare Center and School. I served in this position until I retired at the end of January 2000. The below resume captures most of what I did after I left the military and during my twelve years in the civilian, commercial defense contractor business.

RESUME.

MARK D. BOYATT, RETIRED U.S. ARMY SPECIAL FORCES COLONEL. Mr. Boyatt has over 45 years of management experience both in the military and in civilian organizations. He is well known throughout the Special Operations community. He has served as the Deputy Chief of Staff for Operations, G-3, for the United States Army Special Operations Command from 1996 - 1998 and then as the Deputy Commander, Assistant Commandant and Chief of Staff of the United States Army John F. Kennedy Special Warfare Center and School (USAJFKSWCS) from April 1998 until his retirement in January 2000. From 2000 – 2004 he led the contractor team supporting the development of Special Forces future concepts in the Army SOF Battle Lab and was instrumental in the establishment of the Joint Special Operations Task Force training program at USAJFKSWCS. He has strong socio-cultural and ethnographic experience. Mr. Boyatt was the Deputy Project Manager for the U.S. Army Training and Doctrine Command Human Terrain System Project in 2006 and 2007 where he built and implemented the only successful operationally mature socio-cultural, ethnographic model for training, deploying and supporting Human Terrain Teams. While on active duty, as the Commander, Third Special Forces Group, Boyatt commanded the Army Special Operations Task Force during Operation Uphold Democracy in Haiti 1994-1995. He subsequently authored and narrated a widely distributed video documentary on the role of Special Operations Forces in this operation. He supervised multinational operations throughout the African theater including in South Africa, Zimbabwe, Zambia, Nigeria, Namibia, Uganda, and Senegal. He commanded the 1st

Battalion, 1ˢᵗ Special Forces Group forward deployed on Okinawa, Japan, from 1989-1991 which had an *"in extremis"* mission. He supervised multinational operations throughout the U.S. Pacific Command (PACOM) Theater including in the Philippines, Thailand, Korea, Singapore, Malaysia, Bangladesh, Guam, etc. He has served on the Army Staff in the Pentagon 1987-1989, assigned to the Army Special Operation's Agency (USASOA), Deputy Chief of Staff, Operations (ODCSOPS), where he coordinated a multitude of Army Special Operations issues, both active and reserve, and joint/interagency Special Operations actions. He was involved in the planning for Operation Blue Spoon, the operations in Panama. Over a four-year period from 1976-1980, he has served as the commander of three different Special Forces Operational Detachments "A" in the 5ᵗʰ Special Forces Group (Airborne) --- a GREENLIGHT Special Atomic Demolition Team; a military freefall team; and was one of three BLUELIGHT counter-terrorist assault team leaders. He commanded the first Special Forces Mobile Training Team to Yemen in 1979. He graduated first in his Special Forces Officers Qualification class as the Distinguished Honor Graduate. He has been a guest lecturer and senior mentor supporting the Joint Special Operations University (JSOU), the U.S. Army Command and General Staff College (CGSC), and Joint Special Operations Task Force (JSOTF) programs and supporting various Special Operations Forces Joint Professional Military Education (JPME) forums. With extensive joint and interagency operational experience, he has participated in the operational execution of special operations in the Middle East, the Caribbean and in the Pacific. He is a graduate of the Department of State's Foreign Service Institute Near-East & North Africa Regional Studies Program and attended the Army War College at Carlisle, Pennsylvania, where he published a thesis-level paper that continues to be referenced in the Special Operations community.

Annex K:
Unconventional Warfare Briefing

THREE PHASES OF AN INSURGENCY

I   Latent or Incipient

II   Guerrilla Warfare

III   War of Movement (Conventional Force on Force)

UNCONVENTIONAL CONTINUUM

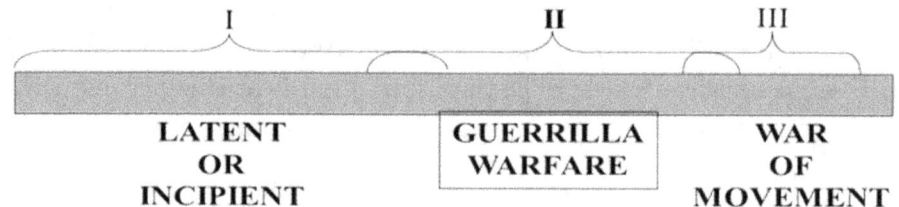

UW STRATEGIC OBJECTIVES

The TARGET of UW is the AUTHORITY of the GOVERNMENT/OCCUPYING POWER

- Undermine domestic and international legitimacy
- Neutralize power/shift power to resistance
- Destroy confidence and will of leadership
- Isolate from international diplomatic and materiel support/gain these for resistance

THE RESISTANCE

- ➢ The individual/group effort to:
    - ▪ Resist
    - ▪ Oppose
        - o Non-violent/violent means
- ➢ To overthrow or cause withdrawal of
    - ▪ Established government
    - ▪ Occupying power
- ➢ May develop if conditions are oppressive enough into an organized resistance movement
- ➢ Success or failure will depend on **THE WILL OF THE PEOPLE**

An INSURGENCY

An organized resistance movement
equals
an insurgency
if
It uses subversion and armed conflict to reach its goal

INSURGENCY vice REVOLUTION

➤ **Insurgents** seek to:
- Establish autonomous territory within borders of the state
- Extract political concessions unobtainable through non-violent means
- Overthrow established government (No follow-on social revolution)

➤ **Revolutionaries** seek:
- Overthrow of existing social order
- Reallocation of power within the state

THE RESISTANCE MOVEMENT

➤ AREA COMMAND
- Command Group
  - Resistance Leader
  - Staff
  - Representatives of:
    Underground
    Auxiliary
    Guerrilla Force
➤ UNDERGROUND
➤ AUXILIARY
➤ GUERRILLA FORCE

THE RESISTANCE MOVEMENT

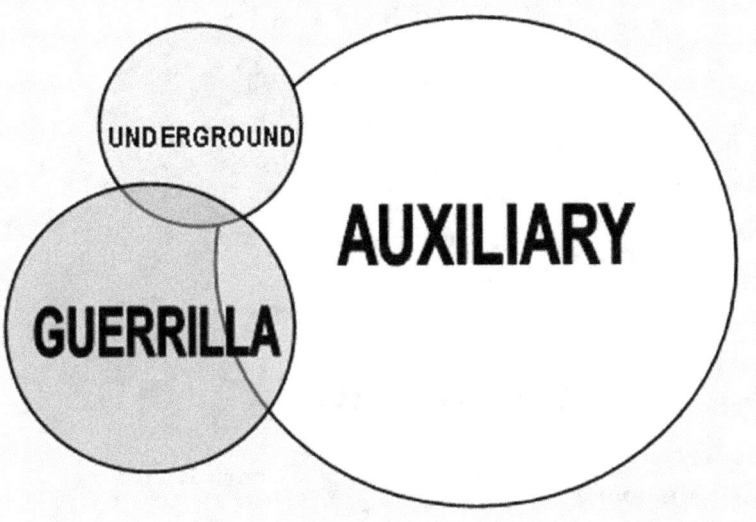

UNDERGROUND

➢ Covert, clandestine arm of resistance
➢ Cellular, compartmented organization
➢ Rural and/or urban based
➢ Internal clandestine support element
➢ Operate in areas denied to guerrillas
➢ Conduct operations not suitable for guerrillas (sabotage, subversion)

THE CELL

➢ Basic Unit of the Underground
➢ Composition -
  o Cell Leader
  o Cell Members
➢ Size depends on assigned functions
➢ Organized on a Geographic or Functional basis

➢ Centralized or Decentralized
➢ Compartmented to protect the Organization

TYPES OF CELLS

❖ Operational Cell
❖ Intelligence Cell
❖ Auxiliary Cell
❖ Parallel Cells
❖ Cells in Series

OPERATIONAL CELL

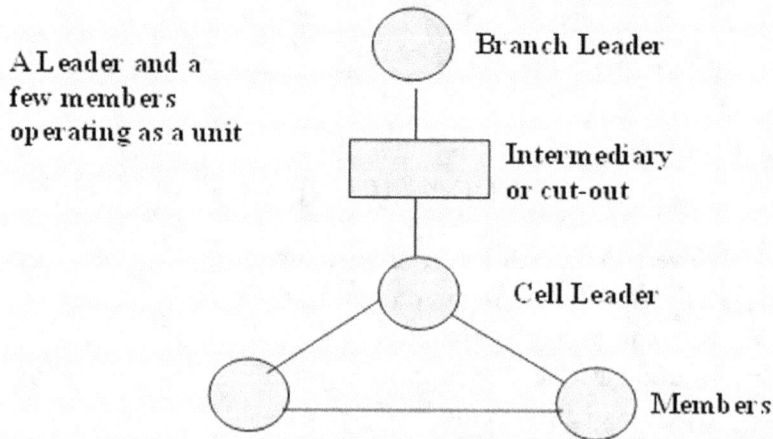

A Leader and a
few members
operating as a unit

Branch Leader

Intermediary
or cut-out

Cell Leader

Members

INTELLIGENCE CELL

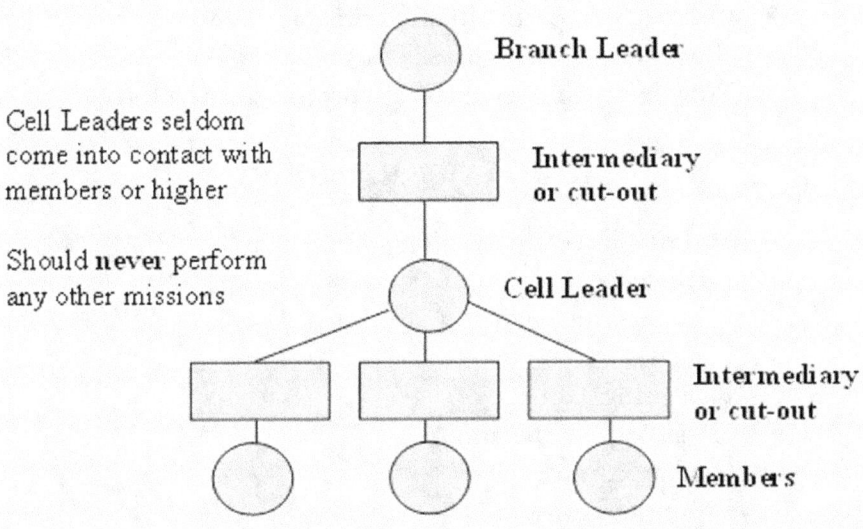

Cell Leaders seldom come into contact with members or higher

Should never perform any other missions

AUXILIARY CELL

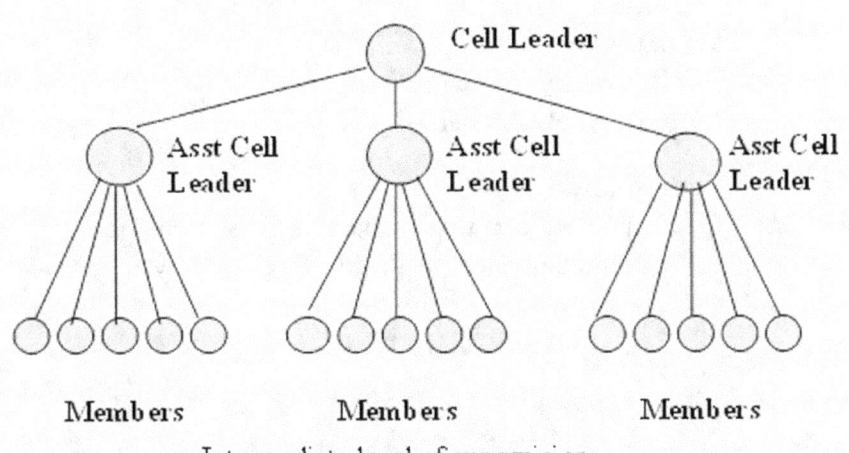

- Intermediate level of supervision
- Little or no compartmentalization

THE AUXILIARY

- ➢ Clandestine support arm of resistance
- ➢ Cellular, compartmentalized organization
- ➢ Rural and/or urban based
- ➢ Provide/organize civilian support for guerrilla force

AUXILIARY MISSIONS

- ➢ Security and early warning
- ➢ Intelligence
- ➢ Counter-intelligence
- ➢ Logistics
- ➢ Recruiting
- ➢ Psychological operations
- ➢ Civilian control
- ➢ Escape and evasion

AUXILIARY MEMBERS

- ➢ "Farmer by day, fighter by night"
- ➢ "Part-time guerrilla"
- ➢ Maintain normal duties/routine
- ➢ NOT auxiliary if providing support
        unwittingly or coerced

- ➢ **Undesirables**:
        X Sympathizers that may be under surveillance
        X Politicians/technicians formerly used by enemy

GUERRILLA FORCE

- ❖ Overt arm of the resistance
- ❖ Military/Paramilitary organization
- ❖ Simplicity, mobility, flexibility, divisibility
- ❖ Organization & Equipment - terrain, resources, objectives
- ❖ Operations - aggressive, surprise attack

GUERRILLA MISSIONS

- ❖ Interdiction
- ❖ Intelligence
- ❖ Support of conventional force operations
  - ✓ Destroy enemy forces
  - ✓ Destroy key C4I
  - ✓ Provide intelligence (scouts)
  - ✓ Secure key terrain for short periods
  - ✓ Deprive enemy of resources
  - ✓ Deception operations
  - ✓ Divert enemy force/tie-up reserves
  - ✓ Interdict LOCs
  - ✓ Demoralize enemy (will to fight)

U.S. SF ROLE IN UW

- ➤ SF provide training, advice and assistance to **existing** indigenous organizations.
- ➤ By Doctrine, SF **do not** create resistance movements (but maybe?)

7 PHASES U.S. SF UW

Phase I	Psychological preparation
Phase II	Initial contact with Resistance
Phase III	Infiltration of SF team
Phase IV	Organization of Resistance
Phase V	Build-up of Guerrilla Force
Phase VI	Employment: Win the fight
Phase VII	Demobilization of the Resistance

Unconventional Continuum: 7 Phases of US Unconventional Warfare

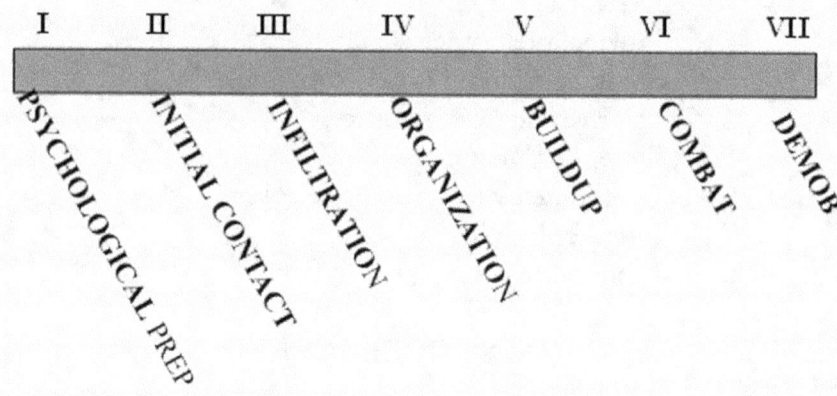

PHASE I
Psychological Preparation

Psychological Operations prepare the resistance organization and civil population in potential UW operational area to accept U.S. Sponsorship and subsequent assistance of SF teams

PHASE II
Initial Contact

- ❖ U.S. Government/resistance coordination for desired U.S. support
- ❖ Conducted by other U.S. agencies
- ❖ Contact made with resistance before SF team infiltrates into the JSOA
- ❖ Arrangements made for reception and initial assistance for SF team

❖ SOC should arrange exfil of a resistance leader (asset) from the operational area

The Asset

❖ A member of the resistance
❖ SF team should be able to debrief while in isolation
❖ May accompany the team on infiltration
❖ Lack of an asset does not prevent infiltration

The Pilot Team

❖ Usually not fewer than four members

Commander	Medic
Intelligence	Radio operator

❖ Duties include:
- Establishing initial contact
- Assessing resistance potential
- Other missions as specified by higher HQ

PHASE III
Infiltration

Remainder of SF Team
❖ Makes contact with the Resistance
❖ Establishes commo with the FOB
❖ Moves to guerrilla base
❖ Begins area assessment - confirm/deny previous assessments

PHASE IV
Organization

❖ Build rapport and credibility
❖ Explain capabilities and limitations
❖ SF team leader and resistance leader agree on command relationship

- ❖ SF team assesses resistance leadership and organization
- ❖ Develop the organization and train cadre

Organization Considerations

- ❖ Religious, Ethnic, Political, and Ideological differences among elements of the population and competing resistance organizations
- ❖ Proposed type and scope of combat operations to include potential targets
- ❖ Degree of U.S. influence with the resistance organization
- ❖ Understand that training will **always** be secondary to security.

PHASE V
Build Up

- ❖ Expansion of infrastructure into effective organization capable of successful combat employment
- ❖ Cadre recruits and trains new members
- ❖ OPSEC is crucial
- ❖ Limited combat operations
- ❖ Develop organization to support future operations

PHASE VI
Combat Employment

- ❖ Interdiction - basic UW combat activity
- ❖ Attack multiple dispersed targets
- ❖ Do not attack targets indiscriminately
- ❖ Raids, Ambushes, Mining, Sniping
- ❖ SF team coordinates activities to complement and support conventional operations
- ❖ Linkup with conventional forces?

Link-up

❖ After link-up with conventional forces, missions may include:
- Economy of Force
- Destroy bypassed enemy units
- Recon & Surveillance
- Provide guides and/or interpreters
- Population Resource Control measures
  * After linkup, resistance forces revert to national control
  * Only occurs if U.S. or Coalition brings in conventional forces

PHASE VII
Demobilization

❖ Planning begins as soon as U.S. Government decides to sponsor a resistance
❖ Resistance members are returned to civilian life or integrated into the national military
❖ Key to long-term strategic success
❖ Take positive measures to prevent resistance members from beginning or participating in further political upheaval
❖ Most neglected phase during planning

Annex L:
U.S. Constitution Timeline

The Constitution of the United States is over 200 years old. Below are some of the important dates that led to the creation of the Constitution:

1765. Stamp Act. Colonial Congress in New York.

1770. "Boston Massacre."

1773. Destruction of tea in Boston Harbor.

1774. September 5. Continental Congress meets in Philadelphia. Boston Port Bill.

1775. April 19. Fight at Lexington and Concord.
May 10. Capture of Ticonderoga. Meeting of Second Continental Congress at Philadelphia.

1775. June 17. Battle of Bunker Hill.
December. Daniel Boone settles in Kentucky.

1776. July 4. Declaration of Independence.
August 27. Battle of Long Island.
December 26. Washington captures Hessians at Trenton.

1777.   June 14. Flag of stars and stripes adopted by Congress.
September 11. Battle of Brandywine.
October 17. Surrender of Burgoyne.
Washington encamps at Valley Forge and Howe occupies
Philadelphia.

1778.   French-American alliance.
June 28. Battle of Monmouth.
December 29. British take Savannah.

1779.   September 23. Naval victory of John Paul Jones.

1780.   May 12. Charleston taken by British.
August 16. Battle of Camden.
October 7. Battle of King's Mountain.

1781.   Adoption of the Articles of Confederation.
October 19. Surrender of Cornwallis at Yorktown.

1782.   November 30. Preliminary treaty of peace.

1783.   September 3. Final treaty of peace signed.
November 25. British army evacuates New York.
December 4. Washington's farewell to his officers.

1786.   Shays's rebellion in Massachusetts.

Ordinance of 1787 adopted.

1787.   May 14. Constitutional Convention meets at Philadelphia.
Sept 17. **Constitution finished and signed by the delegates.**

Rufus Putnam plants first settlement in Ohio.

1788.   June 21. New Hampshire becomes the ninth state to ratify the
Constitution, securing its adoption.

1789.   **March 4. New government goes into operation.**
April 30. Washington inaugurated **first President.**

Annex M:
US History of Regime Change

"I liked this annex a great deal. It certainly illustrates the validity and effectiveness of the theory of trans-generational presence." Frank Emerson

This annex will look at some of the known history of regime changes that were precipitated by the U.S . Most were conducted by conventional force. Only a few were caused by unconventional methods. Few, if any, were through, with or by an indigenous population.

A successful regime change is one that results in a representative government where the military is subservient to the government and voting is both fair and ubiquitous and where the rule of law, freedom and liberty prevail.

There are only a few successful regime changes in which the U.S. has participated.

Successful: Why?

One factor seems to be that the nations that had regime change forced on them had a population with a cohesive national identity and when the government surrendered, the people surrendered also. There was little to no insurgency against the occupying power or the "puppet" regime put in place while reconstruction was implemented.

Also, there was a "success and occupation strategy" developed while the conflict raged that was implemented rapidly with success.

Thirdly, internal and external security was strictly enforced. Internal security was not transferred to the newly formed government until it was 100% prepared and accepted by the people. Then, the external security was continued by the occupying power for generations to allow the new government to mature. The continued occupation, albeit a cooperative endeavor, sent a clear message to any external element that might view the new government as vulnerable, that there was a tripwire there that they did not dare to test.

Most of the successful regime changes of WWII.

- Germany
- Japan
- Italy
- Philippines

Not so successful or total failures:

- Iraq (fragmented)
- Afghanistan (fragmented)
- Yugoslavia (dissolved into factions and fractured)
- Burma (Myanmar) (continuing dictatorship with insurgency)
- China (dictatorship)

Why?

These nations never had a national identity and most were held together by dictatorial internal power and were de facto police states. There was little, if any, feelings of unity with the national government among many of the ethnic or religious factions. They remained resentful of what they saw as oppression.

In effect, once the existing government lost power over the people (regime change), insurgencies sprang up from several different independent segments and the U.S. and allies found themselves in the middle of a civil war. A certain lose/lose situation which continues to play out in some locations.

Additionally, there was no "success and occupation strategy" developed nor implemented. This "strategy" just incoherently evolved...mostly unsuccessfully.

The occupying powers rapidly withdrew, leaving the new government totally vulnerable to both internal and external threats or already compromised into a dictatorship.

- Iraq
- Libya
- Vietnam
- Cambodia
- Burma
- Countries that fell under the Eastern Bloc (Russian) control (WWII)
- China

World War II saw many regime changes, most, if not all, were caused by conventional forces and invasion. The U.S. obviously did not act alone in these regime changes, but the U.S. was the key leader in the post war recovery with the Marshall Plan in Europe. The most compelling reason for success was that the U.S. remained in control and/or provided security, stability and support for more than a generation.

In Germany, we retained military bases into the 21st century...a period of more than 60 years.

In Japan we still retained military bases for almost 70 years.

Of course, critics will say we are only there at the invitation of the host country and they'd be technically correct; however, those countries fully recognize the security blanket the U.S. basing provides them.

From the Office of the Historian, Bureau of Public Affairs, United States Department of State

Marshall Plan

Other short titles:

> Economic Cooperation Act of 1948
> International Children's Emergency Fund Assistance Act of 1948
> Greek-Turkish Assistance Act of 1948
> China Aid Act of 1948

Long title: An Act to promote world peace and the general welfare, national interest, and foreign policy of the United States through economic, financial, and other measures necessary to the maintenance of conditions abroad in which free institutions may survive and remain consistent with the maintenance of the strength and stability of the United States.

Nicknames: Foreign Assistance Act of 1948

Enacted by: the 80th United States Congress

Effective: April 3, 1948

Citations:
Public Law 80-472
Statutes at Large 62 Stat. 137

Legislative history:

- **Introduced in the Senate as** S. 2202
- **Passed the Senate on** March 13, 1948 (71-19)
- **Passed the House on** March 31, 1948 (333-78)
- **Reported by the joint conference committee on** April 1, 1948; **agreed to by the House on** April 2, 1948 (321-78) **and by the Senate on** April 2, 1948 (agreed)
- **Signed into law by President** Harry S. Truman **on** April 3, 1948

Milestones: 1945–1952

Marshall Plan, 1948

In the immediate post-World War II period, Europe remained ravaged by war and thus susceptible to exploitation by an internal and external Communist threat. In a June 5, 1947, speech to the graduating class at Harvard University, Secretary of State George C. Marshall issued a call for a comprehensive program to rebuild Europe. Fanned by the fear of Communist expansion and the rapid deterioration of European economies in the winter of 1946–1947, Congress passed the Economic Cooperation Act in March 1948 and approved funding that would eventually rise to over $12 billion for the rebuilding of Western Europe.

The Marshall Plan generated a resurgence of European industrialization and brought extensive investment into the region. It was also a stimulant to the U.S. economy by establishing markets for American goods. Although the participation of the Soviet Union and East European nations was an initial possibility, Soviet concern over potential U.S. economic domination of its Eastern European satellites and Stalin's unwillingness to open up his secret society to westerners doomed the idea. Furthermore, it is unlikely that the U.S. Congress would have been willing to fund the plan as generously as it did if aid also went to Soviet Bloc Communist nations.

Thus the Marshall Plan was applied solely to Western Europe, precluding any measure of Soviet Bloc cooperation. Increasingly, the economic revival of Western Europe, especially West Germany, was viewed suspiciously in Moscow. Economic historians have debated the precise impact of the Marshall Plan on Western Europe, but these differing opinions do not detract from the fact that the Marshall Plan has been recognized as a great humanitarian effort. Secretary of State Marshall became the only general ever to receive a Nobel Prize for peace. The Marshall Plan also institutionalized and legitimized the concept of U.S. foreign aid programs, which have become an integral part of U.S. foreign policy.

Marshall Plan

(From Wikipedia, the free encyclopedia)

The Marshall Plan (officially the European Recovery Program, ERP) was an American initiative to aid Europe, in which the United States gave

$13 billion (approximately $120 billion in current dollar value- 2013) in economic support to help rebuild European economies after the end of World War II. The plan was in operation for four years beginning in April 1948. The goals of the United States were to rebuild war-devastated regions, remove trade barriers, modernize industry, make Europe prosperous again, and prevent the spread of communism. The Marshall Plan required a lessening of interstate barriers, a dropping of many petty regulations constraining business, and encouraged an increase in productivity, labor union membership, as well as the adoption of modern business procedures.

The Marshall Plan aid was divided amongst the participant states roughly on a per capita basis. A larger amount was given to the major industrial powers, as the prevailing opinion was that their resuscitation was essential for general European revival. Somewhat more aid per capita was also directed toward the Allied nations, with less for those that had been part of the Axis or remained neutral. The largest recipient of Marshall Plan money was the United Kingdom (receiving about 26% of the total), followed by France (18%) and West Germany (11%). Some 18 European countries received Plan benefits. Although offered participation, the Soviet Union refused Plan benefits, and also blocked benefits to Eastern Bloc countries, such as East Germany and Poland. The United States provided similar aid programs in Asia, but they were not called "Marshall Plan."

The initiative is named after Secretary of State George Marshall. The plan had bipartisan support in Washington, where the Republicans controlled Congress and the Democrats controlled the White House with Harry S. Truman as president. The Plan was largely the creation of State Department officials, especially William L. Clayton and George F. Kennan, with help from Brookings Institution, as requested by Senator Arthur H. Vandenberg, chairman of the Senate Foreign Relations Committee. Marshall spoke of an urgent need to help the European recovery in his address at Harvard University in June 1947.

The phrase "equivalent of the Marshall Plan" is often used to describe a proposed large-scale economic rescue program

The reconstruction plan, developed at a meeting of the participating European states, was drafted on June 5, 1947. It offered the same aid to the Soviet Union and its allies, but they refused to accept it, as to do so would be to allow a degree of U.S. control over the Communist economies. In fact, the Soviet Union even prevented its satellite states (i.e. East Germany, Poland, etc.) from accepting. Secretary Marshall became convinced that Stalin had absolutely no interest in helping restore economic health in Western Europe. President Harry Truman signed the Marshall Plan on April 3, 1948, granting $5 billion in aid to sixteen European nations. During the four years that the plan was operational, the U.S. donated $13 billion in economic and technical assistance to help the recovery of the European countries that had joined in the Organization for European Economic Co-operation. In 2013, the equivalent sum reflecting currency inflation since 1948 totaled roughly $148 billion. The $13 billion was in the context of a U.S. GDP of $258 billion in 1948, and was on top of $13 billion in American aid to Europe between the end of the war and the start of the Plan that is counted separately from the Marshall Plan. The Marshall Plan was replaced by the Mutual Security Plan at the end of 1951; that new plan gave away about $7 billion annually until 1961 when it in turn was replaced by a new program.

The ERP addressed each of the obstacles to postwar recovery. The plan looked to the future, and did not focus on the destruction caused by the war. Much more important were efforts to modernize European industrial and business practices using high-efficiency American models, reducing artificial trade barriers, and instilling a sense of hope and self-reliance.

By 1952, as the funding ended, the economy of every participant state had surpassed pre-war levels; for all Marshall Plan recipients, output in 1951 was at least 35% higher than in 1938. Over the next two decades, Western Europe enjoyed unprecedented growth and prosperity, but economists are not sure what proportion was due directly to the ERP, what proportion indirectly, and how much would have happened without it. A common American interpretation of the program's role in European recovery is the one expressed by Paul Hoffman, head of the Economic Cooperation Administration, in 1949, when he told Congress that Marshall aid had provided the "critical margin" on which other investments needed for

European recovery depended. The Marshall Plan was one of the first elements of European integration, as it erased trade barriers and set up institutions to coordinate the economy on a continental level—that is, it stimulated the total political reconstruction of Western Europe.

Belgian economic historian Herman Van der Wee concludes the Marshall Plan was a "great success":

> "It gave a new impetus to reconstruction in Western Europe and made a decisive contribution to the renewal of the transport system, the modernization of industrial and agricultural equipment, the resumption of normal production, the raising of productivity, and the facilitating of intra-European trade

JAPAN

Japan: The U.S. obviously did not act alone in this regime change either, but the U.S. was the key leader in the post war recovery with the occupation of Japan under General MacArthur.

From the Office of the Historian, Bureau of Public Affairs, United States Department of State

Occupation and Reconstruction of Japan, 1945–52

After the defeat of Japan in World War II, the United States led the Allies in the occupation and rehabilitation of the Japanese state. Between 1945 and 1952, the U.S. occupying forces, led by General Douglas A. MacArthur, enacted widespread military, political, economic, and social reforms.

Allied Occupation in Japan after WWII

The groundwork for the Allied occupation of a defeated Japan was laid during the war. In a series of wartime conferences, the leaders of the Allied powers of Great Britain, the Soviet Union, the Republic of China, and the United States discussed how to disarm Japan, deal with its colonies (especially Korea and Taiwan), stabilize the Japanese economy, and prevent the remilitarization of the state in the future. In the Potsdam Declaration, they called for Japan's unconditional surrender; by August of 1945, that objective had been achieved.

In September, 1945, General Douglas MacArthur took charge of the Supreme Command of Allied Powers (SCAP) and began the work of rebuilding Japan. Although Great Britain, the Soviet Union, and the Republic of China had an advisory role as part of an "Allied Council," MacArthur had the final authority to make all decisions. The occupation of Japan can be divided into three phases: the initial effort to punish and reform Japan, the work to revive the Japanese economy, and the conclusion of a formal peace treaty and alliance.

The first phase, roughly from the end of the war in 1945 through 1947, involved the most fundamental changes for the Japanese Government and society. The Allies punished Japan for its past militarism and expansion by convening war crimes trials in Tokyo. At the same time, SCAP dismantled the Japanese army and banned former military officers from taking roles of political leadership in the new government. In the economic field, SCAP introduced land reform, designed to benefit the majority tenant farmers and reduce the power of rich landowners, many of whom had advocated for war and supported Japanese expansionism in the 1930s. MacArthur also tried to break up the large Japanese business conglomerates, or zaibatsu, as part of the effort to transform the economy into a free market capitalist system. In 1947, Allied advisors essentially dictated a new constitution to Japan's leaders. Some of the most profound changes in the document included downgrading the emperor's status to that of a figurehead without political control and placing more power in the parliamentary system, promoting greater rights and privileges for women, and renouncing the right to wage war, which involved eliminating all non-defensive armed forces.

By late 1947 and early 1948, the emergence of an economic crisis in Japan alongside concerns about the spread of communism sparked a reconsideration of occupation policies. This period is sometimes called the "reverse course." In this stage of the occupation, which lasted until 1950, the economic rehabilitation of Japan took center stage. SCAP became concerned that a weak Japanese economy would increase the influence of the domestic communist movement, and with a communist victory in China's civil war increasingly likely, the future of East Asia appeared to be at stake. Occupation policies to address the weakening economy ranged from tax reforms to measures aimed at controlling inflation. However the most serious problem was the shortage of raw materials required to feed Japanese industries and markets for finished goods. The outbreak of the Korean War in 1950 provided SCAP with just the opportunity it needed to address this problem, prompting some occupation officials to suggest that, "Korea came along and saved us." After the UN entered the Korean War, Japan became the principal supply depot for UN forces. The conflict also placed Japan firmly within the confines of the U.S. defense perimeter in Asia, assuring the Japanese leadership that whatever the state of its military, no real threat would be made against Japanese soil.

In the third phase of the occupation, beginning in 1950, SCAP deemed the political and economic future of Japan firmly established and set about securing a formal peace treaty to end both the war and the occupation. The U.S. perception of international threats had changed so profoundly in the years between 1945 and 1950 that the idea of a re-armed and militant Japan no longer alarmed U.S. officials; instead, the real threat appeared to be the creep of communism, particularly in Asia. The final agreement allowed the United States to maintain its bases in Okinawa and elsewhere in Japan, and the U.S. Government promised Japan a bi-lateral security pact. In September of 1951, fifty-two nations met in San Francisco to discuss the treaty, and ultimately, forty-nine of them signed it. Notable holdouts included the USSR, Poland and Czechoslovakia, all of which objected to the promise to support the Republic of China and not do business with the People's Republic of China that was forced on Japan by U.S. politicians.

****

(From Wikipedia, the free encyclopedia)

The Allied **occupation of Japan** at the end of World War II was led by Douglas MacArthur, the Supreme Commander for the Allied Powers, with support from the British Commonwealth. Unlike the occupation of Germany, the Soviet Union was allowed little to no influence over Japan. This foreign presence marked the first time in its history that the nation had been occupied by a foreign power. It transformed the country into a democracy that recalled American "New Deal" priorities of the 1930s politics by Roosevelt. The occupation, codenamed **Operation *Blacklist***, was ended by the San Francisco Peace Treaty, signed on September 8, 1951 and effective from April 28, 1952, after which Japan's independence – with the exception, until 1972, of the Ryukyu Islands – was restored.

According to John Dower, in his book *Cultures of War: Pearl Harbor/ Hiroshima/9-11/Iraq*, the factors behind the success of the occupation were:

> *Discipline, moral legitimacy, well-defined and well-articulated objectives, a clear chain of command, tolerance and flexibility in policy formulation and implementation, confidence in the ability of the state to act constructively, the ability to operate abroad free of partisan politics back home, and the existence of a stable, resilient, sophisticated civil society on the receiving end of occupation policies – these political and civic virtues helped make it possible to move decisively during the brief window of a few years when defeated Japan itself was in flux and most receptive to radical change.*

ITALY

Immediately after WWII, Italian society was largely divided as to how to move forward. For some, the main priority was abolishing the monarchy and establishing a republic, while others wanted to nationalize the northern industrial sectors and implement socialism and communism in Italy. The range of opinions was diverse. The first major post-war political decision in Italy took place in June 1946 when 54% of Italians voted to abolish the monarchy in a popular referendum. In order to prevent possible royalist uprisings, the royal family was expelled from Italy and banned from living within Italian borders.

Italians also elected a Constituent Assembly in 1946 tasked with creating the Italian constitution. The vote returned mainly members of the Christian Democrats Party, the Socialist Party, and the Communist Party, with the Christian Democrats led by Alcide de Gasperi holding a slight edge over its left-leaning compatriots. The constitution this assembly drew up created a bicameral parliamentary republic in Italy with separate judiciary and executive branches, the latter being headed by a president elected by parliament.

The new Italian constitution went into effect January 1, 1948, and set Italy's first open parliamentary elections for later that year. This election was heavily influenced by the United States. At this point, the United States was gifting huge sums of money to Western Europe through the Marshall Plan in the hopes of rebuilding the infrastructure and economies of Western Europe and also hopefully warding off the spread of communism westward from Eastern Europe. Indeed, the United States provided huge sums of money to the Christian Democrats in their campaign and the Marshall Plan's architect, U.S. Secretary of State George C. Marshall, even publicly warned that if the socialists or communists came to power all U.S. aid to Italy would be suspended.

With U.S. help, the Christian Democrats won nearly half of the popular vote and received a majority of the seats in Italy's first republican parliament. With a pro-Western government in charge and U.S. aid secured, Italy rapidly became an economic powerhouse in Europe in the 1950s and 1960s. At the end of the WWII, Italy was a largely rural, agriculture-based society, but with the influx of U.S. cash Italy rapidly industrialized and gained important trading partners throughout the world. Indeed, Italy became a founding member of the European Coal and Steel Community in 1951, an organization which formed the basis for the wider European Economic Community and today's European Union, organizations which fostered and foster economic growth and prosperity throughout the region.

ANNEX N: STARFISH

What are starfish?

Marine scientists have undertaken the difficult task of replacing the beloved starfish's common name with sea star because the starfish is not a fish. It's an echinoderm, closely related to sea urchins and sand dollars. There are some 2,000 species of sea star living in all the world's oceans, from tropical habitats to the cold seafloor. The five-arm varieties are the most common, hence their name, but species with ten, twenty, and even forty arms exist. Beyond their distinctive shape, sea stars are famous for their ability to regenerate limbs, and in some cases, entire bodies. They accomplish this by housing most or all of their vital organs in their arms. Some require the central body to be intact to regenerate, but a few species can grow an entirely new sea star just from a portion of a severed limb.

In their book, Brafman and Beckstrom[166] describe the compelling case for leaderless organizations and one example is Al Qaeda. It does not take much visionary thinking to include all aspects of Islamic fundamentalism and this ideology's pursuit of world domination. The most recent example of this has been the rise of the group calling itself the Islamic State

---

166 *The Starfish and Spider, the Unstoppable Power of Leaderless Organizations,* by Ori Brafman and Rod A. Beckstrom, first published in 2006.

of Syria and Iraq (ISIS). This organization also has a label as the Islamic State of Iraq and the Levant (ISIL).

The geographical term Levant refers to a multi-nation region in the Middle East. It's a land bridge between Turkey to the north and Egypt to the south along the Mediterranean Sea. If you look at a map, in the middle of the nations that comprise the Levant is Israel.

It is still debatable whether or not ISIS is a starfish or a spider. Abu Bakr al-Baghdadi, as the self-proclaimed Caliph Ibrahim, claims to be the successor to the Prophet and the supreme religious authority and absolute political leader of the world's 1.5 billion Muslims. As al-Baghdadi obeys only God, so must all Muslims obey al-Baghdadi. This obviously indicates they have a hierarchical organization which is a spider type organization rather than a leaderless starfish organization. Regardless, ISIS certainly appears to be a rallying point for starfish type Islamic terror organizations.

In the *The Starfish and Spider* referenced above, the authors clearly lay out the failure of centralized organizational structures to deal with decentralized, i.e. starfish, organizations... In fact, a starfish structure can rarely be called an organization; it is more of an ideology, some unifying grievance, a belief system, even ethnocentric rather than geographic. When a centralized organization, for example the U.S. Government or the U.S. military, tries to deal with a starfish structure, it reminds one of the carnival arcade game "whack-a-mole" where every time you hit one mole, two others pop up elsewhere in a never-ending cycle of re-creation and expansion.

So what does this have to do with the uniqueness of Special Forces? As we have discussed in previous chapters and annexes, the uniqueness of Special Forces is its ability and unique mission to accomplish tasks *through, with and by* indigenous populations. In the book, *The Starfish and Spider*, the authors point out that using the same starfish tactics against a starfish structure seems to prove to be the most effective counter.

A thought – you will recognize it is not original ... the only way to overcome or marginalize a sea of starfish is to affect the sea ... take it away, reduce it in size (turn the sea against the starfish), all this is long-term, in many instances, very long term since it probably requires a culture change/evolution … rarely is cultural change revolutionary … even the American revolution took decades to foment.

Other thoughts: The French resistance and underground in WWII essentially was a sea of starfish. Like Al Qaeda, they were independent with mostly local goals and some general goals. While they listened to an outside source for general guidance, received some support from outside sources, and on occasion tried to work in concert, i.e. Normandy invasion, if a "starfish" or even many "starfish" were compromised, it did not stop the resistance and a case can be made that the more brutal the repression, the more starfish were created…active starfish, underground starfish, auxiliary starfish … sound familiar?

In Vietnam, Haiti, Iraq, and Afghanistan, small Special Forces teams through, with and by indigenous populations proved to have significant success in countering starfish type structures. These small SF/indigenous teams operated in much the same manner as the starfish structure. Granted, there was a centralized military structure in place for support, but the actual actions of the teams on the ground were dictated by the local knowledge, people and cultural understanding at the grassroots level. Not only did these small teams track down the local enemy starfish teams and eliminate them, they also were able to directly influence, in a positive manner, the indigenous population. Taking away the sea in which the insurgents swim has always been the key to defeating insurgents. The problem has been that large centralized structures rarely are able to do this for many of the same reasons described in the book. The more centralized an organization becomes, the more it loses touch with the lower or lowest echelons of the organization, in this case the people of a country; thereby rendering them unable to effectively address starfish insurgencies.

Properly using Special Forces to counter starfish structures requires a unique understanding by the centralized organizations of both the U.S. military and our civilian government. These centralized structures must release decision-making to the lowest level. This does not mean there is a lack of guidance or intent as to broad goals and objectives. In fact it requires these centralized hierarchical organizations, primarily the government/interagency to provide the vision and, most importantly, the long-term, multi-administration secession commitment to this long-term vision (in other words, every newly elected administration must be committed to these same long-term goals and continue the support of these efforts). However, where the rubber meets the road, the teams on the ground must be able to make the necessary decisions based on their unique operational environment without second-guessing or interference from the centralized organization. If fact, they must have full support.

Now, other than the manner in which Special Forces are selected, organized, trained and equipped, their effectiveness is based on the fact that these twelve men, although highly trained and probably the twelve deadliest men on the ground in the area, have an incredibly sophisticated, capable, large and multi-functional centralized structure on-call monitoring them to provide every kind of imaginable support needed by the twelve man team - the entire U.S. military and through the interagency process, the entire U.S. government. This is the analogy of the little guy out front with a whole gang of big brothers with guns, bats, muscles, standing behind him. If you mess with the little guy, the big guys kick your butt. This is one of the keys that makes Special Forces effective.

The process of taking on a starfish structure such as Islamic fundamentalism requires a multi-generational approach to effect the ideological pillars of both the indigenous and the U.S. population in order to bring about clear, unambiguous understanding of the threat and, simultaneously effect an evolutionary cultural change in these populations. First, the population of the United States must clearly recognize and understand the threat to our culture and our way of life; second, the same has to be recognized and accepted by other free nations; and third, each starfish cell/structure must be attacked at the lowest level *through, with and by* the local indigenous populations in a manner which wins and converts those populations away from support of this world domination ideology. While Special Forces are at the tip of the spear at the local level, this overall effort requires long-term commitment, not just across successive political administrations, but multi-generational sustained interagency commitment and support.

Annex O:
Special Action Force (SAF)

What is a Special Action Force?

First codified in doctrine in Army Field Manual 31-22, U.S. Army Counterinsurgency Forces dated 12 November 1963, the SAF is defined as:

> ... a specially trained, area-oriented, partially language-qualified, ready force, available to the commander of a unified command[167] for the support of cold, limited and general war operations. SAF organizations may vary in size and capabilities according to theater requirements.

> A SAF consists of a **special forces group** and selected detachments, which may include civil affairs, psychological warfare, engineer, medical, intelligence, military police, and Army Security Agency detachments.

Basic doctrinal guidance pertaining to the SAF concept, as well as the organization and employment of SAF units, was set forth in a Department

---

167 **unified command** — A command with a broad continuing mission under a single commander and composed of significant assigned components of two or more Military Departments (Army, Navy, Air Force, Marines) that is established and so designated by the President, through the Secretary of Defense with the advice and assistance of the Chairman of the Joint Chiefs of Staff. Also called unified combatant command.

of the Army (DA) letter[168]dated 25 November 1963, subject: "Concept for Employment of Special Action Forces (U)" referred to as the DA Concept Paper. As defined in this letter, the SAF was a "specially trained, area oriented, partially language qualified, ready force, available to the commander of a unified command for cold war operations as well as for operations in general or limited war… The SAF consists of special forces units and civil affairs, psychological warfare, engineer, medical, intelligence, military police, and ASA elements." Subsequent to the publication of the DA Concept Paper, six special action forces were organized worldwide: Asia, Latin America, Middle East, Africa, Europe, and a CONUS (Continental United States)-based (reserve)[169] unit. The Europe and CONUS-based (reserved) SAFs consist of special forces groups (SFG) whose only augmentation was Army Security Agency special operations detachments[170].

Asia SAF

> 1st Special Forces Group
> 97th Civil Affairs Group
> 539 Engineer Detachment
> 156 Medical Detachment
> 441 Intelligence Corps Detachment

Africa SAF

> 3rd Special Forces Group
> 1st Civil Affairs Company
> 534th Engineer Detachment
> 705th Intelligence Corps Detachment
> 81st Military Police Detachment
> 19th Psychological Warfare Company

168 Department of the Army (DA) file AGAM –P (M), dated 25 November 1963
169 Document (SECRET NOFORN), Development Status Of Military Counterinsurgency Programs, Including Counterguerrilla Forces, JCS as of 1 August 1964 (U).
170 Study (SECRET), USACDCSWA, November 1964; subject: "Analysis of U.S. Army Special Action Forces (SAF) Augmentation Elements (U)," page 2 and Annex E. This study was conducted during the period May – July 1964 and included an on the ground analysis of augmentation elements attached to the first, third, six, eight special forces groups, which represent the Asia, Africa, mid-East, and Latin America SAF's. 15 of 16 USACDC groups and agencies, service schools and centers with whom this study was formally coordinated concurred in its conclusions and recommendations attached at tab C.

Mid East SAF

> 6th Special Forces Group
> ? Civil Affairs Company
> 535th Engineer Detachment
> 801st Intelligence Corps Detachment
> 82nd Military Police Detachment
> 12th Psychological Warfare Company

Latin America SAF

> 8th Special Forces Group
> 146th Engineer Detachment
> 255th Medical Detachment
> 610th Intelligence Corps Detachment
> 550th Military Police Detachment
> 9th Psychological Warfare Company
> (3rd Civil Affairs Detachment assigned to USARSO)

The 10th Special Forces Group (Europe) and 7th Special Forces Group (CONUS - Base Reserve) had Army Security Agency Special Operations Detachments but were not considered true SAFs.

The Army's only full Special Action Force was organized around the 8th Special Forces Group in 1963 at Fort Gulick, Panama. The 8th Special Forces Group was formed around elements of the 7th Special Forces Group. The 8th SFGA full designation was 8th Special Forces Group (ABN), Special Action Force (SAF), Latin America. In addition to the two line Special Forces companies (all SF companies were re-designated as battalions in 1972), the SAF included the 610th Military Intelligence Detachment, the 255th Medical Detachment, the 550th Military Police Detachment, the 146th Engineer Detachment, an Army Security Agency detachment, and the 9th Psychological Operations Battalion. A mobile training team (MTT) from the 8th Special Forces Group trained and advised the Bolivian Ranger Battalion that captured and killed Che Guevara in the fall of 1967. The 8th SFGA and the 8th SAF were deactivated in June 1972 and became the 3d Battalion, 7th SFGA.

Following the withdrawal of U.S. Army Special Forces-Thailand, the 1st Special Forces Group stationed in Okinawa and its associated detachments- SAF, Asia - were withdrawn from the Pacific. Most of SAF, Asia, including 1st Special Forces Group (-), was inactivated during June 1974.

In a 1965 SAF Study by the Army Combat Developments Command Study titled: Analysis Of The Validity Of Special Action Forces (SAF); Final Draft dated 21 June 1965, states:

ABSTRACT

"This study examines the validity of the concept of the Special Action Force (SAF). Study also examines SAF organizational alternatives, current employment, organizational and doctrinal capabilities, and roles and missions. The analysis invalidates the concept of SAF and recommends that roles and missions presently assigned SAF be reassigned to US Army forces at large. Time frame 1965 – 1970."

FACT SHEET

MAJ Leiter , SOJ5-J 4185

SUBJECT: 1965 SAF Study by Combat Developments Command

FACTS :

1. Study objectives were to determine if SAF structure and doctrine enabled it to preform assigned missions; if current employment was in accordance with assigned missions; if a revision of structure or doctrine was needed; and if a different organizational structure could better fulfill SAF mission; and if a revision of SAF roles and missions was required.

2. Findings and conclusions:

    a. Organizational structure of SF Group is to preform UW mission, revision is needed for counterinsurgency role.

    b. Composition of augmentation elements was not broad

enough in MOS skills or high enough in grade structure to meet the criteria of the MAGGs and Missions of the operational theaters.

c. The prevalent employment of the SAF was not on a task force basis, but on an individual or small MTT basis.

d. The US Army must provide a much broader MOS selection base for counterinsurgency MTTs than existed in the SAF.

e. No organization could be created as an alternative to the SAF which contained all the skills required to meet MTT requirements.

f. SF should be considered primarily a UW organization making such contributions to the US Army counter insurgency mission as it is capable without organizational change or doctrinal orientation away from the primary UW role.

3. The analysis invalidated the concept of SAF and recommended that roles and missions that were assigned SAF be reassigned to US Army forces at large.

As mentioned above, the Army's only full SAF was deactivated in 1972. While the idea of rejuvenating SAFs has been debated for decades, there is significant resistance from the Army to align conventional Army units under the command and control of Special Forces on a continuing basis. The argument made is that forces may be aligned on temporary basis for mission specific reasons, but there is no reason to have a permanently organized SAF. The arguments basically remain the same as in 1965. Unfortunately, this prevents assimilation into the SF culture and does not hold the SF leadership truly responsible, at all levels, for the attached elements.

For the conduct of unconventional warfare, the SAF is an ideal model. As discussed in Chapter 3, UW requires a long term, sustained effort that is regionally focused, but does not necessarily require a large commitment of conventional forces. A Special Forces Group, with a habitually assigned/attached mix of specialty units, integrated with the interagency process is an ideal organization for unconventional warfare. This results in not only trust, but a solid understanding of, and confidence in, operating procedures and methodology.

The current usage of the term "SAF" and the organizations associated with the term is significantly different from the original. The current "SAF" is called security assistance force vice Special Action Force. An example is "ISAF" which stands for either International Security Assistance Force or International Stabilization Assistance Force, depending on the source. The most critical difference is that the Special Action Force was built around a Special Forces Group. The newer security assistance forces are built around conventional units.

Following are some excerpts from doctrinal sources that explains Special Action Forces.

Army Field Manual 31-22, U.S. Army Counterinsurgency Forces dated 12 November 1963, is the first definitive doctrinal source for the Special Action Force.

21. Army Organization

a. (not included)

b. Structurally, the U.S. Army has three tiers of forces upon which the commanders of unified commands, the chiefs of MAAG's/Missions, or in some cases the army attaches, as appropriate, may draw to support or conduct counterinsurgency operations. In the majority of cases, the U.S. elements described below will be employed in an advisory/training role to indigenous forces.

(1) The first tier consists of U.S. Army Special Action Forces (SAF) developed by the Army to support commanders of unified commands. These forces, strategically located, can be provided

with trained replacements from a Base Special Action Force in the Continental United States (CONUS).

(2) The second tier is composed of over seas general purpose TOE units, to include brigade-size backup forces consisting of infantry, armor, armored cavalry, artillery, engineer, psychological warfare, signal, civil affairs, intelligence, military police, aviation, Army Security Agency, medical, and essential support units, which have been designated as back-up forces for the SAF's. Area-oriented, partially language and fully counterinsurgency trained, these backup forces- pro\ride mobile training teams and operational units of sizes and capabilities consistent with mission requirements. Generally, their elements are committed when the capabilities of the MAAG/Mission and/or the SAF are exceeded by the requirements of the country concerned.

(3) The third tier consists of CONUS- based U.S. Army forces, including the base SAF which serves as a rotational base for deployed elements. In consonance with contingency planning, area-oriented and counterinsurgency trained brigade-size backup forces are designated for employment in specific areas as required to assist in pre venting or defeating insurgency. The third tier satisfies requirements that exceed those of the first and second tiers

Section II. THE SPECIAL ACTION FORCE (SAF)

22. General

The SAF is a specially trained, area-oriented, partially language-qualified, ready force, avail able to the commander of a unified command for the support of cold, limited and general war operations. SAF organizations may vary in size and capabilities according to theater requirements.

23. Organization

A SAF consists of a special forces group and selected detachments, which may include civil affairs, psychological warfare, engineer, medical, intelligence, military police, and Army Security Agency detachments. Within the SAF, most of the capabilities of the army as a whole are represented on a small scale in a form specifically designed for counterinsurgency operations. Elements of the SAF are deployed as an advisory/training task ;force to a host country in accordance with requirements stated in the country internal defense plan or to meet the exigencies of an escalading insurgency situation.

24. Command/Control

The organization of the special forces (SF) group is provided with a flexible command and control system which facilitates administration, logistical support and, as required, operations of all elements in the SAF. The SF group headquarters, and the SF operational detachments B and C, each possessing a unit staff, plan and conduct operations as directed within their capabilities. The SAF is commanded by the SF group commander who in turn may be regarded by the commander of the unified command or army component command as his senior counterinsurgency specialist. The SAF augmentation elements, when employed in support of SAF activities, will be either in the SAF chain of command or directly under the MAAG. The establishment of a Special Forces Operational Base (SFOB) with its attendant communications center facilitates operational control of the widely dispersed subordinate elements of the SAF.

25. Characteristics of the SAF.

a. The SAF is specially trained and specifically available for special warfare missions including unconventional warfare, psychological and counterinsurgency operations. It is area oriented and partially language trained.

b. It is maintained in a state of operational readiness.

c. Its members are prepared, from the stand point of training and psychology, to work in remote areas with foreign personnel, including primitive groups, under conditions of relative hardship and danger.

d. It provides a pool of resources from which training assistance and operating teams and forces can be combined on a task force basis to meet the widely varying requirements of counterinsurgency operations.

e. It represents a regional repository of experience in counterinsurgency operations.

Section III. OTHER U.S. ARMY COUNTERINSURGENCY FORCES

26. Backup Forces, Second and Third Tiers

Brigade-size backup forces are organized from selected overseas and CONUS divisions to provide area-oriented and partially language trained mobile training teams, detachments, and operational units as backup for the SAF's and/or MAAG's (par. 21b (2) and (3)). The mission, training and organization of these forces generally parallel that of the SAF; however, since they are normally deployed following an escalation in the level of insurgency, more emphasis is placed on developing combat capabilities.

27. Brigade Organization, Capabilities

Within these forces are specially trained small infantry, artillery and armored cavalry mobile training teams, and engineer, psychological warfare, signal, civil affairs, intelligence, aviation, Army Security Agency, medical, military police, and other support units of varying sizes and capabilities. These teams and units may be deployed and assigned to a deployed SAF or MAAG or, under exceptional circumstances, the entire brigade may be deployed, when required. The elements of this force are capable of training, advising, and providing operational assistance to indigenous regular and paramilitary forces. The tailoring of this force as MTT's is discussed in paragraphs 57 through 59. Training requirements for this force or elements thereof are outlined in paragraph 123.

28. General Purpose Units

In addition to the SAF and brigade-size back up forces discussed above, general purpose CONUS and theater army forces may be deployed to support the activities of the MAAG/ Mission or specified command, in accordance with the requirements of country internal defense plans. Such requirements may include combat support and combat service support units and, under exceptional circumstances, combat units. These units are deployed to countries to support indigenous military and paramilitary forces or U.S. Army units in the conduct of counterinsurgency operations. The primary mission of such units is to provide operational assistance to indigenous forces in cases where the latter do not have the capability of providing their own.

Army Field Manual 31-21 Special Forces Operations - U.S. Army Doctrine dated 14 February 1969, states on page 2-1 in Chap 2, Section II,b.(3) Stability Operations.

The Special Forces group may be assigned to unified and specified commands for the support of stability operations. The group may operate as a separate organization or as a major element of a Special Action Force (SAF).

The organization of the original SAFs was woefully insufficient. They were lacking attached/assigned conventional combat and combat support units such as infantry, aviation, and logistical elements and, of course, dedicated support from the Navy, Air Force and Marines. And, again, repeated is the absolute necessity of dedicated engagement with the interagency process.

Annex P:
OSS Manuals from WWII

Four different OSS field manuals from World War II comprise this Annex. These are provided mostly for historical purposes, but also as a reference to the roots of Special Forces.

The first two manuals, the Simple Sabotage Field Manual and the Special Operations Field Manual, were able to be converted to type from original manuals. The last two manuals, the Operational Groups Field Manual and the Maritime Unit Field Manual, were photocopied from original manuals.

Pages 427 - 430 are translations of the covers of the four manuals.

Page 431 -- Simple Sabotage Field Manual – Strategic Services (Provisional)

Page 468 -- Special Operations Field Manual – Strategic Services (Provisional)

Page 503 -- Operational Groups Field Manual – Strategic Services (Provisional)

Page 533 -- Maritime Unit Field Manual – Strategic Services (Provisional)

Simple Sabotage Field Manual – Strategic Services (Provisional)

Prepared under direction of
The Director of Strategic Services

OSS REPRODUCTION BRANCH   31013

DECLASSIFIED
Authority SecDef Memo dtd 3 Aug 72
Subj: Declass of WWII Records
By (unk) Date 16 June 76

Strategic Services Field Manual No. 3

Office of Strategic Services
Washington, D. C.
17 January 1944

This Simple Sabotage Field Manual - Strategic Services (Provisional) - is published for the information and guidance of all concerned and will be used as the basic doctrine for Strategic Services training for the operations of this subject.

The contents of this manual should be carefully controlled and should not be allowed to come into unauthorized hands.

The instructions may be placed in separate pamphlets or leaflets according to categories of operations but should be distributed with care and not broadly. They should be used as a basis of radio broadcasts only for local and special cases and as directed by the theater commander.

AR 380 – 5, pertaining to the handling of secret documents, will be complied with in the handling of this manual.

(Original signed)
William J. Donovan
Director

Special Operations Field Manual – Strategic Services (Provisional)

DECLASSIFIED
NND 843099
Authority SecDef Memo dtd 3 Aug 72
Subj: Declass of WWII Records
By (unk) Date 16 June 76

Prepared under direction of
The Director of Strategic Services

Strategic Services Field Manual No. 4

Office of Strategic Services
Washington, D. C.
23 February 1944

This Special Operations Field Manual – – Strategic Services (Provisional) is published for the information and guidance of all concerned and will be used as the basic doctrine for strategic services training for such subjects.

It should be carefully noted that Special Operations as defined in this Manual covers the following subjects: (1) sabotage; (2) direct contact with and support of underground resistance groups; (3) conduct of special operations not assigned to other Government agencies and not under direct control of theater or area commanders. Special Operations do not include promotion of, or engagement in, guerrilla activities or subversive maritime activities, which will be the subjects of other provisional basic field manuals.

The contents of this manual should be carefully controlled and should not be allowed to come into unauthorized hands.

AR 380 – 5, pertaining to handling of secret documents, will be complied with in the handling of this manual.

(Original signed)
William J. Donovan
Director

No. 68

Operational Groups Field Manual – Strategic Services (Provisional)

Prepared under direction of
The Director of Strategic Services

OSS REPRODUCTION BRANCH   39707

DECLASSIFIED
Authority NND 843094
By ERC Date 9/17/84

Strategic Services Field Manual No. 6

Office of Strategic Services
Washington, D. C.
25 April 1944

This Operational Groups Field manual – – Strategic Services is made available for the information and guidance of selected personnel and will be used as the basic doctrine for Strategic Services training for the operations of these groups.

The contents of this manual should be carefully controlled and should not be allowed to come into unauthorized hands. The manual will not be taken to advanced basis.

AR 380 – 5, 15 March 1944, pertaining to the handling of secret documents, will be complied with the handling of this manual.

(Original signed)
William J. Donovan
Director

No. 7

Maritime Unit Field Manual – Strategic Services (Provisional)

Prepared under direction of
The Director of Strategic Services

OSS REPRODUCTION BRANCH   47189

DECLASSIFIED
Authority NND 843094
By ERC Date 9/17/84

Strategic Services Field Manual No. 7

Office of Strategic Services
Washington, D. C.
25 April 1944

This Provisional Basic Field Manual for Maritime Unit is made available for the information and guidance of selected personnel and will be used as the basic doctrine for Strategic Services training for the operations of these groups.

The contents of this manual should be carefully controlled and should not be allowed to come into unauthorized hands. The manual will not be taken to advance bases.

AR 380 – 5, pertaining to the handling of secret documents, will be complied with in the handling of this manual.

(Original signed)
William J. Donovan
Director

SIMPLE SABOTAGE
FIELD MANUAL

Strategic Services
(Provisional)

Prepared under direction of
The Director of Strategic Services

Office of Strategic Services
Washington, D.C.
17 January 1944

This Simple Sabotage Field Manual — Strategic Services (Provisional) — is published for the information and guidance of all concerned and will be used as the basic doctrine for Strategic Services training for this subject.

The contents of this Manual should be carefully controlled and should not be allowed to come into unauthorized hands.

The instructions may be placed in separate pamphlets or leaflets according to categories of operations but should be distributed with care and not broadly. They should be used as a basis of radio broadcasts only for local and special cases and as directed by the theater commander.

AR 380-5, pertaining to handling of secret documents, will be complied with in the handling of this Manual.

William J. Donovan

CONTENTS

SIMPLE SABOTAGE

1. *INTRODUCTION*

a. The purpose of this paper is to characterize simple sabotage, to outline its possible effects, and to present suggestions for inciting and executing it.

b. Sabotage varies from highly technical *coup de main* acts that require detailed planning and the use of specially-trained operatives, to innumerable simple acts which the ordinary individual citizen-saboteur can perform. This paper is primarily concerned with the latter type. Simple sabotage does not require specially prepared tools or equipment; it is executed by an ordinary citizen who may or may not act individually and without the necessity for active connection with an organized group; and it is carried out in such a way as to involve a minimum danger of injury, detection, and reprisal.

c. Where destruction is involved, the weapons of the citizen-saboteur are salt, nails, candles, pebbles, thread, or any other materials he might normally be expected to possess as a householder or as a worker in his particular occupation. His arsenal is the kitchen shelf, the trash pile, his own usual kit of tools and supplies. The targets of his sabotage are usually objects to which he has normal and inconspicuous access in everyday life.

d. A second type of simple sabotage requires no destructive tools whatsoever and produces physical damage, if any, by highly indirect means. It is based on universal opportunities to make faulty decisions, to adopt a non-cooperative attitude, and to induce others to follow suit. Making a faulty decision may be simply a matter of placing tools in one spot instead of another. A non-cooperative attitude may involve nothing more than creating an unpleasant situation among one's fellow workers, engaging in bickerings, or displaying surliness and stupidity.

e. This type of activity, sometimes referred to as the "human element," is frequently responsible for accidents, delays, and general obstruction even under normal conditions. The potential saboteur should discover what types of faulty decisions and ... cooperation are *normally* found in this kind of work and should then devise his sabotage so as to enlarge that "margin for error."

2. *POSSIBLE EFFECTS*

a. Acts of simple sabotage are occurring throughout Europe. An effort should be made to add to their efficiency, lessen their detectability, and increase their number. Acts of simple sabotage, multiplied by thousands of citizen-saboteurs, can be an effective weapon against the enemy. Slashing tires, draining fuel tanks, starting fires, starting arguments, acting stupidly, short-circuiting electric systems, abrading machine parts will waste materials, manpower, and time. Occurring on a wide scale, simple sabotage will be a constant and tangible drag on the war effort of the enemy.

b. Simple sabotage may also have secondary results of more or less value. Widespread practice of simple sabotage will harass and de-moralize enemy administrators and police. Further, success may embolden the citizen-saboteur eventually to find colleagues who can assist him in sabotage of greater dimensions. Finally, the very practice of simple sabotage by natives in enemy or occupied territory may make these individuals identify themselves actively with the United Nations war effort, and encourage them to assist openly in periods of Allied invasion and occupation.

3. *MOTIVATING THE SABOTEUR*

a. To incite the citizen to the active practice of simple sabotage and to keep him practicing that sabotage over sustained periods is a special problem.

b. Simple sabotage is often an act which the citizen performs according to his own initiative and inclination. Acts of destruction do not bring him any personal gain and may be completely foreign to his habitually conservationist attitude toward materials and tools. Purposeful stupidity is contrary to human nature. He frequently needs pressure, stimulation or assurance, and information and suggestions regarding feasible methods of simple sabotage.

(1) *Personal Motives*

(a) The ordinary citizen very probably has no immediate personal motive for committing simple sabotage. Instead, he must be made to anticipate indirect personal gain, such as might come with enemy evacuation or destruction of the ruling government group. Gains should be stated as specifically as possible for the area addressed: simple sabotage will hasten the day when Commissioner X and his deputies Y and Z will be thrown out, when particularly obnoxious decrees and restrictions will be abolished, when food will arrive, and so on. Abstract verbalizations about personal liberty, freedom of the press, and so on, will not be convincing in most parts of the world. In many areas they will not even be comprehensible.

(b) Since the effect of his own acts is limited, the saboteur may become discouraged unless he feels that he is a member of a large, though unseen, group of saboteurs operating against the enemy or the government of his own country and elsewhere. This can be conveyed indirectly: suggestions which he reads and hears can include observations that a particular technique has been successful in this or that district. Even if the technique is not applicable to his surroundings, another's success will encourage him to attempt similar acts. It also can be conveyed directly: statements praising the effectiveness of simple sabotage can be contrived which will be published by white radio, freedom stations, and the subversive press. Estimates of the proportion of the population engaged in sabotage can be disseminated. Instances of successful sabotage already are being broadcast by white radio and freedom stations, and this should be continued and expanded where compatible with security.

(c) More important than (a) or (b) would be to create a situation in which the citizen-saboteur acquires a sense of responsibility and begins to educate others in simple sabotage.

(2) *Encouraging Destructiveness*

It should be pointed out to the saboteur where the circumstances are suitable, that he is acting in self-defense against the enemy, or retaliating against the enemy for other acts of destruction. A reasonable amount of humor in the presentation of suggestions for simple sabotage will relax tensions of fear.

(a) The saboteur may have to reverse his thinking, and he should be told this in so many words. Where he formerly thought of keeping his tools sharp, he should now let them grow dull; surfaces that formerly were lubricated now should be sanded; normally diligent, he should now be lazy and careless; and so on. Once he is encouraged to think backwards about himself and the objects of his everyday life, the saboteur will see many opportunities in his immediate environment which cannot possibly be seen from a distance. A state of mind should be encouraged that anything can be sabotaged.

(b) Among the potential citizen-saboteurs who are to engage in physical destruction, two extreme types may be distinguished. On the one hand, there is the man who is not technically trained and employed. This man needs specific suggestions as to what he can and should destroy as well as details regarding the tools by means of which destruction is accomplished.

(c) At the other extreme is the man who is a technician, such as a lathe operator or an automobile mechanic. Presumably this man would be able to devise methods of simple sabotage which would be appropriate to his own facilities. However, this man needs to be stimulated to re-orient his thinking in the direction of destruction. Specific examples, which need not be from his own field, should accomplish this.

(d) Various media may be used to disseminate suggestions and information regarding simple sabotage. Among the media which may be used, as the immediate situation dictates, are: freedom stations or radio; false or .... or leaflets. Broadcasts or leaflets may be directed toward specific geographic or occupational areas, or they may be general in scope. Finally, agents may be trained in the art of simple sabotage, in anticipation of a time when they may be able to communicate this information directly.

(3) *Safety Measures*

(a) The amount of activity carried on by the saboteur will be governed not only by the number of opportunities he sees, but also by the amount of danger he feels. Bad news travels fast, and simple sabotage will be discouraged if too many simple saboteurs are arrested.

(b) It should not be difficult to prepare leaflets and other media for the saboteur about the choice of weapons, time, and targets which will ensure the saboteur against detection and retaliation. Among such suggestions might be the following:

(1) Use materials which appear to be innocent. A knife or a nail file can be carried normally on your person; either is a multi-purpose instrument for creating damage. Matches, pebbles, hair, salt, nails, and dozens of other destructive agents can be carried or kept in your living quarters without exciting any suspicion whatever. If you are a worker in a particular trade or industry you can easily carry and keep such things as wrenches, hammers, emery paper, and the like.

(2) Try to commit acts for which large numbers of people could be responsible. For instance, if you blow out the wiring in a factory at a central fire box, almost anyone could have done it. On-the-street sabotage after dark, such as you might be able to carry out against a military car or truck, is another example of an act for which it would be impossible to blame you.

(3) Do not be afraid to commit acts for which you might be blamed directly, so long as you do so rarely, and as long as you have a plausible excuse: you dropped your wrench across an electric circuit because an air raid had kept you up the night before

and you were half-dozing at work. Always be profuse in your apologies. Frequently you can "get away" with such acts under the cover of pretending stupidity, ignorance, over-caution, fear of being suspected of sabotage, or weakness and dullness due to undernourishment.

(4) After you have committed an act of easy sabotage, resist any temptation to wait around and see what happens. Loiterers arouse suspicion. Of course, there are circumstances when it would be suspicious for you to leave. If you commit sabotage on your job, you should naturally stay at your work.

4. *TOOLS, TARGETS, AND TIMING*

a. The citizen-saboteur cannot be closely controlled. Nor is it reasonable to expect that simple sabotage can be precisely concentrated on specific types of targets according to the requirements of a concrete military situation. Attempts to control simple sabotage according to developing military factors, moreover, might provide the enemy with intelligence of more or less value in anticipating the date and area of notably intensified or notably slackened military activity.

b. Sabotage suggestions, of course, should be adapted to fit the area where they are to be practiced. Target priorities for general types of situations likewise can be specified, for emphasis at the proper time by the underground press, freedom stations, and cooperating propaganda.

(1) *Under General Conditions*

(a) Simple sabotage is more than malicious mischief, and it should always consist of acts whose results will be detrimental to the materials and manpower of the enemy.

(b) The saboteur should be ingenious in using his everyday equipment. All sorts of weapons will present themselves if he looks at his surroundings in a different light. For example, emery dust — a powerful weapon --- may at first seem unobtainable, but if the saboteur were to pulverize an emery knife sharpener or emery wheel with a hammer he would find himself with a plentiful supply.

(c) The saboteur should never attack targets beyond his capacity or the capacity of his instruments. An inexperienced person should not, for example, attempt to use explosives, but should confine himself to the use of matches or other familiar weapons.

(d) The saboteur should try to damage only objects and materials known to be in use by the enemy or to be destined for early use by the enemy. It will be safe for him to assume that almost any product of heavy industry is destined for enemy use, and that the most efficient fuels and lubricants also are destined for enemy use. Without special knowledge, however, it would be undesirable for him to attempt destruction of food crops or food products.

(e) Although the citizen-saboteur may rarely have access to military objects, he should give these preference above all others.

(2) *Prior to a Military Offensive* During periods which are quiescent in a military sense, such emphasis as can be given to simple sabotage might well center on industrial production, to lessen the flow of materials and equipment to the enemy. Slashing a rubber tire on an Army truck may be an act of value; spoiling a batch of rubber in the production plant is an act of still more value.

(3) *During a Military Offensive*

(a) Most significant sabotage for an area which is, or is soon destined to be, a theater of combat operations is that whose effects will be direct and immediate. Even if the effects are relatively minor and localized, this type of sabotage is to be preferred to activities whose effects, while widespread, are indirect and delayed.

(1) The saboteur should be encouraged to attack transportation facilities of all kinds. Among such facilities are roads,

railroads, automobiles, trucks, motor-cycles, bicycles, trains, and trams.

(2) Any communications facilities which can be used by the authorities to transmit instructions or morale material should be the objects of simple sabotage. These include telephone, telegraph and power systems, radio, newspapers, placards, and public notices.

(3) Critical materials, valuable in themselves or necessary to the efficient functioning of transportation and communication, also should become targets for the citizen-saboteur. These may include oil, gasoline, tires, food, and water.

5. *SPECIFIC SUGGESTIONS FOR SIMPLE SABOTAGE*

a. It will not be possible to evaluate the desirability of simple sabotage in an area without having in mind rather specifically what individual acts and results are embraced by the definition of simple sabotage.

b. A listing of specific acts follows, classified according to types of target. This list is presented as a growing rather than a complete outline of the methods of simple sabotage. As new techniques are developed, or new fields explored, it will be elaborated and expanded.

(1) *Buildings*

Warehouses, barracks, offices, hotels, and factory buildings are outstanding targets for simple sabotage. They are extremely susceptible to damage, especially by fire; they offer opportunities to such untrained people as janitors, charwomen, and casual visitors; and, when damaged, they present a relatively large handicap to the enemy.

(a) *Fires* can be started wherever there is an accumulation of inflammable material. Warehouses are obviously the most promising targets but incendiary sabotage need not be confined to them alone.

(1) Whenever possible, arrange to have the fire start after you have gone away. Use a candle and paper combination, setting it as close as possible to the inflammable material you want to burn: From a sheet of paper, tear a strip three or four centimeters wide and wrap it around the base of the candle two or three times. Twist more sheets of paper into loose ropes and place them around the base of the candle. When the candle flame reaches the encircling strip, it will be ignited and in turn will ignite the surrounding paper. The size, heat, and duration of the resulting flame will depend on how much paper you use and how much of it you can cramp in a small space.

(2) With a flame of this kind, do not attempt to ignite any but rather inflammable materials, such as cotton sacking. To light more resistant materials, use a candle plus tightly rolled or twisted paper which has been soaked in gasoline. To create a briefer but even hotter flame, put celluloid such as you might find in an old comb, into a nest of plain or saturated paper which is to be fired by a candle.

(3) To make another type of simple fuse, soak one end of a piece of string in grease. Rub a generous pinch of gunpowder over the inch of string where greasy string meets clean string. Then ignite the clean end of the string. It will burn slowly without a flame (in much the same way that a cigarette burns) until it reaches the grease and gunpowder; it will then flare up suddenly. The grease-treated string will then burn with a flame. The same effect may be achieved by using matches instead of the grease and gunpowder. Run the string over the match heads, taking care that the string is not pressed or knotted. They too will produce a sudden flame. The advantage of this type of fuse is that string burns at a set speed. You can time your fire by the length and thickness of the string you chose.

(4) Use a fuse such as the ones suggested above to start a fire in an office after hours. The destruction of records and other types of documents would be a serious handicap to the enemy.

(5) In basements where waste is kept, janitors should accumulate oily and greasy waste. Such waste sometimes ignites spontaneously, but it can easily be lit with a cigarette or match. If you are a janitor on night duty, you can be the first to report the fire, but don't report it too soon.

(6) A clean factory is not susceptible to fire, but a dirty one is. Workers should be careless with refuse and janitors should be inefficient in cleaning. If enough dirt and trash can be accumulated, an otherwise fireproof building will become inflammable.

(7) Where illuminating gas is used in a room which is vacant at night, shut the windows tightly, turn on the gas, and leave a candle burning in the room, closing the door tightly behind you. After a time, the gas will explode, and a fire may or may not follow.

(b) *Water and miscellaneous*

(1) Ruin warehouse stock by setting the automatic sprinkler system to work. You can do this by tapping the sprinkler heads sharply with a hammer or by holding a match under them.

(2) Forget to provide paper in toilets; put tightly rolled paper, hair, and other obstructions in the W. C. Saturate a sponge with a thick starch or sugar solution. Squeeze it tightly into a ball, wrap it with string, and dry. Remove the string when fully dried. The sponge will be in the form of a tight hard ball. Flush down a W. C. or otherwise introduce into a sewer line. The sponge will gradually expand to its normal size and plug the sewage system.

(3) Put a coin beneath a bulb in a public building during the daytime, so that fuses will blow out when lights are turned on at night. The fuses themselves may be rendered ineffective by putting a coin behind them or loading them with heavy wire. Then a short-circuit may either start a fire, damage transformers, or blow out a central fuse which will interrupt distribution of electricity to a large area.

(4) Jam paper, bits of wood, hairpins, and anything else that will fit, into the locks of all unguarded entrances to public buildings.

(2) *Industrial Production: Manufacturing*

(a) Tools

(1) Let cutting tools grow dull. They will be inefficient, will slow down production, and may damage the materials and parts you use them on.

(2) Leave saws slightly twisted when you are not using them. After a while, they will break when used.

(3) Using a very rapid stroke will wear out a file before its time. So will dragging a file in slow strokes under heavy pressure. Exert pressure on the backward stroke as well as the forward stroke.

(4) Clean files by knocking them against the vise or the workpiece; they are easily broken this way.

(5) Bits and drills will snap under heavy pressure.

(6) You can put a press punch out of order by putting in it more material than it is adjusted for — two blanks instead of one, for example.

(7) Power-driven tools like pneumatic drills, riveters, and so on, are never efficient when dirty. Lubrication points and electric contacts can easily be fouled by normal accumulations of dirt or the insertion of foreign matter.

(b) Oil and lubrication systems are not only vulnerable to easy sabotage, but are critical in every machine with moving parts. Sabotage of oil and lubrication will slow production or stop work entirely at strategic points in industrial processes.

(1) Put metal dust or filings, fine sand, ground glass, emery dust (get it by pounding up an emery knife sharpener) and similar hard, gritty substances directly into lubrication systems. They will scour smooth surfaces, ruining pistons, cylinder walls, shafts, and bearings. They will overheat and stop motors which will need overhauling, new parts, and extensive repairs. Such materials, if they are used, should be introduced into lubrication systems past any filters which otherwise would strain them out.

(2) You can cause wear on any machine by uncovering a filter system, poking a pencil or any other sharp object through the filter mesh, then covering it up again. Or, if you can dispose of it quickly, simply remove the filter.

(3) If you cannot get at the lubrication system or filter directly, you may be able to lessen the effectiveness of oil by diluting it in storage. In this case, almost any liquid will do which will thin the oil. A small amount of sulphuric acid, varnish, water-glass, or linseed oil will be especially effective.

(4) Using a thin oil where a heavy oil is prescribed will break down a machine or heat up a moving shaft so that it will "freeze" and stop.

(5) Put any clogging substance into lubrication systems or, if it will float, into stored oil. Twisted combings of

human hair, pieces of string, dead insects, and many other common objects will be effective in stopping or hindering the flow of oil through feed lines and filters.

(6) Under some circumstances, you may be able to destroy oil outright rather than interfere with its effectiveness, by removing stop-plugs from lubricating systems or by puncturing the drums and cans in which it is stored.

(c) Cooling Systems

(1) A water cooling system can be put out of commission in a fairly short time with considerable damage to an engine or motor, if you put into it several pinches of hard grain, such as rice or wheat. They will swell up and choke the circulation of water, and the cooling system will have to be torn down to remove the obstruction. Sawdust or hair may also be used to clog a water cooling system.

(2) If very cold water is quickly introduced into the cooling system of an overheated motor, contraction and considerable strain on the engine housing will result. If you can repeat the treatment a few times, cracking and serious damage will result.

(3) You can ruin the effectiveness of an air cooling system by plugging dirt and waste into intake or exhaust valves. If a belt-run fan is used in the system, make a jagged cut at least half way through the belt; it will slip and finally part under strain and the motor will overheat.

(d) Gasoline and Oil Fuel. Tanks and fueling engines usually are accessible and easy to open. They afford a very vulnerable target for simple sabotage activities.

(1) Put several pinches of sawdust or hard grain, such as rice or wheat, into the fuel tank of a gasoline engine. The particles will choke a feed line so that the engine will

stop. Some time will be required to discover the source of the trouble. Although they will be hard to get, crumbs of natural rubber, such as you might find in old rubber bands and pencil erasers, are also effective.

(2) If you can accumulate sugar, put it in the fuel tank of a gasoline engine. As it burns together with the gasoline, it will turn into a sticky mess which will completely mire the engine and necessitate extensive cleaning and repair. Honey and molasses are as good as sugar. Try to use about 75-100 grams for each 10 gallons of gasoline.

(3) Other impurities which you can introduce into gasoline will cause rapid engine wear and eventual break-down. Fine particles of pumice, sand, ground glass, and metal dust can easily be introduced into a gasoline tank. Be sure that the particles are very fine, so that they will be able to pass through the carburetor jet.

(4) Water, urine, wine, or any other simple liquid you can get in reasonably large quantities Will dilute gasoline fuel to a point where no combustion will occur in the cylinder and the engine will not move. One pint to 20 gallons of gasoline is sufficient. If salt water is used, it will cause cor-rosion and permanent motor damage.

(5) In the case of Diesel engines, put low flashpoint oil into the fuel tank; the engine will not move. If there al-ready is proper oil in the tank when the wrong kind is added, the engine will only limp and sputter along.

(6) Fuel lines to gasoline and oil engines frequently pass over the exhaust pipe. When the machine is at rest, you can stab a small hole in the fuel line and plug the hole with wax. As the engine runs and the exhaust tube be-comes hot, the wax will be melted; fuel will drip onto the exhaust and a blaze will start.

(7) If you have access to a room where gasoline is stored, remember that gas vapor accumulating in a closed room will explode after a time if you leave a candle burning in the room. A good deal of evaporation, however, must occur from the gasoline tins into the air of the room. If removal of the tops of the tins does not expose enough gasoline to the air to ensure copious evaporation, you can open lightly constructed tins further with a knife, ice pick or sharpened nail file. Or puncture a tiny hole in the tank which will permit gasoline to leak out on the floor. This will greatly increase the rate of evaporation. Before you light your candle, be sure that windows are closed and the room is as air-tight as you can make it. If you can see that windows in a neighboring room are opened wide, you have a chance of setting a large fire which will not only destroy the gasoline but anything else nearby; when the gasoline explodes, the doors of the storage room will be blown open, a draft to the neighboring windows will be created which will whip up a fine conflagration,

(e) Electric Motors. Electric motors (including dynamos) are more restricted than the targets so far discussed. They cannot be sabotaged easily or without risk of injury by unskilled persons who may otherwise have good opportunities for destruction.

(1) Set the rheostat to a high point of resistance in all types of electric motors. They will overheat and catch fire.

(2) Adjust the overload relay to a very high value beyond the capacity of the motor. Then overload the motor to a point where it will overheat and break down.

(3) Remember that dust, dirt, and moisture are enemies of electrical equipment. Spill dust and dirt onto the points where the wires in electric motors connect with terminals, and onto insulating parts. Inefficient transmission

of current and, in some cases, short circuits will result. Wet generator motors to produce short circuits.

(4) "Accidentally" bruise the insulation on wire, loosen nuts on connections, make faulty splices and faulty connections in wiring, to waste electric current and reduce the power of electric motors.

(5) Damage to commutators can reduce the power output or cause short circuiting in direct-current motors: Loosen or remove commutator holding rings. Sprinkle carbon, graphite, or metal dust on commutators. Put a little grease or oil at the contact points of commutators. Where commutator bars are close together bridge the gaps between them with metal dust, or sawtooth their edges with a chisel so that the teeth on adjoining bars meet or nearly meet and current can pass from one to the other.

(6) Put a piece of finely grained emery paper half the size of a postage stamp in a place where it will wear away rotating brushes. The emery paper—and the motor—will be destroyed in the resulting fire.

(7) Sprinkle carbon, graphite or metal dust on slip-rings so that the current will leak or short circuits will occur. When a motor is idle, nick the slip-rings with a chisel.

(8) Cause motor stoppage or inefficiency by applying dust mixed with grease to the face of the armature so that it will not make proper contact.

(9) To overheat electric motors, mix sand with heavy grease and smear it between the stator and rotor, or wedge thin metal pieces between them. To prevent the efficient generation of current, put floor sweepings, oil, tar, or paint between them.

(10) In motors using three-phase current, deeply nick one of the lead-in wires with a knife or file when the machine is at rest, or replace one of the three fuses with a blown-out fuse. In the first case, the motor will stop after running awhile, and in the second, it will not start.

(f) Transformers

(1) Transformers of the oil-filled type can be put out of commission if you pour water, salt water, ... coolant, kerosene into the oil tank.

(2) In air-cooled transformers, block the ventilation by piling debris around the transformer.

(3) In all types of transformers, throw carbon, graphite or metal dust over the outside bushings and other exposed electrical parts.

(g) Turbines for the most part are heavily built, stoutly housed, and difficult of access. Their vulnerability to simple sabotage is very low.

(1) After inspecting or repairing a hydro turbine, fasten the cover insecurely so that it will blow off and flood the plant with water. A loose cover on a steam turbine will cause it to leak and slow down.

(2) In water turbines, insert a large piece of scrap iron in the head of the penstock, just beyond the screening, so that water will carry the damaging material down to the plant equipment.

(3) When the steam line to a turbine is opened for repair, put pieces of scrap iron into it, to be blasted into the turbine machinery when steam is up again.

(4) Create a leak in the line feeding oil to the turbine, so that oil will fall on the hot steam pipe and cause a fire.

(h) Boilers

(1) Reduce the efficiency of steam boilers any way you can. Put too much water in them to make them slow-starting, or keep the fire under them low to keep them inefficient. Let them dry and turn the fire up; they will crack and be ruined. An especially good trick is to keep putting limestone or water containing lime in the boiler; it will deposit lime on the bottom and sides. This deposit will provide very good insulation against heat; after enough of it has collected, the boiler will be completely worthless.

(3) *Production: Metals*

(a) Iron and Steel

(l) Keep blast furnaces in a condition where they must be frequently shut down for repair. In making fire-proof bricks for the inner lining of blast furnaces, put in an extra proportion of tar so that they will wear out quickly and necessitate constant re-lining.

(2) Make cores for casting so that they are filled with air bubbles and an imperfect cast results.

(3) See that the core in a mold is not properly supported, so that the core gives way or the casting is spoiled because of the incorrect position of the core.

(4) In tempering steel or iron, apply too much heat, so that the resulting bars and ingots are of poor quality.

(b) Other Metals

No suggestions available.

(4) *Production: Mining and Mineral Extraction*

(a) Coal

(1) A slight blow against your Davy oil lamp will extinguish it, and to light it again you will have to find a place where there is no fire damp. Take a long time looking for the place.

(2) Blacksmiths who make pneumatic picks should not harden them properly, so that they will quickly grow dull.

(3) You can easily put your pneumatic pick out of order. Pour a small amount of water through the oil lever and your pick will stop working. Coal dust and improper lubrication will also put it out of order.

(4) Weaken the chain that pulls the bucket conveyers carrying coal. A deep dent in the chain made with blows of a pick or shovel will cause it to part under normal strain. Once a chain breaks, normally or otherwise, take your time about reporting the damage; be slow about taking the chain up for repairs and bringing it back down after repairs.

(5) Derail mine cars by putting obstructions on the rails and in switch points. If possible, pick a gallery where coal cars have to pass each other, so that traffic will be snarled up.

(6) Send up quantities of rock and other useless material with the coal.

(5) *Production: Agriculture*

(a) Machinery

(1) See par. 5 *b* (2) (c) , (d) , (e) .

(b) Crops and livestock probably will be destroyed only in areas where there are large food surpluses or where the enemy (regime) is known to be requisitioning food.

(l) Feed crops to livestock. Let crops harvest too early or too late. Spoil stores of grain, fruit and vegetables by soaking them in water so that they will rot. Spoil fruit and vegetables by leaving them in the sun.

(6) *Transportation: Railways*

(a) Passengers

(l) Make train travel as inconvenient as possible for enemy personnel. Make mistakes in issuing train tickets, leaving portions of the journey uncovered by the ticket book; issue two tickets for the same seat in the train, so that an interesting argument will result; near train time, instead of issuing printed tickets write them out slowly by hand, prolonging the process until the train is nearly ready to leave or has left the station. On station bulletin boards announcing train arrivals and departures, see that false and misleading information is given about trains bound for enemy destinations.

(2) In trains bound for enemy destinations, attendants should make life as uncomfortable as possible for passengers. See that the food is especially bad, take up tickets after midnight, call all station stops very loudly during the night, handle baggage as noisily as possible during the night, and so on.

(3) See that the luggage of enemy personnel is mislaid or unloaded at the wrong stations. Switch address labels on enemy baggage.

(4) Engineers should see that trains run slow or make unscheduled stops for plausible reasons.

(b) Switches, Signals and Routing

(l) Exchange wires in switchboards containing signals and switches, so that they connect to the wrong terminals.

(2) Loosen push-rods so that signal arms do not work; break signal lights; exchange the colored lenses on red and green lights.

(3) Spread and spike switch points in the track so that they will not move, or place rocks or close-packed dirt between the switch points. (1) (4) Sprinkle rock salt or ordinary salt profusely over the electrical connections of switch points and on the ground nearby. When it rains, the switch will be short-circuited.

(5) See that cars are put on the wrong trains. Remove the labels from cars needing repair and put them on cars in good order. Leave couplings between cars as loose as possible.

(c) Road-beds and Open Track

(1) On a curve, take the bolts out of the tie-plates connecting to sections of the outside rail, and scoop away the gravel, cinders, or dirt for a few feet on each side of the connecting joint.

(2) If by disconnecting the tie-plate at a joint and loosening sleeper nails on each side of the joint, it becomes possible to move a section of rail, spread two sections of rail and drive a spike vertically between them.

(d) Oil and Lubrication

(1) See 5 *b.* (2) (b) .

(2) Squeeze lubricating pipes with pincers or dent them with hammers, so that the flow of oil is obstructed.

(e) Cooling Systems

(1) See 5 *b* (2) (c) . (f) Gasoline and Oil Fuel

(_!) See 5 *b* (2) (d) .

(g) Electric Motors

(l) See 5 *b* (2) (e) and (f) .

(h) Boilers

(1) See 5 *b* (2) (h) .

(2) After inspection put heavy oil or tar in the engines' boilers, or put half a kilogram of soft soap into the water in the tender.

(i) Brakes and Miscellaneous

(1) Engines should run at high speeds and use brakes excessively at curves and on down hill grades.

(2) Punch holes in air-brake valves or water supply pipes.

(3) In the last car of a passenger train or a front car of a freight, remove the wadding from a journal box and replace it with oily rags.

(7) *Transportation: Automotive*

(a) Roads. Damage to roads [(3) below] is slow, and therefore impractical as a D-day or near D-day activity.

(1) Change sign posts at intersections and forks; the enemy will go the wrong way and it may be miles before he discovers his mistakes. In areas where traffic is composed primarily of enemy autos, trucks, and motor convoys of various kinds, remove danger signals from curves and intersections.

(2) When the enemy asks for directions, give him wrong information. Especially when enemy convoys are in the neighborhood, truck drivers can spread rumors and give false information about bridges being out, ferries closed, and detours lying ahead.

(3) If you can start damage to a heavily traveled road, passing traffic and the elements will do the rest. Construction gangs can see that too much sand or water is put in concrete or that the road foundation has soft spots. Any one can scoop ruts in asphalt and macadam roads which turn soft in hot weather; passing trucks will accentuate the ruts to a point where substantial repair will be needed. Dirt roads also can be scooped out. If you are a road laborer, it will be only a few minutes work to divert a small stream from a sluice so that it runs over and eats away the road.

(4) Distribute broken glass, nails, and sharp rocks on roads to puncture tires.

(b) Passengers

(1) Bus-driver can go past the stop where the enemy wants to get off. Taxi drivers can waste the enemy's time and make extra money by driving the longest possible route to his destination.

(c) Oil and Lubrication

(l) See 5 *b.* (2) (b) .

(2) Disconnect the oil pump; this will burn out the main bearings in less than 50 miles of normal driving.

(d) Radiator

(l) See 5 *b.* (2) (c) .

(e) Fuel

(l) See 5 *b.* (2) (d) .

(f) Battery and Ignition

(l) Jam bits of wood into the ignition lock; loosen or exchange connections behind the switchboard; put dirt in spark plugs; damage distributor points.

(2) Turn on the lights in parked cars so that the battery will run down.

(3) Mechanics can ruin batteries in a number of undetectable ways: Take the valve cap off a cell, and drive a screw driver slantwise into the exposed water vent, shattering the plates of the cell; no damage will show when you put the cap back on. Iron or copper filings put into the cells i.e., dropped into the acid, will greatly shorten its life. Copper coins or a few pieces of iron will accomplish the same and more slowly. One hundred to 150 cubic centimeters of vinegar in each cell greatly reduces the life of the battery, but the odor of the vinegar may reveal what has happened.

(g) Gears.

(1) Remove the lubricant from or put too light a lubricant in the transmission and other gears.

(2) In trucks, tractors, and other machines with heavy gears, fix the gear case insecurely, putting bolts in only half the bolt holes. The gears will be badly jolted in use and will soon need repairs.

(h) Tires

(l) Slash or puncture tires of unguarded vehicles. Put a nail inside a match box or other small box, and set it vertically in front of the back tire of a stationary car; when the car starts off , the nail will go neatly through the tire.

(2) It is easy to damage a tire in a tire repair shop: In fixing flats, spill glass, benzine, caustic soda, or other material inside the casing which will puncture or corrode the

tube. If you put a gummy substance inside the tube, the next flat will stick the tube to the casing and make it unusable. Or, when you fix a flat tire, you can simply leave between the tube and the casing the object which caused the flat in the first place.

(3) In assembling a tire after repair, pump the tube up as fast as you can. Instead of filling out smoothly, it may crease, in which case it will wear out quickly. Or, as you put a tire together, see if you can pinch the tube between the rim of the tire and the rim of the wheel, so that a blow-out will result.

(4) In putting air into tires, see that they are kept below normal pressure, so that more than an ordinary amount of wear will result. In filling tires on double wheels, inflate the inner tire to a much higher pressure than the outer one; both will wear out more quickly this way. Badly aligned wheels also wear tires out quickly; you can leave wheels out of alignment when they come in for adjustment, or you can spring them out of true with a strong kick, or by driving the car slowly and diagonally into a curb.

(5) If you have access to stocks of tires, you can rot them by spilling oil, gasoline, caustic acid, or benzine on them. Synthetic rubber, however, is less susceptible to these chemicals.

(8) *Transportation : Water*

(a) Navigation

(1) Barge and river boat personnel should spread false rumors about the navigability and conditions of the waterways they travel. Tell other barge and boat captains to follow channels that will take extra time, or cause them to make canal detours.

(2) Barge and river boat captains should navigate with exceeding caution near locks and bridges, to waste their time and to waste the time of other craf t which may have to wait on them. If you don't pump the bilges of ships and barges often enough, they will be slower and harder to navigate. Barges "accidentally" run aground are an efficient time waster too.

(3) Attendants on swing, draw, or bascule bridges can delay traffic over the bridge or in the waterway underneath by being slow. Boat captains can leave unattended draw bridges open in order to hold up road traffic.

(4) Add or subtract compensating magnets to the compass on cargo ships. Demagnetize the compass or maladjust it by concealing a large bar of steel or iron near to it.

(b) Cargo

(l) While loading or unloading, handle cargo carelessly in order to cause damage. Arrange the cargo so that the weakest and lightest crates and boxes will be at the bottom of the hold, while the heaviest ones are on top of them. Put hatch covers and tarpaulins on sloppily, so that rain and deck wash will injure the cargo. Tie float valves open so that storage tanks will overflow on perishable goods.

(9) *Communications*

(a) Telephone

(l) At office, hotel and exchange switchboards, delay putting enemy calls through, give them wrong numbers, cut them off "accidentally," or forget to disconnect them so that the line cannot be used again.

(2) Hamper official and especially military business by making at least one telephone call a day to an enemy headquarters; when you get them, tell them you have the

wrong number. Call military or police offices and make anonymous false reports of fires, air raids, bombs.

(3) In offices and buildings used by the enemy, unscrew the earphone of telephone receivers and remove the diaphragm. Electricians and telephone repairmen can make poor connections and damage insulation so that crosstalk and other kinds of electrical interference will make conversations hard or impossible to understand.

(4) Put the batteries under automatic switchboards out of commission by dropping nails, metal filings, or coins into the cells. If you can treat half the batteries in this way, the switchboard will stop working. A whole telephone system can be disrupted if you can put 10 percent of the cells in half the batteries of the central battery room out of order.

(b) Telegraph

(1) Delay the transmission and delivery of telegrams to enemy destinations.

(2) Garble telegrams to enemy destinations so that another telegram will have to be sent or a long distance call will have to be made. Sometimes it will be possible to do this by changing a single letter in a word -for example, chang ing "minimum" to "miximum," so that the person receiving the telegram will not know whether "minimum" or "maximum" is meant.

- Transportation Lines

  (1) Cut telephone and telegraph transmission lines. Damage insulation on power lines to cause interference.

- Mail

- Post office employees can see to it that enemy mail is always delayed by one day or more, that it is put in wrong sacks, and so on.

- Motion Pictures

- Projector operators can ruin newsreels and other enemy propaganda films by bad focusing, speeding up or slowing down the film and by causing frequent breakage in the film.

(2)Audiences can ruin enemy propaganda films by applauding to drown the words of the speaker, by coughing loudly, and by talking.

(3) Anyone can break up a showing of an enemy propaganda film by putting two or three dozen large moths in a paper bag. Take the bag to the movies with you, put it on the floor in an empty section of the theater as you go in and leave it open. The moths will fly out and climb into the projector beam, so that the film will be obscured by fluttering shadows.

Radio

(1) Station engineers will find it quite easy to overmodulate transmissions of talks by persons giving enemy propaganda or instructions, so that they will sound as if they were talking through a heavy cotton blanket with a mouthful of marbles.

(2) In your own apartment building, you can interfere with radio reception at times when the enemy wants everybody to listen. Take an electric light plug off the end of an electric light cord; take some wire out of the cord and tie it across two terminals of a two-prong plug or three terminals of a four-prong plug. Then take it around and put it into as many wall and floor outlets as you can

find. Each time you insert the plug into a new circuit, you will blow out a fuse and silence all radios running on power from that circuit until a new fuse is put in.

(3) Damaging insulation on any electrical equipment tends to create radio interference in the immediate neighborhood, particularly on large generators, neon signs, fluorescent lighting, X-ray machines, and power lines. If workmen can damage insulation on a high tension line near an enemy airfield, they will make ground to-plane radio communications difficult and perhaps impossible during long periods of the day.

(10) *Electric Power*

   (a) Turbines, Electric Motors, Transformers

     (1) See 5 *b* (2) (e) , (f) , and (g) .

   (b) Transmission Lines

     (1) Linesmen can loosen and dirty insulators to cause power leakage. It will be quite easy, too, for them to tie a piece of very heavy string several times back and forth between two parallel transmission lines, winding it several turns around the wire each time. Beforehand, the string should be heavily saturated with salt and then dried. When it rains, the string becomes a conductor, and a short-circuit will result.

(11) *General Interference with Organizations and Production*

   (a) Organizations and Conferences

     (l) Insist on doing everything through "channels." Never permit short-cuts to be taken in order to expedite decisions.

(2) Make "speeches." Talk as frequently as possible and at great length. Illustrate your "points" by long anecdotes and accounts of personal experiences. Never hesitate to make a few appropriate "patriotic" comments.

(3) When possible, refer all matters to committees, for "further study and consideration." Attempt to make the committees as large as possible -never less than five.

(4) Bring up irrelevant issues as frequently as possible.

(5) Haggle over precise wordings of communications, minutes, resolutions.

(6) Refer back to matters decided upon at the last meeting and attempt to re-open the question of the advisability of that decision.

(7) Advocate "caution." Be "reasonable" and urge your fellow-conferees to be "reasonable" and avoid haste which might result in embarrassments or difficulties later on.

(8) Be worried about the propriety of any decision -raise the question of whether such action as is contemplated lies within the jurisdiction of the group or whether it might conflict with the policy of some higher echelon.

(b) Managers and Supervisors

(1) Demand written orders.

(2) "Misunderstand" orders. Ask endless questions or engage in long correspondence about such orders. Quibble over them when you can.

(3) Do everything possible to delay the delivery of orders. Even though parts of an order may be ready beforehand, don't deliver it until it is completely ready.

(4) Don't order new working materials until your current stocks have been virtually exhausted, so that the slightest delay in filling your order will mean a shutdown.

(5) Order high-quality materials which are hard to get. If you don't get them argue about it. Warn that inferior materials will mean inferior work.

(6) In making work assignments, always sign out the unimportant jobs first. See that the important jobs are assigned to inefficient workers of poor machines.

(7) Insist on perfect work in relatively unimportant products; send back for refinishing those which have the least flaw. Approve other defective parts whose flaws are not visible to the naked eye.

(8) Make mistakes in routing so that parts and materials will be sent to the wrong place in the plant.

(9) When training new workers, give incomplete or misleading instructions.

(10) To lower morale and with it, production, be pleasant to inefficient workers; give them undeserved promotions. Discriminate against efficient workers; complain unjustly about their work.

(11) Hold conferences when there is more critical work to be done.

(12) Multiply paper work in plausible ways. Start duplicate files.

(13) Multiply the procedures and clearances involved in issuing instructions, pay checks, and so on. See that three people have to approve everything where one would do.

(14) Apply all regulations to the last letter.

(c) Office Workers

(1) Make mistakes in quantities of material when you are copying orders. Conf use similar names. Use wrong addresses.

(2) Prolong correspondence with government bureaus.

(3) Misfile essential documents.

(4) In making carbon copies, make one too few, so that an extra copying job will have to be done.

(5) Tell important callers the boss is busy or talking on another telephone.

(6) Hold up mail until the next collection.

(7) Spread disturbing rumors that sound like inside dope.

(d) Employees

(1) *Work slowly.* Think out ways to in crease the number of movements necessary on your job: use a light hammer instead of a heavy one, try to make a small wrench do when a big one is necessary, use little force where consider able force is needed, and so on.

(2) Contrive as many interruptions to your work as you can: when changing the material on which you are work-ing, as you would on a lathe or punch, take needless time to do it. If you are cutting, shaping or doing other mea-sured work, measure dimensions twice as often as you need to. When you go to the lavatory, spend a longer time there than is necessary. Forget tools so that you will have to go back after them.

(3) Even if you understand the language, pretend not to understand instructions in a foreign tongue.

(4) Pretend that instructions are hard to understand, and ask to have them repeated more than once. Or pretend that you are particularly anxious to do your work, and pester the foreman with unnecessary questions.

(5) Do your work poorly and blame it on bad tools, machinery, or equipment. Complain that these things are preventing you from doing your job right.

(6) Never pass on your skill and experience to a new or less skillful worker.

(7) Snarl up administration in every possible way. Fill out forms illegibly so that they will have to be done over; make mistakes or omit requested information in forms.

(8) If possible, join or help organize a group for presenting employee problems to the management. See that the procedures adopted are as inconvenient as possible for the management, involving the presence of a large number of employees at each presentation, entailing more than one meeting for each grievance, bringing up problems which are largely imaginary, and so on.

(9) Misroute materials.

(10) Mix good parts with unusable scrap and rejected parts.

(12) *General Devices for Lowering Morale and Creating Confusion*

(a) Give lengthy and incomprehensible explanations when questioned.

(b) Report imaginary spies or danger to the Gestapo or police.

(c) Act stupid.

(d) Be as irritable and quarrelsome as possible without getting yourself into trouble.

(e) Misunderstand all sorts of regulations concerning such matters as rationing, transportation, traffic regulations.

(f) Complain against ersatz materials.

(g) In public treat axis nationals or quislings coldly.

(h) Stop all conversation when axis nationals or quislings enter a cafe.

(i) Cry and sob hysterically at every occasion, especially when confronted by government clerks.

(j) Boycott all movies, entertainments, concerts, newspapers which are in any way connected with the quisling authorities.

(k) Do not cooperate in salvage schemes.

SPECIAL OPERATIONS FIELD MANUAL —

STRATEGIC SERVICES

(Provisional)

WASHINGTON

Prepared under direction of
The Director of Strategic Services

Office of Strategic Services
Washington, D. C.
23 February 1944

This Special Operations Field Manual - Strategic Services (Provisional) is published for the information and guidance of all concerned and will be used as the basic doctrine for Strategic Services training for such subjects.

It should be carefully noted that Special Operations as defined in this Manual covers the following subjects:

(1) sabotage; (2) direct contact with and support of underground resistance groups; (3) conduct of special operations not assigned to other Government agencies and not under direct control of theater or area commanders. Special Operations do not include promotion of, or engagement in, guerrilla activities or subversive maritime activities, which will be the subjects of other pro visional basic field manuals.

The contents of this Manual should be carefully con trolled and should not be allowed to come into unauthorized hands.

AR 380-5, pertaining to handling of secret documents, will be complied with in the handling of this Manual.

William J. Donovan.

TABLE OF CONTENTS

SECTION V -SUPPLY AND COMMUNICATION

SECTION VI -COORDINATION OF SPECIAL OPERATIONS ACTIVITIES WITH THAT OF OTHER OSS BRANCHES AND THE ARMED FORCES AND OTHER AGENCIES OF THE UNITED NATIONS

SECTION VII -PLANS AND ORDER

SPECIAL OPERATIONS FIELD MANUAL
STRATEGIC SERVICES
(Provisional)

SECTION I -PRINCIPLES AND METHODS

1. *THE MISSION , OBJECTIVE, AND IMPLEMENTS*

The mission of the OSS is to plan and operate special services, (including secret intelligence, research and analysis, and morale and physical subversion) to lower the enemy's will and capacity to resist, carried on in support of military operations and in furtherance of the war effort. The mission of the Special Operations Branch is to carry out that part of the OSS mission which can be accomplished by certain physical subversive methods as contrasted with the operations of the Morale Operations, the Operational Groups, and the Maritime Unit. The primary objective of the Special Operations Branch is the destruction of enemy personnel, materiel, and installations.

2. *DEFINITIONS*

a. OVER-ALL PROGRAM FOR STRATEGIC SERVICES ACTIVITIES-a collection of objectives, in order of priority (importance) within a theater or area.

b. OBJECTIVE-a main or controlled goal for accomplishment within a theater or area by Strategic Services as set forth in an Over-all Program.

c. SPECIAL PROGRAM FOR STRATEGIC SERVICES ACTIVITIES-a statement setting forth the detailed missions assigned to one or more Strategic Services branches, designed to accomplish a given objective, together with a summary of the situation and the general methods of accomplishment of the assigned missions.

d. MISSION-a statement of purpose set forth in a special program for the accomplishment of a given objective.

e. Operational Plan - an amplification or elaboration of a special program, containing the details and means...... of carrying out the specified activities.

f. TASK-a detailed operation, usually planned in the field, which contributes toward the accomplishment of a mission.

g. TARGET-a place, establishment, group, or individual toward which activities or operations are directed.

h. THE FIELD-all areas outside of the Western Hemisphere in which Strategic Services activities take place.

i. FIELD BASE-an OSS headquarters in the field, designated by the name of the city in which it is established, e.g., OSS FIELD BASE, Cairo.

j. ADVANCED OR SUB-BASE-an additional base established by and responsible to an OSS field base.

k. OPERATIVE-an individual employed by and responsible to the OSS and assigned under special programs to field activity.

l. AGENT-an individual recruited in the field who is employed and directed by an OSS operative or by a field or sub-base.

m. COVER-an open status, assumed or bona fide, which serves to conceal the secret activities of an operative or agent.

n. Cutout-a person who forms a communicating link between two individuals, for security purposes.

o. OPERATIONAL GROUPS-a small, uniformed party of specially qualified soldiers, organized, trained, and equipped to accomplish the specific missions set forth . below.

p. RESISTANCE GROUPS -individuals associated together in enemy-held territory to injure the enemy by any or all means short of military operations, e.g., by sabotage, espionage, non-cooperation.

q. GUERRILLAS-an organized band of individuals in enemy-held territory, indefinite as to number, which conducts against the enemy operations including those of a military or paramilitary nature.

3. *METHODS*

The methods to be used by Special Operations are all measures needed to destroy enemy personnel, materiel, installations, and his will to resist. The major classifications of SO methods are;

a. Sabotage.

b. Direct contact with and support of underground resistance groups.

c. Special operations not assigned to other governmental agencies and not under direct control of theater or area commanders.

SECTION II -ORGANIZATION

4. *ORGANIZATION IN THE UNITED STATES*

The Special Operations Branch is included under Strategic Services Operations and is responsible for the following:

a. Sabotage.

b. Direct contact with and support of underground resistance groups.

c. Conduct of special operations not assigned to other governmental agencies and not under direct control of theater or area commanders.

d. Organization, equipment, and training of such individuals or organizations as may be required for operations not assigned to other governmental agencies.

5. *ORGANIZATION AT FIELD BASES*

Each field base will normally include an SO section, the head of which is responsible to the Strategic Services Officer in theaters or to the

Chief of OSS Mission in neutral countries, and which will participate in the planning and execution of SO activities in that theater or area. SO personnel both at the base and in the field will be responsible for carrying out the approved .... programs and such additional operations as may be authorized by the theater commander for that theater of area.

6. *ORGANIZATIONAL FUNCTIONS*

a. At headquarters in Washington and in the theaters of operation the SO units, assisted by other OSS units, are responsible for :

Recruiting
Planning
Administration
Staff work
Training
Supply
Liaison

b. SO in its activities will be assisted by the intelligence branches, the operating branches, Services and Communications Branches, Schools and Training Branch, Field Photographic Branch, and other OSS organizations.

7. *ORGANIZATION OF FIELD OPERATIVES*

Field operatives work individually or in groups as required by the mission and objective. Many operatives working with the underground must of necessity operate alone. Carefully selected and trained units will be organized specially for specific coup de main projects.

8. *CONTACT WITH AND SUPPORT OF UNDERGROUND RESISTANCE GROUPS*

SO operatives may assist and train agents for contact with and support of resistance groups. In order to perform this function effectively, they must ascertain the needs of the resistance groups, arrange for communications with the base and assist in the delivery of such supplies as can be obtained. On occasion it may be practical for SO operatives personally to serve as leaders of already organized resistance groups.

SECTION III -PROCUREMENT OF PERSONNEL

9. *ORGANIZATION FOR PROCUREMENT*

The SO Branch is charged with the responsibility for procurement of its personnel. Civilian clerical personnel is procured through the Services Branch, both in the United States and abroad. Other personnel, including military and naval, is procured in the United States through the Personnel Procurement Branch and at foreign bases through the Services Branch. At all times military and naval personnel must come within the approved allotment of grades and ratings for the theater set by Washington Headquarters.

10. *SOURCES FROM WHICH PERSONNEL ARE DRAWN*

SO may recruit civilians of United States or other nationalities. By agreement with the armed forces, members of the United States Army, Navy, and Marine Corps may be assigned to OSS and detailed to SO for service. Members of the armed forces of our Allies may be attached to OSS and detailed to SO for duty, in each case by agreement with the authorities of the nation concerned.

11. TYPES OF PERSONNEL REQUIRED

a. Base personnel will be either military or civilian and are individually selected for their ability to perform special functions.

b. SO agents and operatives are selected for their intelligence, courage, and natural resourcefulness in dealing with resistance groups. In addition they must have stamina to be able to live and move about undetected in their area of operation. Normally, they should be fluent in the local language and be a native of a nationality acceptable to the authorities and people of the area.

SECTION IV -TRAINING

12. *ORGANIZATION FOR TRAINING*

Basic training courses are provided by the Schools and Training Branch. The Special Operations Branch collaborates with that Branch by developing satisfactory training courses for the schools. Training is a continuous process and it is the responsibility of each SO chief, both in the United States and in the field to see that training progresses satisfactorily.

13. *SCOPE OF TRAINING*

Because of the hazardous nature of specialized technical requirements of SO, it is important that every individual in the organization receive a thorough schooling in the work he has to perform. For field operatives and all those having to do with planning, servicing, and commanding field operatives, training starts with the basic school courses which include instruction in secret intelligence and morale operations as well as special operations. Special schooling for each mission is given to the individuals assigned to it. For specific tasks schooling be comes intensive and detailed and concludes in a final briefing or instruction just prior to the execution of the task.

14. *TRAINING OBJECTIVES*

a. FOR OPERATING TECHNIQUES

The SO operative must be able to assume perfect cover or concealment. He must know how to employ underground methods of communication without undue risk to himself or others. He must know how to recruit, incite, train, and direct the operations of agents, saboteurs, resistance groups, and agents provocateur.

b. FOR SABOTAGE TRAINING

The saboteur, according to the methods he is to employ, should be skilled in sabotage by resistance, or by destruction, or against personnel, or by coup de main projects. He should be able to reach his objective, perform the act of sabotage effectively, and either avoid detection or effect an escape. He should preferably be able to incite, organize, train, and lead sabotage groups.

c. MORALE

The maintenance of high morale is the responsibility of all SO commanders and is especially important because of the hazardous, lonely work of SO operatives. From the time a recruit reports for duty until his service is at an end, building up and holding up his morale is an essential training objective for all officers who· have anything to do with the man, SO officers must be personally well-acquainted with each man in their units.

Schools and Training Branch officers will inject morale building into their training courses and SO officers will cooperate with the Schools and Training Branch following the progress of their men in the schools. During periods of inactivity or waiting, SO officers will see to it that men are kept occupied with work or diversions directed toward the tasks on which they will be employed and to the maintenance of their morale. Frequent specific checks of the status of morale of each man and each group will be made by responsible SO officers. Senior officers will inspect the units commanded by junior officers to ensure that morale is maintained.

SECTION V -SUPPLY AND COMMUNICATION

15. THE SPECIAL OPERATIONS SUPPLY PROBLEM

Covering the entire field of sabotage and resistance groups in a number of large theaters of operation means that SO is confronted with a complicated and extensive problem of supply. It will be necessary to obtain thousands of standard items included in the supply tables of the armed forces and in addition many special items necessary to sabotage, underground communication, and resistance groups. Clothing, food, medicines, arms, ammunition, demolition materials, communication equipment, naval equipment, air equipment, money, and other supplies will be necessary to SO activity.

16. ORGANIZATION FOR SUPPLY

The OSS Services Officer at field bases or in Washington fills requisitions for supplies, money, and transportation. It will not always be possible to communicate with the Services Officer, especially in active service in the field where supplies may be needed on the spot and immediately. To meet these emergencies SO officers and operatives may be supplied with special funds or through the theater commander authority may be obtained to requisition on vouchers from civilian and other sources. It is essential that all responsible SO officers and operatives have a thorough training in the handling of supplies, transportation, and money.

17. SUPPLIES FOR SABOTEURS AND RESISTANCE GROUPS

One of the greatest obstacles to underground and resistance activity is the difficulty of obtaining needed equipment, and one of the most important functions of SO is to see that the underground and resistance groups receive adequate equipment for effective operations. SO officers and operatives should maintain a continuous survey of the supply requirements of the underground and resistance groups they deal with, report such requirements to the theater or other commander, and make every effort to see that their needs are satisfied.

18. PAYMENT AND SUBSIDIES

Special funds are provided for the financial support of underground and resistance personnel. Great care must be exercised in disbursing funds for these purposes as oftentimes an individual activated by money may not be a stable character.

19. RADIO AND OTHER SIGNAL EQUIPMENT

The Communications Branch of OSS is the normal source of supply for radio and other signal equipment. All equipment of this type must be obtained through this source.

20. TRANSPORTATION

a. Arrangements for transportation of such SO military and civilian personnel as have been requested by the theater commander from the United States to theaters of operation are made through the transportation officer of the theater officer's staff. The necessary passports are secured from the Special Relations Office. Arrangements for overseas shipment of material are made through the Cargo Unit of the Services Branch.

b. Transportation of SO personnel and cargo within theaters is arranged by the Services Officer on the staff of the Strategic Services Officer. When movement of personnel or cargo is required.....where OSS services officers are not available, arrangements for transportation should be made through channels of the Army or Navy.

SECTION VI - COORDINATION OF SPECIAL OPERATIONS ACTIVITY WITH THAT OF OTHER OSS BRANCHES AND THE ARMED FORCES AND OTHER AGENCIES OF THE UNITED NATIONS

21. COOPERATION WITH OTHER OSS BRANCHES

a. GENERAL

The activities of the branches of OSS are interdependent. SO activities must be correlated with those of intelligence and the other operating branches. SO is part of the OSS team and all of its activities must be planned and executed as part of the OSS program.

b. INTELLIGENCE

SI, X-2, R&A, and FN supply information to SO. Such information will include information from the intelligence services of the armed forces and our allies. SO should obtain its own operational intelligence from the underground and resistance organizations with which they are in contact. Much of the information which SO uncovers will be useful to the intelligence services and others and should be turned over to SI. To avoid duplication of effort and the risk of discovery by the enemy, SO and SI activities in the field will be coordinated for the benefit of both services.

c. MORALE OPERATIONS

The functions of MO an SO will often overlap. Activities of SO may have an effect on the morale of our friends or enemies and SO personnel may be required to assist in MO activities in the field. This will be necessary where MO will not have a field organization, and when MO will train SO personnel to execute MO missions. Sabotage and activities of resistance groups will increase in extent and effectiveness as a resistance spirit is increased by morale operations. MO and SO must work together as each will often be able to aid the other. SO will often require the development of attitudes or states of mind and will request MO to cooperate.

22. COOPERATION WITH SIMILAR AGENCIES OF ALLIED GOVERNMENTS

Our Allies have agencies which in whole or in part parallel the functions of OSS. The governments-in-exile of enemy-occupied countries all have intelligence organizations and are in active communication with the under ground and resistance groups in occupied areas. It is the duty of OSS and SO to cooperate with the similar agencies of our Allies. It will often be necessary for SO to be the subordinate teammate of an agency of an Allied govern ment. Every effort must be made to avoid the frictions and misunderstandings which can develop so easily when agencies of Allied governments are working together on the same task.

23. COOPERATION WITH THE ARMED FORCES

The fact that the Strategic Services are under the command of the theater commander is not enough to ensure that OSS will most effectively play its part as a member of the military team. It is the responsibility of Strategic Services Officers and special operations officers and operatives to insure that all plans and activities are integrated with the plans of the theater commander. Military plans may call for drastic and sudden changes in the special operations plan and it will be necessary for operatives and officers to conform.

24. COOPERATION WITH GOVERNMENT AGENCIES

Political, diplomatic, and administrative branches of our government and the governments of our Allies participate in the war effort at home and abroad and SO operations must conform to the accepted policies and programs of these agencies. By political and diplomatic activity and through the supply of foods, medicines, and other materials, the government agencies are often in a position to assist in special operations activity. SO must never perform functions reserved to other government agencies except when duly authorized.

SECTION VII -PLANS AND ORDERS

25. *IMPORTANCE OF PLANS AND ORDERS*

SO activities must conform to the missions laid down in OSS special programs or in approved projects to be incorporated in special programs. Based upon these missions, SO must prepare, in coordination with all branches of OSS, operational plans for the accomplishment of those missions. SO must see to it that SO plans are coordinated with those of other branches. SO personnel and units must always be prepared to act promptly and decisively in furtherance of those plans when an opportunity presents itself. Unless plans are based on accurate information and worked out in exact detail, SO operatives and agents will be working at a great disadvantage. Slipshod planning will result in discovery by the enemy, heavy casualties, and failure. A failure means that SO methods will be revealed to the enemy, putting him on guard, and making it difficult or impossible to succeed after the failure.

26. *ORGANIZATION AND RESPONSIBILITY FOR THE PREPARATION OF PLANS AND ORDERS*

a. The over-all responsibility for OSS planning is stated in Section IV, Provisional Basic Field Manual for Strategic Services.

b. Within the scope of approved Strategic Services programs, the chief of the SO Branch in Washington or at a field base is responsible for the preparation of operational plans and orders covering SO activities.

Similarly, the commander or chief of any SO activity in the field is responsible for the preparation of operational plans and orders for the personnel engaged in that activity.

27. *PROCEDURE IN OPERATIONAL PLANNING*

Planning is a continuous process in which all responsible officers participate. It will be the duty of the chief of SO branch or seetio11 to develop operational plans covering the missions included in Strategic Services programs. He will also prepare operational plans for activities which the theater commander desires to have accomplished in connection with military operations, and which have not yet been included in OSS special programs. Within the limits of security control a description of such activities will be sent to OSS, Washington, to be included in OSS special programs, which are to be executed within that theater. The process of preparing operational plans and orders will vary widely according to the situation. A plan may consist of a simple verbal recommendation and an order may be an equally simple verbal instruction. Another plan may call for months of detailed preparation and the development of the corresponding orders may likewise entail laborious work. Procedure must never impede effective operation, and when the preparation of formal orders threatens to slow down action, oral orders m1Jst be used. The United States War Department Staff Officers Field Manual, FM 101-5, may be consulted with respect to forms for operational orders. The Strategic Services detachments within the theaters are subject to the direction and control of the theater commander and an adherence to military procedure will facilitate OSS work.

SECTION VIII -SABOTAGE TECHNIQUES

28. *DEFINITION*

Special Operations sabotage includes all secret physical subversive activity which destroys or impairs the effectiveness of enemy resources, production, personnel, materiel, and installations.

29. *PLANNING SABOTAGE*

The planning of sabotage will cover a large range of subjects from the most simple act to the highly scientific operation involving inconsiderable original research. Once a sabotage task has been decided upon, careful plans should be prepared for its accomplishment. The enemy will always have a defense against sabotage and no plan can succeed unless this defense is penetrated successfully. Even in the most violent and open sabotage, surprise, deception, and withdrawal are fundamental to planning,

30. *TRAINING OF SABOTEURS*

For all types of sabotage, including the most elementary, the personnel .... should be thoroughly trained in the use of sabotage implements and devices as well as concealment, deception, and withdrawal. To ... specific sabotage task individuals or groups should be specially selected, trained, and rehearsed. The details of basic train ing for sabotage are covered in the courses of the Schools and Training Branch of OSS. For the training of operatives and agents for specific tasks, information and assistance will be obtained from the intelligence services of OSS who will provide information from all other available sources, military, governmental, and civil.

31. *TYPES OF SABOTAGE*

a. INDUSTRIAL SABOTAGE

Industrial sabotage includes attacks on natural resources such as mines, oil wells, and water supply; attacks on processing and handling facilities such as refineries, smelters, factories, and warehouses; public utilities such as electric, telephone, railroad, road, water, and gas systems; and, essential supplies such as forage, foods, and medicines. Physical attacks on management and labor personnel are part of industrial sabotage.

b. MILITARY SABOTAGE

Military sabotage includes attacks on lines of communication, supplies, installations, equipment, materiel, and personnel. Included are roads, railroads, waterways, and their equipment; aircraft, airports, and their installations; radio, telephone, and telegraph systems; food, water, arms, ammunition, medical, and other supplies; key personnel, staffs, sentries, outposts, bridge and other guards.

C. POLITICAL AND PUBLIC SABOTAGE

Political and public physical sabotage covers the liquidation or physical harassment of political and administrative leaders and physical interference with their effectiveness, the demoralization or terrorization of the population by physical means, and physical attacks on collaborationists.

32. *METHODS OF SABOTAGE*

a. SABOTAGE APPLIED TO INDIVIDUALS

Includes liquidation, capture, delays, interferences, and physical attacks on personnel.

b. SABOTAGE BY DESTRUCTION

Thousands of destructive methods are available including explosions, fires, floods, wrecks, accidents, leaks, breaks, overwork of machinery, maladjustment of machinery, and the adulteration of lubricants, fuels and products.

c. SABOTAGE BY RESISTANCE

Physical resistance by riots and mob action is best conducted by native resistance groups. SO contributes by giving support, supplies, and when necessary, leadership. MO contributes by inciting and instructing resistance groups to acts which impede the enemy's military progress, such as absenteeism, slow-down in production, and other acts of passive resistance and simple sabotage. Sabotage by resistance may result in overlapping functions of MO and SO. Hence, in this field MO and SO must cooperate and coordinate their activities. (See the Provisional Basic Field Manual for Morale Operations.)

d. Coup de MAIN PROJECTS

Coup de main operations are usually attacks against important targets and are executed by a carefully selected and trained group of SO operatives.

e. DEFENSE MISSIONS

The defense mission is one that is designed to prevent the destruction of installations by the retreating · enemy. This includes protection of important bridges and tunnels; wire communications, including wires, transformers, repeater stations; power plants, radio stations, water and sewage systems. It also includes activities to prevent the mining of roads by the enemy, the blowing up of supply dumps, as well as other activities that will prevent the enemy from impeding the progress of the invading forces. Resistance groups, under the guidance of SO operatives, will be the primary agency in the accomplishment of defense missions.

SECTION IX-MISCELLANEOUS SPECIAL OPERATIONS FUNCTIONS

33. *ADDITIONAL FUNCTIONS*

As a member of the OSS-Military Team SO may be called upon to perform a variety of functions in support of the Armed Forces, other branches of OSS and governmental agencies of the United States or its allies.

34. *MORALE OPERATIONS ACTIVITY*

SO may be required to execute field activity for MO. MO activity may include: physical activity for MO effects; the subversion of important individuals; the distribution of subversive pamphlets, posters, or the marking up of slogans; the creation of riots and disturbances; the work of agents provocateur; the spreading of rumors; incitement to resistance; and countering the effects of enemy morale operations.

35. *INTELLIGENCE ACTIVITY*

SI may call upon SO to gather information and to transmit it. X-2 may ask SO operatives to assist in discovering and neutralizing the work of enemy intelligence agents.

36. *ASSISTANCE TO THE ARMED FORCES*

SO may be called upon by theater and other commanders to perform special activities such as to provide guides, interpreters, couriers, and signal men, and to defend or protect installations within the enemy areas. In support of the military plan SO may be required to create diversions with false signals, sabotage, and attacks by resistance groups for the purpose of deceiving the enemy.

37. *DIRECT CONTACT WITH AND SUPPORT OF UNDERGROUND RESISTANCE GROUPS*

SO will maintain liaison with resistance groups; to encourage, instruct, and direct them, and to supply them with munitions, food, medicines, communication equipment, and other materiel.

38. *SPECIAL OPERATIONS NOT ASSIGNED TO OTHER GOVERNMENTAL AGENCIES AND NOT UNDER THE DIRECT CONTROL OF THEATER OR AREA COMMANDERS*

From neutral areas or in areas not under a military commander, SO may recruit and train personnel or conduct operations in enemy or enemy-occupied countries as directed by Strategic Services in Washington, Chief of the OSS Mission and at field bases. For this type of operation, instructions must be clear and explicit to make sure that SO does not overstep its authority or clash with any other agency, or provoke undesirable diplomatic or political complications. The Chief of the Diplomatic Mission should be advised of such contemplated operations.

SECTION X-THE SELECTION OF SPECIAL OPERATIONS TASKS AND MISSIONS

39. *TYPES OF TASKS*

In sabotage and in contact with and support of resistance groups there is a large field of possible SO tasks, including:

a. ORGANIZATIONAL TASKS-the recruiting of agents, gaining contact with and establishing good relations with such groups, assisting in their training, organization, leadership and supply.

b. OPERATIONAL TASKS

(1) Sabotage of enemy resources, productive facilities, personnel, materiel, and installations, as well as protection of vital installations and equipment required by our own forces and the civilian population.

(2) Miscellaneous special operations tasks in support of the other branches of OSS and the Armed Forces and governmental agencies of the United States and its Allies.

40. *SELECTION OF MISSIONS TO COORDINATE WITH THE MILITARY PLAN*

As SO is a member of the OSS-Military Team it is necessary that its activities always be in proper relationship to the military plan of the commander. The status of military activities will have a direct and important bearing on the type of special operations engaged in.

a. DURING A RELATIVELY STATIC OR PREPARATORY PHASE OF MILITARY ACTIVITY

(1) Such a phase may extend over a long period of time during which the opposing forces will be gathering strength or breaking down resistance by bombing from the air and submarine warfare, or maneuvering for strategic advantages on the flanks or by the clearing of lines of communication. During a preparatory phase the activities to be engaged in depend on the situation. However, attacks on military communications, installations, and personnel can be effective during a preparatory phase when the enemy is operating in extremely hostile occupied territory, far from its home base, with limited and vulnerable lines of communication. Under such favorable circumstances, activities of resistance groups can make it extremely costly for the enemy to hold the territory and maintain communications.

(2) Industrial sabotage will reach its greatest effectiveness during a preparatory phase of military activity and the primary objectives should be those facilities whose destruction will cause maximum inconvenience to the enemy. The selection of industries to attack will depend on their relative importance to the war effort and this will depend upon the over-all production position of the enemy. Only a careful and accurate survey of the production picture, industry by industry, will enable SO to determine what objectives to attack and then a full knowledge of manufacturing techniques will be necessary before the best targets can be selected. As a general rule, critical materials and sources of supply, bottlenecks of production and vital .... transportation systems should be selected. The .... should not preclude the application of general sabotage to anything and everything which may hurt the enemy, if and when included as part of an approved program. These activities should be very carefully coordinated with air intelligence and the air bombing program.

(3) SO may also contribute to an MO program of encouraging slow-downs, mistakes, confusion, demoralization, absenteeism, riots, disturbances, and resistance of all kinds as long as they do not interfere with calculated attacks on the more important objectives.

b. DURING AND JUST PRECEDING A PERIOD OF INTENSIVE MILITARY ACTIVITY

(1) A period of intensive military activity may include air, land, or sea battles or combined operations; offensives, retreats or sieges; warfare of movement or position; landings or river crossings; and the campaign may extend over large or small areas of land or water and involve large or small forces. During such a phase SO activity should be concentrated on those missions which will give direct and immediate aid to the armed forces.

(2) Missions may include attacks on enemy personnel, materiel, and communications and they may include defenses of

communications and installations which the commander may wish to protect from enemy demolition.

(3) The selection of specific missions will depend on the situation and the military plan. Under one set of circumstances, it may be necessary for SO to concentrate all its efforts on blocking enemy transportation. When the enemy forces are not too strong and are operating in a hostile territory, a general organized resistance on the part of the civilian population may give the greatest help to the military commander. In selecting missions, every possibility should be considered and carefully examined in relation to other responsibilities and the military plans before recommendations are made.

41. *AUTHORIZED MISSIONS*

In general, SO activities will fall within the scope of its prescribed functions, as described in pars. 1 and 3, Section I. In the field, these may be modified as the theater commander requires. However, all SO missions must be included in approved programs covering the accomplishment of definite objectives.

42. *TASKS SHOULD BE PRACTICAL*

Unless it is reasonably feasible to accomplish the task assigned with the personnel and equipment available, such SO task should not be undertaken. This does not mean that SO should be unwilling to take risks. SO should always be on the offensive, planning and executing its activities in an aggressive spirit and willing to accept considerable losses and to risk failure.

43. *MISSIONS MUST BE APPROVED BY THE MILITARY COMMANDER*

The responsibility for success of military operations rests with the commander. For security reasons, it will not be possible for SO to be acquainted with all of the military plans. It is essential, therefore, that all

SO missions within theaters be acceptable to the theater commander and be approved by him.

44. CHECK LIST

In *Appendix "A"* there are summarized in the form of a check list a number of the more important points that may have been presented in this manual. This check list may serve as a brief list of reminders to SO personnel to assist them in the course of their work.

APPENDIX "A"

SPECIAL OPERATIONS FIELD MANUAL - STRATEGIC SERVICES
(Provisional)
CHECK LIST
For SO (Washington)
PLANNING

1. *AUTHORITY*

Does the projected activity conform to approved Strategic Services special programs or to additional activities approved by competent authority for inclusion in special programs?

2. *PLANNNG IN IMPLEMENTATION OF PROGRAMS*

a. Is planning complete, covering tests as to suitability, feasibility, and practicability?

b. Have provisions been made for:

    (1)   Coordination of planning with appropriate allied agencies?

    (2)   Recruiting and training of necessary personnel?

    (3)   Equipment, supplies, funds, and administrative services?

(4) Adequate communications?

(5) Transportation to the theater?

c. Have SO plans been coordinated with those of other OSS branches to ensure perfect teamwork and to avoid duplication?

d. Have these plans been approved by appropriate authority?

e. Has all pertinent intelligence been forwarded to the field for use in current and further operational plans to be made there?

f. Has the field been informed of the steps being taken by the various branches of OSS, Washington, for the implementation of the approved special program?

g. Have all standing instructions in respect of SO activities been complied with?

SUPPLIES: PROCUREMENT, TRAINING, AND EQUIPPING OF PERSONNEL

3. *SUPPLIES*

a. Has the field been consulted regarding supply requirements for the special programs?

b. Based on that information have lists of supplies and equipment required for the projected activities been prepared and submitted as a requisition to Procurement and Supplies Branch?

c. Has close liaison been maintained all the way with Procurement and Supply to determine:

(1) Availability of supplies and equipment?

(2) Time required to obtain such material?

d. Has the base been notified of what part of the supplies will be sent from Washington?

e. Has branch chief in the field been notified to initiate requests for supplies and equipment as soon as need can be foreseen?

f. Has the field been informed of new special devices and weapons that have become available since plans were made, and have descriptions of their functions and operating details been sent to the field, as well as the quantities available?

g. Has provision been made for adequate funds for the activities under this program?

4. *SUPPLIES OF OSS FUNDS AND SPECIAL EQU IPMENT FOR RESISTANCE GROUPS*

- Has the field provided detailed information regarding needs of the resistance elements for money, supplies, and equipment.

(1) What is available from stocks at the base?

(2) What has to be shipped from the U.S.?

b. Have all needed steps been taken to obtain these materials through Services -Procurement and Supply?

5. *SHIPMENT OF SUPPLIES*

a. Has theater commander approval been received from field for shipment of supplies and equipment?

b. Has field been informed of:

(1) Schedule of shipment of supplies and equipment?

(2) Shortages in the shipment?

6. *PERSONNEL AND EQUIPMENT*

· Has personnel about to be sent abroad in connection with prospective activities been examined individually for :

(1) Proper training?

(2) Proper inoculations for overseas service?

(3) Regular equipment and special equipment?

(4) Careful security check?

b. Has plausible "cover" been worked out and approved?

7. *TRAINING OF PERSONNEL*

a. Has continuous contact been kept by the SO officers with men in training? Has that contact been maintained in a manner consistent with security?

b. Has special training for the specific assignment been completed satisfactorily?

c. Has the trainee been informed as far as possible consistent with security, of his proposed assignment?

d. Has indoctrination of personnel been completed?

e. Has special emphasis been placed on security throughout the training course?

f. Are you satisfied with the security and discretion of the individual?

g. Has the individual been thoroughly ..... in his "cover" story?

h. Has provision been made for utilizing this personnel in event of delay in transportation?

8. *REPORTS*

Have you arranged with the field to send you detailed reports of :

a. Operational plans made in the implementation of special programs?

b. Successes or failures in the field in the effort to carry out the missions?

c. Effectiveness of any special devices?

d. Any new methods developed for the use of special devices?

e. Status of personnel by activities under programs?

f. Cooperation received from pertinent allied organizations?

g. Supply of resistance forces:

    (1) Supplied directly by OSS?

    (2) Supplied directly by the theater commander?

9. *TRANSPORTATION OF PERSONNEL*

a. Has theater commander approval been given to transportation schedules for personnel?

b. Have all the proper documents been prepared and all authorizations received?

c. Has overseas security check been made by OSS, Washington?

d. Has final security check been made?

e. Has final inspection been made of physical condition and equipment of personnel?

f. Has the field been notified, giving names, grades of personnel being sent, as well as the numbers that are to follow, if any, to complete the allotment for the projected activity?

CHECK LIST
For SO (Theater)
PLANNING

1. *AUTHORITY*

Does the projected activity conform to approved Strategic Services special programs or to additional activities approved by competent authority for inclusion in special programs?

2. *PLANNING IN IMPLEMENTATION OF PROGRAMS*

a. Is operational planning complete, covering tests as to suitability, feasibility, and practicability?

b. Have provisions been made for:

(1) Coordination of planning with appropriate allied agencies?

(2) Recruitment and training of necessary additional personnel?

(3) Equipment, supplies, funds, and administrative services?

(4) Adequate communications?

(5) Transportation to, within, and from the area of action?

c. Have SO plans been coordinated with those of other OSS branches to ensure perfect teamwork and to avoid duplication?

d. Has the plan been checked against pertinent intelligence from all sources?

e. Have instructions been included in the plan for training of personnel and indoctrination in security and responsibility in the projected activity?

f. Has provision been made in the plan for prompt reports of field personnel to base:

(1) Information obtained?

(2) Progress of activities?

(3) Additional assistance required supplies, funds, equipment, personnel?

g. Has provision been made in the plan for the inclusion in the required biweekly reports on all activities to SO in Washington, of:

(1) Copies of operational plans as soon as security conditions permit?

(2) Effectiveness of any special devices?

(3) New methods developed for the use of special devices?

(4) Status of personnel -by activities under programs?

(5) Cooperation received from pertinent allied organizations?

SUPPLIES: PROCUREMENT, TRAINING, AND EQUIPPING OF PERSONNEL

3. *SUPPLIES*

a. Have requirements for supplies and equipment been carefully worked out?

b. Have arrangements been made with Services to obtain in the theater what is available there from American and allied military supplies?

c. Has Services requisitioned the remaining needs from Procurement and Supplies Branch in Washington?

d. Has the final approved list been checked as to time required to get such material to the field?

e. Have descriptions of functions and operating details of latest OSS weapons been received?

f. Has requisition been made for these weapons?

g. Have required funds been requisitioned?

h. Have steps been taken to obtain required amount of foreign currency?

i. Have arrangements been made for adequate disguise and cover for personnel?

SUPPLIES OF OSS FUNDS AND SPECIAL EQUIPMENT FOR RESISTANCE GROUP

a. Is a continuing check kept of needs of resistance groups for funds, equipment, and supplies?

b. What is available from stocks at base?

c. What has to be shipped from the United States?

d. Have arrangements been made for a continuous supply service to the resistance groups?

4. *SHIPMENT OF SUPPLIES*

a. Has proper requisition been made for items mentioned in "4" above?

b. Has theater commander approval been forwarded to Washington for shipment of items?

c- Has schedule of shipments been worked out with Washington?

5. *PERSONNEL AND EQUIPMENT*

Has personnel on arrival been examined individually for :

a. Morale;

b. Physical condition;

c. Equipment;

d. Training;

e. Indoctrination;

f. Security?

6. *TRAINING OF PERSONNEL*

For personnel trained at the base, have the following points been checked carefully:

a. Has continuous contact been kept by SO officers with men in training? Has that contact been maintained in a manner consistent with security?

b. Has special training for the specific assignment been completed satisfactorily?

c. Has the trainee been informed ...... as possible, consistent with security of his proposed assignment?

d. Is the indoctrination complete?

e. Has special emphasis been placed on security throughout the training course?

f. Are you satisfied with the security and discretion of the individual?

TRANSPORTATION OF PERSONNEL

7. *AUTHORIZATION FOR TRANSPORTATION*

a. Have all the proper documents been prepared consistent with the individual's cover or protection and his proposed activities?

b. Has the individual a supply of money consistent with his cover?

c. Have arrangements for transportation of the individual to destination been worked out with military authorities?

d. Have arrangements been made to ensure establishment of the individual's secret communications with the base?

e. Have all measures covering security of individual's departure been taken?

f. Have arrangements been made for the individual's withdrawal in case of necessity or when his task is completed?

OPERATIONAL GROUPS FIELD MANUAL

– STRATEGIC SERVICES

(Provisional)

Strategic Services Field Manual No. 6

SECRET

Office of Strategic Services

Washington, D. C.

25 April 1944

This Operational Groups Field Manual — Strategic Services is made available for the information and guidance of selected personnel and will be used as the basic doctrine for Strategic Services training for the operations of these groups.

The contents of this manual should be carefully controlled and should not be allowed to come into unauthorized hands. The manual will not be taken to advance bases.

AR 380-5, 15 March 1944, pertaining to the handling of secret documents, will be complied with the handling of this manual.

William J. Donovan

Director

TABLE OF CONTENTS

SECRET

OPERATIONAL GROUPS FIELD MANUAL — STRATEGIC SERVICES

SECTION I — INTRODUCTION

1. *SCOPE AND PURPOSE OF MANUAL*

This manual sets forth the authorized functions, operational principles, methods, and organization of Operational Groups (OG's) as a part of OSS operations. Its purpose is to guide Strategic Services personnel responsible for planning, training, and operations in the proper employment of OG's.

2. *DEFINITIONS*

a. OVER-ALL PROGRAM FOR STRATEGIC SERVICES ACTIVITIES — a collection of objectives, in order of priority (importance) within a theater or area.

b. OBJECTIVE — a main or controlling goal for accomplishment within a theater or area by Strategic Services as set forth in an Over-all Program.

c. SPECIAL PROGRAM FOR STRATEGIC SERVICES ACTIVITIES — a statement setting forth the detailed missions assigned to one or more Strategic Services branches, designed to accomplish a given objective, together with a summary of the situation and the general methods of accomplishment of the assigned missions.

d. MISSION — a statement of purpose set forth in a special program for the accomplishment of a given objective.

e. OPERATIONAL PLAN — an amplification or elaboration of a special program, containing the details and means of carrying out the specified activities.

f. TASK — a detailed operation, usually planned in the field, which contributes toward the accomplishment of a mission.

g. TARGET — a place, establishment, group, or individual toward which activities or operations are directed.

1

h. THE FIELD — all areas outside of the United States in which Strategic Services activities take place.

i. FIELD BASE — an OSS headquarters in the field, designated by the name of the city in which it is established, e.g., Strategic Services Field Base, Cairo.

j. ADVANCED OR SUB-BASE — an additional base established by and responsible to an OSS field base.

k. OPERATIVE — an individual employed by and responsible to the OSS and assigned under special programs to field activity.

l. AGENT — an individual recruited in the field who is employed and directed by an OSS operative or by a field or sub-base.

m. RESISTANCE GROUPS — individuals associated together in enemy-held territory to oppose the enemy by any or all means short of military operations, e.g., by sabotage, non-cooperation.

n. GUERRILLAS — an organized band of individuals in enemy-held territory, indefinite as to number, which conducts against the enemy irregular operations, including those of a military or quasi-military nature.

3. OPERATIONAL GROUPS

a. DEFINITION

OPERATIONAL GROUPS: a small, uniformed party of specially qualified soldiers, organized, trained, and equipped to accomplish the specific missions set forth below.

b. AUTHORITY

Among the functions assigned by Joint Chiefs of Staff directive to the Office of Strategic Services are the following, which are applicable to Operational Groups:

(1) The organization and conduct of guerrilla warfare.

(2) The use of the organization and facilities of the OSS by the theater commander in his theater or

area in any manner and to the maximum extent desired by him.

c. MISSIONS OF OPERATIONAL GROUPS

The mission of Operational Groups is:

(1) To organize, train, and equip resistance groups in order to convert them into guerrillas, and to serve as the nuclei of such groups in operations against the enemy, as directed by the theater commander.

(2) In addition, under authority granted to the theater commander by the JCS Directive, Operational Groups may be used to execute independent operations against enemy targets as directed by the theater commander.

SECTION II — ORGANIZATION

4. ORGANIZATION IN WASHINGTON

a. Operational Groups are organized in Washington along strictly military lines. There is a commanding officer, responsible to the Strategic Services Operations Officer, and a staff consisting of an executive officer, an S-1 (personnel), and S-2 (intelligence and security), an S-3 (plans and training), an S-4 (supply), and a medical officer (chief surgeon and medical supply officer). There is also a training staff of variable size consisting of semi-permanent senior instructors, and junior instructors who are assigned to field duty with OG's after they have trained their successors.

b. OG Headquarters, Washington, has no direct command over OG's in the field, since they are under control and direction of the theater commander through the strategic services officer. The primary function of the OG organization in Washington is to service OG's in the field with trained personnel and supplies. OG Headquarters, Washington, also has the administrative responsibility of maintaining coordinated chronological record of OG activities.

5. *ORGANIZATION IN THE FIELD*

a. THE OPERATIONAL GROUP

(1) TABLE OF ORGANIZATION

The Operational Groups, consisting of 4 officers and 30 men, is the basic unit of OG organization. An OG normally consists of 2 sections of 2 squads each. The T/O of a typical OG is as follows:

Captain (1), commanding
First Lieutenant (3), including:
 Second-in-command of the OG (1)
 Section leader (2)
Technical sergeant (2), including:
 Second-in-command of sections (2)
Staff Sergeant (6), including:
 Squad leader (4)
 Medical technician (2)
Corporal or technician fifth grade (22), including:
 Scout (16)
 Code clerk (1)
 Courier (1)
 Radio operator (4)
Aggregate (all ranks): 34

(2) TABLE OF EQUIPMENT

In addition to standard Army clothing, OG members are issued special garments appropriate to the climate and terrain in their country of operations. Each Operational Group has a special Table of Equipment (T/E), showing the arms and other articles to be carried. This T/E varies with the theater for which the OG is bound and the missions it is expected to accomplish.

(3) SS EQUIPMENT

(a) SS weapons and demolition equipment are issued to OG's through SS supply channels in the theater, as required by their missions.

(b) Communications equipment carried by OG's consists of SS radio sets which are issued through SS supply channels in the theater.

(4) MOTORIZED VEHICLES

Although motorized vehicles are not part of the organic equipment of an OG, they may be issued in the theater when required by a mission and when it is feasible to introduce and maintain such vehicles in the area of operations.

b. THE FIELD SERVICE HEADQUARTERS

(1) TABLE OF ORGANIZATION

The Field Service Headquarters (FSHQ) is the next higher echelon of command above the Operational Group. An FSHQ is roughly comparable to the Army's battalion headquarters, and the FSHQ commanding officer directs the operations of from two to five OG's. An FSHQ is normally located outside of, but in proximity to, the enemy-held territory in which several OG's are operating. However, when conditions permit, FSHQ will be established in the area of operations. The T/O consists of the following:

Major (1), commanding
Captain (1), medical officer
First lieutenant (3), including:
    Adjutant (1)
    Communications officer (1)
    Supply officer (1)
First sergeant (1)
Technical Sergeant (6), including:
    Signal non-commissioned officer (3)
    Supply non-commissioned officer (2)
    Replacement (1)
Corporal or technician, fifth grade (16), including:
    Armorer (1)
    Automobile mechanic (1)
    Clerk typist (2)
    Code clerk-courier (6)
    Radio operator (6)
Aggregate (all ranks): 28

(2) TABLE OF EQUIPMENT

In addition to standard Army clothing, FSHQ personnel are issued special garments appropriate to the climate and terrain in their country of operations. Each FSHQ has a special T/E, showing the arms and other articles to be carried. This T/E varies with the theater in which the FSHQ is to operate and the missions it is expected to execute.

(3) SS EQUIPMENT

(a) SS weapons and demolitions equipment are issued to an FSHQ as required, through SS supply channels in the theater.

(b) Communications equipment for an FSHQ consists of SS radio sets which are issued through SS supply channels in the theater.

(4) MOTORIZED VEHICLES

Motorized vehicles are part of the organic equipment of an FSHQ and are issued through SS and military supply channels in the theater, provided it is feasible to introduce and maintain such vehicles in the area of FSHQ operations.

c. AREA HEADQUARTERS (Headquarters at OSS Field Base)

(1) TABLE OF ORGANIZATION

An Area Headquarters (AHQ), or Headquarters at OSS field base, is the next higher echelon of command above the FSHQ. It operates under direction and control of the SS officer at the OSS field base. The normal T/O of an AHQ is as follows:

Lieutenant Colonel (1), OG commanding officer
Captain (1), executive officer
First lieutenant (1), operations officer
First sergeant (1)
Technical sergeant (1), signal non-commissioned officer
Corporal or technician, fifth grade (3), including:
Clerk-typist (1)
Code clerk-courier (1)

Motorcyclist (1)

Aggregate (all ranks): 8

(2) TABLE OF EQUIPMENT

In addition to the standard Army clothing issued to personnel of the AHQ, each AHQ has a special
T/E, showing the arms and other articles to be carried. This T/E is variable, depending on the theater
of operations.

(3) SS EQUIPMENT

(a) Stockpiles of SS weapons and demolitions
equipment are normally set up at an AHQ to supply Field Service Headquarters and OG's in areas
of operations.

(b) Since the AHQ is located at an OSS field
base, communications to and from AHQ are generally handled by the field base message center.

(4) MOTORIZED VEHICLES

Motorcycles, trucks, and trailers needed for
operations at AHQ are supplied through SS and military supply channels in the theater.

SECTION III — PERSONNEL

6. ORGANIZATION FOR RECRUITMENT

a. Members of OG's procured in the United States
are officers or enlisted men who have been inducted into
the Army through regular channels. Under War Department approval, and within War Department allotment of grades and ratings, selection is made of such
personnel by trained interviewers of the Personnel Procurement Branch (PPB), OSS, according to specifica-
tions submitted by Headquarters, Operational Groups,
Washington. PPB interviewers examine the civil and
military records of likely candidates and hold personal
interviews. Candidates who are acceptable are ordered
to an SS area to begin training, pending security clearance. This procedure in no way violates security, as the

7

SECRET

training initially given is an extension of Army training. No specialized strategic services instruction is given until the security check has been completed.

b. It will sometimes be necessary to procure OG personnel directly in the theater where they will operate. This procedure is applicable when persons cannot be found in the United States who are qualified in a particular language, knowledge of a certain locality, and other essentials. When an OG must be staffed in the theater, the work of procurement will usually be done by a cadre from the U.S. consisting normally of 2 officers and 5 men, with the following T/O: 1 captain, 1 first lieutenant, 1 first sergeant, 1 staff sergeant, 1 sergeant, and 2 radio operator technicians, fourth or fifth grade (specification serial No. 777). This cadre will attempt to recruit and train in the theater sufficient personnel to comprise standard OG's of 4 officers and 30 men each. However, the T/O may be reduced in strength for OG's recruited in the field depending on the availability of qualified personnel. Civilians recruited for OG's in the field will be enlisted or commissioned in the Army of the U.S. and will wear its uniform. The procurement of all personnel for OG's within theaters must be within the limitations of authorized grades and ratings.

7. QUALIFICATIONS OF OG PERSONNEL

The following considerations will govern selection of personnel for Operational Groups:

a. WILLINGNESS TO PERFORM HAZARDOUS DUTY

Because of the nature of their assignments, all members of OG's must be willing to undertake unusual and dangerous risks. Candidates must be adequately informed of the hazards they may expect, and must be accepted only on a volunteer basis.

b. LANGUAGE ABILITY

It is normally preferable that the candidate speak the required language as a native tongue, or with great fluency. In some cases, however, e.g., radio operators, language facility must be sacrificed for other valuable qualifications.

c. FAMILIARITY WITH COUNTRY OF OPERATIONS

Since OG's may have to enter territory without benefit of a friendly local reception committee, previous acquaintance with the country of operations is highly desirable, especially if such acquaintance is of recent date. OG personnel with friends or relatives who might provide concealment and guidance are especially valuable.

d. SKILLS

As many men as possible in each OG should be qualified in certain specialized fields. Previous training on radio, demolitions, weapons, scouting, or fieldcraft is a particularly desirable qualification in a candidate.

e. PHYSICAL CONDITION

The rigorous character of their work demands that OG personnel satisfy the same physical requirements as men accepted for parachute training in the Army.

f. POLITICAL SYMPATHIES

Persons charged with procurement of OG personnel must use great care in the case of individuals who are sympathetic to particular political movements or factions within the country of their origin. The readiness and ability of such individuals to get along harmoniously with the movement or faction in the area of operations must be carefully determined in advance. In certain areas, however, where disputes are bitter, and the areas of rivals not delineated, it is more desirable to staff an OG with American citizens whose language ability is somewhat imperfect rather than with ex-natives of the area who have pronounced political attachments.

g. CHARACTER TRAITS

While the risks involved tend to make OG work appeal to young men, the success of OG assignments

SECRET

is not the result of daring and bravado alone. Accordingly, candidates will be selected whose past records, civilian and military, give evidence of stability and good judgment.

h. ARMY TRAINING

Except for certain specially qualified persons recruited in the field (see paragraph 6.b.) candidates must have completed basic training before being accepted for OG work. Candidates who have also had combat training are preferable.

SECTION IV — TRAINING

8. GENERAL PROCEDURE

OG training is an intensive course of specialized instruction in the weapons, techniques, and methods of operation appropriate for a small, self-sufficient band of men who may be required to live and fight in the manner of guerrillas. OG training comes under the general supervision of the Schools and Training Branch, but the actual instruction is given by OG personnel, based on schedules drawn up by the OG training officer. An OG is assembled prior to the start of training according to the common foreign language of its members; thereafter, the group trains, lives and operates as a unit. The officers who will lead an OG in the field assists in training its personnel. The training period in the U.S. is normally three weeks. One additional week is allowed for the clearance of administrative details. The group is then ready for embarkation to the theater of operations. An OG is rarely used immediately upon its arrival overseas. The normal time delay involved is utilized for further training, as dictated by the particular mission to be performed. This training will emphasize tactical problems and may include parachute jumping or amphibious operations if either of these means of entry is to be used. Overseas training is usually conducted by OG officers.

9. TRAINING OBJECTIVES

The objectives of OG training are as follows:

a. To train specially qualified bi-lingual officers and enlisted men in the techniques and skills required to execute their prescribed missions in enemy or enemy-occupied territory.

b. To weld this personnel into an efficient, mobile, self-sufficient unit capable of:

(1) organizing and training local resistance groups with a view to converting them into guerrillas;

(2) supplying such guerrillas withs arms, ammunition, demolition, communication equipment, food, medical supplies, and money;

(3) serving as nuclei in planning and execution by native elements of attacks against enemy forces or installations, as directed by the theater commander;

(4) executing independent operations, usually of a "hit-and-run" character, against enemy targets as directed by the theater commander.

c. To develop in each member of an Operational Group the physical strength, individual initiative, and ability to improvise, which his missions will demand.

10. CURRICULUM

a. Members of Operational Groups should receive adequate training in the following subjects:

(1) Map study, including map sketching map-and-compass problems, direction-finding by field expedients, study of aerial photos.

(2) Scouting and patrolling, including instruction and practice in use of physical cover, reconnaissance, signalling, infiltration.

(3) Close combat (armed and unarmed), including knife-fighting.

(4) Physical conditioning, including swimming, toughening exercises, and obstacle course runs.

(5) Fieldcraft, including camouflage, living off the land, preparation of shelter and food.

(6) Hygiene and camp sanitation.

(7) Tactics, including basic maneuvers and tactical principles, discussion and practice in small-group operations and methods of guerrilla warfare, day and night problems, planning and execution of airborne raids, street and village fighting, jungle fighting (when applicable).

(8) Demolitions, including explosives, incendiaries, booby traps, field expedients, delayed action charges, multiple charges, charges for special purposes.

(9) Weapons, including function, stripping, cleaning, and firing of .30 cal. M1 rifle, cal. .30 carbine, cal. .30 machine gun, cal. .50 machine gun, Browning automatic rifle, cal. .45 pistol, Sten gun, cal. .45 submachine gun, grenade launcher, 2.36-inch anti-tank rocket launcher (bazooka), Marlin submachine gun, 60 mm. mortar, 81 mm. mortar, hand grenades. Also the function and firing of enemy weapons with which group may come into contact.

(10) Principles and practice of first aid, especially under combat conditions.

(11) Enemy motor transportation, including operation and repair of enemy motorcycles, trucks, automobiles, half-tracks, and other vehicles with which group may come into contact.

(12) Enemy organization, including lectures on enemy military and political structure, uniforms, insignia, procedure in interrogating prisoners, methods of espionage and counter-espionage.

(13) Methods of organizing and training civilians in the techniques of guerrilla warfare; indoctrination as to correct general attitude and behavior toward the civilians.

(14) Identification of enemy and Allied planes, tanks, and other vehicles.

(15) Care of clothing and equipment.

(16) Security, including precautions to be observed in U.S., in the theater, and in area of operations.

(17) Problems of supply, including the procedure of procuring supplies from OSS stocks, methods of packaging, and the details regarding the introduction and receipt of cargo into the zone of operations.

b. The basic training of OG's preparation will be supplemented in the theater immediately prior to operations by a detailed briefing on topography, battle order, friendly and hostile groups that may be encountered, and other matters pertinent to the operation to be performed.

c. In addition to the training outlined in paragraph a. above, radio operators for each OG should receive intensive practice in code, operational procedure, and repair of their equipment.

11. *MAINTENANCE OF MORALE*

In view of the extreme hazards of OG operations, maintenance of morale assumes a special importance. Every effort should be made throughout the training period to keep the aggressive spirit and confidence of OG personnel at a high level. The men should be kept steadily occupied, either with training tasks or with organized group recreation. Following the completion of their training, OG's will be shipped to their theater of operations as expeditiously as possible, to avoid the staleness and dissatisfaction which inevitably result from idleness or a monotonous repetition of training. All means available will be used to foster intimate friendship, mutual confidence, and teamplay among members of the group, and a strong feeling of trust between officers and men.

13

SECTION V — OPERATIONS

12. *GENERAL*

a. OG's operate only in enemy or enemy-occupied territory. Their primary function is in connection with guerrillas. They have no operational function in neutral territory.

b. The following operational distinctions exist between the OG and SO Branches:

(1) While SO operating personnel may or may not be members of the armed forces, may or may not be in uniform, and operate as individuals or in small groups, OG personnel are always members of the armed forces, always operate in uniform, and conduct operations as a unit. When any individual OG personnel is selected to perform SO tasks and function, he will operate under cover and will become part of SO personnel.

(2) OG's, being military organizations, operate in accordance with military principles and on occasion will deliberately engage hostile armed forces. On the other hand, SO personnel in enemy-held territory operate under cover, except in unusual circumstances, and attempt to avoid all contact with enemy forces.

(3) Both OG and SO personnel deal with resistance groups. SO carries on a strictly covert relationship with such groups and organizes them for such tasks as attritional sabotage. OG's on the other hand, train, organize, and equip resistance groups to operate as guerrillas against enemy forces.

13. *TYPES OF OG OPERATIONS*

a. As set forth in paragraph 3-c, OG's have two broad missions. These missions determine the pattern of their operations.

(1) The primary mission of OG's is to organize, train, and equip resistance groups in order to convert

them into guerrillas, and to serve as the nuclei of such groups in operations against the enemy as directed by the theater commander.

(a) *Organizing*

Normally before OG's enter a territory contact must have been established with resistance elements, and their potentialities and needs for supplies and equipment ascertained. This can be accomplished by use of OSS clandestine agents, primarily SO, or by representatives abroad of resistance elements who are brought out for this purpose. Such resistance elements range from small, loosely organized and poorly equipped bands of individuals to large quasi-military organizations with insufficient equipment. When organization is inadequate, the main function of OG's is to weld the individuals into a guerrilla unit that can contribute to the support of military operations. Organizing such guerrilla units may involve selecting leaders, assigning individuals or units to various areas of operation, constituting demolition or sabotage teams as the situation may require, providing for communications and courier services. While providing guidance and over-all direction is an OG responsibility, the actual leadership will usually be entrusted to local individuals. Where guerrilla activity is already well developed, the OG's work of organizing consists primarily of coordinating the operations of guerrilla bands with allied military plans. In certain areas, OG's may encounter guerrillas whose effectiveness is reduced by partisan differences. Although OG's will avoid local political controversy and will emphasize their essentially military role, they may, by their ability to furnish supplies, be effective in achieving a measure of coordinated effort among estranged groups.

(b) *Training*

The work of OG's will be mainly with civilians who are largely ignorant of military dis-

15

cipline, tactics, and weapons. Briefly stated, the
training objective of OG's is to transform these
resisters into efficient guerrillas. Within the limitations of local conditions, OG's must find ways to
instruct and give practice to the patriots in such
subjects as the use of weapons, close combat,
scouting and patrolling, demolition, radio operation, first aid, sabotage, and physical conditioning.
For obvious reasons this training should, if possible,
be conducted in areas unoccupied by enemy troops,
such as isolated mountain or forest regions. One of
the most important OG training tasks will be in-
doctrinating civilians in the necessity of avoiding
premature action and preserving their numbers
for coordinated use at the proper time.

(c) *Equipping*

Need for additional equipment will often
arise after arrival of OG's in the zone of operations.
OG officers will transmit requisitions or requests
for requirements either to their Field Service Headquarters, if established, or the OSS field base.

(d) *Serving as Operational Nuclei for Guerrilla Warfare*

In theaters where active military operations are being conducted, the plans covering
guerrilla operations, including supply, must be
approved by the theater commander. In areas
where military operations are not being conducted,
the nature and timing of guerrilla operations conducted by native groups under OG direction will be
coordinated insofar as possible with the desires of
the theater commander. In some areas it may be
desirable to attack industrial or other targets at
the earliest possible moment; in other regions, the
theater commander may consider it essential for
the groups to remain inactive until they can be
employed in support of Allied military operations.
In either case, the authorized function of OG's is to
serve as the core of a larger group composed pre-

16

dominantly of members of the local population. As indicated in paragraph **5**, OG's are sub-divided into sections and squads. These smaller units will attempt to insure proper leadership and guidance for the native guerrillas whom they have trained. Typical operations by these groups might include tasks such as attacks on and demolition of a power-house or oil dump as well as the marking and hold-ing of landing beaches and cutting of enemy communications.

(2) The secondary mission of OG's is to execute operations, usually of a "hit-and-run" character, against enemy targets as directed by the theater commander. It will be seen that this mission takes in a broad range of activity. Thus, OG's might conceiv-ably be used by the theater commander to: attack an enemy headquarters; harass an enemy withdrawal; destroy enemy stores; blow up a factory; demolish a radar installation—or any one of a number of similar tasks. It is characteristic of OG operations under this category that they may or may not be closely tied in to large-scale military operations.

14. *OPERATIONAL PROBLEMS*

a. CONTACT WITH RESISTANCE GROUPS

OG's assigned to organize and train resistance ele-ments into guerrillas usually will enter the area of operations only after preliminary contact thru clandes-tine agents with such groups has been established and arrangements made for reception of the OG's. This con-tact may be made by SO or SI operatives or agents.

b. ENTRY INTO AREA OF OPERATIONS

The manner of entry will be determined by the terrain of the area of operations, the tightness of enemy surveillance, and the transportation available. Entry may be made by parachute, by small boat or submarine, or by infiltration of an enemy area on foot. OG's will be given special training in the theater, appropriate to the

17

means of entry chosen. OG's will normally be received and guided at the point and time of entry by sympathizers with whom contact has previously been established (paragraph a above).

c. COMMUNICATIONS

As soon after entry as is feasible, OG's will make radio contact with FSHQ, if established, or with the base, according to an arranged schedule for periodic future contact. Communications will be maintained by FSHQ with all OG's functioning in the area of operations which it controls, as well as with Area Headquarters at the field base. Messages to and from Area Headquarters are handled by the field base message center. OG's will not normally attempt to communicate with any higher echelon than FSHQ. When an OG is divided into squads which operate in separate parts of the same area, contact may have to be maintained with the commanding officer of the group by radio. However, because of the risks of location by the enemy, radio traffic should be kept to a minimum. Elements of an OG may find it possible to keep in touch with each other more securely by establishing a courier service, utilizing local civilians, rather than by using radio. OG's in enemy-held territory will normally operate on foot, although in some isolated areas enemy surveillance may be so light as to permit a limited use of horses or even local motorized vehicles.

d. SUPPLY

OG's usually carry into an area of operations only such equipment as they need for their own use. OG's will survey the local status of supply, and, basing estimates upon needs previously reported and consequent preliminary plans for supply of the resistance forces, will report any additional immediate requirements by priorities. They should also report on whether the previously agreed place and means for introduction of supplies is feasible and should furnish necessary modifications.

e. CONCEALMENT

Since OG personnel operate in uniform they must

rely on concealment and secrecy to safeguard their operations. Concealment is of particular importance to OG's because they are small in number and can be severely weakened by the loss of even a few men. Prior to their entry, OG's should be issued camouflage clothing appropriate to the season and terrain. OG's will be obliged in most cases to avoid cities and towns where the enemy or his agents may be encountered. Semi-permanent concealment in mountainous or forested areas may be available, and native sympathizers will be induced to provide hiding-places in their homes and barns when this is feasible. In some areas enemy controls may be so rigid as to compel OG's to keep on the move, changing bivouac sites frequently.

f. SECURITY

The enemy has established efficient espionage and counter-espionage organizations in all the occupied countries. These networks, coupled with the enemy-controlled local police and local informers, will frequently be more dangerous to the security of OG's than will the enemy's regular troops. Before OG's enter an area all possible investigations will be made as to the security of the resistance groups with whom OG's are working, but OG's must be alert to the danger of possible penetration by enemy agents. OG's should have contact only with those individuals whom resistance group leaders can personally vouch for as loyal. So far as possible, the location and operations of OG personnel should be kept secret from the families of resistance group members who are being trained and organized by OG's.

SECTION VI — COOPERATION OF OG WITHIN OSS AND WITH OTHER ORGANIZATIONS

15. COOPERATION WITH THE INTELLIGENCE SERVICE

a. The planning and execution of OG missions are based upon reliable intelligence, furnished primarily by the SI and X-2 Branches and the Research and Analysis Branch (R&A). Liaison between OG and these branches is maintained in Washington and in the theaters; it is most important in the theaters because all operational planning for OG's is done there. R&A provides basic intelligence with respect to topography, industrial targets, the structure of enemy military and political organization, and the attitudes of the people in the area of OG operations. For briefing purposes, SI furnishes up-to-the-minute intelligence concerning locations of enemy units and installations in the area of operations, the strength, location, and personnel of guerrilla and resistance groups that will be encountered, and such other data as is pertinent to the mission at hand. X-2 supplements this with intelligence regarding enemy espionage agents and networks which may jeopardize OG operations.

b. Although procurement of intelligence is not normally an OG task, OG's functioning behind enemy lines will frequently obtain information by reconnaissance and from the local population which will be relayed through channels to the appropriate OSS and military intelligence organizations.

16. COOPERATION WITH OTHER OSS OPERATIONS BRANCHES

a. OG must work in closest collaboration with SO. The integration of OG operations with this branch is achieved in Washington through the strategic services Operations officer, and in the field by the strategic services officer for each theater.

b. OG operations must be largely dependent upon SO operatives and agents who develop preliminary contacts with and make preliminary investigations of underground resistance groups prior to the entry of OG's into an area of operations.

17. COOPERATION WITH SIMILAR AGENCIES OF ALLIED NATIONS

Cooperation as to any joint activities with other Allied organizations conducting irregular warfare will be arranged through the strategic services officer.

SE~~C~~RET

SECTION VII — PLANNING

18. *PLANNING IN WASHINGTON*

<u>a</u>. Special Programs covering OG activities in a Theater of Operations are incorporated into OSS Over-all Programs. In the Over-all Program for a given theater, the objectives for all the OG branches concerned are set forth in order of importance. The Special OG Programs state the missions to be performed by OG to attain the objectives listed in the Over-all Program, present a brief summary of the situation bearing on the missions in question, and prescribe in a general way the plan to be followed. These Special OG Programs are drawn up jointly by the Strategic Services Planning Staff and the OG Branch, and are presented to the Strategic Services Planning Group for approval. Upon approval by the Planning Group, the Programs are submitted to the Director, OSS, for his consideration and approval before being transmitted to the theater or senior American commander in the field through the strategic services officer.

<u>b</u>. Upon approval of theater commanders, OG Programs establish priorities for OG operations in the field. In conformity with these programs, OG prepares detailed operational plans.

<u>c</u>. When plans covering OG activities in the field are made which are not in furtherance of missions set forth in Special Programs, such plans are reported to OSS, Washington, for consideration and incorporation into an appropriate program, consistent with security control.

19. *PLANNING IN THEATERS OF OPERATIONS*

Operational planning for OG's is performed in the field, in the implementation of missions of approved special programs covering OG activities. Such planning should cover the details listed in paragraph 14. The nature of OG operations makes teamwork essential and requires that planning be executed in the most minute detail possible.

20. *CHECK LIST*

In Appendix "A" there are summarized in the form of a check list a number of the more important points that have been presented in this manual. This check list may serve as a brief list of reminders to OG personnel to assist them in the course of their work.

APPENDIX "A"

TO

OPERATIONAL GROUPS FIELD MANUAL —

STRATEGIC SERVICES

CHECK LIST FOR OG OPERATIONS

This check list is designed to assist the OG Branch, Washington, and Operational Groups in the field in planning, training, and operating.

FOR OG, WASHINGTON

1. *PROCUREMENT OF PERSONNEL*

a. Is the request for procurement and training of personnel for OG's approved by proper authority?

b. Does the allotment of officers and enlisted men to OG permit the procurement of the numbers requested by the strategic services officer?

c. Are qualified individuals available in the U.S. Army?

d. Can suitable personnel be procured in the time available?

e. Have detailed requests been submitted to the Personnel Procurement Branch, OSS, for procurement of personnel?

f. Is the OSS area in which the OG's are initially to be received properly staffed and equipped to receive them?

g. Have the required numbers of suitable personnel been procured and dispatched to the holding area?

h. Have personnel been procured for Field Service Headquarters?

2. *TRAINING*

a. Have all members of the OG's received basic military training?

b. Are suitable OG instructors available and assigned?

c. Has training schedule been coordinated with Schools and Training Branch?

d. Does the standard curriculum for OG's require addition of specialized training for a particular Group? If so, where is it to be accomplished?

e. Is the training area prepared to receive the OG's?

f. Are there any unqualified or unsuitable individuals who should be dropped from the OG's? Are replacements available?

g. Has training accomplished its objectives?

h. Are abilities properly recognized by assignment of ranks and grades within the groups?

i. Has the strategic services officer been informed of the training given OG's to be assigned to his theater?

j. Has personnel of Field Service Headquarters been given adequate training?

3. *SUPPLY AND EQUIPMENT*

a. Has each member of the OG's complete standard army clothing and equipment and special items of individual equipment prescribed?

b. Has each OG complete equipment as prescribed by its approved T E?

c. Has each Field Service Headquarters the equipment and supplies prescribed by its T E?

23

d. Has each Area Headquarters the equipment and supplies prescribed by its T/E?

e. Is special OSS equipment required for the OG's available in the theater?

(1) If so, have requisitions been received and when will the equipment and supplies be shipped? Has the strategic services officer been given complete information?

f. Is any equipment requisitioned unavailable? When will it be available? Has the strategic services officer been informed?

g. What is the schedule of future shipments of supplies and equipment?

h. Is a Table of Equipment sent to the Port of Embarkation with each OG?

4. *MORALE*

a. What is the state of morale in the OG's during training?

b. Is personal contact maintained with the trainees and are facilities available for handling individual morale cases?

c. Are the trainees conscious of the seriousness and the importance of the work?

d. Are periods for rest, relaxation, and diversion provided?

e. Has the schedule been arranged so that there will be no prolonged periods of idleness?

f. Will the OG's depart for the theater promptly after the training period? If early departure is impossible have further training or useful duties been scheduled?

5. *SECURITY*

a. Has each member of the OG's received a security check while he is at the holding area and prior to his specialized OG training?

24

SECRET

b. Has the trainee evidenced a sufficient appreciation of security in training?

c. Has each member of the OG's received a security check for overseas service?

6. TRANSPORTATION

a Have all arrangements been completed to transport the OG's to the theater promptly after training is completed?

(1) Theater commander's approval?

(2) T/O's and T/E's complete?

(3) Inoculations and physical examinations completed?

b. Has an OG roster been sent to the strategic services officer?

c. Has the strategic services officer been informed when additional personnel requested will be transported?

7. REPORTS

a. Are reports on OG operations received from the field?

b. Do reports indicate that the operations of OG's conform to approved Strategic Services over-all and special programs?

c. Are the reports from the field complete and in the prescribed form?

25

CHECK LIST

FOR OG's, THEATER

1. PLANNING

a. Do the projected operations conform to approved Strategic Services over-all and special programs?

b. Has the operational plan been approved and co-ordinated by proper authority?

c. Is all available intelligence considered and plans kept up to date?

d. Has a system of supply been determined?

2. PERSONNEL

a. Is Field Service Headquarters present and organized to administer control over OG's?

b. Are the OG's up to strength? If not, can the required additional personnel be procured in the theater?

c. Is the organization of OG's complete and in conformity with the T/O?

d. Have the personnel of the OG's been inspected individually to determine their morale and physical fitness?

3. TRAINING

a. Have the OG's received all specialized training required for the tasks assigned?

b. Has the training of specialists been adequate to enable them to perform their individual duties?

c. Has the training of the personnel of Field Service Headquarters and Area Headquarters prepared these organizations properly to perform their functions?

26

SECRET

4. SUPPLY AND EQUIPMENT

a. Are the OG's, Field Service Headquarters, and Area Headquarters fully equipped in conformity with the T/E's?

b. Is the required special OSS equipment available? If not, have requisitions been submitted? When will it be received?

c. Is the individual equipment of the OG's complete and in order?

d. Has a detailed supply plan been made for each task?

5. REPORTS

a. Have detailed reports, within the limits of security control, been sent to OSS, Washington?

27

Nº 7

MARITIME UNIT FIELD MANUAL –

STRATEGIC SERVICES
(Provisional)

Prepared under direction of
The Director of Strategic Services

SECRET

SECRET

MARITIME UNIT FIELD MANUAL
– STRATEGIC SERVICES
(Provisional)

Strategic Services Field Manual No. 7

SECRET

SECRET

Office of Strategic Services

Washington, D. C.

18 July 1944

This Provisional Basic Field Manual for Maritime Unit is made available for the information and guidance of selected personnel and will be used as the basic doctrine for Strategic Services training for the operations of these groups.

The contents of this manual should be carefully controlled and should not be allowed to come into unauthorized hands. The manual will not be taken to advance bases.

AR 380—5, pertaining to the handling of secret documents, will be complied with in the handling of this manual.

William J. Donovan

Director

TABLE OF CONTENTS

SECRET

MARITIME UNIT FIELD MANUAL
STRATEGIC SERVICES
(Provisional)

SECTION I—INTRODUCTION

1. *SCOPE AND PURPOSE OF THE MANUAL*

This manual sets forth the authorized functions, operational plans, methods, and organization of Maritime Units (MU) as a part of OSS operations. Its purpose is to guide Strategic Services personnel responsible for planning, training, and operations in the proper employment of Maritime Units.

2. *DEFINITIONS*

a. OVER-ALL PROGRAM FOR STRATEGIC SERVICES ACTIVITIES—a collection of objectives, in order of priority (importance) within a theater or area.

b. OBJECTIVE—a main or controlling goal for accomplishment within a theater or area by Strategic Services as set forth in an Over-All Program.

c. SPECIAL PROGRAM FOR STRATEGIC SERVICES ACTIVITIES—a statement setting forth the detailed missions assigned to one or more Strategic Services branches, designed to accomplish a given objective, together with a summary of the situation and the general methods of accomplishment of the assigned missions.

d. MISSION—a statement of purpose set forth in a special program for the accomplishment of a given objective.

e. OPERATIONAL PLAN—an amplification or elaboration of a special program, containing the details and means of carrying out the specified activities.

f. TASK—a detailed operation, usually planned in the field, which contributes toward the accomplishment of a mission.

g. TARGET—a place, establishment, group, or individual toward which activities or operations are directed.

1

h. THE FIELD—all areas outside of the United States in which strategic services activities take place.

i. FIELD BASE—an OSS headquarters in the field, designated by the name of the city in which it is established, e.g., OSS Field Base, London.

j. ADVANCED OR SUB-BASE—an additional base established by and responsible to an OSS Field Base, London.

k. OPERATIVE—an individual employed by and responsible to the OSS and assigned under special programs to field activity.

l. AGENT—an individual recruited in the field who is employed and directed by an OSS operative or by a field or sub-base.

m. PARENT CRAFT—the medium by which personnel and supplies are transported from the base to within Maritime Unit operational distance of their objective.

SECTION II—OPERATIONS AND METHODS

3. MISSIONS

    a. To conduct clandestine ferrying.

    b. To conduct maritime sabotage.

    c. To provide military tactical assistance.

    d. To conduct special training by Maritime Unit.

4. CLANDESTINE FERRYING

    a. GENERAL—Penetrations into and departures from enemy areas by water will be the specific responsibility of MU. The responsibility essentially will be to effect the transfer of personnel, supplies, and communications from water to land and land to water. Such ferrying which will normally be clandestine may be considered in two stages: approach and departure by parent craft, transfer to and from parent craft.

    b. APPROACH TO ENEMY SHORE—This can be by a parent craft of sufficient range and other characteristics necessary to get within small boat or swimming distance of enemy shore. Parent craft may be submarine, de-

2

stroyer, torpedo boat, or other conveyances. Parent craft may be detailed by U.S. Navy or other Allied armed forces either for specific tasks or regular operations. Parent craft may also be native or other vessels acquired by OSS.

c. TRANSFER OF PERSONNEL AND MATERIEL TO AND FROM PARENT CRAFT TO SHORE—This may be by swimming, surfboard, rubber boat, dinghy, or other small surface craft.

5. MARITIME SABOTAGE

Maritime sabotage against enemy shipping and shipping installations in harbors, roadsteads, canals, and rivers, will be executed with limpets and other special underwater demolitions and with standard demolitions. Special Maritime Groups of swimmers are trained to conduct underwater sabotage. However, MU personnel will also participate in maritime sabotage by ferrying demolitions parties to targets or target areas.

6. MILITARY TACTICAL ASSISTANCE

a. GENERAL—Where unique techniques and abilities of MU (such as underwater approach and clandestine ferrying and maritime sabotage) are required by a military commander in his theater, such aid by MU shall be furnished as requested of OSS by the theater commander.

b. SPECIAL TACTICAL AIDS—MU sections, when adequately manned at the theater base, may render the following clandestine aid to military operations: (1) hydrographic and beach reconnaissance; (2) establishing navigation aids, especially close to shore; (3) infiltration and exfiltration of personnel.

7. SPECIAL TRAINING BY MARITIME UNIT

a. GENERAL—MU will assist Schools and Training Branch by providing instructors and equipment for the training of other OSS personnel and military personnel in special MU techniques, upon request.

b. OSS PERSONNEL—Where operatives or agents have to be infiltrated or exfiltrated by water, they will be

3

trained (usually in the theater) by S&T to enable them to effect the transition from water to shore and vice versa. MU will provide instructors and equipment to assist in such training. Other MU techniques will be taught to OSS personnel of other branches as required for their special tasks.

c. MILITARY PERSONNEL—Where specific MU techniques and equipment are of special use to military commanders in their theater and where training in MU techniques is requested by the military commander through OSS, the MU Section in the theater will provide instructors and equipment to assist S&T in such training.

8. EQUIPMENT

a. Specially designed equipment for use under water and on the surface includes self-contained breathing devices, motor propelled surfboards, swim suits, swim fins, two and eight place kayaks, depth gauge, underwater luminous compass, underwater flashlight, electric waterproof motor for use on surf boards and rubber boats. Detailed descriptions of this special equipment are given in a secret pamphlet "Underwater Operations" prepared for the Maritime Unit, December 1943.

b. Standard military and OSS demolitions are used. A principal type is the limpet; the OSS magnetic type and the "pin up" limpet. Military equipment and supplies, such as rations, clothing, small arms, ammunition, and the like will be supplied from U.S. Army or Navy sources in the theaters. Special OSS explosives and equipment will be supplied by Services Branch, OSS.

SECTION III—ORGANIZATION AND PLANNING

9. BRANCH AND FIELD BASE ORGANIZATION

a. WASHINGTON—The Chief of MU Branch, Washington, is directly responsible to the Deputy Director, SSO for the carrying out of MU operations. He is assisted by a Deputy Chief, an Operations Officer, a Supply Officer, and a Personnel Officer. Liaison in Washington with

4

British Commander Combined Operations is maintained through appropriate officers of that nation in contact with the Chief, MU, or any representative designated by him.

b. ORGANIZATION OF FIELD BASES—

(1) The organization of MU at OSS field bases will vary in accordance with local conditions and requirements, but generally they will reflect the structure of the MU Branch, Washington.

(2) The MU Section of an OSS field base is headed by a Chief who is responsible to the Strategic Services Officer.

(3) The Operations Officer of the MU Section of an OSS field base is responsible for planning and coordination of operations with naval vessels detailed to OSS tasks. In the case of naval units, they will be administratively and operationally under the Navy.

(4) All activities of a field base in a theater of operations are under the control and direction of the theater commander.

10. *PLANNING AND ORGANIZATION FOR OPERATIONS*

a. The approved OSS over-all and special programs establish the objectives and missions for MU. Operational plans are developed by MU in the field in conformity with the approved special programs.

b. The MU section in the field assembles personnel and equipment required to accomplish specific missions based upon operational plans developed in accordance with approved special programs.

c. All MU plans and operations are coordinated with the activities of other branches by the Chief of the MU Branch in Washington, and by the Chief of the MU sections at the various field bases. MU advises and assists other branches on any project with maritime phases.

d. MU Branch in Washington is to be kept fully informed of all MU plans and projects for operations originating in the field.

5

SECTION IV—PERSONNEL

11. *REQUIREMENTS*

a. The duties of personnel selected for MU activities divide into four general types:

(1) Staff work at the branch in Washington or in the MU Section at a field base.

(2) Assisting S&T in instruction in special MU techniques.

(3) Maritime operations.

(4) Special underwater swimming activities.

b. For all of these types of activities personnel should be such that the MU special training can be assimilated and employed effectively. For the first three types of duties it is important that the personnel have seafaring experience, particularly with small boats. For the special underwater swimming activities, exceptional swimming ability is a specific requirement.

c. The principal sources for the types of personnel required for MU activities are the U. S. Navy, Marine Corps, and Coast Guard. Competent personnel with special skills are also taken from the Army and civil life.

12. *RECRUITING*

Personnel for MU activities is secured through the regular OSS channels. Requests for personnel are submitted to the OSS Personnel Procurement Branch. This branch makes all arrangements for procuring Army and civilian personnel and forwards requests for Navy, Marine Corps, and Coast Guard personnel to the Naval Command, OSS.

SECTION V—TRAINING

13. *BASIC TRAINING*

a. The basic training for all MU personnel includes the following subjects:

(1) Day and night landings (and reembarkations) through surf.

(2) Swimming in surf and under water.

6

(3) Handling and maintenance of small boats (rubber boats, kayaks, caiques, etc.)

(4) Navigation, piloting, seamanship.

(5) Reading of maps, charts and aerial photographs.

(6) Hydrographic and beach reconnaissance.

(7) Maritime sabotage instruments and methods.

(8) Harbor and beach defenses.

(9) Demolitions.

(10) Small arms (sub-machine guns, pistol, carbine, rifle, MG).

(11) Operation and simple maintenance of outboard and marine motors.

(12) Operation and care of special MU underwater and surface gear.

(13) Signaling.

(14) Hand-to-hand combat.

(15) Types and designs of ships.

(16) Geography of area of operations.

b. For all types of MU personnel recruited in the U. S., basic training in all subjects is given in the U. S.

c. Personnel recruited overseas are given basic training and specialized training at field schools established in the various theaters.

d. MU instruction for special courses in MU techniques is made available especially in the field to other branches of the OSS and on request to military and naval personnel not assigned to OSS.

14. *SPECIALIZED TRAINING*

a. "Operational Personnel" are specially trained and equipped for special duties such as clandestine ferrying, maritime sabotage, and military tactical assistance. Such advanced training is normally given by MU instructors at field bases.

b. "Special Maritime Groups" of swimmers are given intensive training in underwater swimming (normally a minimum of six months). They are organized and trained specifically for underwater operations and therefore should be used only for tasks for which this special training is required.

7

APPENDIX "A"

EXAMPLES OF TYPICAL MU OPERATIONS

1. *INTRODUCTION*

No attempt is made herein to assess the reasoning and considerations which must precede the assignment of a task to a particular section of an OSS Field Base. This Appendix will serve to illustrate several typical Maritime Unit operations.

2. *MARITIME SABOTAGE (1)*

a. PROBLEM—It is desired to attack an enemy vessel moored in the channel of a hostile harbor.

b. SOLUTION—Task is assigned to Maritime Unit Section of OSS Field Base, since weighing of all factors concerned indicates that underwater sabotage attack presents greatest likelihood of success.

(1) *Personnel*

Since underwater swimming is required, two Special Maritime Group (SMG) men are assigned the task.

(2) *Method of Attack*

It is planned that one man will affix limpets to the side of the vessel, while the other will secure plastic charges to the fore and aft anchor cables. Use of lungs, swim suits, depth gauges, compasses and fins is required.

(3) *Penetration of Harbor*

(a) This is executed by parent craft (submarine, or surface vessel, depending upon circumstances assigned by Theater Commander) which transports the SMG men to

(1) Rendezvous point where friendly native fishermen may pick them up, secrete them, take them into harbor and return them to rendezvous point after they had finished affixing explosives with twelve-hour time charges under cover of darkness, or

8

(2) Rendezvous point and putting them over the side in inflated surfboard. This would be used to take the men within underwater swimming distance of target, then deflated, secured perhaps to a channel marker so that it may be regained, reinflated by special CO_2 bottle and used to rendezvous with parent craft on return, or

(3) Within actual underwater swimming distance of the target.

3. MARITIME SABOTAGE (2)

a. PROBLEM—It is desired to destroy an important lock (or dock, or bridge) in an enemy canal. Heavy guard prevents approach from shore.

b. SOLUTION—Task is assigned to MU Section of OSS Field Base, as underwater approach appears to be only reasonably safe method of attempting attack.

(1) *Personnel*

An MU operative (trained as member of Special Maritime Group), thoroughly conversant with the locality, language, customs of the natives and highly trained in demolition, work is selected.

(2) *Method of Attack*

Attack will be made under water and will require the use of lungs, fins, swim suits, gauges, compass and the handling of explosives and fuses under water.

(3) *Penetration*

Operative is parachuted into locality with his equipment.

4. CLANDESTINE FERRYING (1)

a. PROBLEM—It is desired to land an OSS Operational Group on a hostile beach so that they may penetrate inland to contact guerrilla forces.

b. SOLUTION—The task of ferrying is assigned to the Maritime Unit of OSS Field Base.

(1) *Personnel*

A group of ten OG's is turned over to the Maritime Unit for several days intensive training in landing through surf. Four Maritime Unit men are assigned responsibility for delivery of OG's.

(2) *Approach*

A suitable parent ship is assigned to this particular task. It transports the OSS men to within several hundred yards off shore of landing point on beach under cover of darkness. Two 8-man kayaks are assembled and put over the side. In each are two MU men, five OG's and equipment. The OG's are landed after one MU man has gone over the side and swum in to assure that reception committee of guerrillas with whom rendezvous has been established are on hand and that landing has been made at correct point. Similar technique is followed to evacuate personnel from beaches.

5. *CLANDESTINE FERRYING* (2)

a. PROBLEM—It is desired to land two native SI agents in an enemy port.

b. SOLUTION—Task of ferrying is assigned to Maritime Unit Section of OSS Field Base.

(1) *Personnel*

One MU operative, operating under cover as a native fisherman is assigned responsibility for task.

(2) *Method of Penetration*

The MU operative is in command of a felucca with a reliable crew of natives. This vessel regularly engages in off shore fishing and delivers catch into nearest port, village or harbor every several days. This craft delivers the two SI agents directly into port of their objective, all personnel concerned being under cover as natives.

6. *CLANDESTINE FERRYING* (3)

a. PROBLEM—It is desired to establish communications with partisan groups on a coastal island which

10

must be approached through enemy-controlled waters. The purpose is to supply them continuously with arms, ammunition, food and medicines.

b. SOLUTION—Task is assigned to Maritime Unit Section of OSS Field Base.

(1) *Personnel*

The MU section has trained a number of natives to act as crews for native caiques with under cover MU operatives as commanding officers. Three such vessels with crews are assigned responsibility.

(2) *Method*

Under cover as fishing boats and native ferries, these vessels accomplish their assigned mission by continuous ferrying of supplies to objective.

11